NTA UGC NET

Computer Science (Paper II)

Latest Edition
Practice Kit

10 Tests
10 Mock Test

Based On Real Exam Pattern

✓ Thoroughly Revised and Updated

✓ Detailed Analysis of all MCQs

Title	: NTA UGC NET Computer Science (Paper II)
Author Name	: Mr. Rohit Manglik
Published By	: EduGorilla Community Pvt. Ltd.
Publishers Address	: 12/651, First Floor Opp. Arvindo Park, Near Jama Masjid, Indira Nagar, Lucknow, Uttar Pradesh-226016, India

Copyright EduGorilla

ISBN : 978-93-90257-34-8

Second Edition

Disclaimer EduGorilla

Compiled and created by EduGorilla Community Pvt. Ltd

Printed By EduGorilla Community Pvt. Ltd.

ROHIT MANGLIK
CEO, EduGorilla

Dear Applicants,

People say *"Success comes to those who work hard."* But I've seen people working hard for their exams day in and day out for marginal success. While others succeed in their examinations by putting in just half the work. So are they God Gifted? No! I believe that it's because they work *smart* and not just *hard*. Similarly, for your exams, you should strategize your preparation so as to increase the likelihood of success. Well with EduGorilla get ready to increase your *chances of selection* in your exam by *16x*.

EduGorilla helps you in not only working *hard* but also working in a *smart and strategic* manner. With EduGorilla's preparation package, you get a chance to make your exam preparation easy, and a fun learning path towards selection. Finding the right path to your preparations can be difficult if you don't know in which direction to head. Don't worry, we have you covered! EduGorilla will be your guide to success in your journey. With our Preparation Package, you can prepare strategically and beat the exam in just one attempt.

EduGorilla's Preparation Package includes-

- **Test Series**
- **Books**

Our preparation package is handcrafted as per the latest changes, expert opinions, and students' discretion. Thus, enabling you to get through each stage of the selection process for your exam.

Our Books are designed by the teachers and experts of the respective exam with a combined 150+ years of experience; to provide you with easy, efficient, and effective learning. Our books are smart, in the sense that not only do they give you the answers to the questions but also provide similar questions for practice.

EduGorilla's competent Test Series gives you real-time experience and confidence through which you can clear your offline or online exam in just one attempt. We currently host 83,000+ mock tests for 1,440+ competitive and academic exams.

Thus, EduGorilla misses no chance to assist you in your preparation and covers all stages of the exam, so that you don't have to look anywhere else.

We provide complete preparation packages for defense, banking, teaching, and other National & State-Level exams. Hence, it doesn't matter which exam you aspire to because you will reach your success.

ALL THE BEST !

Let EduGorilla be your Guide to Success.

Rohit Manglik,
Founder and CEO, EduGorilla

INTRODUCTION

EduGorilla focuses on guiding students to succeed in their examinations. With that in mind, our book, titled "NTA UGC NET : Computer Science (Paper II)", has been drafted through the collective efforts of our distinguished experts with 150+ years of combined experience. This book consists of questions that are created following the latest changes in the syllabus and exam pattern. We compiled the book on the basis of questions that are most likely to appear in the UGC NET Computer Science. Through EduGorilla's "NTA UGC NET : Computer Science (Paper II)" your chances of success will increase 16x.

EduGorilla does this through our Complete Preparation Package. This package consists of well-conceptualized and structured content in the form of questions that are tailor-made according to your needs and will help you practice for exams in a smart way by pinpointing all the necessary information. It also provides hints and solutions, along with a smart answer sheet for your self-evaluation. You can assess your shortcomings and work accordingly on areas that may require more of your attention.

EduGorilla promises to help you succeed in your examination and accomplish your dream goals. We believe in our aspirants and see them at the top of the merit list. And the first step towards the top is to start preparing with us. EduGorilla's "NTA UGC NET : Computer Science (Paper II)" includes the following attributes.

➤ Well-Researched Content

➤ Top-Notch Quality

➤ Detailed Answers and Analysis

➤ Smart Answer Sheet

➤ Exam Relevant Questions

Therefore, EduGorilla fortifies your preparation and makes it durable enough to help you stand tall and beat the examination.

UGC NET Computer Science
Scan QR code for Eligibility, Exam Pattern, Syllabus and more.

Book ID: 0186

TABLE OF CONTENTS

Q.1 A reduced state table has 18 rows. The minimum number of Flips flops needed to implement the sequential machine is:

A. 18   **B.** 9   **C.** 5   **D.** 4

Q.2 Which of the following statements are true?

(a) Depth-first search is used to traverse a rooted tree.
(b) Pre-order, Post-order and In-order are used to list the vertices of an ordered rooted tree.
(c) Huffman's algorithm is used to find an optimal binary tree with given weights.
(d) Topological sorting provides a labelling such that the parents have larger labels than their children.

A. (a) and (b)   **B.** (c) and (d)
C. (a), (b) and (c)   **D.** (a), (b), (c) and (d)

Q.3 Consider a language A, defined over the alphabet $\Sigma = \{0,1\}$ as $A = \{0^{[n/2]}1^n : n >= 0\}$
The expression [n/2] means the floor of n/2 or what you get by rounding n/2 down to the nearest integer.
Which of the following is not an example of a string in A?

A. 011   **B.** 0111   **C.** 0011   **D.** 001111

Q.4 File access mechanism refers to the manner in which the records of a file may be accessed. There are several ways to access files, which among the following is not a file access method.

A. Sequential   **B.** Indexed
C. Linked   **D.** Direct/Rando

Q.5 Database applications were built directly on top of file system to overcome which of the following drawback(s) of using file-systems?

(a) Data redundancy and inconsistency
(b) Difficulty in accessing data
(c) Data isolation
(d) Integrity problems

A. (a)   **B.** (a) and (d)
C. (a), (b) and (c)   **D.** (a), (b), (c) and (d)

Q.6 The following program computes the sum of which of the following series?

```
#include <stdio.h>
main( )
{int i, inp;
float x, term = 1, sum = 0;
scanf('%d %f ', & inp, &x);

for(i = 1; i <= inp; i++)
{
term = term * x/i;    sum = sum + term ;
}
printf('Result = %f\n', sum);
}
```

A. $x + x^2/2 + x^3/3 + x^4/4 + \ldots$

B. $x + x^2/2! + x^3/3! + x^4/4! + \ldots$
C. $1 + x^2/2 + x^3/3 + x^4/4 + \ldots$
D. $1 + x^2/2! + x^3/3! + x^4/4! + \ldots$

Q.7 With 3 Boolean variables, how many Boolean expressions can be formed.

A. 256   **B.** 257   **C.** 258   **D.** 259

Q.8 In C++, which of the following system-provided functions is called when no handler is provided to deal with an exception?

A. terminate()   **B.** unexpected()
C. abort()   **D.** kill()

Q.9 Consider a system having 'm' resources of the same type. These resources are shared by processes P_1, P_2 and P_3 which have peak demands of 2, 5 and 7 resources, respectively. Deadlock will **not** occur for what value of 'm'?

A. 28   **B.** 14   **C.** 13   **D.** 7

Q.10 In a paging system, it takes 30 ns to search Translation Look-aside Buffer (TLB) and 90 ns to access the main memory. If the TLB hit ratio is 70%, then the effective memory access time is

A. 148 ns   **B.** 147 ns   **C.** 120 ns   **D.** 84 ns

Q.11 There are three processes P_1, P_2 and P_3 sharing a semaphore for synchronising a variable. Initial value of semaphore is one. Assume that negative value of semaphore tells us how many processes are waiting in queue.

Processes access the semaphore in the following order.
(a) P_2 needs to access
(b) P_1 needs to access
(c) P_3 needs to access
(d) P_2 exits critical section
(e) P_1 exits critical section
The final value of semaphore will be

A. 0   **B.** 1   **C.** -1   **D.** -2

Q.12 Which of the following scheduling algorithms may cause starvation?
a. First-come-first-served
b. Round robin
c. Priority
d. Shortest process next
e. Shortest remaining time first

A. a, c and e   **B.** c, d and e
C. b, d and e   **D.** b, c and d

Q.13 1's complement can be easily obtained by using _______.

A. Comparator   **B.** Invertor
C. Adder   **D.** Subtractor

Q.14 Which of the following statements is **false** with respect to microwaves?

A. Electromagnetic waves have frequencies from 300 GHz to

400 THz.

B. Propagation is line-of-sight.

C. Very high-frequency waves cannot penetrate walls.

D. Use of certain portions of the band requires permission from authorities.

Q.15 Which of the following is **not** a congestion policy at network layer?

A. Flow Control Policy

B. Packet Discard Policy

C. Packet Lifetime Management Policy

D. Routing Algorithm

Q.16 Four channels are multiplexed using TDM. If each channel sends 100 bytes/second and we multiplex 1 byte per channel, then the bit rate for the link is

A. 400 bps   **B.** 800 bps   **C.** 1600 bps   **D.** 3200 bps

Q.17 An analog signal has a bit rate of 8000 bps and a baud rate of 1000. Then, analog signal has ____ signal elements and carries ____ data elements in each signal.

A. 256, 8 bits   **B.** 128, 4 bits

C. 256, 4 bits   **D.** 128, 8 bits

Q.18 Outputs x_1, x_2 and x_3 from the 8 $\times$ 3 priority encoder are used to provide a vector address of the form $101x_1x_2x_300$. What is the second highest priority vector address in hexadecimal, if the vector addresses are starting from the one with the highest priority?

A. BC   **B.** A4   **C.** BD   **D.** AC

Q.19 A network with bandwidth of 10 Mbps can pass only an average of 12,000 frames per minute with each frame carrying an average of 10,000 bits. What is the throughput of this network?

A. 1 Mbps   **B.** 2 Mbps   **C.** 10 Mbps   **D.** 12 Mbps

Q.20 Consider the following statements regarding relational database model.

(a) NULL values can be used to opt a tuple out of enforcement of a foreign key.

(b) Suppose that table T has only one candidate key. If Q is in 3NF, then it is also in BCNF.

(c) The difference between the project operator (Π) in relational algebra and the SELECT keyword in SQL is that if the resulting table/set has more than one occurrences of the same tuple, then Π will return only one of them, while SQL SELECT will return all.

One can determine that

A. (a) and (b) are true

B. (a) and (c) are true

C. (b) and (c) are true

D. (a), (b) and (c) are true

Q.21 Relational database schema normalisation is **not** for

A. reducing the number of joins required to satisfy a query

B. eliminating uncontrolled redundancy of data stored in the database

C. eliminating number of anomalies that could otherwise occur with inserts and deletes

D. ensuring that functional dependencies are enforced

Q.22 The minimum number of two input AND gates and two input OR gates are required to realize

Y = BD+CE+AB ?

A. 2, 2   **B.** 4, 2   **C.** 3, 2   **D.** 2, 3

Q.23 How many strings of 5 digits have the property that the sum of their digits is 7?

A. 270   **B.** 330   **C.** 495   **D.** 545

Q.24 What will be the hexadecimal value in the register ax (32 bits) after executing the following instructions?

```
mov al, 15
mov ah, 15
xor al, al
mov cl, 3
shr ax, cl
Codes
```

A. 0F00 h   **B.** 0F0F h   **C.** 01E0 h   **D.** FFFF h

Q.25 The octal equivalent of the binary number 1011101011 is

A. 7353   **B.** 1353   **C.** 5651   **D.** 5657

Q.26 The translator which performs macro calls expansion is called

A. macro processor

B. micro pre-processor

C. macro pre-processor

D. dynamic linker

Q.27 In 8085, which of the following performs: load register pair immediate operation?

A. LDAX rp   **B.** LHLD addr

C. LXI rp, data   **D.** INX rp

Q.28 In a positive-edge-triggered JK flip-flop, if J and K both are high, then what will be the output on the rising edge of the clock?

A. No change   **B.** Set

C. Reset   **D.** Toggle

Q.29 Consider the following statements related to compiler construction.

I. Lexical analysis is specified by context free grammar and implemented by pushdown automata.

II. Syntax analysis is specified by regular expressions and implemented by finite-state machine.

Which of the above statements is/are correct?

A. Only I   **B.** Only II

C. Both I and II   **D.** Neither I nor II

Q.30 Which of the following non-functional quality attributes is **not** highly affected by the architecture of the software?

A. Performance   **B.** Reliability

C. Usability   **D.** Portability

Q.31 In software testing, how are the error, fault and failure related to one another?

A. Error leads to failure, but fault is not related to error and failure.

B. Fault leads to failure, but error is not related to fault and failure.

C. Error leads to fault, and fault leads to failure.

D. Fault leads to error, and error leads to failure.

Q.32 Cohesion is an extension of

A. abstraction concept

B. refinement concept

C. information hiding concept

D. modularity

Q.33 A software design pattern used to enhance the functionality of an object at run-time is

A. adapter

B. decorator

C. delegation

D. proxy

Q.34 Which of the following is **not** a software process model?

A. Prototyping

B. Iterative

C. Time boxing

D. Glass boxing

Q.35 The process of dividing an analog signal into a string of discrete outputs, each of constant amplitude, is called

A. strobing

B. amplification

C. conditioning

D. quantisation

Q.36 In a typical mobile phone system with hexagonal cells, it is forbidden to reuse a frequency band in adjacent cells. If 840 frequencies are available, then how many can be used in a given cell?

A. 280

B. 110

C. 140

D. 120

Q.37 _________ uses electronic means to transfer funds directly from one account to another, rather than by cheque or cash.

A. M-banking

B. E-banking

C. O-banking

D. C-banking

Q.38 In XML, we can specify the frequency of an element by using which of the following symbols?

A. + * !

B. # * !

C. +* ?

D. - * ?

Q.39 Which of the following arguments are **not** valid?

(a) 'If Gora gets the job and works hard, then he will be promoted. If Gora gets promotion, then he will be happy. He will not be happy, therefore, either he will not get the job or he will not work hard'.

(b) 'Either Puneet is not guilty or Pankaj is telling the truth. Pankaj is not telling the truth, therefore, Puneet is not guilty'.

(c) If n is a real number such that n > 1, then $n^2 > 1$. Suppose that $n^2 > 1$, then n > 1.

A. (c)

B. (b) and (c)

C. (a), (b) and (c)

D. (a) and (b)

Q.40 If all the production rules have single non-terminal symbol on the left side, the grammar defined is:

A. Context-free grammar

B. Context-sensitive grammar

C. Unrestricted grammar

D. Phrase grammar

Q.41 A 4-bit synchronous UP counter is holding a state 0101. What will be the count after 27th clock pulse?

A. 0101

B. 0001

C. 1111

D. 0000

Q.42 In Activity-Selection problem, each activity 'i' has a start time 's_i' and a finish time 'f_i', where $s_i \leq f_i$. Activities 'i' and 'j' are compatible, if

A. $s_i \geq f_j$

B. $s_j \geq f_i$

C. $s_i \geq F_j$ or $S_j \geq F_i$

D. $s_i \geq f_j$ and $s_j \geq f_i$

Q.43 Suppose that a disk drive has 5000 cylinders, numbered 0 to 4999. The drive is currently serving a request at cylinder 143, and the previous request was at cylinder 125. The queue of pending requests, in FIFO order, is 86, 1470, 913, 1774, 948, 1509, 1022, 1750, 130

Starting from the current head position, what is the total distance (in cylinders) that the disk arm moves to satisfy all the pending requests, for each of the following disk- scheduling algorithms?

FCFS

SSTF

SCAN

A. 7081, 1745, 9769

B. 7081, 1745, 7081

C. 1745, 1004, 9600

D. 9769, 1745, 7081

Q.44 Which of the following is used to make an abstract class?

A. Making at least one member function as pure virtual function

B. Making at least one member function as virtual function

C. Declaring as abstract class using virtual keyword

D. Declaring as abstract class using static keyword

Q.45 In C++, polymorphism requires

A. inheritance only

B. virtual functions only

C. references only

D. inheritance, virtual functions and references

Q.46 Consider a system with twelve magnetic tape drives and processes P_1, P_2 and P_3. Process P_1 requires maximum ten tape drives, process P_2 may need as many as four tape drives and P_3 may need up to nine tape drives. Suppose that at time t_1, process P_1 is holding five tape drives, process P_2 is holding two tape drives and process P_3 is holding three tape drives. At time t_1, system is in

A. safe state

B. unsafe state

C. deadlocked state

D. starvation state

Q.47 If the period of a signal is 1000 ms, then what is its frequency in kilohertz?

A. 10–3 KHz

B. 10–2 KHz

C. 10–1 KHz

D. 1 KHz

Q.48 Race conditions in critical sections can be avoided if

A. the critical section is treated as an atomic instruction

B. proper thread synchronization using locks

C. proper thread synchronization atomic variables

D. All of the above

Q.49 Which of the following things are considered to be very important to design the algorithm.

A. Modularity of program

B. Maintainability
C. Security
D. All of the above

Q.50 System calls are usually invoked by using which of the following?
A. Privileged instruction
B. Indirect jump
C. Software interrupt
D. Polling

Q.51 A slotted ALOHA network transmits 200 bits frames using a shared channel with 200 kbps bandwidth. If the system (all stations put together) produces 1000 frames per second, then the throughput of the system is

A. 0.268   **B.** 0.468   **C.** 0.368   **D.** 0.568

Q.52 If link transmits 4000 frames per second and each slot has 8 bits, then the transmission rate of circuit of this TDM is

A. 64 Kbps   **B.** 32 Mbps   **C.** 32 Kbps   **D.** 64 Mbps

Q.53 In a fast Ethernet cabling, 100 base-TX uses ___ cable and the maximum segment size of 100 base-TX is ____ metres.

A. twisted pair, 100   **B.** twisted pair, 200
C. fibre optic, 1000   **D.** fibre optic, 2000

Q.54 Which of the following is/are restriction(s) in classless addressing?
A. The number of addresses need to be a power of 2.
B. The mask needs to be included in the address to define the block.
C. The starting address must be divisible by the number of addresses in the block.
D. All of the above

Q.55 In link state routing algorithm, after construction of link state packets, new routes are computed using
A. DES algorithm   **B.** Dijkstra's algorithm
C. RSA algorithm   **D.** Packets

Q.56 If for a given Binary Search Tree (BST) the pre-order traversal is $41,23,11,31,62,50,73$. Then which of the following is its post-order traversal?
A. 11,31,23,50,73,62,41
B. 31,11,23,50,41,62,73
C. 11,31,50,23,73,62,41
D. 11,31,23,50,62,73,41

Q.57 Integrity constraints ensure that changes made to the database by authorised users do not result into loss of data consistency. Which of the following statements is/are true regarding the examples of integrity constraints?
(A) An instructor ID number cannot be null, provided instructor ID number being primary key.
(B) No two citizens have same Adhar ID.
(C) Budget of a company must be zero.
A. (A), (B) and (C) are true.
B. (A) is false, but (B) and (C) are true.
C. (A) and (B) are true, but (C) is false.
D. (A), (B) and (C) are false.

Q.58 Consider a schema R(ABCD) and functional dependencies $A \to B,\ C \to D$. The decomposition of R into R₁(AB) and R₂(CD) is
A. dependency preserving, but not lossless join
B. dependency preserving and lossless join
C. lossless join, but not dependency preserving
D. neither dependency preserving nor lossless join

Q.59 Consider a database table R with attributes A and B. Which of the following SQL queries is illegal?
A. SELECT A FROM R;
B. SELECT A, COUNT(*) FROM R;
C. SELECT A, COUNT(*) FROM R GROUP BY A;
D. SELECT A, B, COUNT(*) FROM R GROUP BY A, B;

Q.60 In propositional logic, P ↔ Q is equivalent to (Where ~ denotes NOT)
A. ~(P ∨ Q) ∧ ~ (Q ∨ P)
B. (~P ∨ Q) ∧ (~Q ∨ P)
C. (P ∨ Q) ∧ (Q ∨ P)
D. ~(P ∨ Q) → ~(Q ∨ P)

Q.61 Directions: Match the following.

(a) Size oriented metrics	(i) Uses number of external interfaces as one of the measurement parameters
(b) Function oriented metrics	(ii) Originally designed to be applied to business information systems
(c) Extended function point metrics	(iii) Derived by normalising quality and/or productivity measures by considering the size of the software
(d) Function point	(iv) Uses algorithm characteristics as one of the measurement parameters

A. (a) - (iii), (b) - (iv), (c) - (i), (d) - (ii)
B. (a) - (ii), (b) - (i), (c) - (iv), (d) - (iii)
C. (a) - (iv), (b) - (ii), (c) - (iii), (d) - (i)
D. (a) - (iii), (b) - (i), (c) - (iv), (d) - (ii)

Q.62 If X is a binary number which is power of 2, then the value of X & (X - 1) is
A. 11....11   **B.** 00.....00   **C.** 100.....0   **D.** 000.....1

Q.63 Postfix to infix operations is performed on the following expression. Using stack we need to perform the set of PUSH and POP operations depending upon the operator or operand in the expression. At a certain point, the top of the stack is $"s - t".$

How many push and pop operations are performed till that moment.

$$pqr + -st - uv - w + *$$

A. 6,8   **B.** 8,6   **C.** 6,6   **D.** 8,8

Q.64 The RST 7 instruction in 8085 microprocessor is equivalent to
A. CALL 0010 H   **B.** CALL 0034 H
C. CALL 0038 H   **D.** CALL 003C H

Q.65 Which of the following statement(s) regarding a linker software is/are true?
I. A function of a linker is to combine several object modules into a single load module.

II. A function of a linker is to replace absolute references in an object module by symbolic references to locations in other modules.

A. Only I
B. Only II
C. Both I and II
D. Neither I nor II

Q.66 Which of the following statements is/are true?
(i) The grammar S →SS | a is ambiguous (where S is the start symbol).
(ii) The grammar S →0S1 | 01S | e is ambiguous (the special symbol e represents the empty string and S is the start symbol).
(iii) The grammar (where S is the start symbol)

S →T/U

T →x S y ? xy ? e

U →yT

generates a language consisting of the string yxxyy.

A. Only (i) and (ii)
B. Only (i) and (iii)
C. Only (ii) and (iii)
D. All of these

Q.67 The major shortcoming of waterfall model is the
A. difficulty in accommodating changes after requirement analysis
B. difficulty in accommodating changes after feasibility analysis
C. system testing
D. maintenance of system

Q.68 In CRC based design, a CRC Team consists of
(a) one or two users representatives
(b) several programmers
(c) project co-ordinators
(d) one or two system analysts

A. (a) and (c)
B. (a), (b), (c) and (d)
C. (a), (c) and (d)
D. (a), (b) and (d)

Q.69 Which of the following design matrics is used to measure the compactness of the program in terms of lines of code?

A. Consistency
B. Conciseness
C. Efficiency
D. Accuracy

Q.70 The relational model feature is that there
A. Is no need for primary key data
B. Is much more data independence than some other database models
C. Are explicit relationships among records
D. Are tables with many dimensions

Q.71 Requirements established during requirements analysis are validated against developed software in

A. validation testing
B. integration testing
C. regression testing
D. system testing

Q.72 Dining philosopher's problem is a
A. producer-consumer problem
B. classical IPC problem
C. starvation problem
D. synchronisation primitive

Q.73 Which of the following logic families is well suited for high-speed operations?

A. TTL
B. ECL
C. MOS
D. CMOS

Q.74 Which of the following tags is an extension to HTML that can enclose any number of Javascript statements?

A. <SCRIPT>
B. <BODY>
C. <HEAD>
D. <TITLE>

Q.75 Related fields in a database are grouped to form a
A. Data file
B. Data record.
C. Menu
D. document type language

Q.76 Consider an implementation of unsorted single linked list. Suppose, it has its representation with a head and a tail pointer (i.e. pointers to the first and last nodes of the linked list), then which of the following operations **cannot** be implemented in O(1) time?

A. Insertion at the front of the linked list.
B. Insertion at the end of the linked list.
C. Deletion of the front node of the linked list.
D. Deletion of the last node of the linked list.

Q.77 If there are n integers to sort and each integer has d digits and each digit is in the set {1, 2, ..., k}, then radix sort can sort the numbers in

A. $O(d\ n\ k)$
B. $O(d\ n^k)$
C. $O((d + n)k)$
D. $O(d(n + k))$

Q.78 Consider a sequence F_{00} defined as

$F_{00}(0) = 1$, $F_{00}(1) = 1$

$$F_{00}(n) = \frac{10 \times F_{00}(n-1)+100}{F_{00}(n-2)} \ for\ n \geq 2$$

What shall be the set of values of the sequence F_{00}?

A. (1, 110, 1200)
B. (1, 110, 600, 1200)
C. (1, 2, 55, 110, 600, 1200)
D. (1, 55, 110, 600, 1200)

Q.79 Which of the following are advantage of CD-ROM as a storage media?

A. CD-ROM is an inexpensive way to store large amount of data and information
B. CD-ROM disks retrieve data and information more quickly than magnetic disks do
C. CD-ROMS make less errors than magnetic media
D. All of these

Q.80 Assume that an integer and a pointer each takes 4 bytes. Also, assume that there is no alignment in objects. Predict the output of the following program.

```
#include<iostream>
using namespace std;
class Test
{
static int x;
int *ptr;
int y;
};
int main()
```

```
{
Test t;
cout << sizeof(t) << " ";
cout << sizeof(Test *);
}
```

A. 12 4   **B.** 12 12   **C.** 8 4   **D.** 8 8

Q.81 In an operating system, indivisibility of operation means

A. operation is interruptable
B. race-condition may occur
C. processor cannot be pre-empted
D. All of the above

Q.82 An ideal sort is an in-place-sort whose additional space requirement is

A. $O(\log_2 n)$ **B.** $O(n \log_2 n)$
C. $O(1)$ **D.** $O(n)$

Q.83 In 3G network, W-CDMA is also known as UMTS. The minimum spectrum allocation required for W-CDMA is

A. 2 MHz   **B.** 20 KHz   **C.** 5 KHz   **D.** 5 MHz

Q.84 This set of Microprocessor Multiple Choice Questions & Answers (MCQs) focuses on "Numeric Processor 8087 -1".
1. The unit that executes all the numeric processor instructions in 8087 is

A. Control unit
B. ALU
C. Numeric extension unit
D. None of the mentioned

Q.85 Consider the following two statements.
(A) Data scrubling is a process to upgrade the quality of data, before it is moved into data warehouse.
(B) Data scrubling is a process of rejecting data from data warehouse to create indexes.
Which of the following options is correct?

A. (A) is true, but (B) is false.
B. (A) is false, but (B) is true.
C. Both (A) and (B) are false.
D. Both (A) and (B) are true.

Q.86 Suppose ORACLE relation R(A, B) currently has tuples {(1, 2), (1, 3), (3, 4)} and relation S(B, C) currently has {(2, 5), (4, 6), (7, 8)}. Consider the following two SQL queries SQ_1 and SQ_2.

SQ_1: Select *
From R Full Join S
On R.B = S.B;

SQ_2 : Select *
From R Inner Join S
On R.B = S.B;

The numbers of tuples in the result of the SQL query SQ_1 and the SQL query SQ_2 are given by

A. 2 and 6, respectively
B. 6 and 2, respectively
C. 2 and 4, respectively
D. 4 and 2, respectively

Q.87 Consider the following two well-formed formulas in prepositional logic.

$$F_1: P \Rightarrow \neg P$$
$$F_2: (P \Rightarrow \neg P) \lor (\neg P \Rightarrow P)$$

Which of the following statements is correct?

A. F_1 is satisfiable and F_2 is valid
B. F_1 is unsatisfiable, but F_2 is satisfiable
C. F_1 is unsatisfiable and F_2 is valid
D. F_1 and F_2 are both satisfiable

Q.88 Suppose counting semaphore s having value If 19P, 12V and 3P operation perform respectively on s. then after performing these operation value of s will be ____. Assuming the initial value of s be 15.

A. 1   **B.** 5   **C.** 8   **D.** 7

Q.89 Which of the following are the principle tasks of the linker?
I. Resolve external references among separately compiled program units.
II. Translate assembly language to machine code.
III. Relocate code and data relative to the beginning of the program.
IV. Enforce access-control restrictions on system libraries.

A. I and II   **B.** I and III   **C.** II and III   **D.** I and IV

Q.90 Which of the following 8085 microprocessor hardware interrupts has the lowest priority?

A. RST 6.5   **B.** RST 7.5   **C.** TRAP   **D.** INTR

Q.91 Directions: Match the following.

Addressing mode	Location of operand
a. Implied	i. Registers which are in CPU
b. Immediate	ii. Register specifies the address of the operand
c. Register	iii. Specified in the register
d. Register indirect	iv. Specified implicitly in the definition of instruction

A. a - iv, b - iii, c - i, d - ii
B. a - iv, b - i, c - iii, d - ii
C. a - iv, b - ii, c - i, d - iii
D. a - iv, b - iii, c - ii, d - i

Q.92 For a program of k variables, boundary value analysis yields _____ test cases.

A. 4k - 1   **B.** 4k   **C.** 4k + 1   **D.** 2^k - 1

Q.93 Which of the following process models is also called as classic life cycle model?

A. Waterfall model   **B.** RAD model
C. Prototyping model   **D.** Incremental model

Q.94 The control unit functions in

A. establishing communication between CPU and memory
B. coordinating the internal coprocessor execution
C. reads and writes memory operands
D. all of the mentioned

Q.95 Which of the following is the run time for traversing all the nodes of a binary search tree with n nodes and printing them in an order?

A. $O(lg\ n)$ **B.** $O(n\ lg\ n)$ **C.** $O(n)$ **D.** $O(n^2)$

Q.96 Directions: Match the following with reference to object oriented modelling.

List - I	List - II
(a) Polymorphism	(i) Picking both operator and attributes with operations appropiate to model and object
(b) Inheritance	(ii) Hiding implementation details of methods from users of objects
(c) Encapsulation	(iii) Using similar operations to do similar things
(d) Abstraction	(iv) Creating new classes from existing class

A. (a) - (iv), (b) - (iii), (c) - (i), (d) - (ii)
B. (a) - (iii), (b) - (iv), (c) - (i), (d) - (ii)
C. (a) - (iii), (b) - (i), (c) - (ii), (d) - (iv)
D. (a) - (iv), (b) - (iii), (c) - (ii), (d) - (i)

Q.97 A function template in C++ provides _____ level(s) of generalisation.

A. 4 **B.** 3 **C.** 2 **D.** 1

Q.98 Consider the following three SQL queries (Assume the data in the people table).
(a) Select name from people where age > 21.
(b) Select name from people where height > 180.
(c) Select name from people where age > 21 or height > 180.
If the SQL queries (a) and (b) return 10 rows and 7 rows in the result set, respectively, then what is one possible number of rows returned by the SQL query (c)?

A. 3 **B.** 7 **C.** 10 **D.** 21

Q.99 The number of flip-flops required to design a modulo-272 counter is

A. 8 **B.** 9 **C.** 11 **D.** 27

Q.100 Consider the following statements:

S_1 : Ethernet frame include checksum field.

S_2 : ARP request is normally broadcast and ARP reply is normally unicast.

S_3 : Differential Manchester encoding has a transition at the middle of each bit. Which of the above statement is correct?

A. S_1 and S_2 only **B.** S_3 only
C. S_1 and S_3 only **D.** S_2 and S_3 only

// Smart Answer Sheet //

Correct Percentage of students who answered correctly. **Skipped** Percentage of students who skipped.

Q.	Ans.	Correct / Skipped	Q.	Ans.	Correct / Skipped	Q.	Ans.	Correct / Skipped	Q.	Ans.	Correct / Skipped	Q.	Ans.	Correct / Skipped
1	C	28.94 % / 3.54 %	17	A	27.97 % / 28.3 %	33	B	20.1 % / 31.51 %	49	D	39.07 % / 35.37 %	65	A	15.27 % / 37.46 %
2	D	32.64 % / 13.18 %	18	B	26.69 % / 29.74 %	34	D	29.58 % / 32.0 %	50	C	32.8 % / 34.56 %	66	D	18.49 % / 37.94 %
3	C	38.26 % / 16.4 %	19	B	22.67 % / 28.94 %	35	D	20.58 % / 32.47 %	51	C	19.13 % / 35.53 %	67	A	26.21 % / 37.13 %
4	C	31.51 % / 19.62 %	20	D	14.47 % / 29.42 %	36	A	15.59 % / 33.93 %	52	C	26.05 % / 36.17 %	68	C	18.81 % / 37.94 %
5	D	43.41 % / 18.17 %	21	A	24.6 % / 28.29 %	37	B	54.5 % / 32.32 %	53	A	20.9 % / 36.17 %	69	B	19.94 % / 37.62 %
6	B	22.35 % / 20.74 %	22	A	22.03 % / 28.45 %	38	C	22.99 % / 32.96 %	54	D	33.92 % / 35.85 %	70	B	25.08 % / 37.3 %
7	A	45.02 % / 20.41 %	23	B	22.99 % / 30.71 %	39	A	14.95 % / 33.28 %	55	B	35.69 % / 36.17 %	71	A	28.46 % / 37.78 %
8	A	25.56 % / 19.13 %	24	C	19.45 % / 32.48 %	40	A	30.71 % / 32.79 %	56	A	15.11 % / 36.34 %	72	B	18.01 % / 37.46 %
9	C	27.33 % / 20.74 %	25	B	41.16 % / 30.87 %	41	D	18.33 % / 33.12 %	57	C	32.8 % / 36.81 %	73	B	21.38 % / 38.11 %
10	B	26.21 % / 22.99 %	26	C	29.58 % / 30.71 %	42	C	31.19 % / 34.24 %	58	A	18.97 % / 36.82 %	74	A	44.05 % / 36.98 %
11	A	24.76 % / 24.28 %	27	C	26.21 % / 31.19 %	43	A	18.49 % / 33.6 %	59	B	15.43 % / 36.34 %	75	B	39.07 % / 37.14 %
12	B	28.62 % / 23.95 %	28	D	33.44 % / 30.71 %	44	A	18.65 % / 34.24 %	60	B	26.85 % / 36.65 %	76	D	15.59 % / 38.43 %
13	B	35.85 % / 25.89 %	29	D	12.06 % / 31.03 %	45	D	35.05 % / 33.44 %	61	D	12.38 % / 36.98 %	77	D	13.67 % / 37.94 %
14	A	17.68 % / 26.05 %	30	C	24.6 % / 31.19 %	46	B	17.36 % / 34.57 %	62	B	20.42 % / 37.78 %	78	A	19.13 % / 38.59 %
15	A	18.17 % / 25.88 %	31	C	35.85 % / 31.35 %	47	A	17.52 % / 35.53 %	63	B	21.06 % / 37.14 %	79	A	9.81 % / 37.14 %
16	D	14.79 % / 26.69 %	32	C	21.86 % / 31.68 %	48	D	35.85 % / 34.09 %	64	C	22.99 % / 37.62 %	80	C	20.58 % / 38.91 %

Q.	Ans.	Correct		Q.	Ans.	Correct		Q.	Ans.	Correct		Q.	Ans.	Correct		Q.	Ans.	Correct
		Skipped				Skipped				Skipped				Skipped				Skipped
81	A	11.09 %		85	A	24.92 %		89	B	26.37 %		93	A	36.82 %		97	C	21.54 %
		36.98 %				38.1 %				38.42 %				36.49 %				37.14 %
82	C	16.56 %		86	D	9.0 %		90	D	22.51 %		94	D	37.62 %		98	C	25.72 %
		37.78 %				38.43 %				38.1 %				36.98 %				37.78 %
83	D	13.02 %		87	A	16.24 %		91	A	21.22 %		95	C	17.36 %		99	B	21.06 %
		38.43 %				38.58 %				36.98 %				36.34 %				37.78 %
84	C	17.52 %		88	B	23.63 %		92	C	22.67 %		96	B	38.59 %		100	D	14.79 %
		38.27 %				38.43 %				37.78 %				37.13 %				35.21 %

//Hints and Solutions//

1. For sequential machine min no. of flip flop = $\log_2 n = \log_2 18 = 4.16$

Hence minimum 5 will be required.

2.

- Depth-first search is used to traverse a rooted tree. **Correct**

- Pre-order, Post-order and In-order are used to list the vertices of an ordered rooted tree. **Correct**

- Huffman's algorithm is used to find an optimal binary tree with given weights. **Correct**

- Topological sorting provides a labelling such that the parents have larger labels than their children. **Correct**

So, option (D) is correct.

3. If n = 2
$[n/2] = [1] = 1$ i.e. Language is : 011
If n = 3
$[n/2] = [1.5] = 1$ i.e. Language is : 0111
If n = 4
$[n/2] = [2] = 2$ i.e. Language is : 001111
Hence, options (A), (B) and (C) are possible, but (C) is not possible.
So, option (C) is correct.

4. The three file access methods are

1) Sequential Access

2) Direct/Indirect Access

3) Indexed sequential Access

The three space Allocation methods are

1) contigous Allocation

2) linked Allocation

3) Indexed Allocation

5. Database applications were built directly on top of file system to overcome the following drawbacks of using file-systems.

- **Data redundancy and inconsistency** is the concept of repetition of data, i.e. each data may have more than a single copy. We can overcome it with the help of normalisation.

- **Difficulty in accessing data** can be overcome by different types of queries, i.e. procedural and non-procedural queries.

- **Data isolation** can be removed by join, etc.

- **Integrity problems** are the compulsory conditions which should be satisfied by every data value present in the relational table at any instance of time to ensure that the database consists of only meaningful and relevant data. There are four types of integrity constraints:

- Domain constraints: Every attribute should have values within its defined domain.

- Key constraints: There should be a primary key for every relational table.

- Entity integrity constraints: No null values should be there for primary keys.

- Referential integrity constraints: In relational model, when two tables are related to each other with the help of some common attributes, the value of referencing attribute should be present in the referenced attribute, else it should be null.

So, option (D) is correct.

6. For i = 1:
term = term * x/i = 1 * x/1 = x
sum = sum + term = x
For i = 2:
term = x * x/2 = $x^2/2$
sum = x + $x^2/2$
For i = 3:
term = $x^2/2$ * x/3 = $x^3/3!$
sum = x + $x^2/2!$ + $x^3/3!$ and so on ...
So, option (B) is correct.

7. Number of possible functions with n variable.
$$= 2^{x^n}$$
Here $n = 3$.
$$2^{z^3} = 2^z = 256$$

8. This function is automatically called when no catch handler can be found for a thrown exception, or for some other exceptional circumstance that makes impossible to continue the exception handling process.

9. Peak demands of p_1, p_2, p_3 are 2,5 and 7.

allocate 1 less than peak demand i.e,, p_1 --> 1 ,p_2-->4 ,p_3-->6

the number of resources for which deadlock occurs is 1+4+6 = 11

Add one to the number of resources we get 12 ,the value for which deadlock will not occur . (13 is nearest possible answer)

10. Correct Answer : 70% tlb hit ratio 30 ns to search tlb

(0.7 ✕30) in hit case: to find the page

0.3 ✕(90+30) in miss case: to find the page

90 ns to access the data from main memory

so total time:

(0.7 ✕ 30)+ (0.3 ✕ (90+30)) + 90 = 147

11.

1. P_2 needs to access decreases semaphore by 1, new value will be 0 (no one is waiting)

2. P_1 needs to access decreases semaphore by 1, new value will be -1 (one process is waiting)

3. P_3 needs to access decreases semaphore by 1, new value will be -2 (2 process are waiting)

4. P_2 exits critical section increases semaphore by 1, new value will be -1 (one process is waiting)

5. P_1 exits critical section increases semaphore by 1, new value will be 0 (no process is waiting)

So, option (A) is correct.

12. The following scheduling algorithms may cause starvation:

- First-come-first-served- No starvation

- Round Robin- No starvation

- Priority- starvation if higher priority process called again and again, lower priority starves

- Shortest process next -starvation possible

- Shortest remaining time first -starvation possible as its a preemptive version of shortest process next casuing apotential for longer processes to starve.

13. With the help of an inverter the1's complement is easily obtained. Since, during the operation of1's complement, 1is converted into 0 and vice-versa and this is well suited for the inverter.

Hence, the correct option is (B).

14. The frequencies are between 300 MHz to 300 GHz.

15. Network layer congestion policy are:

1)Virtual circuits vs datagram inside the subnet

2)Packet sequencing and service policy

3)Packet discard policy

4)Routing algorithm

5)Packet lifetime management

16. Number of channels = 4

1 byte is multiplexed with each channel i.e. each frame carries 1 byte and we have 4 channel, so the size of each frame is 1 $\times$ 4 byte = 4 bytes 32 bits.

Channel sends 100 frames per seconds. So, the bit rate will be 100 $\times$ 4 bytes i.e. 3200 bits/seconds.

So, option (D) is correct.

17. Analog signal has a bit rate of 8000 bps and a baud rate of 1000.

So, each signal will clearly carry bit rate / baud rate bits. i.e. 8000 / 1000 = 8 bits and 28= 256 signal.

So, option (A) is correct.

18. priority encoder 8 x 3 gives equivalent bits for digits from 0-7

given vector address 101 x_1 x_2 x_3 00

first highest priority 101 0 00 00 i.e A0 (since vector addresses are starting from the one with the highest priority $x_1=x_2=x_3=0$)

second highest priority 1010 0100 i.e A4 ($x_1=x_2=0,x_3=1$)

so ans will be B

19. Throughput is amount of data moved successfully from one place to another place.

i.e. 12,000 frames per minute. Each Frame is carrying 10,000 bits

So, 12,000 $\times$ 10,000 / 60 seconds.

= 2 $\times$ 1000000 bits / seconds.

= 2 Mbps.

So, option (B) is correct

20. IN relational database model:

(a) NULL values can be used to opt a tuple out of enforcement of a foreign key.Correct

(b) Suppose that table T has only one candidate key. If Q is in 3NF, then it is also in BCNF.Correct

(c) The difference between the project operator (Π) in relational algebra and the SELECT keyword in SQL is that if the resulting table/set has more than one occurrences of the same tuple, then Π will return only one of them, while SQL SELECT will return all.Correct

So, option (D) is correct.

21. Relational database schema normalization is NOT for reducing the number of joins required to satisfy a query.

relational database schema normalization goal is

1) eliminating redundancy

2)functional dependencies should preserved

3) Eliminating number of anomalies that could otherwise occur with inserts and deletes(lossless join)

So A should be answer.

22. Y = BD+CE+AB here 3 and gate and 2 or gate [we can minimize 1 AND gate]

Y = B(D + A)+ CE

Now we see that 2 AND Gate and 2 OR Gate required.

23. We have to make string which have sum = 7.There are:

2,2,1,1,1 = 5! / 2! $\times$ 3! = 10

2,2,2,1,0 = 5! / 3!   = 20

3,1,1,1,1 = 5! / 4!   = 5

3,2,1,1,0 = 5! / 2!   = 60

3,2,2,0,0 = 5! / 2! $\times$ 2! = 30

3,3,1,0,0 = 5! / 2! $\times$ 2! = 30

4,2,1,0,0 = 5! / 2!   = 60

4,3,0,0,0 = 5! / 3!   = 20

4,1,1,1,0 = 5! / 3!   = 20

5,1,1,0,0 = 5! / 2! $\times$ 2! = 30

5,2,0,0,0 = 5! / 3!   = 20

6,1,0,0,0 = 5! / 3!   = 20

7,0,0,0,0 = 5! / 4!   = 5

total = 10 + 20 + 5 + 60 + 30 + 30 + 60 + 20 + 20 + 30 + 20 + 20 + 5 = 330.

So, option (B) is correct.

Alternative method –

Lets digits are a, b, c, d, and e. Therefore,

a + b + c + d + e = 7

Total number of combinations are $^{(n-1+r)}C_{(r)}$ = $^{(5-1+7)}C_7$ = $^{11}C_7$ = $^{11}C_4$ = 330.

24. in assembly AX=AH+BL

AL is the lower 8 bits

AH is the higher bits 8

HERE AL and Ah both contains 15 or F so AX contains 0F0F or 0000 1111 0000 1111

XOR AL AL will return 0 in AL

so AX becomes 0000 1111 0000 0000

MOV CL,3 will store 3 in CL

shr ax,cl will shift right ax by 3

so 0000 1111 0000 0000 will become 0000 0001 1110 0000 or 01E0 in hexadecimal i.e

01E0 h

Hence the correct option is (C)

25. Explanation: First we will make pair of 3 bits from LSB :

ie- 1 011 101 011

now convert these bits into decimal and that will be

1 – 1

011 – 3

101 – 5

011 – 3

so the answer will be 1353.

So, option (B) is correct.

26. The translator which performs macro calls expansion is called Macro pre – processor. A Macro processor is a program that copies a stream of text from one place to another, making a systematic set of replacements as it does so. ... It is called micro pre-processor because it allows us to add macros.

27. LDAX – Load accumulator indirect(This instruction copies the contents of that memory location into the accumulator.)

LHLD – Load H and L register direct (This instruction loads the contents of the 16- bit memory location into the H and L register pair.)

LXI – Load register pair immediate(The instruction loads 16-bit data in the register pair designated in the operand.)

INX – Increment register pair by 1.(It will increment the register value by 1.)

So, option (C) is correct.

28. When J = 1 and K = 1 , The output continuously Toggles from 1 to 0 and 0 to 1.

At the end Output is indeterminate. This condition is called as Race around Condition. This happens when Propagation Delay is less than the Pulse width.

29. Both statement are wrong becoz lexical analyser uses finite autometa so it uses regular grammer ,whose expression will be for example letter(letter + digit)* , where as syntax tree uses context free grammer which uses pda.

30. The answer should be C usability it should not be highly affected by the architecture of the software as it is basic things rest options are extra features offered by s/w and may be highly affected by the architecture of the software.

31.

- ans is C error leads to fault and fault leads to error
- Error is deviation from actual and expected value.
- It represents mistake made by people.
- Fault is incorrect step, process or data definition in a computer program which causes the program to behave in an unintended or unanticipated manner.
- It is the result of the error.
- Bug is a fault in the program which causes the program to behave in an unintended or unanticipated manner.
- It is an evidence of fault in the program.
- Failure is the inability of a system or a component to perform its required functions within specified performance requirements.
- Failure occurs when fault executes.
- A defect is an error in coding or logic that causes a program to malfunction or to produce incorrect/unexpected results.
- A defect is said to be detected when a failure is observed.

32. Cohesion is a natural extension of the information hiding concept. A module that performs tasks that are related logically is logically cohesive. When a module contains tasks that are related by the fact that all must be executed with the same span of time, the module exhibits temporal cohesion.

33. Decorator is used to enhancing the functionality of an object at run-time, i.e., it allows you to add new behaviour to other objects at run-time.

So, option (B) is correct.

34. ans is D no such model named glassboxing however glassbox testing is there

A and B are well known process models

In time boxing model, development is done iteratively as in the iterative enhancement model. However, in time boxing model, each iteration is done in a timebox of fixed duration.

35.

- The process of dividing an analog signal into a string of discrete outputs, each of constant amplitude, is called Quantization.

- The process of enhancing an analog signal is called Amplification.

- Irregular behaviour or jerk or loss of continuity in analog signal is called Strobing.

- Conditioning is a process of manipulating an analog signal in a way that prepares it for the next stage of processing.

So, option (D) is correct.

36. Hexagonal cells means each cell has six neighbors.

If the central cell uses frequency A, its six neighbors can use B, C, B, C, B, and C respectively.

In other words, only 3 unique cells are needed.

Consequently, each cell can have 840/3= 280 frequencies

37. clearly (B) E-banking or net banking is the answer.

38. + symbol for one or more time.

* for 0 or more time.

? for zero or more time.

39. Option A let

- p: Gora get the job
- q: he works hard
- r: he will be promoted
- s: he will be happy

So we have $p \cap q \rightarrow r, r \rightarrow s$ which will give us $\neg s \rightarrow \neg r$ (by contrapositive law) and $\neg r \rightarrow \neg(p \cap q)$. Now $\neg s$ is given so it implies $\neg r$ and so we have $\neg p \vee \neg q$ i.e either he does not get the job or he does not work hard. So it is valid

Option B valid as EXACTLY one of two statements must be true. Given one statement is not true so other must be true

Option C not valid. Here we have $a \Rightarrow b$. But this does not always mean $b \Rightarrow a$.

Hence **A and B are valid C is no valid** so Option A is correct .

40. If all the production rules have single non-terminal symbol on the left side, the grammar defined is Context free grammar

i.e. V $\rightarrow$ (T +V) +

41. After every modulus the initial state will repeat hence after 16 clock pulses the counter holds the same state i.e decimal 5

The remaining clock pulses 27-16=11,so the final state is 11+5=16

For this counter means 0000.

42. Two activities arecompatible if they can be completed in some order and don't overlap in time. To complete two activities,STARTtime of one activity must be greater than or equal toFINISHtime of other activity i.e one activity must start only after other finishes. So,

Si > = Fj or Sj > = Fi:

43. The total seek time is sum of difference between successive head positions.

The FCFS schedule is 143, 86, 1470, 913, 1774, 948, 1509, 1022, 1750, 130. The total seek distance is 7081.

The SSTF schedule is 143, 130, 86, 913, 948, 1022, 1470, 1509, 1750, 1774. The total seek distance is 1745.

The SCAN schedule is 143, 913, 948, 1022, 1470, 1509, 1750, 1774, 4999, 130, 86. The total seek distance is 9769.

44. Making at least one member function as pure virtual function

45. Answer should be D.

The word polymorphism means having many forms. Typically, polymorphism occurs when there is a hierarchy of classes and they are related by inheritance. C++ polymorphism means that a call to a member function will cause a different function to be executed depending on the type of object that invokes the function.

in C++ polymorphism indicates the form of member function that can be changed at run time such member functions are called virtual functions and the corresponding class is called polymorphic class. the objects of the polymorphic class , addressed by pointers change at run time and responds differently for the same message

46. System is in UNSAFE state

P_1 holds 5 tapes

P_2 holds 2 tapes

P_3 holds 3 tapes

Total 10 tapes are allocated and 12-10=2 tapes are free

P_1 requires maximum 10 tape drives; It needs 10-5 =5 more tapes

P_2 may need as many as 4 tape drives. It needs 4-2=2 more tapes.

P_3 may need as many as 9 tape drives. It needs 9-3=6 more tapes.

We can allocate 2 free tapes to P_2.

P_2 will complete execution and release all its resources including 4 tapes.

Even if we allocate 4 tapes to P_1 or P_3 they cannot complete execution because P_1 nees 5 more taps while P_3 needs 6 more tapes.

System is in unsafe state.!!!

$$T = 1000msec$$
$$= 1000 \times 10^{-3}sec$$
$$= 1sec$$

47. frequency $f = \frac{1}{T} = 1Hz$
$$= \frac{1}{1000}KHz$$
$$= 10^{-3}KHz$$

48. Race conditions in critical sections can be avoided if the critical section is treated as an atomic instruction. Also, proper thread synchronization using locks or atomic variables can prevent race conditions.

49. Modularity of program,Maintainability, Security are important to design the algorithm.

50. Privileged instruction cannot be the answer as system call is done from user mode and privileged instruction cannot be done from user mode.

51. For pure aloha Throughput(S) = Ge-2G.

For Slotted aloha Throughput(S) = Ge-G. (it is maximum at G = 1).

i.e. S = 1 ✕ e-1.

S = 1 / e.

S = 1 / 2.71

S = 0.368.

So, option (C) is correct

52. Transmission rate = frame rate * no of bits in a slot.

Frame rate = 4000 frames per second

# of bits in a slot = 8 bit

TDM = 4000 ✕ 8 bps = 32 Kbps.

So, option (C) is correct.

53. 100 Base TX, Fast Ethernet, transmits data at 100 Mbps. Segment size is 100 meter and it uses twisted pair cable. Base stands for baseband.

So, option (A) is correct.

54. In classless addressing :

- The number of addresses needs to be a power of 2
- The mask needs to be included in the address to define the block
- The starting address must be divisible by the number of addresses in the block

D is answer.

55. Dijkstra's algorithm

Link state protocols, sometimes called shortest path first or distributed database protocols, are built around a well-known algorithm from graph theory, E. W. Dijkstra's shortest path algorithm, which is is a graph search algorithm that solves the single-source shortest path problem for a graph with non-negative edge path costs, producing a shortest path tree. This algorithm is often used in routing and as a subroutine in other graph algorithms.

56. Binary Search Tree (BST):

Pre-order traversal: $41,23,11,31,62,50,73$

In order traversal: It is the sorted order of the nodes.

So, in order traversal for above BST is:

$11,23,31,41,50,62,73$

BST formation with pre-order and in-order traversal:

The first node of pre-order traversal is the root.

Then whatever comes the left-hand side of the root in in-order traversal will be the left subtree of the root.

Whatever comes on the right side of root in in-order traversal will be the right subtree of root.

The tree will become:

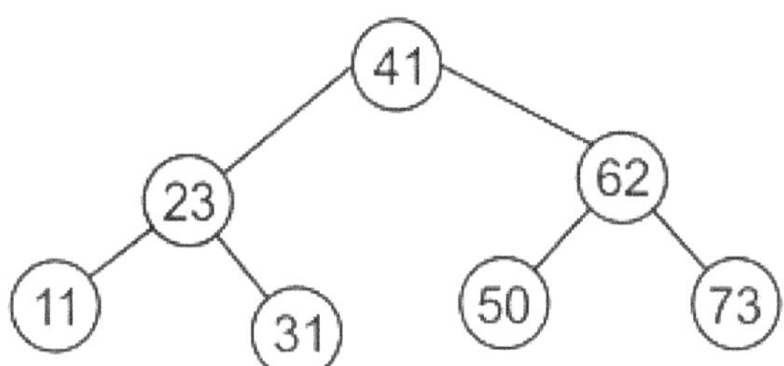

Now, we have to find the post order traversal of this tree:

Algorithm:

1) Traverse the left subtree

2) Traverse the right subtree

3) Visit the root

So, post order traversal will be: $11,31,23,50,73,62,41$

Hence, the correct option is (A).

57. (A) An instructor Id. No. cannot be null, provided Instructor Id No. being primary key. Correct by Codd's rule

(B) No two citizens have same Adhar-Id. Correct because Adhar is identification for citizens so it must be unique

(C) Budget of a company must be zero. We cant say or it is not necessarily true

So, option (C) is correct.

58. Dependency Preserving Decomposition:

Decomposition of R into R_1 and R_2 is a dependency preserving decomposition if closure of functional dependencies after

decomposition is same as closure of of FDs before decomposition.

A simple way is to just check whether we can derive all the original FDs from the FDs present after decomposition.

In the above question R(A, B, C, D) is decomposed into R_1 (A, B) and R_2(C, D) and there are only two FDs A -> B and C -> D. So, the decomposition is dependency preserving

Lossless-Join Decomposition:

Decomposition of R into R_1 and R_2 is a lossless-join decomposition if at least one of the following functional dependencies are in F+ (Closure of functional dependencies)

$R_1 \cap R_2 \rightarrow R_1$

  OR

$R_1 \cap R_2 \rightarrow R_2$

In the above question R(A, B, C, D) is decomposed into R_1(A, B) and R_2(C, D), and $R_1 \cap R_2$ is empty. So, the decomposition is not lossless.

59. SELECT A FROM R; **legal query**

SELECT A, COUNT(*) FROM R; **Illegal query** because we can't SELECT A, COUNT(*) unless it is grouped by A.

SELECT A, COUNT(*) FROM R GROUP BY A; **legal query**

SELECT A, B, COUNT(*) FROM R GROUP BY A, B; **legal query**

So, option (B) is correct.

60. $P \leftrightarrow Q$

$(P \rightarrow Q) \wedge (Q \rightarrow P)$

$(\sim P \vee Q) \wedge (\sim Q \vee P)$

B is answer.

61. a-iii is directly implied

b-i function oriented metrics measuring the following parameters:-

•Number of user inputs:

Each user input that provides distinct application oriented data to the software is counted.

•Number of user outputs:

Each user output that provides application oriented information to the user is counted. In this context output refers to reports, screens, error messages, etc.

•Number of user inquiries:

An inquiry is defined as an on-line input that

Results in the generation of some immediate software response in the form of an on-line output. Each distinct inquiry is counted.

•Number of files:

Each logical master file (i.e., a logical grouping of data that may be one part of a large database or a separate file) is counted.

•Number of external interfaces:

All machine readable interfaces (e.g., data files on storage media) that are used to transmit information to another system.

c-iv A function point extension called feature points, is a superset of the function point measure that can be applied to systems and engineering software applications.The feature point measure accommodates applications in which algorithmic complexity is high. Real-time, process control and embedded software applications tend to have high algorithmic complexity and are therefore amenable to the feature point.

d-ii A function point is a "unit of measurement" to express the amount of business functionality an information system (as a product) provides to a user. Function points are used to compute a functional size measurement (FSM) of software. The cost (in dollars or hours) of a single unit is calculated from past projects.

62. let $X=2^3=8=1000$

then $X-1=7=0111$

now $X\&(X-1)=0000$

(here & is bitwise AND= If both bits in the compared position of the bit patterns are 1, the bit in the resulting bit pattern is 1, otherwise 0)

So answer is B.

63. When there is an operand PUSH it on the stack, when there is an operator, POP top two operands from the stack and perform the operation and push the result back.

Here are the steps followed:

1) 3 PUSH

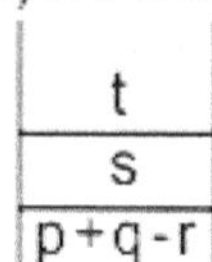

2) 2 POP, 1 PUSH

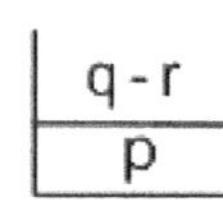

3) 2 POP, 1 PUSH

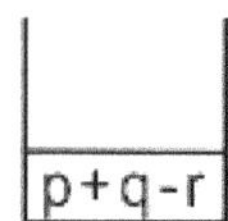

4) 2 PUSH

5) 2 POP, 1 PUSH

Total push operations $= 8$

Total Pop operations $= 6$

Hence, the correct option is (B).

64.

Interrupt	Vector Address

RST$_0$	0000H
RST$_1$	0008H
	0010H
RST$_2$	0018H
RST$_3$	
	0020H
RST$_4$	0028H
RST$_5$	
	0030H
RST$_6$	0038H
RST$_7$	

So, option (C) is correct answer.

65. A linker is computer software that combine two or more file generated by compiler into a single executable file.

Option I is correct but II option doesn't resemble linker.

66. We can generate more than 1 parse tree for a single string from the grammars. For statement (iii)

S → U

U → yT

yT → yxSy

yxSy → yxTy

yxTy → yxxyy

All statement are correct.

So, option (D) is correct.

67. The main drawback of the waterfall model is the difficulty of accommodating change after the process is underway. In principle, a phase has to be complete before moving onto the next phase. Waterfall model problems include:

1) Difficult to address change

Inflexible partitioning of the project into distinct stages makes it difficult to respond to changing customer requirements. Therefore, this model is only appropriate when the requirements are well-understood and changes will be fairly limited during the design process. Few business systems have stable requirements.

2) Very few real-world applications

The waterfall model is mostly used for large systems engineering projects where a system is developed at several sites. In those circumstances, the plan-driven nature of the waterfall model helps coordinate the work.

68. ans should be C in critical review committe , the CRC team must consist

1)one or two users representative

2)project co-ordinators

3)system analyst

need of programmers is not there as they can be co-ordianted later by project co-ordinators

69. McCall's Software Metrics - (Subjective)

*Auditability - The ease with which conformance to standards can be checked.

*Accuracy - The precision of computations and control.

*Communication commonality - The degree to which standard interfaces, protocols, and bandwidth are used.

*Completeness - The degree to which full implementation of required function has been achieved.

*Conciseness - The compactness of the program in terms of lines of code.

*Consistency - The use of uniform design and documentation techniques throughout the software development project.

*Data commonality - The use of standard data structures and types throughout the program.

*Error tolerance - The damage that occurs when the program encounters an error.

*Execution efficiency - The run-time performance of a program.

*Expandability - The degree to which architectural, data, or procedural design can be extended.

*Generality - The breadth of potential application of program components.

*Hardware independence - The degree to which the software is decoupled from the hardware on which it operates.

*Instrumentation - The degree to which the program monitors its own operation and identifies errors that do occur.

*Modularity - The functional independence (Chapter 13) of program components.

*Operability - The ease of operation of a program.

*Security - The availability of mechanisms that control or protect programs and data.

*Self-documentation - The degree to which the source code provides meaningful documentation.

*Simplicity - The degree to which a program can be understood without difficulty.

*Software system independence - The degree to which the program is independent of nonstandard programming language features, operating system characteristics, and other environmental constraints.

*Traceability - The ability to trace a design representation or actual program component back to requirements.

*Training - The degree to which the software assists in enabling new users to apply the system.

70. In relational model data is stored in tables and if we talk about data independence it is one of the major feature of DBMS which holds in all DBMS models.

71. According to the Capability Maturity Model (CMMI-SW v1.1),

Software Verification: The process of evaluating software to determine whether the products of a given development phase satisfy the conditions imposed at the start of that phase. [IEEE-STD-610]

Software Validation: The process of evaluating software during or at the end of the development process to determine whether it satisfies specified requirements.

72. Answer must be B

*The simple description of the problem:

*Five silent philosophers sit at a round table with bowls of spaghetti.Forks are placed between each pair of adjacent philosophers.

*Each philosopher must alternately think and eat.

*However, a philosopher can only eat spaghetti when he has both left and right forks.

*Each fork can be held by only one philosopher and so a philosopher can use the fork only if it is not being used by another philosopher.

*After he finishes eating, he needs to put down both forks so they become available to others.

*A philosopher can take the fork on his right or the one on his left as they become available, but cannot start eating before getting both of them.

*Eating is not limited by the remaining amounts of spaghetti or stomach space; an infinite supply and an infinite demand are assumed.

*The problem is how to design a discipline of behavior (a concurrent algorithm) such that no philosopher will starve; i.e., each can forever continue to alternate between eating and thinking, assuming that no philosopher can know when others may want to eat or think.

73. ECL remains for Emitter-Coupled Logic. It is intended for greatly fast application. It is appropriate for substantial centralized server PC that requires high number of operation every second.

74. ans must be 1)SCRIPT

```
<script>

document.getElementById("demo").innerHTML = "Hello JavaScript!";

</script>
```

rest options are part of a normal HTML document

75. Related data fields in a database are grouped to form a data record.

(A record is a collection of related fields)

76. Deletion of the last node of the linked list, we need address of second last node of single linked list to make NULL of its next pointer. Since we can not access its previous node in singly linked list, so need to traverse entire linked list to get second last node of linked list.

So, option (D) is correct.

77. Look at the above link on how algo works.

Lets consider there are 'K' buckets (as given).

Now, for each digit you repeat the following:

1) place the digit of each number in the appropriate bin. - ø(n)

2) append all the 'K' bins sequentially.

Thus, for a single digit, its ø(n+k),

For 'd' digits, its ø(d(n+k))

78. $F_{00}(2) = \dfrac{10 \times F_{00}(1) + 100}{F_{00}(0)} = \dfrac{10 \times 1 + 100}{1} = 110$

$F_{00}(3) = \dfrac{10 \times F_{00}(2) + 100}{F_{00}(1)} = \dfrac{10 \times 110 + 100}{1} = 1200$

So, Option (A) is correct.

79. CD-ROM is an inexpensive way to store large amount of data and information

80. For a compiler where pointers take 4 bytes, the statement "sizeof(Test *)" returns 4 (size of the pointer ptr).

The statement "sizeof(t)" returns 8. Since static is not associated with each object of the class, we get (8 not 12).

81. Any operation which is indivisible requires processor until it executes entirely. If processor decides to perform some other operation or service some other request like interrupt, the operation will be left to the current state and might never be executed entirely, ever. However, the state of operation might be or might not be consistent, but the operation is anyways reduced and violates the property of indivisible operation.

Race condition is an undesirable situation where two or more process attempts to modify same data at almost same time, which is a concept of multithreading.

82. In place sort are those sorts which doesn't need extra space it uses own space and in case if space is required then it is O(1).

83. In 3G network, W-CDMA is also known as UMTS. The minimum spectrum allocation required for W-CDMA is 5 MHz.

So, option (D) is correct.

84. The 8087 is divided into two sections namely control unit and numeric extension unit in which the numeric extension unit executes all the numeric processor instructions.

Hence the correct option is (C).

85. Data Scrubling (Data Cleaning.):-The process of removing data in a database that is incorrect, incomplete, improperly formatted, or duplicated before sending it into data warehouse.

86. inner join gives the record of two tables based on = condition

here R.B=S.B holds for 2 records when B=2 and B=4 hence its result w hence 2

for SQ_2 Full Join or full outer join gives the result of left outer join(all rows of left table whether there is match or not) + right outer join(all rows of right table whether there is match or not with the left) now both table has 3 records but there are 2 match and 2 mismatch

hence SQ_1 will give 4 records

So answer is option D.

87. The concept behind this solution is:

a) Satisfiable

If there is an assignment of truth values which makes that expression true.

b) UnSatisfiable

If there is no such assignment which makes the expression true

c) Valid

If the expression is Tautology

Here, P => Q is nothing but –P v Q

F_1: P => -P = -P v –P = -P

F_1 will be true if P is false and F_1 will be false when P is true so F_1 is Satisfiable

F_2: (P => -P) v (-P => P) which is equals to (-P v-P) v (-(-P) v P) = (-P) v (P) =

Tautology

So, F_1 is Satisfiable and F_2 is valid

Option (a) is correct.

88. If we perform 19P, 12V and 3P then

Value of s =15-19+12-3 =5

89. They are the principle tasks of the linker

I. Resolve external references among separately compiled program units.

III. Relocate code and data relative to the beginning of the program.

90. Correct answer is (D).

Hardware interrupts: The 8085 microprocessor has five hardware interrupt inputs (five pins). They are TRAP, RST 7.5, RST 6.5, RST 5.5 , and INTR in the decreasing order of priority. If two or more interrupts go high at the same time, the 8085 will service them on priority basis.

TRAP	RST 7.5	RST6. 5	RST 505	INTR
Edge triggered & level triggered	Edge triggered	Level triggered	Level triggered	Level triggered
Non-maskable. It can be masked only by resetting the microprocessor.	Maskable . DI instructio n	Maskable . DI and SIM instructio n	Maskable . DI and SIM instructio n	Maskable . DI and SIM instructio n

0024 H	003 CH	0034 H	002 CH	Not vectored

91. Implied is implicitly defined. So a→4

immediate mode takes directly the value contained in a register in CPU. So b→1

very direct c. Register →3 Specified in the register

and register indirect means that, it will first go to the register and get the Address, where the actual operand is residing

so d→2

so matching all these we get B is the correct answer

now you may have a doubt

i. Registers which are in CPU

iii. Specified in the register are same thing!!!!

but specified in register means ,operand specified in register. Suppose suppose i get an indirect addressing which referes me to A register, then again i am referred to register B that means it was directly not specified in register

and Direct addressing is not option 1, coz whatever direct and indirect is, registers will always will be in CPU..so that is pointless

92. For a program of k variables boundary value analysis yields 4 × k + 1 test

Robustness testing yields 6 × k + 1

worst case testing yields 5 × k.

So, option (C) is correct.

93. The Waterfall Model was first Process Model to be introduced.

- It is also referred to as a linear-sequential life cycle model.
- It is very simple to understand and use. In a waterfall model, each phase must be completed fully before the next phase can begin.
- This type of model is basically used for the for the project which is small and there are no uncertain requirements.
- At the end of each phase, a review takes place to determine if the project is on the right path and whether or not to continue or discard the project.
- In this model the testing starts only
- after the development is complete.
- In waterfall model phases do not overlap.

94. The control unit is used for establishing communication between CPU and memory and coordinating the internal coprocessor execution.

95. Printing the elements in an order means the elements should be printed in sorted order and we know inorder traversal of BST takes gives the sorted order and takes O(n) time.The recurrence involved is :

T(n) = 2T(n/2) + c for balanced BST which on solving gives O(n) and also for skewed tree T(n) = T(n-1) + c which also on solving gives O(n) time.Hence (C) is the correct option.

96. a. Polymorphism---->Using similar operations to do similar things

b. Inheritance -----> Create new classes from existing class

c.Encapsulation---->Hiding implementation details of methods from users of objects

d.Abstraction--->Picking both operator and attributes with operations appropriate to model an object

97. A function template in C++ provides 2 level of generalization.

98. When set a and set b all rows are distinct ans would be = 10+7 = 17

When set b is subset of set a than

10+7-7 = 10

Only these two options are preferable.

99. Remember with 'n' no. of flip-flop you can get upto max. modulo-[2n] counter.

Since 2 9 = 512 > 272 it can satisfy the condition

100. S_1 : Ethernet frame include CRC not checksum.

S_2 : ARP request is broadcast and reply is unicast.

S_3 : Differential Manchester encoding has a transition at the middle of each bit. S_2 and S_3 both are true.

Mock Test 02

Q.1 Consider the graph given below:

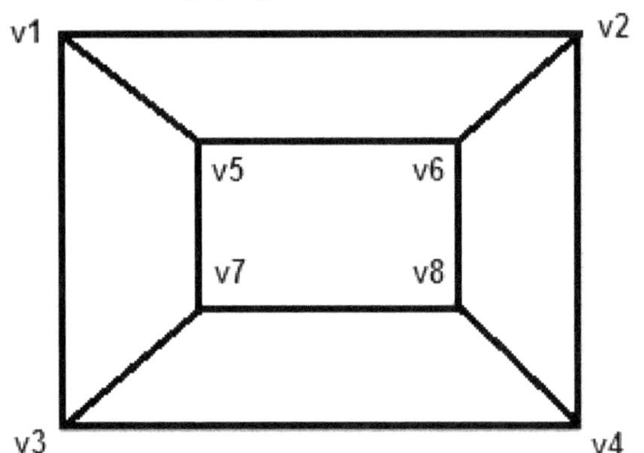

The two distinct sets of vertices, which make the graph bipartite are:

A. (v1, v4, v6); (v2, v3, v5, v7, v8)
B. (v1, v7, v8); (v2, v3, v5, v6)
C. (v1, v4, v6, v7); (v2, v3, v5, v8)
D. (v1, v4, v6, v7, v8); (v2, v3, v5)

Q.2 Which is not functionality of computer network

A. Error control   **B.** Access control
C. flow control   **D.** none

Q.3 How many committees of five people can be chosen from 20 men and 12 women such that each committee contains at least three women?

A. 75,240   **B.** 52,492   **C.** 41,800   **D.** 9,900

Q.4 The number of disk pages access in B-tree search, where h is height, n is the number of keys, and t is the minimum degree, is:

A. $\Theta(\log_n h \times t)$ **B.** $\Theta(\log_t n \times h)$
C. $\Theta(\log_h n)$ **D.** $\Theta(\log_t n)$

Q.5 Given two sequences X and Y:
X = < a, b, c, b, d, a, b >
Y = < b, d, c, a, b, a >
The longest common subsequence of X and Y is:

A. < b, c, a >   **B.** < c, a, b >
C. < b, c, a, a >   **D.** < b, c, b, a >

Q.6 Consider the following two statements:
(a) A publicly derived class is a sub-type of its base class.
(b) Inheritance provides for code reuse.

A. Both the statements (a) and (b) are correct.
B. Neither of the statements (a) and (b) is correct.
C. Statement (a) is correct and (b) is incorrect.
D. Statement (a) is incorrect and (b) is correct.

Q.7 Which of the following graphic primitives is/are considered as the basic building blocks of computer graphics?
(a) Points
(b) Lines
(c) Polylines
(d) Polygons

A. (a) only   **B.** (a) and (b)
C. (a), (b) and (c)   **D.** (a), (b), (c) and (d)

Q.8 What is the output of the following program?
(Assume that the appropriate preprocessor directives are included and there is no syntax error.)

```
main ( )
{ char S[ ] = ABCDEFGH;
printf (%C, *(&S[3]));
printf (%s, S + 4);
printf (%u, S);
/* Base address of S is 1000 */
}
```

A. ABCDEFGH1000   **B.** CDEFGH1000
C. DDEFGHH1000   **D.** DEFGH1000

Q.9 A system has four processes and five allocatable resources. The current allocation and maximum needs are as follows:

	Allocated	Maximum	Available
Process A	1 0 2 1 1	1 1 2 1 3	0 0 x 1 1
Process B	2 0 1 1 0	2 2 2 1 0	
Process C	1 1 0 1 0	2 1 3 1 0	
Process D	1 1 1 1 0	1 1 2 2 1	

The smallest value of x for which the above system is in safe state is _________.

A. 1   **B.** 3   **C.** 2   **D.** 0

Q.10 A virtual memory has a page size of 1K words. There are eight pages and four blocks. The associative memory page table contains the following entries:

Page	Block
0	3
2	1
5	2
7	0

Which of the following lists of virtual addresses (in decimal) will not cause any page fault if referenced by the CPU?

A. 1024, 3072, 4096, 6144
B. 1234, 4012, 5000, 6200
C. 1020, 3012, 6120, 8100
D. 2021, 4050, 5112, 7100

Q.11 Match the following with respect to various memory management algorithms:

List - I	List - II
(a) Demand paging	(i) degree of multiprogramming
(b) Segmentation	(ii) working set
(c) Dynamic partitions	(iii) supports user view of memory
(d) Fixed partitions	(iv) compaction

- **A.** (a) - (iii), (b) - (iv), (c) - (ii), (d) - (i)
- **B.** (a) - (ii), (b) - (iii), (c) - (i), (d) - (iv)
- **C.** (a) - (iv), (b) - (iii), (c) - (ii), (d) - (i)
- **D.** (a) - (ii), (b) - (iii), (c) - (iv), (d) - (i)

Q.12 A CPU handles interrupt by executing interrupt service subroutine _________.

- **A.** by checking interrupt register after execution of each instruction
- **B.** by checking interrupt register at the end of the fetch cycle
- **C.** whenever an interrupt is registered
- **D.** by checking interrupt register at regular time interval

Q.13 In Unix, the login prompt can be changed by changing the contents of the file _________.

A. contrab   **B.** init   **C.** gettydefs   **D.** inittab

Q.14 Consider Round Robin scheduling algorithm with the time quantum of 2. There are 5 processes for which their process id, arrival time and burst time is given as

Process id	Arrival time	Burst time
P0	2	2
P1	1	4
P2	0	1
P3	3	5
P4	4	3

Average waiting time and completion of execution of the processes

- **A.** 4.75 & P4 before P3
- **B.** 3.80 & P3 before P4
- **C.** 3.80 & P4 before P3
- **D.** 4.75 & P3 before P4

Q.15 What will be the position of hosts which have taken services from DHCP server, when DHCP server goes down?

- **A.** There will be no communication of hosts with other hosts
- **B.** There will be communication among the hosts limited time
- **C.** Communication among the hosts will take place outsides the network
- **D.** Communication among the hosts is only possible by IP address

Q.16 The combination of an IP address and a port number is known as _________.

- **A.** network number
- **B.** socket address
- **C.** subnet mask number
- **D.** MAC address

Q.17 What will be the output at PORT1, if the following program is executed?

```
MVI B, 82H
MOV A, B
MOV C, A
MVI D, 37H
OUT PORT1
HLT
```

A. 37H   **B.** 82H   **C.** B9H   **D.** 00H

Q.18 Consider a subnet with 720 routers. If a 3-level hierarchy is choosen with 8 clusters, each containing 9 regions of 10 routers, then total number of entries in the routing table is _________.

A. 25   **B.** 27   **C.** 53   **D.** 72

Q.19 In classful addressing, the IP addresses with 0 (zero) as network number

- **A.** refers to the current network
- **B.** refers to broadcast on the local network
- **C.** refers to broadcast on a distant network
- **D.** refers to loopback testing

Q.20 Which of the following is incorrect in C++?
(1) Upon writing overloaded function, it must be coded for each usage.
(2) Upon writing function template, it is coded only once.
(3) It is difficult to debug macros.
(4) Templates are more efficient than macros.

- **A.** (1) and (2)
- **B.** (1), (2) and (3)
- **C.** (3) and (4)
- **D.** All are correct.

Q.21 Match the following database terms to their respective functions:

List - I	List - II
(a) Normalisation	(i) Enforces match of primary key to foreign key
(b) Data dictionary	(ii) Reduces data redundancy in a database
(c) Referential integrity	(iii) Defines view(s) of the database for particular user(s)
(d) External schema	(iv) Contains metadata describing database structure

- **A.** (a) - (iv), (b) - (iii), (c) - (i), (d) - (ii)
- **B.** (a) - (ii), (b) - (iv), (c) - (i), (d) - (iii)
- **C.** (a) - (ii), (b) - (iv), (c) - (iii), (d) - (i)
- **D.** (a) - (iv), (b) - (iii), (c) - (ii), (d) - (i)

Q.22 Consider the following database table:
```
Create table test(
one integer,
two integer,
primary key(one),
unique(two),
check(one >= 1 and <= 10), check(two >= 1 and <= 5) );
```
How many data records/tuples atmost can be contained in this table?

A. 5   **B.** 10   **C.** 15   **D.** 50

Q.23 In propositional logic, given P and P $\rightarrow$ Q, we can infer _________.

A. ~ Q   **B.** Q   **C.** P ∧ Q   **D.** ~ P ∧ Q

Q.24 'If my computations are correct and I pay the electric bill, then I will run out of money. If I don't pay the electric bill, the power will be turned off. Therefore, if I don't run out of money and the power is still on, then my computations are incorrect.' Convert this argument into logical notations using the variables c, b, r, p for propositions of computations, electric bills, out of money and the power, respectively. (Where ¬ means NOT)

A. If $(c \wedge b) \rightarrow r$ and $\neg b \rightarrow \neg p$, then $(\neg r \wedge p) \rightarrow \neg c$
B. If $(c \vee b) \rightarrow r$ and $\neg b \rightarrow \neg p$, then $(r \wedge p) \rightarrow c$
C. If $(c \wedge b) \rightarrow r$ and $\neg p \rightarrow b$, then $(\neg r \vee p) \rightarrow \neg c$
D. If $(c \vee b) \rightarrow r$ and $\neg b \rightarrow \neg p$, then $(\neg r \wedge p) \rightarrow \neg c$

Q.25 A dynamic RAM has refresh cycle of 32 times per msec. Each refresh operation requires 100 nsec and a memory cycle requires 250 nsec. What percentage of memory's total operating time is required for refreshes?

A. 0.64   **B.** 0.96   **C.** 2.00   **D.** 0.32

Q.26 In 8085 microprocessor, which of the following flag(s) is/are affected by an arithmetic operation?

A. AC flag only   **B.** CY flag only
C. Z flag only   **D.** AC, CY, Z flags

Q.27 In 8085 microprocessor, the address bus is of _________ bits.

A. 4   **B.** 8   **C.** 16   **D.** 32

Q.28 Loop unrolling is a code optimisation technique that

A. avoids tests at every iteration of the loop
B. improves performance by decreasing the number of instructions in a basic block
C. exchanges inner loops with outer loops
D. reorders operations to allow multiple computations to happen in parallel

Q.29 8085 microprocessor has ____ bit ALU.

A. 32   **B.** 16   **C.** 8   **D.** 4

Q.30 There are four bus routes between A and B; and three bus routes between B and C. A man can travel round-trip in number of ways by bus from A to C via B. If he does not want to use a bus route more than once, in how many ways can he make round trip?

A. 72   **B.** 144   **C.** 14   **D.** 19

Q.31 Which of the following is/are **CORRECT** statement(s) about version and release?
I. A version is an instance of a system, which is functionally identical but non-functionally distinct from other instances of a system.
II. A version is an instance of a system, which is functionally distinct in some way from other system instances.
III. A release is an instance of a system, which is distributed to users outside of the development team.
IV. A release is an instance of a system, which is functionally identical but non-functionally distinct from other instances of a system.

A. I and III   **B.** II and IV   **C.** I and IV   **D.** II and III

Q.32 Javascript and Java have similar names because _________ is/are true.

(a) syntax used in Javascript is loosely based on syntax used in Java
(b) Javascript is a stripped down version of Java
(c) Java and Javascript originated from the Island of Java

A. (a) only   **B.** (a), (b) and (c)
C. (a) and (b)   **D.** (a) and (c)

Q.33 Which of the following statements is incorrect?

A. Pareto analysis is a statistical method used for analysing causes, and is one of the primary tools for quality management.
B. Reliability of a software specifies the probability of failure-free operation of that software for a given time duration.
C. The reliability of a system can also be specified as the Mean Time To Failure (MTTF).
D. In white-box testing, the test cases are decided from the specifications or the requirements.

Q.34 Which of the following statements, related to the requirement phase in Software Engineering is incorrect?

A. 'Requirement validation' is one of the activities in the requirement phase.
B. 'Prototyping' is one of the methods for requirement analysis.
C. 'Modelling-oriented approach' is one of the methods for specifying the functional specifications.
D. 'Function points' is one of the most commonly used size metric for requirements.

Q.35 Which of the following character sets is used in Windows 2000 operating system?

A. 8 bit ASCII   **B.** Extended ASCII
C. 16 bit UNICODE   **D.** 12 bit UNICODE

Q.36 Match the following w.r.t. programming language:

List - I	List - II
(a) JAVA	(i) Dynamically object oriented
(b) Python	(ii) Statically non-object oriented
(c) Prolog	(iii) Statically object oriented
(d) ADA	(iv) Dynamically non-object oriented

A. (a) - (iii), (b) - (i), (c) - (ii), (d) - (iv)
B. (a) - (ii), (b) - (i), (c) - (iii), (d) - (iv)
C. (a) - (i), (b) - (iv), (c) - (iii), (d) - (ii)
D. None of these

Q.37 Is there any difference in the speed of execution between linear serach(recursive) vs linear search(Iterative)?

A. Both execute at same speed
B. Linear search(recursive) is faster
C. Linear search(Iterative) is faster
D. Cant be said

Q.38 Consider a Standard Additive Model consisting of rules of the following form:
If x is A_i and y is B_i, then z is C_i.
Given crisp inputs x = x_0, y = y_0, the output of the model is:

A. $z = \sum_i \mu_{Ai}(x_0)\mu_{Bi}(y_0)\mu_{Ci}(z)$
B. $z = \sum_i \mu_{Ai}(x_0)\mu_{Bi}(Y_0)$
C. $z = $centroid $\sum_i \mu_{Ai}(x_0)\mu_{Bi}(Y_0)\mu_{Ci}(z)$

D. $z =$ centroid $\sum_i \mu_{Ai}(x_0)\mu_{Bi}(Y_0)$

Q.39 In general, in a recursive and non-recursive implementation of a problem (program)

A. both time and space complexities are better in recursive than in non-recursive program

B. both time and space complexities are better in non-recursive than in recursive program

C. time complexity is better in recursive version but space complexity is better in non-recursive version of the program

D. space complexity is better in recursive version but time complexity is better in non-recursive version of the program

Q.40 Which of the following is the solution of the given recurrence relation?

T(n) ≤ {θ(1) if n ≤ 80

T(n) ≤ { T(n/s) + T((7n/10) + 6) + O(n), if n ≥ 80

A. O(lg n)
B. O(n)
C. O(n lg n)
D. None of the above

Q.41 Let the number of instructions executed between page fault be directly proportional to the number of page frames allocated to a program. If the available memory is doubled, then the mean interval between page faults also doubles. Further, consider that a normal instruction takes one microsecond, but if a page fault occurs, it takes 2,001 microseconds. If a program takes 60 seconds to run, during which time it gets 15,000 page faults, then how long would it take to run, if twice as much memory were available?

A. 60 seconds
B. 30 seconds
C. 45 seconds
D. 10 seconds

Q.42 Which of the following concurrency protocols ensures both conflict serialisability and freedom from deadlock?
(a) z - phase locking
(b) Time stamp - ordering

A. Both (a) and (b)
B. (a) only
C. (b) only
D. Neither (a) nor (b)

Q.43 Which of the following is/are correct with reference to abstract class and interface?
(a) A class can inherit only one abstract class but may inherit several interfaces.
(b) An abstract class can provide complete and default code but an interface has no code.

A. (a) is true.
B. (b) is true.
C. Both (a) and (b) are true.
D. Neither (a) nor (b) is true.

Q.44 Which of the following, in C++, is inherited in a derived class from base class?

A. Constructor
B. Destructor
C. Data members
D. Virtual method

Q.45 Let P_i and P_j be two processes, R be the set of variables read from memory, and W be the set of variables written to memory. For the concurrent execution of two processes P_i and P_j, which of the following conditions is not true?

A. $R(P_i) \cap W(P_j) = \Phi$
B. $W(P_i) \cap R(P_j) = \Phi$
C. $R(P_i) \cap R(P_j) = \Phi$
D. $W(P_i) \cap W(P_j) = \Phi$

Q.46 Function of memory management unit is
A. address translation
B. memory allocation
C. cache management
D. All of the above

Q.47 Consider three CPU intensive processes P_1, P_2, P_3 which require 20, 10 and 30 units of time, arrive at times 1, 3 and 7, respectively. Suppose operating system is implementing Shortest Remaining Time First (preemptive scheduling) algorithm, then ____ context switches are required (suppose context switch at the beginning of Ready queue and at the end of Ready queue are not counted).

A. 3
B. 2
C. 4
D. 5

Q.48 LRU page replacement is used with four page frames and eight pages. How many page faults will occur with the reference string 0172327103 if the four frames are initially empty?

A. 6
B. 7
C. 8
D. 5

Q.49 A unix file system has 1 KB blocks and 4-byte disk addresses. What is the maximum file size if i-nodes contain 10 direct entries and one single, double and triple indirect entries each?

A. 32 GB
B. 64 GB
C. 16 GB
D. 1 GB

Q.50 Which of the following is true?
A. The code that changes the system clock runs in user mode.
B. Context switching between two kernel threads has about the same overhead as that between two user processes.
C. A thread can be blocked on multiple condition variables simultaneously.
D. None of the above

Q.51 A device is sending out data at the rate of 2000 bps. How long does it take to send a file of 1,00,000 characters?

A. 50 seconds
B. 200 seconds
C. 400 seconds
D. 800 seconds

Q.52 A network with bandwidth of 10 Mbps can pass only an average of 15,000 frames per minute with each frame carrying an average of 8,000 bits. What is the throughput of this network?

A. 2 Mbps
B. 60 Mbps
C. 120 Mbps
D. 10 Mbps

Q.53 What is the size of the 'total length' field in IPv4 datagram?

A. 4 bits
B. 8 bits
C. 16 bits
D. 32 bits

Q.54 In the case of parallelization, Amdahl's law states that if P is the proportion of a program that can be made parallel and (1 - P) is the proportion that cannot be parallelized, then the maximum speed-up that can be achieved by using N processors is:

A. $\dfrac{1}{(1-P)+N\cdot P}$
B. $\dfrac{1}{(N-1)P+P}$

C. $\dfrac{1}{(1-P)+\frac{P}{N}}$ **D.** $\dfrac{1}{(P)+\frac{(1-P)}{N}}$

Q.55 The distributed system is a collection of (P) and communication is achieved in distributed system by (Q), where (P) and (Q) are

A. loosely coupled hardware on tightly coupled software and disk sharing, respectively

B. tightly coupled hardware on loosely coupled software and shared memory, respectively

C. tightly coupled software on loosely coupled hardware and message passing, respectively

D. loosely coupled software on tightly coupled hardware and file sharing, respectively

Q.56 Which of the following statements is **false** about weak entity set?

A. Weak entities can be deleted automatically when their strong entity is deleted.

B. Weak entity set avoids data duplication and consequent possible inconsistencies caused by duplicating the keys of the strong entity.

C. A weak entity set has no primary keys, unless attributes of the strong entity set on which it depends are included.

D. Tuples in a weak entity set are not partitioned according to their relationship with tuples in a strong entity set.

Q.57 An attribute A of datatype varchar(20) has value 'Ram' and the attribute B of datatype char(20) has value 'Sita' in oracle. The attribute A has ____ memory spaces and B has ____ memory spaces.

A. 20, 20   **B.** 3, 20   **C.** 3, 4   **D.** 20, 4

Q.58 Reasoning strategies used in expert systems include __________.

A. forward chaining, backward chaining and problem reduction

B. forward chaining, backward chaining and boundary mutation

C. forward chaining, backward chaining and back propagation

D. backward chaining, problem reduction and boundary mutation

Q.59 The clausal form of the disjunctive normal form $\times A \vee \times B \vee \times C \vee D$ is:

A. $A \wedge B \wedge C \Rightarrow D$

B. $A \vee B \vee C \vee D \Rightarrow$ true

C. $A \wedge B \wedge C \wedge D \Rightarrow$ true

D. $A \wedge B \wedge C \wedge D \Rightarrow$ false

Q.60 Blind image deconvolution is __________.

A. combination of blur identification and image restoration

B. combination of segmentation and classification

C. combination of blur and non-blur image

D. None of the above

Q.61 A ripple counter is a/an

A. synchronous counter

B. asynchronous counter

C. parallel counter

D. None of the above

Q.62 In the architecture of the 8085 microprocessor, match the following:

List - I	List - II
(a) Process unit	(i) Interrupt
(b) Instruction unit	(ii) General purpose register
(c) Storage and interface unit	(iii) ALU
	(iv) Timing and control

A. (a) - (iv), (b) - (i), (c) - (ii)

B. (a) - (iii), (b) - (iv), (c) - (ii)

C. (a) - (ii), (b) - (iii), (c) - (i)

D. (a) - (i), (b) - (ii), (c) - (iv)

Q.63 Which of the following statements is false?

A. Top-down parsers are LL parsers where first L stands for left-to-right scan and second L stands for leftmost derivation.

B. (000)* is a regular expression that matches only strings containing an odd number of zeroes, including the empty string.

C. Bottom-up parsers are in the LR family, where L stands for left-to-right scan and R stands for rightmost derivation.

D. The class of context-free languages is closed under reversal, i.e. if L is any context-free language, then the language $L^R = \{w^R; w \in L\}$ is context-free.

Q.64 The register that stores the bits required to mask the interrupts is _____.

A. status register

B. interrupt service register

C. interrupt mask register

D. interrupt request register

Q.65 How are the status of the carry, auxiliary carry and parity flag affected if the write instruction

MOV A,#9C

ADD A,#64H

A. CY=0,AC=0,P=0   **B.** CY=1,AC=1,P=0

C. CY=0,AC=1,P=0   **D.** CY=1,AC=1,P=1

Q.66 The ISO quality assurance standard that applies to Software Engineering is:

A. ISO 9000 : 2004   **B.** ISO 9001 : 2000

C. ISO 9002 : 2001   **D.** ISO 9003 : 2004

Q.67 Which of the following are external qualities of a software product?

A. Maintainability, reusability, portability, efficiency, correctness

B. Correctness, reliability, robustness, efficiency, usability

C. Portability, interoperability, maintainability, reusability

D. Robustness, efficiency, reliability, maintainability, reusability

Q.68 In perspective projection (from 3D to 2D), objects behind the centre of projection are projected upside down and backward onto the view-plane. This is known as ____.

A. topological distortion

B. vanishing point

C. view confusion
D. perspective foreshortening

Q.69 Which of the following tags in HTML is used to surround information such as signature of the person who created the page?
A. <body></body>
B. <address></address>
C. <strong></strong>
D. <em></em>

Q.70 What will be the output of the following Unix command?
$rm chap0[1 - 3]
A. Remove file chap0[1 - 3]
B. Remove file chap01, chap02, chap03
C. Remove file chap[1 - 3]
D. None of the above

Q.71 Which of the following statements is/are true with reference to the way of describing XML data?
(a) XML uses DTD to describe the data.
(b) XML uses XSL to describe the data.
(c) XML uses a description node to describe the data.

A. Only (a)
B. Only (b)
C. Both (a) and (b)
D. Both (a) and (c)

Q.72 The end points of a given line are (0, 0) and (6, 18). Compute each value of y as x steps from 0 to 3, by using equation of straight line.
A. For x = 0, y = 0; x = 1, y = 3; x = 2, y = 6; x = 3, y = 9
B. For x = 0, y = 1; x = 1, y = 3; x = 2, y = 4; x = 3, y = 9
C. For x = 0, y = 2; x = 1, y = 3; x = 2, y = 6; x = 3, y = 9
D. For x = 0, y = 0; x = 1, y = 3; x = 2, y = 4; x = 3, y = 6

Q.73 The maximum number of nodes in a binary tree of level k, k ≥1 is :
A. 2^k+1
B. 2^{k-2}
C. 2^k-1
D. $2^{k+1}-1$

Q.74 The average case occurs in the Linear Search Algorithm when
A. the item to be searched is somewhere in the middle of the array
B. the item to be searched is not in the array
C. the item to be searched is in the last of the array
D. the item to be searched is either in the last or is not in the array

Q.75 Which of the following statements regarding the features of the object-oriented approach to databases are true?
(a) The ability to develop more realistic models of the real world.
(b) The ability to represent the world in a non-geometric way.
(c) The ability to develop databases using natural language approaches.
(d) The need to split objects into their component parts.
(e) The ability to develop database models based on location rather than state and behaviour.
A. (a), (b) and (c)
B. (b), (c) and (d)
C. (a), (d) and (e)
D. (c), (d) and (e)

Q.76 Given: x = 7.5, j = -1.0, n = 1.0, m = 2.0
The value of - - x + j = = x > n > = m is:
A. 0
B. 1
C. 2
D. 3

Q.77 The output of the 4-to-1 MUX shown in below is

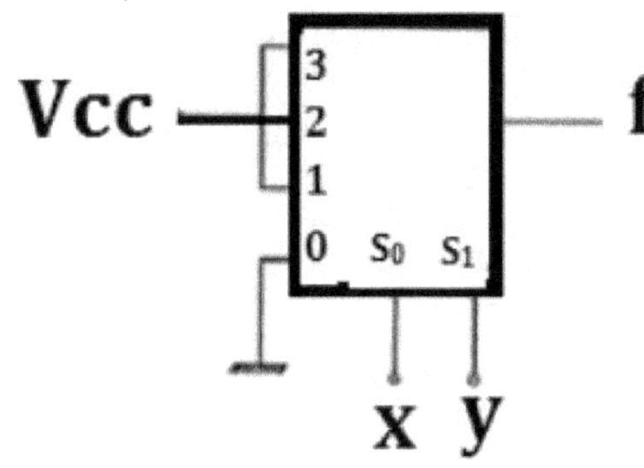

A. $xy + x$
B. $x + y$
C. $x + y$
D. $xy + x$

Q.78 Drop Table cannot be used to drop a Table referenced by __________ constraint.
(a) primary key
(b) sub key
(c) super key
(d) foreign key
A. (a)
B. (a), (b) and (c)
C. (d)
D. (a) and (d)

Q.79 Which of the following steps is/are **not** required for analog to digital conversion?
(a) Sensing
(b) Conversion
(c) Amplification
(d) Conditioning
(e) Quantisation
A. (a) and (b)
B. (c) and (d)
C. (a), (b) and (e)
D. None of the above

Q.80 In Unix operating system, special files are used to
A. buffer data received in its input from where a process reads
B. provide a mechanism to map physical device to file names
C. store list of file names plus pointers associated with i-nodes
D. store information entered by a user application program or utility program

Q.81 An attacker sits between the sender and the receiver, and captures the information and re-transmits to the receiver after some time without altering the information. This attack is called _____.
A. denial of service attack
B. masquarade attack
C. simple attack
D. complex attack

Q.82 An assertion is a predicate expressing a condition we wish database to always satisfy. The correct syntax for assertion is
A. CREATE ASSERTION 'ASSERTION Name' CHECK 'Predicate'
B. CREATE ASSERTION 'ASSERTION Name'

C. CREATE ASSERTION, CHECK 'Predicate'

D. SELECT ASSERTION

Q.83 Consider the following three tables R, S and T. In this question, all the join operations are natural joins (⋈).

(π) is the projection operation of a relation.

R	
A	B
1	2
3	2
5	6
7	8
9	8

S	
B	C
6	2
2	4
8	1
8	3
2	5

T	
A	C
7	1
1	2
9	3
5	4
3	5

Which of the following is one of the possible answer tables?

A.

A	B	C
1	2	4
1	2	5
3	2	4
3	2	5
5	6	2
7	8	1
7	8	3
9	8	1
9	8	3

B.

A	B	C
1	2	2
3	2	5
5	6	4
7	8	1
9	8	3

C.

A	B	C
1	6	2
3	2	5
5	2	4
7	8	1
9	8	3

<table>
<tr><td>A</td><td>B</td><td>C</td></tr>
<tr><td>3</td><td>2</td><td>5</td></tr>
<tr><td>7</td><td>8</td><td>1</td></tr>
<tr><td>9</td><td>8</td><td>3</td></tr>
</table>

D.

Q.84 Match the following:

List - I	List - II
(a) $(p \rightarrow q) \Leftrightarrow (\neg q \rightarrow \neg p)$	(i) Contrapositive
(b) $[(p \wedge q) \rightarrow r] \Leftrightarrow [p \rightarrow (q \rightarrow r)]$	(ii) Exportation law
(c) $(p \rightarrow q) \Leftrightarrow [(p \wedge \neg q) \rightarrow o]$	(iii) Reductio ad absurdum
(d) $(p \leftrightarrow q) \Leftrightarrow [(p \rightarrow q) \wedge (q \rightarrow p)]$	(iv) Equivalence

A. (a) - (i), (b) - (ii), (c) - (iii), (d) - (iv)
B. (a) - (ii), (b) - (iii), (c) - (i), (d) - (iv)
C. (a) - (iii), (b) - (ii), (c) - (iv), (d) - (i)
D. (a) - (iv), (b) - (ii), (c) - (iii), (d) - (i)

Q.85 A context free grammar for $L = \{w \mid n_0(w) > n_1(w)\}$ is given by:
A. $S \rightarrow 0|0S|1SS$
B. $S \rightarrow 0S|1S|0SS|1SS|0|1$
C. $S \rightarrow 0|0S|1SS|S1S|SS1$
D. $S \rightarrow 0S|1S|0|1$

Q.86 Which of the following is/are the principle components of a memory-tube display?
(a) Flooding gun
(b) Collector
(c) Phosphorus grains
(d) Ground
A. (a) and (b)
B. (c) only
C. (d) only
D. All of the above

Q.87 A design concept refinement is a
A. top-down approach
B. complementary of abstraction concept
C. process of elaboration
D. All of the above

Q.88 For a weak entity set to be meaningful, it must be associated with another entity set in combination with some of their attribute values. Such a set is called as

A. neighbour set
B. strong entity set
C. owner entity set
D. weak set

Q.89 Which of the following is not Linear Data Structure-
A. Array
B. Queue
C. Tree
D. Linked List

Q.90 Adaptive maintenance is a maintenance which _______.
A. corrects errors that were not discovered till testing phase
B. is carried out to port the existing software to a new environment
C. improves the system performance
D. Both (2) and (3)

Q.91 An Operating System (OS) crashes on the average once in 30 days, i.e. the Mean Time Between Failures (MTBF) = 30 days. When this happens, it takes 10 minutes to recover the OS, i.e. the Mean Time To Repair (MTTR) = 10 minutes. The availability of the OS with these reliability figures is approximately:
A. 96.97% **B.** 97.97% **C.** 99.009% **D.** 99.97%

Q.92 If we push data onto the stack then the stack pointer
A. increases with every push
B. decreases with every push
C. increases & decreases with every push
D. none of the mentioned

Q.93 Which Among the following is Static Data Structure-
A. Linked List
B. Queue
C. Stack
D. Array

Q.94 To determine the efficiency of an algorithm, the time factor is measured by counting
A. micro seconds
B. number of key operations
C. number of statements
D. kilobytes of algorithm

Q.95 Match the following:

(a) Forward reference table	(i) Assembler directive
(b) Mnemonic table	(ii) Uses array data structure
(c) Segment register table	(iii) Contains machine OP code
(d) EQU	(iv) Uses linked list data structure

A. (a) - (ii), (b) - (iii), (c) - (iv), (d) - (i)
B. (a) - (iii), (b) - (iv), (c) - (ii), (d) - (i)
C. (a) - (iv), (b) - (i), (c) - (iii), (d) - (ii)
D. (a) - (iv), (b) - (iii), (c) - (ii), (d) - (i)

Q.96 When the inheritance is private, the private methods in base class are _______ in the derived class (in C++).
A. inaccessible
B. accessible
C. protected
D. public

Q.97 Consider a full adder with the following input values.
(a) $x = 1$, $y = 0$ and C_i(carry input) = 0
(b) $x = 0$, $y = 1$ and $C_i = 1$
Compute the values of S(sum) and C_o(carry output) for the above input values.
A. $S = 1$, $C_o = 0$ and $S = 0$, $C_o = 1$

B. $S = 0$, $C_o = 0$ and $S = 1$, $C_o = 1$

C. $S = 1$, $C_o = 1$ and $S = 0$, $C_o = 0$

D. $S_o = 0$, $C_o = 1$ and $S = 1$, $C_o = 0$

Q.98 A DMA controller transfers 32 bit words to memory using cycle stealing. The words are assembled from a device that transmits characters at a rate of 4,800 characters per second. The CPU is fetching and executing instructions at an average rate of one million instructions per second. How much will the CPU slow down because of the DMA transfer?

A. 0.6%   **B.** 0.12%   **C.** 1.2%   **D.** 2.5%

Q.99 Directions: Consider the following statements.

(a) Boolean expressions and logic networks correspond to labelled acyclic digraphs.

(b) Optimal boolean expressions may not correspond to simplest networks.

(c) Choosing essential blocks first in a Karnaugh map and then, greedily choosing the largest remaining blocks to cover may not give an optimal expression.

Which of these statement(s) is/are correct?

A. (a) only   **B.** (b) only

C. (a) and (b)   **D.** (a), (b) and (c)

Q.100 Directions: Match the following port numbers with their uses.

List - I	List - II
(a) 23	(i) World Wide Web
(b) 25	(ii) Remote login
(c) 80	(iii) USENET news
(d) 119	(iv) E-mail

A. (a) - (iv), (b) - (i), (c) - (ii), (d) - (iii)

B. (a) - (ii), (b) - (i), (c) - (iv), (d) - (iii)

C. (a) - (ii), (b) - (iv), (c) - (iii), (d) - (i)

D. (a) - (ii), (b) - (iv), (c) - (i), (d) - (iii)

// Smart Answer Sheet //

Correct Percentage of students who answered correctly. **Skipped** Percentage of students who skipped.

Q.	Ans.	Correct / Skipped	Q.	Ans.	Correct / Skipped	Q.	Ans.	Correct / Skipped	Q.	Ans.	Correct / Skipped	Q.	Ans.	Correct / Skipped
1	C	49.62 % / 12.98 %	17	B	33.59 % / 37.4 %	33	B	23.66 % / 38.94 %	49	C	31.3 % / 41.22 %	65	B	27.48 % / 41.99 %
2	D	34.35 % / 33.59 %	18	A	25.95 % / 35.12 %	34	C	22.14 % / 39.69 %	50	D	16.79 % / 38.94 %	66	B	41.22 % / 42.75 %
3	B	32.06 % / 37.41 %	19	A	32.82 % / 36.65 %	35	C	28.24 % / 39.7 %	51	C	20.61 % / 39.7 %	67	B	22.14 % / 41.98 %
4	D	20.61 % / 33.59 %	20	D	30.53 % / 35.88 %	36	D	15.27 % / 39.69 %	52	A	27.48 % / 41.99 %	68	C	19.85 % / 43.51 %
5	D	32.82 % / 37.41 %	21	B	53.44 % / 33.58 %	37	C	24.43 % / 39.69 %	53	C	25.95 % / 38.17 %	69	B	23.66 % / 42.75 %
6	A	48.09 % / 35.88 %	22	B	30.53 % / 34.36 %	38	C	29.77 % / 41.22 %	54	C	29.77 % / 42.75 %	70	A	22.9 % / 43.51 %
7	B	31.3 % / 35.11 %	23	B	25.95 % / 37.41 %	39	B	24.43 % / 40.46 %	55	C	25.95 % / 43.52 %	71	D	27.48 % / 41.99 %
8	D	35.88 % / 35.11 %	24	A	35.11 % / 38.94 %	40	B	30.53 % / 36.65 %	56	D	26.72 % / 39.69 %	72	A	20.61 % / 43.51 %
9	C	25.19 % / 37.41 %	25	D	19.85 % / 39.69 %	41	C	29.01 % / 41.98 %	57	B	35.88 % / 41.22 %	73	C	27.48 % / 45.8 %
10	C	28.24 % / 39.7 %	26	D	36.64 % / 38.93 %	42	C	31.3 % / 39.69 %	58	A	28.24 % / 38.94 %	74	A	35.88 % / 41.98 %
11	D	22.9 % / 34.35 %	27	C	37.4 % / 36.65 %	43	C	37.4 % / 41.23 %	59	A	22.14 % / 41.98 %	75	A	22.14 % / 39.69 %
12	A	32.06 % / 35.12 %	28	A	18.32 % / 38.93 %	44	C	35.11 % / 38.94 %	60	A	29.77 % / 41.22 %	76	A	22.14 % / 41.98 %
13	C	31.3 % / 35.88 %	29	C	27.48 % / 36.64 %	45	C	34.35 % / 40.46 %	61	B	41.22 % / 39.7 %	77	B	32.06 % / 43.51 %
14	C	32.06 % / 35.88 %	30	A	25.19 % / 34.35 %	46	A	16.03 % / 36.64 %	62	B	44.27 % / 41.23 %	78	C	32.82 % / 42.75 %
15	B	31.3 % / 35.88 %	31	D	29.01 % / 40.46 %	47	A	29.01 % / 42.75 %	63	B	25.95 % / 44.28 %	79	D	18.32 % / 41.99 %
16	B	38.93 % / 35.12 %	32	A	23.66 % / 37.41 %	48	B	38.17 % / 41.22 %	64	C	41.22 % / 40.46 %	80	B	18.32 % / 43.51 %

Q.	Ans.	Correct / Skipped	Q.	Ans.	Correct / Skipped	Q.	Ans.	Correct / Skipped	Q.	Ans.	Correct / Skipped	Q.	Ans.	Correct / Skipped
81	A	26.72 % / 43.51 %	85	C	25.19 % / 45.04 %	89	C	35.11 % / 42.75 %	93	D	30.53 % / 45.04 %	97	A	21.37 % / 44.28 %
82	A	35.11 % / 44.28 %	86	D	40.46 % / 42.75 %	90	B	20.61 % / 41.99 %	94	B	35.11 % / 44.28 %	98	B	27.48 % / 48.09 %
83	D	17.56 % / 42.75 %	87	D	35.88 % / 37.4 %	91	D	26.72 % / 44.27 %	95	D	23.66 % / 45.81 %	99	D	31.3 % / 45.8 %
84	A	28.24 % / 43.52 %	88	C	28.24 % / 43.52 %	92	A	39.69 % / 43.52 %	96	A	29.01 % / 40.46 %	100	D	35.88 % / 38.17 %

//Hints and Solutions//

1. A **Bipartite Graph** is a graph whose vertices can be divided into two independent sets, U and V such that every edge (u, v) either connects a vertex from U to V or a vertex from V to U. In other words, for every edge (u, v), either u belongs to U and v to V, or u belongs to V and v to U. We can also say that there is no edge that connects vertices of same set.
(v1, v4, v6, v7); (v2, v3, v5, v8) is a bipartite graph vertices set.
So, option (C) is correct.

2. If any data frame is lost during transferring through network, error control mechanism notify the receiver & sender about this and helps sender resend the lostdata frame.

Access control mechanism handles access of many device into a same link at a given time.

In flow control after receiving & processing data, receiver host sends an acknowledgement message to the sender host to maintain data flow errorless.

Hence the correct option is (D).

So all option are functionality of network in data link layer

3. We can select 5 people from 20 men and 12 women having at least 3 women.
$^{12}C_3 \times {}^{20}C_2 + {}^{12}C_4 \times {}^{20}C_1 + {}^{12}C_5 \times {}^{20}C_0$
$= 220 \times 190 + 495 \times 20 + 792$
$= 52,492$
So, option (B) is correct.

4. The number of disk pages accessed by B-tree search
is $\Theta(h) = \Theta(\log_t n)$, where h is the height of the B-tree and n is the number of keys in the B-tree.

Hence, option D is the correct answer.

5. A subsequence is a sequence that can be derived from another sequence by deleting some elements without changing the order of the remaining elements. Longest common subsequence (LCS) of two sequences is a subsequence, with maximal length, which is common to both the sequences.
So, the longest common subsequence of X and Y is < b, c, b, a >.
So, option (D) is correct.

6. A publicly derived class is a subtype of its base class.

Inheritance provides for code reuse.

So, option (A) is correct.

7. Points(Co-ordinate) and lines are the basic building blocks of computer graphics.

Hence the correct option is (B).

8. printf("%C", *(&S[3])); = D

    printf("%s", S+4); = EFGH

    printf("%u", S); = 1000

Hence the correct option is (D).

9. here need matrix for all process is given below (by (Max - allocated))

for A 0 1 0 0 2   B 0 2 1 0 0   C 1 0 3 0 0
D 0 0 1 1 1

available is 0 0 x 1 1

So only D can execute for any no of x as A,B or C need at least one instance of either of first 2 resource

if x=1 then D can be executed and will release its allocated resource which is 1 1 1 1 0 then available matrix will become 1 1 2 2 1 but with this neither of (A,B,C) process can be executed as their need matrix is not less than or equal to available matrix so it will result in unsafe state.

if x=2

then D can be executed and will release its allocated resource which is 1 1 1 1 0 then available matrix will become 1 1 3 2 1 now Process C (with need 1 0 3 0 0) can be executed and release its allocated resources (1 1 0 1 0) and then available matrix will become 2 2 3 3 1 so B can be executed and then A (assuming some minor mistake in last resource) hence it is safe state.

So answer is C, x=2

Note :- process A can not be executed for any no of x as its fifth resource need is 2 which can not be fulfilled.

Hence the correct option is (C).

10. We have 8 pages in the memory and 4 blocks:

0-1023 (0)

1024-2047 (1)

2048-3071 (2)

3072-4095 (3)

4096-5119 (4)

5120-6143 (5)

6144-7167 (6)

7168-8191 (7)

option (A) will string 1,3,4,6 so page fault will occur.

option (B) will string 1,3,4,6 so page fault will occur.

option (C) will string 0,2,5,7 so page fault will occur.

option (D) will string 1,3,4,6 so page fault will occur.

So, option (C) is correct.

11. a. Demand paging Working Set

b. Segmentation supports user view of memory

c. Dynamic partitions compaction

d. Fixed partitions degree of multiprogramming

Dynamic partion (variable partion): where external fragmentation is the problem and solution is compaction

Fixed partitions: the degree of multiprograming is restricted by no of partitions in the memory

Hence the correct option is (D).

12. Hardware detects interrupt immediately, but CPU acts only after its current instruction. This is followed to ensure integrity of instructions.

Hence the correct option is (A).

13. The gettydefs file supplies the getty command with information about various terminal attributes, such as the default initialization and the login message. The gettydefs file contains single line entries that are separated by blank lines. Each entry contains five fields; each field is separated by a number sign (#). You can indicate comments in the file by putting a number sign (#) at the beginning of a line.

When the getty command is invoked, it scans the gettydefs file for the first entry with a matching identifier field (see below). If the gettydefs file cannot be opened, internal default settings are used. If a match is found, then the matching entry is parsed, and the terminal attributes are set based on the fields specified in the entry. If a match is not found, the first gettydefs file entry is used; therefore the first entry in gettydefs must be the default entry. The maximum length of each entry is 255 characters.

Hence the correct option is (C).

14.

Process id	Arrival time	Burst time	Compilation time	Turn around time	Waiting time
P0	2	2	5	3	1
P1	1	4	9	8	4
P2	0	1	1	1	0
P3	3	5	15	12	7
P4	4	3	15	10	7

0	1	3	5	7	9	11	13	14	15
P2	P1	P0	P3	P1	P4	P3	P4		P3

Process scheduling queue

P2	P1	P0	P3	P1	P4	P3	P4	P3

Average waiting time = 19/5 = 3.8

Hence the correct option is (C).

15. Dynamic Host configuration Protocol – DHCP – assigns an IP address to a client for a limited period of time, this address is then saved in a database. When the DHCP Server goes down, that client can still use the allocated IP address for a limited period of time.

Hence the correct option is (B).

16. The combination of an IP address and a port number is called a socket address. The client socket address defines the client process uniquely just as the server socket address defines the server process uniquely.

Hence the correct option is (B).

17. MVI B, 82H   // move immediate 82 in hexadecimal to register B

MOV A, B   // move value of B 82 in hexa to acc A

MOV C, A   // move value of A to register C

MVI D, 37H   // move immediate the value 37 in hexa to register D

OUT PORT1   // output the value of port1 i.e of acc A hence 82 H will be the output

HLT //halt the computer

Hence the correct option is (B).

18. Eight clusters, each containing 9 regions of 10 routers is a 3 level hierarchy.

Each router needs 10 entries for local router, 8 entries for routing the other regions and for distant cluster it need 7 enrties.

i.e. total 10 + 8 + 7 = 25 entries.

So, option (A) is correct.

19. In a classful addressing, the IP addresses with 0 (zero) as network number refers to the current network.

For more information on Classful IP address ReferIP Addressing | Introduction and Classful Addressing

Option (A) is correct.

20. C++ is a general purpose programming language and widely used now a days for competitive programming. It has imperative, object-oriented and generic programming features. C++ runs on lots of platform like Windows, Linux, Unix, Mac etc.

(1) Upon writing overloaded function, it must be coded for each usage.

(2) Upon writing function template, it is coded only once.

(3) It is difficult to debug macros.

(4) Templates are more efficient than macros.

Hence the correct option is (D).

21. Normalization - Reduces data redundancy in a database

Data Dictionary - Contains metadata describing database structure

Referential Integrity - Enforces match of primary key to foreign key

External Schema - Defines view(s) of the database for particular user(s)

Hence the correct option is (B).

22. As one is primary key and it varies from 1 to 10 , So using one atmost 10 tuples can be there. When we take two into consideration it varies from 1 to 5 and is unique, which implies it can be NULL. Hence the number of tuples will be 10, with two being NULL in five of them.

Hence the correct option is (B).

23. P -> Q ans P infer to Q

 Using : Modus Ponens

Hence the correct option is (B).

24. (a) if $(c \wedge b) \rightarrow r$ and $\neg b \rightarrow \neg p$, then $(\neg r \wedge p) \rightarrow \neg c$

"If my computations are correct and I pay the electric bill, then I will run out of money. If I don't pay the electric bill, the power will be turned off. Therefore, If I don't run out of money and the power is still on then my computations are incorrect."

(b) if $(cvb) \rightarrow r$ and $\neg b \rightarrow \neg p$, then $(r \wedge p) \rightarrow c$

"If my computations are correct or I pay the electric bill, then I will run out of money. If I don't pay the electric bill, the power will be turned off. Therefore, If I run out of money and the power is still on then my computations are correct."

(c) if $(c \wedge b) \rightarrow r$ and $\neg p \rightarrow \neg b$, then $(\neg r \vee p) \rightarrow \neg c$

"If my computations are correct and I pay the electric bill, then I will run out of money. If the power turned off then i will not pay the electric bill. Therefore, If I don't run out of money or the power is still on then my computations are incorrect."

(d) if $(c \vee b) \rightarrow r$ and $\neg b \rightarrow \neg p$, then $(\neg r \wedge p) \rightarrow \neg c$

"If my computations are correct or I pay the electric bill, then I will run out of money. If I don't pay the electric bill, the power will be turned off. Therefore, If I don't run out of money and the power is still on then my computations are incorrect."

Hence,Option(A) if $(c \wedge b) \rightarrow r$ and $\neg b \rightarrow \neg p$, then $(\neg r \wedge p) \rightarrow \neg c$.

Hence the correct option is (A).

25. Memory cycle time = 250nsec = 250×10^{-9} s

Number of refreshes in 1 msec = 32

=>Number of refreshes in 1 s = 32000

=> Number of refreshes in 250×10^{-9} s = $32000 \times 250 \times 10^{-9}$

= 8×10^{-3}

Time taken by 1 refresh cycle = 100 nsec = 100×10^{-9} = 10^{-7} s

=> Time taken by 8×10^{-3} refresh cycles = $8 \times 10^{-3} \times 10^{-7}$

= 8×10^{-10} sec

Hence percentage of time for refresh = $8 \times 10^{-10}/250 \times 10^{-9}$ x100%

= 0.32 %

Hence the correct option is (D).

26. AC, CY, Z flags-

Auxiliary Carry (AC): In an arithmetic operation, when a carry is generated by digit D_3 and passed to digit D_4, the AC flag is set. Generally this flag is used internally for Binary Coded Decimals (BCD).

Carry flag (CY): After an addition of two numbers, if the sum in the accumulator is larger than eight bits, then the flip-flop uses to indicate a carry called the Carry flag – which is set to one.

Zero Flag (Z): When an arithmetic operation results in zero , the flip-flop called the Zero flag - which is set to one.

Hence the correct option is (D).

27. ADDRESS BUS:

It is a group of wires or lines that are used to transfer the addresses of Memory or I/O devices. It us unidirectional.

In Intel 8085 microprocessor, Address bus was of 16 bits. This means that Microprocessor 8085 can transfer maximum 16 bit address which means it can address 65,536 different memory locations. This bus is multiplexed with 8 but data bus. So, the most significant bits (MSB) of address goes through Address bus and LSB goes through multiplexed data bus.

Hence the correct option is (C).

28. Loop unrolling, also known as loop unwinding, is a loop transformation technique that attempts to optimize a program's execution speed at the expense of its binary size, which is an approach known as space–time tradeoff. The transformation can be undertaken manually by the programmer or by an optimizing compiler.

Hence the correct option is (A).

29. The Intel 8085 ("eighty-eighty-five") is an 8-bit microprocessor produced by Intel and introduced in 1976.

Hence the correct option is (C).

30. There are 4 bus routes from A to B and 3 routes from B to C.

Therefore, there are 4 × 3 = 12 ways to go from A to C.

It is round trip so the man will travel back from C to A via B.

It is restricted that man cannot use same bus routes from C to B and B to A more than once.

Thus, there are 2 × 3 = 6 routes for return journey.

Therefore, the required number of ways = 12 × 6 = 72.

Hence, the correct option is (A).

31. A version is an instance of a system, which is functionally distinct in some way from other system instances.

A release is an instance of a system, which is distributed to users outside of the development team.

So, option (D) is correct.

32. Clearly statement C is not true which implies choice B, D are out also statement B is not true as they are different languages.

Although they are different languages, JavaScript's syntax is loosely based on Java.

Hence correct answer is (A).

33. Reliability of a software specifies the probability of failure-free operation of that software for a given time duration.

Hence the correct option is (B).

34. 'Modelling-oriented approach' is one of the methods for specifying the functional specifications." related to the requirement phase in Software Engineering is incorrect.

Hence the correct option is (C).

35. Since Windows 2000 offers a nice Unicode API and supports non-BMP characters. It usesUnicode strings implemented as wchar_t* strings (LPWSTR). wchar_t is 16 bits long on Windows and so it uses UTF-16: non-BMP characters are stored as two wchar_t (a surrogate pair), and the length of a string is the number of UTF-16 units and not the number of characters.

Windows 95, 98 an Me had also Unicode strings, but were limited to BMP characters: they usedUCS-2 instead of UTF-16.

Hence the correct option is (C).

36. What is Object oriented Programming?

Object-oriented programming (OOP) is based on the concept of "objects", which may contain data (attributes), and code (methods).

What is dynamic Programming?

Dynamic programming language is a class of high-level programming languages which, at runtime, execute many common programming behaviors that static programming languages perform during compilation.

eg: adding new code, modify the type etc.
Dynamic languages are frequently (but not always) referred to as "scripting languages"

a JAVA: -Statically Object Oriented

b Python:- Dynamically Object Oriented

c Prolog:- Dynamically Object Oriented

d ADA: -Statically Non Object Oriented

Hence the correct option is (D).

37. The Iterative algorithm is faster than the latter as recursive algorithm has overheads like calling function and registering stacks repeatedly.

Hence the correct option is (C).

38. STANDARD ADDITIVE MODEL (SAM) includes the centroid defuzzification technique. here

IF x is AND y is THEN z is

Given crisp inputs x= x_0, y = y_0,

$$z = centroid \sum_i \mu\, Ai(X_0)\mu Bi(Y_0)\mu Ci(Z)$$

Hence the correct option is (C).

39. In general, in a recursive and non-recursive implementation of a problem (program) both time and space complexities are better in non-recursive than in recursive program. In some program recursive implementation gives worst case scenario too. So, recursive implementation does not guarantee for best case all the time.

So, optipon (B) is correct.

40. Assuming that s is a constant or 5 is misprinted as s:

Given question can be reduced as:

$T(n) = T([n/s]) + T(7n/10 + 6) + O(n)$

$\leq c[n/s] + c(7n/10 + 6) + O(n)$

$\leq c((n/s) + 7cn/10 + 6c + O(n)$

$\leq cn$

We can say T(n)

$T(n) = O(n)$

Hence the correct option is (B).

41. Normal instruction takes 1 micro second 10^{-6} sec

instruction with page fault takes 2001 micro seconds so p.f take 2000 microsecond

now given program takes 60 sec and there were 15000 p.f

so time taken by page faults= 15000x2000 micro seconds=30 sec

rest 30 sec are consumed by program execution

if memory is doubled than the mean interval between the page faults is also doubled(and hence p.f rate will be reduced by half) so when earlier 30 sec were needed by program instructions and 30 sec of p.f

now program execution takes 30 sec and p.f will take 15 sec($15000 \times 2000 \times 10^{-3}$)/2

so total time =30+15 =45 sec

Hence the correct option is (C).

42. 2 Phase Locking (2PL) is a concurrency control method that guarantees serializability. The protocol utilizes locks, applied by a transaction to data, which may block (interpreted as signals to stop) other transactions from accessing the same data during the transaction's life. 2PL may be lead to deadlocks that result from the mutual blocking of two or more transactions. See the following situation, neither T_3 nor T_4 can make progress.

T_3	T_4
Lock-X(B)	
Read(B)	
B:B-50	
Write(B)	
	Lock-S(A)
	Read(A)
	Lock-S(B)
Lock-X(A)	

Timestamp-based concurrency control algorithm is a non-lock concurrency control method. In Timestamp based method, deadlock cannot occur as no transaction ever waits.

Hence the correct option is (C).

43. An interface is an empty shell, there are only the signatures of the methods, which implies that the methods do not have a body. The interface can't do anything. It's just a pattern so b is true

he key technical differences between an abstract class and an interface are:

Abstract classes can have constants, members, method stubs (methods without a body) and defined methods, whereas interfaces can only have constants and methods stubs.

Methods and members of an abstract class can be defined with any visibility, whereas all methods of an interface must be defined as public (they are defined public by default).

When inheriting an abstract class, a concrete child class must define the abstract methods, whereas an an abstract class can extend another abstract class and abstract methods from the parent class don't have to be defined.

Similarly, an interface extending another interface is not responsible for implementing methodsfrom the parent interface. This is because interfaces cannot define any implementation.

A child class can only extend a single class (abstract or concrete), whereas an interface can extend or a class can implement multiple other interfaces so a is true

A child class can define abstract methods with the same or less restrictive visibility, whereas a class implementing an interface must define the methods with the exact same visibility (public).

Hence the correct option is (C).

44. Data members in C++ is inherited in a derived class from base class

Constructor is a member function of a class which initializes objects of a class. In C++,Constructor is automatically called when object(instance of class) create.It is special member function of the class.

Destructor is a member function which destructs or deletes an object.

Virtual methods is a method which is redefined(Over-riden) in derived class

So, option (C) is correct.

45. For a concurrent execution there should be no read-write ,write-write or write-read conflict.

as given option (a),(b) and (d) depicts the same which true option.

C represent the two simultaneous read operation of the process with no intersection variables which may not be case.

hence C is false.

46. A memory management unit (MMU), sometimes called paged memory management unit (PMMU), is a computer hardware unit having all memory references passed through itself, primarily performing the translation of virtual memory addresses to physical addresses.

Hence the correct option is (A).

47. p_1 ,p_2, p_3 are three process

Arrival time of p_1 is 1 so we made to run p_1 at time 1

now p_1 is run for 2 units (upto 3) new process arrived with less B.T ,so switch happens to p_2 ----- (1)

p_2 run till completion since there are no shorter jobs available ,then switch happens to p_1---- (2)

again p_1 is run since it has burst time (18) < burst time of p_3 (30)

completion of p_1, switch happens to p_3 run till completion. ----- (3)

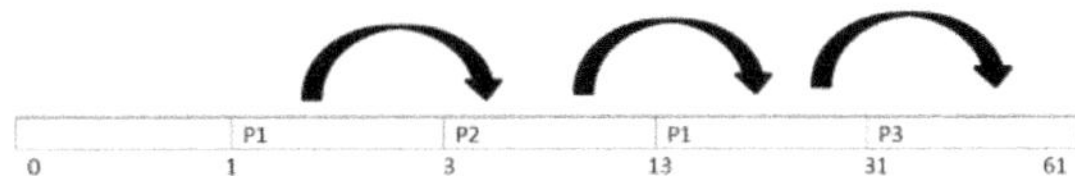

	P1	P2	P1	P3
0	1	3	13	31 61

Hence the correct option is (A).

48.

1	2	3	4	5	hit	hit	hit	6	7
0	0	0	0	3	3	3	3	0	0
	1	1	1	1	1	1	1	1	1
		7	7	7	7	7	7	7	7
			2	2	2	2	2	2	3

Total page fault = 7

Hence the correct option is (B).

49. Direct block entry

One direct block entry points 1 KB

So 10 direct block entries can point 1 x 10 =10 KB

Single indirect block:

We have 4 bytes address

So number of blocks in indirect block= 1 KB/4 = 256 blocks

– So one indirect block entry can point 256 ✕ 1 KB = 256 KB

Double-indirect block:

Similarly – 256 ✕ 256 ✕ 1 KB = 64 MB

• **Triple Indirect block:**

– 256 ✕ 256 ✕ 256 ✕ 1 KB = 16 GB

Total file size = 16 GB + 64 MB+256 KB+ 10 KB ~ 16 GB

===

Tip : For competitive exams, speed matters. Maximum file size is mostly depends on triple block entries only and for faster approximate answer we need to calculate triple indirect block only.

256 ✕ 256 ✕ 256 ✕ 1 KB = 16 GB

Hence the correct option is (C).

50. (A) is False: It requires a privileged instruction to change the clock.

(B) is False: A context switch between two user processes require crossing the protection boundary twice, whereas a context switch between two kernel threads does not require crossing the protection boundary.

(C) is False: In a monitor, there is no primitive that allows a thread to wait on two condition variables.

Hence the correct option is (D).

51. File of 100,000 character will take 8 ✕ 100,000 = 800,000 bits.

Device sends the data @ 2000 bps.

2000 bits take 1 sec.

1 bit will take 1 / 2000 second.

800,000 bits will take 800,000 ✕ (1 / 2000) = 400 sec.

So, option (C) is correct.

52. A network with 10 Mbps bandwidth can pass 15,000 frames and each frame carries 8,000 bit i.e. 120,000,000 bits per minute.

i.e. 120,000,000 / 60 = 2,000,000 = 2 Mbps.

So, option (A) is correct.

53. The Total Length field is the total length of the IPv4 datagram in bytes. Using this field and the IHL field can indicate where the data portion of the datagram starts, and its length. Because this is a 16-bit field, the maximum size of an IPv4 datagram (including header) is 65,535 bytes.

Hence the correct option is (C).

54. Amdahl's law states that if P is the proportion of a program that can be made parallel and (1-P) is the proportion that cannot be parallelized, then the maximum speed-up that can be achieved by using N processors is: $\dfrac{1}{(1-P)+\dfrac{P}{N}}$

Hence the correct option is (C).

55. hardware is loosely coupled and software is tightly coupled

Distributed computing is a field of computer science that studies distributed systems. A distributed system is a model in which components located on networked computers communicate and coordinate their actions by passing messages.

Hence the correct option is (C).

56.

- We want to avoid the data duplication and consequent possible inconsistencies caused by duplicating the key of the strong entity.

- Weak entities reect the logical structure of an entity being dependent on another entity.

- Weak entities can be deleted automaticallywhen their strong entity is deleted.

- Weak entities can be stored physically with their strong entities.

D is incorrect statement. so the choice will be D.

Hence the correct option is (D).

57. varchar will acquire the exact memory of attribute and it varies from tuple to tuple while char will acquire memory space which is define at the time of table creation it is fixed: varchar(20) 'Ram' will take 3 and 'Sita' will take 20 character space in memory.

Hence the correct option is (B).

58. Forward chaining, backward chaining and problem reduction

- forward chaining: Expert system is driven by the antecedent (left hand side)

- backward chaining. : Expert system is driven by the consequent (right hand side)

Hence the correct option is (A).

59. It should be clausal form rather than casual

as we know A->B is equivalent to ~AVB now checking option A

A∧B∧C⇒D applying above equivalence

~(A∧B∧C)V D   applying de-morgans law

=> ~A V ~B V ~C V D which is given in the question hence answer is A.

Hence the correct option is (A).

60. Blind image deconvolution is combination of blur identification and image restoration.

Hence the correct option is (A).

61. A ripple counter is an asynchronous counter where only the first flip-flop is clocked by an external clock. All subsequent flip-flops are clocked by the output of the preceding flip-flop. Asynchronous counters are also called ripple-counters because of the way the clock pulse ripples it way through the flip-flops.

Hence the correct option is (B).

62. ALU is the arithmetic logic unit and it involves the processing of input into the desired output.

Timing and control instruction is covered in the instruction unit of the microprocessor.

There are some general-purpose registers in the storage and interface unit.

While an interrupt is a signal to the processor which required attention from the processor, an interrupt is serviced on the basis of priority and need.

Hence the correct option is (B).

63. Top-down parsers are LL parsers where first L stands for left – to – right scan and second L stands for a leftmost derivation.**Correct**

(000)* is a regular expression that matches only strings containing an odd number of zeroes, including the empty string.Incorrect (000)* will generate ε, 000, 000000, 000000000, ... multiples of 3 which include odd and even strings, so this is **incorrect.**

Bottom-up parsers are in the LR family, where L stands for left – to – right scan and R stands for rightmost derivation. **Correct**

The class of context – free languages is closed under reversal. That is, if L is any context – free language, then the language $L^R = \{w^R ; w \in L\}$ is context – free. **Correct**

Hence the correct option is (B).

64. The register that stores the bits required to mask the interrupts is Interrupt mask register.

The register that stores the bits required for Status is Status register

The register that stores the bits required to service the interrupts is Interrupt service register

The register that stores the bits required to request the interrupts is Interrupt request register

Hence the correct option is (C).

65. On adding 9C and 64, a carry is generated from D_3 and from the D_7 bit so CY and AC are set to 1. In the result, the number of 1's present are even so parity flag is set to zero.

Hence the correct option is (B).

66. ISO quality assurance standard applies to software engineering is ISO 9000:2000. Q. The ISO quality assurance standard that applies to software engineering is ISO 9000:2000.

Hence the correct option is (B).

67. External Quality Characteristics:

Correctness, Usability, Efficiency, Reliability, Integrity, Adaptability, Accuracy, and Robustness.

Internal Quality Characteristics:

Maintainability, Flexibility, Portability, Re-usability, Readability, Testability, and Understandability.

Hence the correct option is (B).

68.

- In perspective projection (from 3D to 2D), objects behind the centre of projection are projected upside down and backward onto the view-plane. This is known as view confusion.

- Vanishing point: Where all parallel points appear to meet is called vanishing point.

- Perspective foreshortening: As we move from centre of projection size of object varies inversely with distance, this is known as perspective foreshortening.

- Topological Distortion: A line segment joining a point lying in front of the viewer to a point in back of the viewer is projected to a broken line of infinite extent. This is known as topological distortion.

Hence the correct option is (C).

69. The address element provides contact information for a document or part of a document. Information provided by address may include the names of the document's maintainers, links to the maintainers' Web pages, e-mail addresses for feedback, postal addresses, phone numbers, and so on. The address element is not appropriate for all postal and e-mail addresses; it should be reserved for providing such information about the contact people for the document.

The address element has been around since the HTML3 spec was drafted in 1995, and it continues to survive in the latest drafts of HTML5. But nearly fifteen years after its creation, it's still causing confusion among developers. So how should we be using address in our documents?

<address> </address> tag in HTML is used to surround information, such as signature of the person who created the page.

Hence the correct option is (B).

70. Square brackets can surround a choice of single characters (i.e., one digit or one letter) you'd like to match. For example, [Cc]hapterwould match either Chapter or chapter, but [ch]apter would match either capter or hapter. Use a hyphen (-) to separate a range of consecutive characters. For example, chap[1-3] would match chap1,chap2, or chap3.

But if escape sequence(\) is used then it literally matches with that after \

so $rm chap0

$$1 - 3$$

will remove

Remove file chap0[1-3]

Hence the correct option is (A).

71. XML uses Document Type Definition(DTD) to describe the data. DTD is specified document defining and constraining definition and XML uses a description node to describe the data.

Extensible Stylesheet Language(XSL) is used to transform and render the XML document.

Statement (a) and (c) are correct.

Hence the correct option is (D).

72. Equation of line passing through 2 points (x_1,y_1) ,(x_2,y_2) is y-y_1=$(y_2$-$y_1)$ $\times$ $(x$-$x_1)$/$(x_2$-$x_1)$

So here equation of line is y-0=(18-0)(x-0)/(6-0) =>y=3x

So when x=0 y=0

x=1 y=3

x=2 y=6

x=3 y=9

Hence the correct option is (A).

73. $2^{(h+1)}$-1 example: let a binary tree be of height 2 then total nodes is at level 0: 1 node, at level 1: 2 nodes and at level 2: 4 nodes. Hence total will be : 1+2+4=7 e.i., $2^{(2+1)}$-1=8-1=7

and here k=h+1

so maximum number of nodes with k- level -->

2^k -1

Hence the correct option is (C).

74.

- The average case occurs in the Linear Search Algorithm when the item to be searched is in some where middle of the Array.

- The best case occurs in the Linear Search Algorithm when the item to be searched is in starting of the Array.

- The worst case occurs in the Linear Search Algorithm when the item to be searched is in end of the Array.

Hence the correct option is (A).

75. THE following statements are true

The ability to develop more realistic models of the real world. (a)

The ability to represent the world in a non-geometric way. (b)

The ability to develop databases using natural language approach (c)

Hence correct answer is option (A).

76. $--x+j==x>n>=m$

$6.5 +(-1.0) ==6.5 > 1.0 >= 2.0$

$5.5 == 1 > = 2.0$

$3.5 == 0$

Hence the correct option is (A).

77. Here, Vcc Corresponds to 1, So equivalent expression will be

$f(x, y) = xy'.1 + x'y.1+ xy.1= y+ xy' = x + y$

78. Foreign key should be answer because this key is used only to create the referential integrity constraint so we cannot drop the table .

Hence the correct option is (C).

79. the steps which are required are

1)sampling, quantization(in choice C) , amplification(in choice B) ,conversion(in choice A,D)

every option contains at least one of these 3 hence answer should be none of these.

Hence the correct option is (D).

80. provides a mechanism to map physical device to file names

Windows and DOS also have special files.

provide simple interfaces between drivers and peripheral devices such as printers and serial ports.

Hence the correct option is (B).

81. An attacker sits between the sender and receiver and captures the information and re-transmits to the receiver after some time without altering the information. This attack is called as Denial of service attack.

A Masquerade attack is a type of attack where the attacker pretends to be an authorized user of a system in order to gain access to it or to gain greater privileges than they are authorized for.

Hence the correct option is (A).

82. CREATE ASSERTION 'ASSERTION Name' CHECK 'Predicate' is the proper syntax for applying constraints

for example This SQL statement creates an assertion to demand that there's no more than a single president among the employees:

create assertion AT_MOST_ONE_PRESIDENT as CHECK

((select count(*)   from EMP e   where e.JOB = 'PRESIDENT') < = 1)

Hence the correct option is (A).

83. (A) option is option return all possible results after natural join but it does not involve the table t during natural join so false

In (B)option record 5 6 4 and record 1 2 2 not possible in result so false.

In (C) option record 5 2 4 abd record 1 6 2 nit possible after natural join of table.

In (D) option it contain partial result after joining all three table.

So (D) option should be answer.

84.

- $(p \rightarrow q) \Leftrightarrow (\neg q \rightarrow \neg p)$ is Contrapositive

- $[(p \wedge q) \rightarrow r] \Leftrightarrow [p \rightarrow (q \rightarrow r)]$ is exportation law.

- $(p \rightarrow q) \Leftrightarrow [(p \wedge \neg q) \rightarrow o]$ is Reduction and absurdum

- $(p \leftrightarrow q) \Leftrightarrow [(p \rightarrow q) \wedge (q \rightarrow p)]$ is Equivalence.

Hence the correct option is (A).

85. A. S→0|0S|1SS (false since 10001 can't generate)

B. S→0S|1S|0SS|1SS|0|1 (false since generates 1)

C. S→0|0S|1SS|S1S|SS1 (true)

D. S→0S|1S|0|1 (false since 1+ generated)

Hence the correct option is (C).

86. The principle components of a memory-tube display are flooding gun, collector, phosphorus grains and ground.

So, option (D) is correct.

87. Refinement is surely a Top-Down approach as we are extracting a particular type Like from Person entity to S/w engineer

Refinement Process of elaboration. Start with the statement of function defined at the abstract level, decompose the statement of function in a step wise fashion until programming language statements are reached.

Hence the correct option is (D).

88. Every weak entity must be associated with an identifying entity; that is, the weak entity set is said to be existence dependent on the identifying entity set. The identifying entity set is said to own the weak entity set that it identifies. It is also called as owner entity set.

Hence the correct option is (C).

89. A data structure is called linear if all of its elements are arranged in the linear order. In linear data structures, the elements are stored in non-hierarchical way where each element has the successors and predecessors except the first and last element.

Example- Array, Linked List, Stack, Queue.

Tree is not a Linear Data Structure.

Hence the correct option is (C).

90. Adaptive maintenance: Modification of a software product performed after delivery to keep a software product usable in a changed or changing environment.

Hence the correct option is (B).

91. System crashes once in 30 days and need 10 minutes to get repaired.

Either convert 30 days into minute or 10 minute into days

30 days = 30 $\times$ 24 $\times$ 60 minute

fraction of time system is not available = (10 / (30 $\times$ 24 $\times$ 60)) $\times$ 100 = 0.023%

Availability = 100 – 0.023 = 99.97%

Hence the correct option is (D).

92. If we push elements onto the stack then the stack pointer increases with every push of element.

Hence the correct option is (A).

93. A static data structure is an organization or collection of data in memory that is fixed in size. This results in the maximum size needing to be known in advance, as memory cannot be reallocated at a later point. Arrays are a prominent example of a static data structure.

So, Static Data Structure is array.

Hence the correct option is (D).

94. Time is measured by counting the number of key operations such as comparisons in the sorting algorithm.

Hence the correct option is (B).

95. a-iv, b-iii, c-ii, d-i

a. Forelward Reference Table -Uses linked list data structure

b. Mnemonic Table   -Contains machine OP code

c. Segment Register Table -Uses array data structure

d. EQU   -Assembler directive

Hence the correct option is (D).

96. Inaccessible in the derived class.

only public or protected members are inherited.

Hence the correct option is (A).

97. In full adder:

For input x, y and C_i

$S_o = x \oplus y \oplus C_i$

$C_o = xy + C_i(x + y)$

For x = 1, y = 0 and C_i(carry input) = 0

i.e. $S_o = 1 \oplus 0 \oplus 0 = 1$.

$C_o = 1 \times 0 + 0(1 + 0) = 0$.

For x = 0, y = 1 and $C_i = 1$

i.e. $S_o = 0 \oplus 1 \oplus 1 = 0$

$C_o = 0 \times 1 + 1(0 + 1) = 1$.

Hence the correct option is (A).

98. 1 character=1 byte

32 bit word= 4byte

4800 bytes in 1 sec

So for 1 byte it takes 1/4800 sec

So for 4 byte word it takes 1/1200 sec

So 1200 words are transferred in 1 sec through cycle stealing

and given 1 million instructions are fetching and executing in 1 sec out of which 1200 words are executing through cycle stealing so

% of slow down or cycle wasted in dma transfer = (1200/1000000) $\times$ 100

=0.12%

Hence the correct option is (B).

99. (a) Boolean expressions and logic networks correspond to labelled acyclic digraphs.

(b) Optimal boolean expressions may not correspond to simplest networks.

(c) Choosing essential blocks first in a Karnaugh map and then, greedily choosing the largest remaining blocks to cover may not give an optimal expression.

All are correct.

Hence the correct option is (D).

100. a. 23(TELNET) ii. Remote login

b. 25(SMTP)   iv. E-mail

c. 80 (HTTP) i. World wide web

d. 119   iii. USENET news

Hence the correct option is (D).

Q.1 Let us suppose from given statistics, it is known that meningitis causes stiff neck 50% of the time. The proportion of persons having meningitis is $\dfrac{1}{50000}$ and the proportion of people having stiff neck is $\dfrac{1}{20}$. Find the percentage of people who had meningitis and complain about stiff neck.

A. 0.01%   **B.** 0.02%   **C.** 0.04%   **D.** 0.05%

Q.2 Directions: Match the following terms.

List - I	List - II
(a) Vacuous proof	(i) Proof that the implication $p \to q$ is true, based on the fact that p is false.
(b) Trivial proof	(ii) Proof that the implication $p \to q$ is true, based on the fact that q is true.
(c) Direct proof	(iii) Proof that the implication $p \to q$ is true, that proceeds by showing that q must be true, when p is true.
(d) Indirect proof	(iv) Proof that the implication $p \to q$ is true, that proceeds by showing that p must be false, when q is false.

A. (a) - (i), (b) - (ii), (c) - (iii), (d) - (iv)
B. (a) - (ii), (b) - (iii), (c) - (i), (d) - (iv)
C. (a) - (iii), (b) - (ii), (c) - (iv), (d) - (i)
D. (a) - (iv), (b) - (iii), (c) - (ii), (d) - (i)

Q.3 Let P(m, n) be the statement 'm divides n' where the universe of discourse for both the variables is the set of positive integers. Determine the truth values of the following propositions.

(a) $\exists m \ \forall P(m, n)$

(b) $\forall n P(1, n)$

(c) $\forall m \forall n P(m, n)$

A. (a) - True, (b) - True, (c) - False
B. (a) - True, (b) - False, (c) - False
C. (a) - False, (b) - False, (c) - False
D. (a) - True, (b) - True, (c) - True

Q.4 The inorder traversal of the following tree is

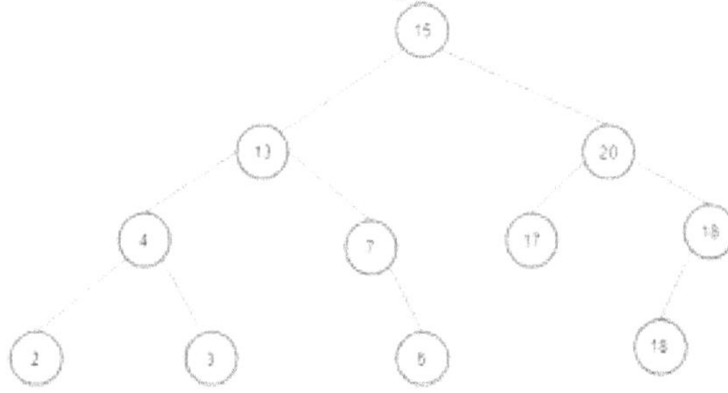

A. 2 3 4 6 7 13 15 17 18 18 20
B. 20 18 18 17 15 13 7 6 4 3 2
C. 15 13 20 4 7 17 18 2 3 6 18

D. 2 4 3 13 7 6 15 17 20 18 18

Q.5 Floyd-Warshall algorithm utilises _________ to solve the all-pairs shortest paths problem on a directed graph in _________ time.

A. greedy algorithm, θ (V^3)
B. greedy algorithm, θ (V^2 lgn)
C. dynamic programming, θ (V^3)
D. dynamic programming, θ (V^2 lgn)

Q.6 Language model used in LISP is

A. functional programming
B. logic programming
C. object oriented programming
D. All of the above

Q.7 If a function is friend of a class, then which of the following is **incorrect**?

A. A function can only be declared a friend by a class itself.
B. Friend functions are not members of a class, they are associated with it.
C. Friend functions are members of a class.
D. It can have access to all members of the class, even private ones.

Q.8 Module design is used to maximise cohesion and minimise coupling. Which of the following is the key to implement this rule?

A. Inheritance   **B.** Polymorphism
C. Encapsulation   **D.** Abstraction

Q.9 Directions: Match the following for unix system calls.

List - I	List - II
(a) exec	(i) Creates a new process
(b) brk	(ii) Invokes another program overlaying memory space with a copy of an executable file
(c) wait	(iii) Increases or decreases the size of data region
(d) fork	(iv) Synchronises with termination of child process

A. (a) - (ii), (b) - (iii), (c) - (iv), (d) - (i)
B. (a) - (iii), (b) - (ii), (c) - (iv), (d) - (i)
C. (a) - (iv), (b) - (iii), (c) - (ii), (d) - (i)
D. (a) - (iv), (b) - (iii), (c) - (i), (d) - (ii)

Q.10 A bridge has access to _________ address in the same network.

A. Physical   **B.** Network
C. Datalink   **D.** Application

Q.11 Directions: Consider the following reference string.
0 1 2 3 0 1 4 0 1 2 3 4

If FIFO page replacement algorithm is used, then the number of page faults with three page frames and four page frames are ______ and ______, respectively.

A. 10, 9   **B.** 9, 9   **C.** 10, 10   **D.** 9, 10

Q.12 The CPU of a system, having 1 MIPS execution rate, needs 4 machine cycles on an average for executing an instruction. Fifty percent of cycles use a memory bus. A memory read/write employs one machine cycle. For execution of the program, a system utilises 90 percent of the CPU time. For block data transfer, an IO device is attached to the system while CPU executes the background programs continuously. What is the maximum IO data transfer rate, if programmed IO data transfer technique is used?

A. 500 Kbytes/sec   **B.** 2.2 Mbytes/sec
C. 125 Kbytes/sec   **D.** 250 Kbytes/sec

Q.13 Match the following in Unix file system:

List - I	List - II
(a) Boot block	(i) Information about file system
(b) Super block	(ii) Information about file
(c) Inode table	(iii) Storage space
(d) Data block	(iv) Code for making OS ready

A. (a) - (iv), (b) - (i), (c) - (ii), (d) - (iii)
B. (a) - (i), (b) - (iii), (c) - (ii), (d) - (iv)
C. (a) - (iii), (b) - (i), (c) - (ii), (d) - (iv)
D. (a) - (iv), (b) - (ii), (c) - (i), (d) - (iii)

Q.14 Which among the following is correct in case of Spatial locality?
A. It cannot be referenced again
B. It can be referenced again
C. It gets referenced to nearby location
D. None of Above

Q.15 Which of the following transmission techniques guarantees that data packets will be received by the receiver in the same order in which they were sent by the sender?
A. Broadcasting   **B.** Unicasting
C. Packet switching   **D.** Circuit switching

Q.16 Suppose, a digitised voice channel is made by digitising 8 kHz bandwidth analog voice signal. It is required to sample the signal at twice the highest frequency (two samples per hertz). What is the bit rate required, if it is assumed that each sample requires 8 bits?
A. 32 kbps   **B.** 64 kbps   **C.** 128 kbps   **D.** 256 kbps

Q.17 Consider a 32-bit microprocessor, with a 16-bit external data bus, driven by an 8 MHz input clock. Assume that this microprocessor has a bus cycle, whose minimum duration equals four input clock cycles. What is the maximum data transfer rate for this microprocessor?
A. 8×10^6 bytes/sec   **B.** 4×10^6 bytes/sec
C. 16×10^6 bytes/sec   **D.** 4×10^9 bytes/sec

Q.18 Suppose, transmission rate of a channel is 32 kbps. If there are '8' routes from source to destination and each packet p contains 8000 bits, then total end to end delay in sending packet P is

A. 2 sec   **B.** 3 sec   **C.** 4 sec   **D.** 1 sec

Q.19 Which of the following protocols allows the transfer of multimedia messages in electronic mail?
A. IMAP   **B.** SMTP   **C.** POP3   **D.** MIME

Q.20 What do you call the data which improves the performance and accessibility of the database?
A. Index
B. User data
C. Application metadata
D. Data dictionary

Q.21 A relation R = {A, B, C, D, E, F, G} is given with following set of functional dependencies.
F = {AD → E, BE → F, B → C, AF → G}
Which of the following is a candidate key?
A. A   **B.** AB   **C.** ABC   **D.** ABD

Q.22 In the indexed scheme of blocks to a file, the maximum possible size of the file depends on
A. the number of blocks used for index and the size of index
B. size of blocks and size of address
C. size of index
D. size of block

Q.23 Boolean function [~(~p ∧ q) ∧ ~(~p ∧ ~q)] ∨ (p ∧ r)] is equal to the Boolean function
A. q   **B.** p ∧ r   **C.** p ∨ q   **D.** p

Q.24 The relation schemas R_1 and R_2 form a lossless join decomposition of R, if and only if
(a) $R_1 \cap R_2 \to (R_1 - R_2)$
(b) $R_1 \to R_2$
(c) $R_1 \cap R_2 \to (R_2 - R_1)$
(d) $(R_2 \to R_1) \cap R_2$
A. (a) and (b) happens   **B.** (a) and (d) happens
C. (a) and (c) happens   **D.** (b) and (c) happens

Q.25 The equivalent hexadecimal notation for octal number 2550276 is
A. FADED   **B.** AEOBE   **C.** ADOBE   **D.** ACABE

Q.26 Octal number 326.4 is equivalent to
A. $(214.2)_{10}$ and $(D6.8)_{16}$
B. $(212.5)_{10}$ and $(D6.8)_{16}$
C. $(214.5)_{10}$ and $(D6.8)_{16}$
D. $(214.5)_{10}$ and $(D6.4)_{16}$

Q.27 which of the following is decidable problem for Context free languages
A. Emptiness problem
B. Completeness problem
C. Equality problem
D. None of the above

Q.28 The context free grammar given by
S → XYX

$X \rightarrow aX|bX|\lambda$

$Y \rightarrow bbb$

generates the language which is defined by regular expression

A. (a + b) * bbb

B. abbb(a + b)*

C. (a + b) * (bbb)(a + b)*

D. (a + b)(bbb)(a + b)*

Q.29 Which of the following phases of compiler generates stream of atoms?

A. Syntax analysis

B. Lexical analysis

C. Code generation

D. Code optimisation

Q.30 Directions: Match the following.

List - I	List - II
(a) Flood gun	(i) An electron gun designed to flood the entire screen with electrons.
(b) Collector	(ii) Partly energised by flooding gun, stores the charge generated by the writing gun.
(c) Ground	(iii) Used to discharge the collector.
(d) Phosphorus grains	(iv) Used in memory-tube display and similar to those used in standard CRT.
(e) Writing gun system	(v) Used in memory-tube display and basically the same as the electron gun used in a conventional CRT.

	(a)	(b)	(c)	(d)	(e)
(1)	(i)	(ii)	(iii)	(iv)	(v)
(2)	(ii)	(iii)	(i)	(iv)	(v)
(3)	(iii)	(i)	(ii)	(v)	(iv)
(4)	(iv)	(v)	(i)	(ii)	(iii)

A. (1) **B.** (2) **C.** (3) **D.** (4)

Q.31 _______ is subject oriented, integrated, time variant and non-volatile collection of data in support of management decisions.

A. Data mining

B. Web mining

C. Data warehouse

D. Database Management System

Q.32 In data mining, classification rules are extracted from

A. data

B. information

C. decision tree

D. database

Q.33 A software design is highly modular, if cohesion is

A. functional and coupling is data type

B. coincidental and coupling is data type

C. sequential and coupling is content type

D. functional and coupling is stamp type

Q.34 Verification

A. refers to the set of activities that ensure that software correctly implements a specific function

B. gives answer to the question - Are we building the product right?

C. requires execution of software

D. both (1) and (2)

Q.35 The Liang-Barsky line clipping algorithm uses the parametric equation of a line from (x_1, y_1) to (x_2, y_2) along with its infinite extension which is given as

$x = x_1 + \Delta x.u$

$y = y_1 + \Delta y.u$,

where $\Delta x = x_2 - x_1$, $\Delta y = y_2 - y_1$ and u is the parameter with $0 < u < 1$.

A line AB with end points A(-1, 7) and B(11, 1) is to be clipped against a rectangular window with $x_{min} = 1$, $x_{max} = 9$, $y_{min} = 2$ and $y_{max} = 8$. The lower and upper bound values of the parameter u for the clipped line using Liang-Barsky algorithm is given as

A. (0, 2/3)

B. (1/6, 5/6)

C. (0, 1/3)

D. (0, 1)

Q.36 When an algorithm is written in the form of a programming language, it becomes a _______

A. Flowchart

B. Program

C. Pseudo code

D. Syntax

Q.37 What is the number of principal vanishing point(s) along with their direction for the standard perspective transformation?

A. One in the direction K

B. Two in the directions I and J

C. Three in the directions I, J and K

D. Two in the directions J and K

Q.38 Queue follows which methodology for storing the data items.

A. Last-In-First-Out (LIFO)

B. First-In-First-Out (FIFO)

C. First-In-Last-Out (FILO)

D. None of these

Q.39 Consider a Hamiltonian Graph (G) with no loops and parallel edges. Which of the following is true with respect to this graph?

(a) deg (v) ≥ n/2, for each vertex of G

(b) |E(G)| ≥ 1/2(n - 1)(n - 2) + 2 edges

(c) deg (v) + deg (w) ≥ n, for every n and v not connected by an edge

A. (a) and (b)

B. (b) and (c)

C. (a) and (c)

D. (a), (b) and (c)

Q.40 The hash function used in double hashing is of the form

A. $h(k, i) = (h_1(k) + h_2(k) + i) \bmod m$

B. $h(k, i) = (h_1(k) + h_2(k) - i) \bmod m$

C. $h(k, i) = (h_1(k) + i \times h_2(k)) \bmod m$

D. $h(k, i) = (h_1(k) - i \times h_2(k)) \bmod m$

Q.41 An all-pairs shortest-paths problem is efficiently solved using

A. Dijkstra algorithm

B. Bellman-Ford algorithm

C. Kruskal algorithm

D. Floyd-Warshall algorithm

Q.42 The number of nodes of height h in any n element heap is

A. h

B. z^h

C. $ceil\left(\frac{n}{z^h}\right)$

D. $ceil\left(\frac{n}{z^{h+1}}\right)$

Q.43 The following 'C' statement int * f [ ] ( );
declares

A. a function returning a pointer to an array of integers

B. array of functions returning pointers to integers

C. a function returning an array of pointers to integers

D. an illegal statement

Q.44 A recursive function h, is defined as follows.

$$h(m) = k, \text{ if } m = 0$$
$$= 1, \text{ if } m = 1$$
$$= 2h(m-1) + 4h(m-2), \text{ if } m \geq 2$$

If the value of h(4) is 88, then the value of k is

A. 0   **B.** 1   **C.** 2   **D.** -1

Q.45 Pumping lemma is generally used for proving :

A. A given frammar is regular

B. A given grammar is not regular

C. whether two given regular expressions are equivalent or not

D. none

Q.46 Unix Operating System Kernel maintains two key data structures related to processes, the process table and the user structure. Now, consider the following two statements.
I. The process table is resident all the time and contains information needed for all processes, even those that are not currently in memory.
II. The user structure is swapped or paged out when its associated process is not in memory, in order not to waste memory on information that is not needed.
Which of the following options is correct with reference to the above statements?

A. Only (I) is correct.

B. Only (II) is correct.

C. Both (I) and (II) are correct.

D. Both (I) and (II) are incorrect.

Q.47 An operating system supports a paged virtual memory, using a central processor with a cycle time of one microsecond. It costs an additional one microsecond to access a page, other than the current one. Pages have 1000 words and the paging device is a drum that rotates at 3000 revolutions per minute and transfers one million words per second. Further, one percent of all instructions executed accessed a page, other than the current page. The instruction that accessed another page, 80% accessed a page already in memory and when a new page was required, the replaced page was modified 50% of the time. What is the effective access time on this system, assuming that the system is running only one process and the processor is idle during drum transfers?

A. 30 microseconds

B. 34 microseconds

C. 60 microseconds

D. 68 microseconds

Q.48 Suppose, there are four processes in execution with 12 instances of a resource R in a system. The maximum need of each process and current allocation are given below.

Process	Max. need	Allocation
P1	8	3
P2	9	4
P3	5	2
P4	3	1

With reference to current allocation, is the system safe? If so, what is the safe sequence?

A. No

B. Yes, $P_1P_2P_3P_4$

C. Yes, $P_4P_3P_1P_2$

D. Yes, $P_2P_1P_3P_4$

Q.49 Which of the following statements is **false** for Multi Level Feedback Queue processor scheduling algorithm?

A. Queues have different priorities.

B. Each queue may have different scheduling algorithm.

C. Processes are permanently assigned to a queue.

D. This algorithm can be configured to match a specific system under design.

Q.50 In Unix, the command to enable execution permission for file 'mylife' by all is

A. Chmod ugo + X myfile

B. Chmod a + X myfile

C. Chmod + X myfile

D. All of the above

Q.51 Directions: Match the following.

List - I	List - II
(a) Spooling	(i) Allows several jobs in memory to improve CPU utilisation
(b) Multiprogramming	(ii) Access to shared resources among geographically dispersed computers in a transparent way
(c) Time sharing	(iii) Overlapping I/O and computations
(d) Distributed computing	(iv) Allows many users to share a computer simultaneously by switching processor frequently

	(a)	(b)	(c)	(d)
(1)	(iii)	(i)	(ii)	(iv)
(2)	(iii)	(i)	(iv)	(ii)
(3)	(iv)	(iii)	(ii)	(i)
(4)	(ii)	(iii)	(iv)	(i)

A. (1)   **B.** (2)   **C.** (3)   **D.** (4)

Q.52 The maximum payload of a TCP segment is

A. 65,535 bytes

B. 65,515 bytes

C. 65,495 bytes   **D.** 65,475 bytes

Q.53 Directions: Match the following.

List - I	List - II
a. Session layer	i. Virtual terminal software
b. Application layer	ii. Semantics of the information transmitted
c. Presentation layer	iii. Flow control
d. Transport layer	iv. Management of dialogue control

A. a - iv, b - i, c - ii, d - iii
B. a - i, b - iv, c - ii, d - iii
C. a - iv, b - i, c - iii, d - ii
D. a - iv, b - ii, c - i, d - iii

Q.54 Directions: Consider the following statements.

A. High speed Ethernet works on optic fibre.

B. A point to point protocol over Ethernet is a network protocol for encapsulating PPP frames inside Ethernet frames.

C. High speed Ethernet does not work on optic fibre.

D. A point to point protocol over Ethernet is a network protocol for encapsulating Ethernet frames inside PPP frames.

Which of the following is correct?

A. A and B are true, C and D are false.
B. A and B are false, C and D are true.
C. A, B, C and D are true.
D. A, B, C and D are false.

Q.55 An attacker sits between customer and banker and captures the information from the customer and retransmits it to the banker by altering the information. This attack is called as

A. masquerade attack
B. replay attack
C. passive attack
D. denial of service attack

Q.56 Which of the following are the two modes of IP security?

A. Transport and certificate
B. Transport and tunnel
C. Certificate and tunnel
D. Preshared and transport

Q.57 In multithreading, which of the following statements is correct?

A. All threads of a process share same address space and resources
B. Creation of a new thread only involves allocating a new stack and a new Thread Control Block.
C. Both A. and B.
D. Neither A. nor B.

Q.58 Which of the following statements is **false** about Normal Forms?

A. Lossless preserving decomposition into 3NF is always possible.
B. Lossless preserving decomposition into BCNF is always possible.
C. Any relation with two attributes is in BCNF.

D. BCNF is stronger than 3NF.

Q.59 The STUDENT information in a university is stored in the relation STUDENT (Name, SEX, Marks, DEPT_Name).
Consider the following SQL Query SELECT DEPT_Name from STUDENT, where SEX = 'M' group by DEPT_Name having avg (Marks)>SELECT avg (Marks) from STUDENT.
It returns the name of the department for which the average marks of

A. male students are more than the average marks of students in the same department
B. male students are more than the average marks of students in the university
C. male students are more than the average marks of male students in the university
D. students are more than the average marks of male students in the university

Q.60 Which of the following relation is undecidable?

A. $P \subset NP$ **B.** $P \supset NP$
C. $P = NP$ **D.** Both (B) and (C)

Q.61 A multiplexer combines four 100 Kbps channels using a time slot of 2 bits. What is the bit rate?

A. 100 Kbps   **B.** 200 Kbps
C. 400 Kbps   **D.** 1000 Kbps

Q.62 Which of the following statements is **incorrect** for a Windows Multiple Document Interface (MDI)?

A. Each document in an MDI application is displayed in a separate child window within the client area of the application's main window.
B. An MDI application has three kinds of windows - a frame window, an MDI client window and number of child windows.
C. An MDI application can support more than one kind of document.
D. An MDI application displays output in the client area of the frame window.

Q.63 The content of the accumulator, after the execution of following 8085 assembly language program, is

```
MVI A, 42H
MVI B, 05H
UGC: ADD B
DCR B
JNZ UGC
ADI 25H
HLT
```

A. 82H   **B.** 78H   **C.** 76H   **D.** 47H

Q.64 The simplified SOP (Sum Of Product) form of the Boolean expression (P + Q' + R').(P + Q' + R).(P + Q + R') is

A. (P'.Q + R')   **B.** (P + Q'.R')
C. (P'.Q + R)   **D.** (P.Q + R)

Q.65 Given the following grammars.
$G_1: S \to AB|aaB$
$A \to aA \mid \in$
$B \to bB \mid \in$
$G_2: S \to A|B$
$A \to aAb \mid ab$

$B \rightarrow abB \mid \in$

Which of the following is correct?

A. G_1 is ambiguous and G_2 is unambiguous grammar

B. G_1 is unambiguous and G_2 is ambiguous grammar

C. Both G_1 and G_2 are ambiguous grammars

D. Both G_1 and G_2 are unambiguous grammars

Q.66 In compiler optimisation, operator strength reduction uses mathematical identities to replace slow math operations with faster operations. Which of the following code replacements is an illustration of operator strength reduction?

A. Replace $P + P$ by $2 \times P$ or replace $3 + 4$ by 7

B. Replace $P \times 32$ by $P << 5$

C. Replace $P \times 0$ by 0

D. Replace $(P << 4) - P$ by $P \times 15$

Q.67 Which of the following is most efficient to perform arithmetic operations on numbers?

A. Sign-magnitude   **B.** 1's complement

C. 2's complement   **D.** 9's complement

Q.68 In Data mining, _____ is a method of incremental conceptual clustering.

A. STRING   **B.** COBWEB

C. CORBA   **D.** OLAD

Q.69 Discovery of cross sales opportunities is called as

A. association   **B.** visualisation

C. correlation   **D.** segmentation

Q.70 Directions: Match the following.

List - I	List - II
(a) Joint Application Design (JAD)	(i) Delivers functionality in rapid iteration measured in weeks and needs frequent communication, development, testing and delivery
(b) Computer Aided Software Engg	(ii) Reusable applications generally with one specific function. It is closely linked with idea of web services and service oriented architecture.
(c) Agile development	(iii) Tools to automate many tasks of SDLC
(d) Component based technology	(iv) A group based tool for collecting user requirements and creating system design. It is mostly used in analysis and design stages of SDLC.

A. a-i, b-iii, c-ii, d-iv   **B.** a-iv, b-iii, c-i, d-ii

C. a-iii, b-iv, c-i, d-ii   **D.** a-iii, b-i, c-iv, d-ii

Q.71 _____ model is preferred for software development when the requirements are not clear.

A. Rapid Application Development

B. Rational Unified Process

C. Evolutionary Model

D. Waterfall Model

Q.72 Which of the following is **false** regarding the evaluation of computer programming languages?

A. Application oriented features

B. Efficiency and readability

C. Software development

D. Hardware maintenance cost

Q.73 Directions: Match the following with respect to Input/Output management.

List - I	List - II
a. Device controller	i. Extracts information from the controller register and stores it in data buffer
b. Device driver	ii. I/O scheduling
c. Interrupt handler	iii. Performs data transfer
d. Kernel I/O subsystem	iv. Processing of I/O request

A. a - iii, b - iv, c - i, d - ii

B. a - ii, b - i, c - iv, d - iii

C. a - iv, b - i, c - ii, d - iii

D. a - i, b - iii, c - iv, d - ii

Q.74 Which of the following statements is correct?

(A) Strategic value of data mining is timestamping.

(B) Information collection is an expensive process in building an expert system.

A. Both (A) and (B) are false.

B. Both (A) and (B) are true.

C. (A) is true, (B) is false.

D. (A) is false, (B) is true.

Q.75 In Java, when we implement an interface method, it must be declared as

A. private   **B.** protected

C. public   **D.** friend

Q.76 Given the symbols A, B, C, D, E, F, G and H with the probabilities 1/30, 1/30, 1/30, 2/30, 3/30, 5/30, 5/30 and 12/30, respectively. The average Huffman code size (in bits) per symbol is

A. $\frac{67}{30}$ **B.** $\frac{70}{30}$ **C.** $\frac{76}{30}$ **D.** $\frac{78}{30}$

Q.77 Directions: Consider the following transportation problem.

	W1	W2	W3	Supply
F1	16	20	12	200
F2	14	8	18	160
F3	26	24	16	90
Demand				

The initial basic feasible solution of the above transportation problem using Vogel's Approximation Method (VAM) is given below.

	W1	W2	W3	Supply
F1	16(140)	20	12(60)	200
F2	14(40)	8(120)	18	160
F3	26	24	16(90)	90
Demand				

The solution of the above problem

A. is a degenerate solution

B. is an optimum solution

C. needs to improve

D. is an infeasible solution

Q.78 Aliasing, in the context of programming languages, refers to

A. multiple variables having the same location

B. multiple variables having the same identifier

C. multiple variables having the same value

D. use of same variable

Q.79 Directions: Match the following with reference to functional programming history.

a. Lambda calculus	i. Church, 1932
b. Lambda calculus as programming language	ii. Wordsworth, 1970
c. Lazy evaluation	iii. Haskel, 1990
d. Type classes	iv. Mecarthy, 1960

A. a - iv, b - i, c - iii, d - ii

B. a - i, b - iv, c - ii, d - iii

C. a - iii, b - ii, c - iv, d - i

D. a - ii, b - i, c - iv, d - iii

Q.80 Consider a file currently consisting of 50 blocks. Assume that the file control block and the index block is already in memory. If a block is added at the end (and the block information to be added is stored in memory), then how many disk I/O operations is/are required for indexed (single-level) allocation strategy?

A. 1   **B.** 101   **C.** 27   **D.** 0

Q.81 Optical fibre uses reflection to guide light through a channel, in which angle of incidence is _______ the critical angle.

A. equal to   **B.** less than

C. greater than   **D.** less than or equal to

Q.82 In a fully-connected mesh network with 10 computers, total _____ number of cables are required and _____ number of ports are required for each device.

A. 40, 9   **B.** 45, 10   **C.** 45, 9   **D.** 50, 10

Q.83 A pure ALOHA Network transmits 200 bit frames using a shared channel with 200 Kbps bandwidth. If the system (all stations put together) produces 500 frames per second, then the throughput of the system is

A. 0.384   **B.** 0.184   **C.** 0.286   **D.** 0.586

Q.84 How many of the following statements are true?

1) The intersection of two regular languages is infinite is decidable.

2) Whether a given context free language is regular is decidable.

3) Whether a given grammar is context free is not decidable.

4) Finiteness problem of regular language is decidable.

A. I only   **B.** II only

C. I and II only   **D.** I, II and III only

Q.85 The Relation Vendor Order (V_no, V_ord_no, V_name, Qty_sup, unit_price) is in 2NF because

A. Non_key attribute V_name is dependent on V_no which is part of composite key

B. Non_key attribute V_name is dependent on Qty_sup

C. Key attribute Qty_sup is dependent on primary_key unit price

D. Key attribute V_ord_no is dependent on primary_key unit price

Q.86 DBMS provides the facility of accessing data from a database through

A. DDL   **B.** DML   **C.** DBA   **D.** Schema

Q.87 Consider the statement.

Either $-2 \leq x \leq -1$ or $1 \leq x \leq 2$.

The negation of this statement is

A. x < - 2 or 2 < x or - 1 < x < 1

B. x < -2 or 2 < x

C. -1 < x < 1

D. x ≤ -2 or 2 < x or -1 < x < 1

Q.88 Consider the relations R(A, B) and S(B, C) and the following four relational algebra queries over R and S.

I. $\pi_{A,B}(R \bowtie S)$

II. $\pi_B(S)R \bowtie$

III. $R \cap \left(\pi_A(R) \times \pi_B(S)\right)$

IV. $\pi_A R_{.B}(R \times S)$, where $R.B$ refers to the column B in table R

One can determine that

A. I, III and IV are the same query

B. II, III and IV are the same query

C. I, II and IV are the same query

D. I, II and III are the same query

Q.89 How many of the following problem is decidable?

A) Does a given program ever produce an output.

B) If L is CFL, Then L' is also CFL.

C) Given a CFG, G , L(G) = {empty}.

D) If L is a recursive language, then , is L' also recursive.

A. 1   **B.** 2   **C.** 3   **D.** 4

Q.90 Which of the following strings would match the regular expression $p + [3 - 5] \times [xyz]$?

I. p443y

II. p6y

III. 3xyz

IV. p35z

V. p353535x

VI. ppp5

A. I, III and VI only   **B.** IV, V and VI only

C. II, IV and V only   **D.** I, IV and V only

Q.91 The quick design of a software that is visible to end users leads to

A. iterative model   **B.** prototype model

C. spiral model   **D.** waterfall model

Q.92 If s_1 is the total number of modules defined in the program architecture and s_3 is the number of modules whose correct function depends on prior processing, then the number of modules **not** dependent on prior processing is

A. $1 + (s_3/s_1)$ **B.** $1 - (s_3/s_1)$

C. $1 + (s_1/s_3)$ **D.** $1 - (s_1/s_3)$

Q.93 Which of the following is **not** included in waterfall model?

A. Requirement analysis

B. Risk analysis

C. Design

D. Coding

Q.94 The extent to which a software tolerates the unexpected problems is termed as

A. accuracy   **B.** reliability

C. correctness   **D.** robustness

Q.95 A data cube C has n dimensions and each dimension has exactly p distinct values in the base cuboid. Assume that there are no concept hierarchies associated with the dimensions. What is the maximum number of cells possible in the data cube C?

A. p^n **B.** p

C. $(2^n - 1)p + 1$ **D.** $(p + 1)^n$

Q.96 Directions: Match the following types of variables with the corresponding programming languages.

(a) Static variables	(i) Local variables in Pascal
(b) Stack dynamic	(ii) All variables in APL
(c) Explicit heap dynamic	(iii) Fortran 77
(d) Implicit heap dynamic	(iv) All objects in JAVA

A. (a) - (i), (b) - (iii), (c) - (iv), (d) - (ii)

B. (a) - (iv), (b) - (i), (c) - (iii), (d) - (ii)

C. (a) - (iii), (b) - (i), (c) - (iv), (d) - (ii)

D. (a) - (ii), (b) - (i), (c) - (iii), (d) - (iv)

Q.97 Consider an un-directed graph G, where self-loops are not allowed. The vertex set of G is {(i, j) | 1 < i < 12, 1 < j < 12}. There is an edge between (a, b) and (c, d), if |a - c| < 1 or | b - d | < 1. The number of edges in this graph is

A. 726   **B.** 796   **C.** 506   **D.** 616

Q.98 Assume that the program 'P' is implementing parameter passing with 'call by reference'. What will be printed by following print statements in P?

```
Program P( )
{
x = 10;
y = 3;
funb (y, x, x)
print x;
print y;
}
funb (x, y, z)
{
y = y + 4;
z = x + y + z;
}
```

A. 10, 7   **B.** 31, 3   **C.** 10, 3   **D.** 31, 7

Q.99 Which of the following statements is/are true regarding some advantages that an object-oriented DBMS (OODBMS) offers over a relational database?

I. An OODBMS avoids the 'impedance mismatch' problem.

II. An OODBMS avoids the 'phantom' problem.

III. An OODBMS provides higher performance concurrency control than most relational databases.

IV. An OODBMS provides faster access to individual data objects, once they have been read from disk.

A. II and III only   **B.** I and IV only

C. I, II, and III only   **D.** I, III and IV only

Q.100 The cyclomatic complexity of a flow graph V(G), in terms of predicate nodes, is

(1) P + 1

(2) P - 1

(3) P - 2

(4) P + 2, where P is the number of predicate nodes in flow graph V(G).

A. (1)   **B.** (2)   **C.** (3)   **D.** (4)

// Smart Answer Sheet //

Correct Percentage of students who answered correctly. **Skipped** Percentage of students who skipped.

Q.	Ans.	Correct / Skipped	Q.	Ans.	Correct / Skipped	Q.	Ans.	Correct / Skipped	Q.	Ans.	Correct / Skipped	Q.	Ans.	Correct / Skipped
1	B	28.26 % / 16.31 %	17	B	34.78 % / 43.48 %	33	A	29.35 % / 39.13 %	49	C	32.61 % / 43.48 %	65	C	35.87 % / 44.56 %
2	A	26.09 % / 40.21 %	18	A	32.61 % / 42.39 %	34	D	43.48 % / 43.48 %	50	D	30.43 % / 43.48 %	66	B	33.7 % / 48.91 %
3	A	28.26 % / 38.04 %	19	D	42.39 % / 38.04 %	35	B	29.35 % / 47.82 %	51	B	39.13 % / 40.22 %	67	C	33.7 % / 44.56 %
4	D	50.0 % / 36.96 %	20	A	34.78 % / 40.22 %	36	B	31.52 % / 45.65 %	52	C	23.91 % / 41.31 %	68	B	25.0 % / 44.57 %
5	C	42.39 % / 39.13 %	21	D	44.57 % / 40.21 %	37	A	14.13 % / 41.3 %	53	A	38.04 % / 42.39 %	69	A	15.22 % / 46.74 %
6	A	22.83 % / 34.78 %	22	A	34.78 % / 34.79 %	38	B	39.13 % / 46.74 %	54	A	41.3 % / 43.48 %	70	B	27.17 % / 43.48 %
7	B	29.35 % / 32.61 %	23	D	18.48 % / 38.04 %	39	C	21.74 % / 39.13 %	55	B	21.74 % / 43.48 %	71	C	32.61 % / 44.56 %
8	C	28.26 % / 33.7 %	24	C	43.48 % / 40.22 %	40	C	27.17 % / 41.31 %	56	B	36.96 % / 42.39 %	72	D	40.22 % / 46.74 %
9	A	39.13 % / 34.78 %	25	C	43.48 % / 44.56 %	41	D	41.3 % / 39.13 %	57	A	19.57 % / 43.47 %	73	D	20.65 % / 44.57 %
10	A	20.65 % / 42.39 %	26	C	30.43 % / 42.4 %	42	C	22.83 % / 42.39 %	58	B	30.43 % / 43.48 %	74	B	42.39 % / 47.83 %
11	D	34.78 % / 36.96 %	27	A	29.35 % / 40.22 %	43	B	21.74 % / 43.48 %	59	B	28.26 % / 45.65 %	75	C	31.52 % / 45.65 %
12	D	14.13 % / 40.22 %	28	C	36.96 % / 41.3 %	44	C	33.7 % / 45.65 %	60	C	22.83 % / 50.0 %	76	C	28.26 % / 47.83 %
13	A	36.96 % / 40.21 %	29	A	18.48 % / 38.04 %	45	B	25.0 % / 43.48 %	61	C	20.65 % / 44.57 %	77	B	38.04 % / 51.09 %
14	C	33.7 % / 35.87 %	30	A	34.78 % / 36.96 %	46	C	31.52 % / 45.65 %	62	D	14.13 % / 44.57 %	78	A	20.65 % / 46.74 %
15	D	30.43 % / 38.05 %	31	C	34.78 % / 40.22 %	47	B	19.57 % / 47.82 %	63	C	18.48 % / 47.82 %	79	B	22.83 % / 51.08 %
16	C	30.43 % / 41.31 %	32	C	38.04 % / 39.13 %	48	C	41.3 % / 43.48 %	64	B	34.78 % / 44.57 %	80	A	20.65 % / 45.65 %

Q.	Ans.	Correct		Q.	Ans.	Correct		Q.	Ans.	Correct		Q.	Ans.	Correct		Q.	Ans.	Correct
		Skipped				Skipped				Skipped				Skipped				Skipped
81	C	27.17 %		85	A	28.26 %		89	B	23.91 %		93	B	50.0 %		97	C	20.65 %
		44.57 %				50.0 %				50.0 %				46.74 %				45.65 %
82	C	30.43 %		86	B	34.78 %		90	D	16.3 %		94	D	36.96 %		98	B	23.91 %
		48.92 %				46.74 %				51.09 %				46.74 %				48.92 %
83	B	30.43 %		87	A	18.48 %		91	B	35.87 %		95	D	18.48 %		99	B	19.57 %
		45.66 %				48.91 %				47.83 %				48.91 %				46.73 %
84	B	27.17 %		88	D	15.22 %		92	B	28.26 %		96	C	21.74 %		100	A	21.74 %
		50.0 %				44.56 %				47.83 %				44.56 %				45.65 %

//Hints and Solutions//

1. According to Bayes theorem,

$$P(B \mid A) = \frac{P(A|B) \times P(B)}{P(A)}$$

$$P(A) = \frac{1}{20}$$

$$P(B) = \frac{1}{5000}$$

We know that meningitis causes stiff neck 50% of the time i.e.

$$P(A \mid B) = 0.5$$

$$P(B \mid A) = \frac{\frac{0.5 \times 1}{50000}}{\frac{1}{20}}$$

$$= 0.02\%$$

So, option (B) is correct.

2.

- Vacuous proof is a proof in which the implication $p \to q$ is true, based on the fact that p is false.

- Trivial proof is a proof in which the implication $p \to q$ is true, based on the fact that q is true.

- Direct proof is a proof in which the implication $p \to q$ is true, that proceeds by showing that q must be true, when p is true.

- Indirect proof is a proof in which the implication $p \to q$ is true, that proceeds by showing that p must be false, when q is false.

So, option (A) is correct.

3. $\exists m \forall n P(m, n)$: There exist some m which divide all n. True

$\forall n P(1, n)$ Every n is divided by 1. True

$\forall m \forall n P(m, n)$ Every m divides every n. False

So, option (A) is correct.

4. In inorder traversal, first we traverse left node, then root node and finally the right node.

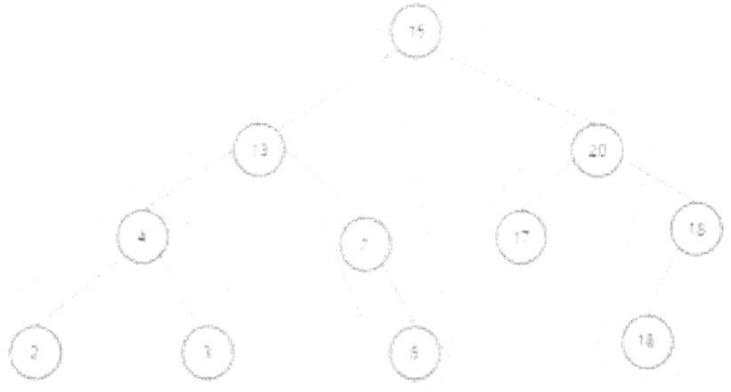

In the given tree, first we go to the leftmost node, then its root and after that, to the right.

So, 2 4 3 13 7 6 15 17 20 18 18.

In the other options, inorder property has been violated.

So, option (D) is correct.

5. Floyd-Warshall algorithm utilises dynamic programming to solve all-pairs shortest paths problem on a directed graph in θ (V³) time.

Option (C) is correct.

6. LISP is a functional language

Useful properties of a functional languages are:

1.Evaluates an expression and use the result

2.Call functions

3.Related to Mathematics and the theory of functions

4.Side effect free

Hence the correct option is (A).

7. friend function is not a member of class it works as a bridge between 2 classes

one of the most convenient and controversial feature of C++ is allowing non -memeber function to access even the private members of a class using friend function or friend classes . It permits a function or all the functions of another class to access a different class's private members

In object-oriented programming, a friend function, that is a "friend" of a given class, is a function that is given the same access than methods to private and protected data.

A friend function is declared by the class that is granting access, so friend functions are part of the class interface, like methods. Friend functions allow alternative syntax to use objects, for instance f(x) instead of x.f(), or g(x,y) instead of x.g(y). Friend functions have the same implications on encapsulation than methods.

Hence the correct option is (B).

8. We know that the Golden rule in Module design is used to maximize cohesion and minimize coupling.

Encapsulation is the key to implement this rule.

Hence the correct option is (C).

9. exec replaces the current program in the current process, without forking a new process.

brk() and sbrk() change the location of the program break, which defines the end of the process's data segment.

The parent process may then issue a wait system call, which suspends the execution of the parent process while the child executes. When the child process terminates, it returns an exit status to the operating system, which is then returned to the waiting parent process. The parent process then resumes execution.

fork --Creates new process

Hence the correct option is (A).

10. A bridge operates at the data link layer, giving it access to the physical address of all stations connected to it.

So Answer is physical addresses.

Hence, the correct option is (A).

11. For frame size =3

0 1 2 3 0 1 4 0 1 2 3 4

F F F F F F F H H F F H

Total 9 page fault

For Frame Size =4

0 1 2 3 0 1 4 0 1 2 3 4

F F F F H H F F F F F F

Total 10 page fault

Hence the correct option is (D).

12. CPU speed 1MIPS=10^6 instruction per sec

1 Cpu instruction =4 machine cycles(Avg)

1 memory read/access = 1 machine cycle

CPU utilization =90%

Programmed I/O

each byte transfer requires 4 cycles (instructions)

in status

check status

Branch

Read/Write data

max data transfer rate CPU speed /4 = 10^6/4=250 kbytes/sec

Hence the correct option is (D).

13. (a) Boot block -- (iv) Code for making OS ready

(b) Super block-- (i) Information about file system

(c) Inode table --(ii) Information about file

(d) Data block --(iii) Storage space

Each file system contains:

1. a boot block located in the first few sectors of a file system. The boot block contains the initial bootstrap program used to load the operating system.

Typically, the first sector contains a bootstrap program that reads in a larger bootstrap program from the next few sectors, and so forth.

2. a super block describes the state of the file system: the total size of the partition, the block size, pointers to a list of free blocks, the inode number of the root directory, magic number, etc.

3. a linear array of inodes (short for index nodes"). There is a one to one mapping of files to inodes and vice versa. An inode is identified by its inode number", which contains the information needed to find the inode itself on the disk

Thus, while users think of files in terms of file names, Unix thinks of files in terms of inodes.

4. data blocks blocks containing the actual contents of files

Hence the correct option is (A).

14. It is observed that Spatial locality can referenced same value or related value many times. The implication with spatial locality is that in this, we will predict with reasonable accuracy about instructions and data in a program for near future which depends on access in recent past.

Hence the correct option is (C).

15. Circuit switching transmission technique guarantees that data packets will be received by the receiver in the same order in which they were sent by the sender because path is fixed and all packet goes through that path in same order .

Hence the correct option is (D).

16. Bandwidth of analog channel is 8K/Sec.

Required sample 2 samples/hz. =2s.

one sample is 8 bit.

so bit rate = (8k) $\times$2 $\times$(8 bit)=128 kbps.

Hence the correct option is (C).

17. Since minimum bus cycle duration = 4 clock cycles

Bus clock = 8 MHz

Then, maximum bus cycle rate = 8 M / 4 = 2 M/sec

Data transferred per bus cycle = 16 bit = 2B

Data transfer rate per second = bus cycle rate $\times$ data per bus cycle = 2 M $\times$ 2 = 4 $\times$ 106 B/sec

Hence the correct option is (B).

18. Since there are 8 routes we can send 8 packets (8 $\times$8000 bits) simultaneously

Total end to end delay= Transmission time = $\dfrac{8 \times 8000}{32 \times 1000}$ = 2 sec

Hence the correct option is (A).

19. Internet Message Access protocol (IMAP) is used to retrieve email from mail server.

Simple Mail Transfer Protocol (SMTP) is a internet standard for email communication.

Multimedia Internet Mail Extensions(MIME) protocol allows the transfer of multimedia messages.

POP3(Post Office Protocol) is the most recent version of a standard protocol for receiving e-mail.

Hence the correct option is (D).

20. Indexes are special lookup tables that the database search engine can use to speed up data retrieval. Simply put, an index is a pointer to data in a table. An index in a database is very similar to an index in the back of a book.

Hence the correct option is (A).

21. Given Relation is R = ABCDEFG

Take options:

1.A = A

2.AB = ABC

3.ABC = ABC

4.ABD = ABDEFCG (ABCDEFG)

ABD will be the candidate keys.

Hence the correct option is (D).

22. In Index allocation size of maximum file can be derived like following:

No. of addressable blocks using one Index block (A)= Size of block / Size of block address

No. of block addresses available for addressing one file (B)=

No. of Maximum blocks we can use for the Index $\times$ No. of addressable blocks using one Index block (A)

Size of File = B $\times$ Size of Block

So, it is clear that:

Hence the correct option is (A).

23. We have Boolean function:

$[\sim(\sim p \wedge q) \wedge \sim(\sim p \wedge \sim q)] \vee (p \wedge r)]$

$= [(p \vee \sim q) \wedge (p \vee q) \vee (p \wedge r)]$

$= [p \vee (p \wedge q) \vee (p \wedge \sim q) \vee (p \wedge r)]$

$= p[1 \vee q \vee \sim q \vee r]$

$= p$

So, option (D) is correct.

24. Correct answer is C.

e.g $R_1=(a,b,c,d)$ $R_2=(c,d,e,f)$

$R_1-R_2=(a,b)$, $R_2-R_1=(e,f)$

$R_1 \cap R_2 =c,d$

 c,d is common to both relation ,now to be lossless c,d must be a superkey in at least one of the relation R_1 and R_2

According to option C it is superkey in both relation so it is lossless.

Hence the correct option is (C).

25. 2550276 = 010 101 101 000 010 111 110

0 1010 = A 1101= D 0000= 0 1011= B 1110= E

Hence the correct option is (C).

26. Option C Is Correct.

$(326.4)_8 = 8^2 \times 3 + 8^1 \times 2 + 8^0 \times 6 . 8^{-1} \times 4 = (214.5)_{10}$

To convert in hexa decimal i assume you already familiar with the conventional way there is also a shortcut which is only applicable if one base can be written in the power of another base eg.($r_1)m = r_2$

$(326.4)_8 = (011010110.100)_2$ here we expanded every digit in three bits

3	2	6	.	4
011	010	110	.	100

$(011010110.100)_2 = (D6.8)_{16}$ here we grouped every 4 bits (radix point taken as reference)

0000	1101	0110	.	1000
0	D	6	.	8

Hence the correct option is (C).

27. In context of Context free language, only emptiness problem is decidable. Rests are undecidable.

28. looking at X-> aX | bX | eps

we see that X is generating (a+b)*

now simply replacing X by (a+b)*

and Y by bbb in S-> XYX

we get (a+b)*bbb(a+b)*

Hence the correct option is (C).

29. Syntax Analysis generates stream of atoms. Lexical Analysis is the first phase of compiler also known as scanner. It converts the input program into a sequence of Tokens.

Hence the correct option is (A).

30. Already given in proper matching order.

Hence the correct option is (A).

31. A data warehouse is a subject-oriented, integrated, time-variant and non-volatile collection of data in support of management's decision making process. Subject-Oriented: A data warehouse can be used to analyze a particular subject area. For example, "sales" can be a particular subject.

Hence the correct option is (C).

32. a decision tree can be used to visually and explicitly represent decisions and decision making. In data mining, a decision tree describes data but not decisions; rather the resulting classification tree can be an input for decision making.

Hence the correct option is (C).

33. cohesion is functional and coupling is data type

as we know our aim is to maximize cohesion and minimize coupling .

strongest form of cohesion is functional cohesion (when parts of a module are grouped because they all contribute to a single well-defined task of the module)

weakest form of coupling is data coupling (when modules share data through, for example, parameters)

Hence the correct option is (A).

34. Verification refers to the set of activities that ensure that software correctly implements a specific function and gives answer to the question – Are we building the product right ? but it does not requires execution of software.

So, option (D) is correct.

35. first we will calculate Δx and Δy:

i.e. $\Delta x = x_2 - x_1$

$= 11 - (-1)$

$= 11 + 1$

$= 12$.

$\Delta y = y_2 - y_1$

$= 1 - 7$

$= -6$

Now $P_1 = -\Delta x = -12$

$P_2 = \Delta x = 12$

$P_3 = -\Delta y = 6$

$P_4 = \Delta y = -6$

$Q_1 = x_1 - x_{min} = -1 - 1 = -2$

$Q_2 = x_{max} - x_1 = 9 - (-1) = 9 + 1 = 10$.

$Q_3 = y_1 - y_{min} = 7 - 2 = 5$.

$Q_4 = y_{max} - y_1 = 8 - 7 = 1$.

$P_1, P_4 < 0$ and $P_2, P_3 > 0$.

Intially: $t_1 = 0, t_2 = 1$

$t_1 = max(0, Q_1 / P_1, Q_4 / P_4)$

$= max(0, 2 / 12, 1 / -6)$

$= 1 / 6$.

$t_2 = min(1, Q_1 / P_1, Q_4 / P_4)$

$= min(1, 10 / 12, 5 / 6)$.

$= 5 / 6$.

i.e. u ranges between (1 / 6, 5 / 6).

So, option (B) is correct.

36. An algorithm becomes a program when it is written in the form of a programming language. Thus, any program is an algorithm.

Hence the correct option is (B).

37. In this case the view plane normal N is vector K. since N.I =0 and N.J=0, so there are no vanishing points in the direction I and J. on the other hand N.K = K.K = 1. thus there is only one principal vanishing point and it is in K direction.

STANDARD PERSPECTIVE PROJECTION

A perspective transformation is the transformation from one three space in to another three space. In contrast to the parallel transformation , in perspective transformations parallel lines converge, object size is reduced with increasing distance from the center of projection, and non uniform foreshortening of lines in the object as a function of orientation and the distance of the object from the center of projection occurs. All of these effects laid the depth perception of the human visual system., but the shape of the object is not preserved. Perspective drawings are characterized by perspective foreshortening and vanishing points .Perspective foreshortening is the illusion that object and lengths appear smaller as there distance from the center of projection increases. The illusion that certain sets of parallel lines appear to meet at a point is another feature of perspective drawings. These points are called vanishing points .Principal vanishing points are formed by the apparent intersection of lines parallel to one of the three x,y or z axis. The number of principal vanishing points is determined by the number of principal axes interested by the view plane

Perspective Anomalies

1. Perspective foreshortening- The farther an object is from the center of projection ,the smaller it appears

2. Vanishing Points- Projections of lines that are not parallel to the view plane (i.e. lines that are not perpendicular to the view plane normal) appear to meet at some point on the view plane. This point is called the vanishing point. A vanishing point corresponds to every set of parallel lines. Vanishing points corresponding to the three principle directions are referred to as "Principle Vanishing Points (PVPs)". We can thus have at most three PVPs. If one or more of these are at infinity (that is parallel lines in that direction continue to appear parallel on the projection plane), we get 1 or 2 PVP perspective projection.

Hence the correct option is (A).

38. Queue is opened at both end therefore it follows First-In-First-Out (FIFO) methodology for storing the data items.

Hence the correct option is (B).

39. In an Hamiltonian Graph (G) with no loops and parallel edges:

According to Dirac's theorem in a n vertex graph, deg (v) ≥ n / 2 for each vertex of G.

According to Ore's theorem deg (v) + deg (w) ≥ n for every n and v not connected by an edge is sufficient condition for a graph to be hamiltonian.

If $|E(G)| ≥ 1 / 2 \times [(n - 1) (n - 2)]$ then graph is connected but it doesn't guaranteed to be Hamiltonian Graph.

(a) and (c) is correct regarding to Hamiltonian Graph.

So, option (C) is correct.

40. $h(k, i) = (h_1(k) + i \times h_2(k))$ mod m is used in double hashing is of the form. Rest other option does not used in double hashing.

Hence the correct option is (C).

41. An all-pairs shortest-paths problem is efficiently solved using Floyd-Warshall algorithm.

For more information on all-pairs shortest-paths problem and its solution using Floyd-Warshall algorithm Refer:Dynamic Programming | Set 16 (Floyd Warshall Algorithm)

Hence the correct option is (D).

42. We can prove it by taking random example.

if we take n=9 and required h=3(e.g.)

then according to option d it will produce answer as (9/16=1(ceil))..and that is not correct.

If we consider option C--(9/8=2) which is correct.

Hence the correct option is (C).

43. int (*f())[ ];

[] it represents Array Subscript

() it represents function Subscript

* it represents pointer

[] and () has same precedence and they are Left to right associative .

so a/c to precedence and associative f first becomes function

*f() shows that function f is returning a pointer

then we went to [] a/c to associativity then complete declaration put together becomes

A function f returning a pointer to an array of integers.

Hence the correct option is (B).

44. given that

h(m)=k, if m=0

= 1, if m=1

= 2h(m-1) + 4h(m-2), if $m \geq 2$

If the value of h(4) is 88 then the value of k is

h(4)=2h(3)+4h(2)=2(2h(2)+4h(1))+4h(2)
=8h(2)+8h(1)=8(2h(1)+4h(0))+8h(1)=24h(1)+32h(0)=24+32k=88
=>k=2

Hence the correct option is (C).

45. If a grammar doesn't satisfy pumping lemma , then it is surely not regular.

If satisfy pumping lemma , then it may or may not be regular.

Hence , option (b) is correct.

46. The process table is resident all the time and contain information needed for all processes, even those that are not currently in memory. this is TRUE kernel store all PCB(Process Control Block).

Hence the correct option is (C).

47. Effective access time = 0.99 $\times$ (1 μs) + 0.8 $\times$.02 μs + 0.001 $\times$ (10000 μs + 1000 μs) + 0.001 $\times$ (20000 μs + 2000 μs)

= (0.99 +0.016+22.0+11.0) μs

= 34 μs

Hence the correct option is (B).

48.

- P_1 holds 3 resources
- P_2 holds 4 resources
- P_3 holds 2 resources
- P_4 holds 1 resource
- Total 3+4+2+1 = 10 resources are allocated and 12-10=2 resources are free
- P_1 requires maximum 8 resources; It needs 8-3 =5 more tapes
- P_2 requires maximum 9 resources; It needs 9-4 =5 more tapes
- P_3 requires maximum 5 resources; It needs5-2 =3 more tapes
- P_4 requires maximum 3 resources; It needs 3-1 = 2 more tapes

We can allocate 2 free resources to P_4.

P_4 will complete execution and release all its resources. Now total 3 resoucres are free.

We can allocate 3 free resources to P_3.

P_3 will complete execution and release all its resources. Now total 5 resoucres are free.

We can allocate 5 free resources to P_1.

P_1 will complete execution and release all its resources. Now total 8 resoucres are free.

We can allocate 5 free resources to P_2.

P_2 will complete execution and release all its resources.

System is in safe state.!!!

The sequence is $P_4P_3P_1P_2$

Hence the correct option is (C).

49. C is not true.

Processes are not permanently assigned to a queue they can very between queues as their priorities change.

Rest 3 options are true.

Hence the correct option is (C).

50. all three commands are used to enable execution permission chmod (change mode) X for execution

ugo (user group other) and + for add

a(all) and + for add

only + for all

Hence the correct option is (D).

51. Spooling--iii. Overlapping I/O and computations.

Multiprogramming--- Allows several jobs in memory to improve CPU utilization.

Time sharing---Allows many users to share a computer simultaneously by switching processor frequently.

Distributed computing---Access to shared resources among geographically dispersed computers in a transparent way.

Hence the correct option is (B).

52. The maximum payload of a TCP segment is 65,495 bytes. Why was such a strange number chosen? Maximum IP packet is 65,535 bytes, out of which 20 is used for IP headers. TCP header is 20 bytes.

Hence the correct option is (C).

53. Session layer maintains multiple connections and synchronisation since we know session is a combination of multiple connections and hence it is associated with dialog control management

Application layer is the topmost layer in TCP/IP protocol stack.Hence is related to software related things.

Presentation layer presents the data in proper format for transmission so it is concerned with semantics of the data.

Lastly transport layer deals with flow control and congestion control mainly.

Hence the correct option is (A).

54. The cable types used for various Ethernet types are:

Ethernet (10 Mbps) : Coaxial, twisted pair, optical fiber

Fast Ethernet (100 Mbps):twisted pair, optical fiber

Gigabit Ethernet (1000 Mbps) : twisted pair, optical fiber

10 gigabit Ethernet (10000 Mbps) : twisted pair, optical fiber

Thus A is true C is False.

The Point-to-Point Protocol over Ethernet   (PPPoE) is used to encapsulate PPP frames inside Ethernet frames

Thus B is true D is false.

Hence the correct option is (A).

55. Replay attack: An attacker spies the communication between sender and receiver and retransmits the information later. Perfect example is question itself. An attacker sits between customer and banker and captures the information from the customer and retransmits to the banker by altering the information .

Masquerade attack: Attacker uses a fake identity to gain unauthorized access to the system. Attacker steals password of Hrithik Roshan's mail ID and sends fake mails to Kangana Ranaut. For receiver (Kangana) , the mails seems to be legitimate as it come from valid mail ID.

Passive attack: Attacker monitors the target system for its vulnerabilities. (eg:open ports). The purpose is solely to gain information about the target and no data is changed on the target.

Eg: Stealing Neighbour's Wifi if it is not password protected.

Denial of service attack: Attacker sends a lot of requests to the target system so that it will be overloaded and will not be available for legitimate users.

Eg; Attacker sends a large number of connection requests to the server. Server will be hanged by serving each request and allocating resources. No other client can connect with the server for a period of time.

Hence the correct option is (B).

56. IPsec can be implemented in a host-to-host transport mode, as well as in a network tunneling mode.

In transport mode, only the payload of the IP packet is usually encrypted and/or authenticated. The routing is intact, since the IP header is neither modified nor encrypted.

In tunnel mode, the entire IP packet is encrypted and/or authenticated. It is then encapsulated into a new IP packet with a new IP header. Tunnel mode is used to create virtual private networks for network-to-network communications, host-to-network communications and host-to-host communications.

Hence the correct option is (B).

57. Creation of new thread requires allocation of new stack,registers and TCB.Threads share the same address space,code,data, permission, resources.

Hence the correct option is (A).

58. It is not always possible to decompose a table in BCNF and preserve dependencies. For example, a set of functional dependencies {AB –> C, C –> B} cannot be decomposed in BCNF. See this for more details.

Hence the correct option is (B).

59. The SQL query:

SELECT DEPT_Name from STUDENT where SEX = 'M' group by DEPT_Name having avg (Marks)>SELECT avg (Marks) from STUDENT.

will return The average marks of male students is more than the average marks of students in the University.

So, option (B) is correct.

60. We know that P class problem is proper subset of NP class so option A) is decidable.

Option (B) is not correct hence it is decidable. But whether P=NP is correct or not as it is still unknown.

61. The link carries 50000 frames per sec as each frame contains 2 bits per channel (100 kbps/2=50kbps)

frame duration is therefore 1/50000 sec= 20 microseconds

Bit rate =frame rate x no of bits per frame =50000x 8 =400 kbps

Hence the correct option is (C).

62. In Windows Multiple Document Interface (MDI):

Each document in an MDI application is displayed in a separate child window within the client area of the application's main window.Correct.

An MDI application has three kinds of windows namely a frame window, an MDI client window and number of child windows.Correct.

An MDI application can support more than one kind of document.Correct.

An MDI application displays output in the client area of the frame window.Incorrect.

Hence the correct option is (D).

63. A is taking accumulator...

A= 4 $\times$ 16 + 2 = 66 in decimal

B= 5 in decimal

Loop runs from B=5 to 1

So 66 + 5 +4 +3+2+1

That is 81 + 25H = 81 + 37 =118

In binary ..

01110110 = 76H

Hence the correct option is (C).

64. See following :

$$(P + Q' + R') \cdot (P + Q' + R) \cdot (P + Q + R') = \prod(3,2,1) = \sum(0,4,5,6,7)$$

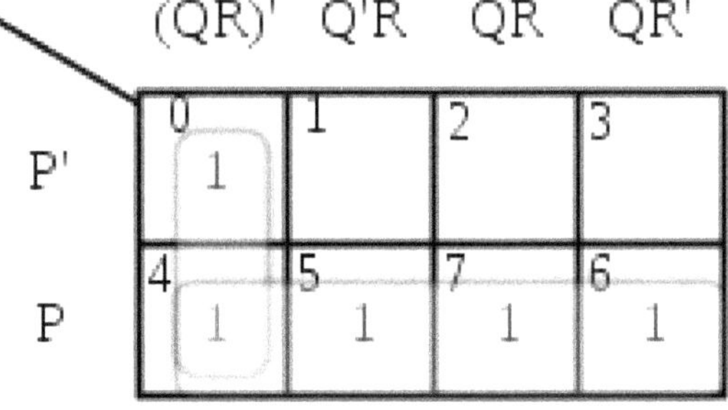

From the K-map, POS form is :

$$P + Q' \cdot R'$$

Hence the correct option is (B).

65. Both are ambiguous...

G_1: S→AB|aaB

A→a|Aa

B→b

To generatte string "aab"

S->AB ->AaB -> aaB -> aab

S->aaB->aab

So ambiguous...

G_2: S→aSbS|bSaS|λ

Generate" abab "

S->aSbS -> abS->abaSbS -> abab

S->aSbS->aSb->abSaSb ->abab

So ambiguous.

Hence the correct option is (C).

66. Strength Reduction : Replace expensive operations with less expensive but equivalent operations.

For Example : Multiplication is more expensive operation than addition.

Shift operation is less expensive operation than Multiplication/Division.

2 $\times$3 CAN BE REPLACED WITH 2+2+2 .

OPTION A : We are replacing less expensive operation with more expensive operation which is not right. So Option 1 is incorrect.

Option B : We are replacing Multiplication (Expensive Operation) With Shift(Less expensive) . So this is OK

Option : C Both are equivalent

Option D: Replacing shift(Less Expensive) with Multiplication . This is Wrong

Hence the correct option is (B).

67. The two's complement form is more suitable to perform arithmetic operations as there is no need to involve the sign of the number into consideration.

Hence the correct option is (C).

68. COBWEB is an incremental system for hierarchical conceptual clustering. COBWEB was invented by Professor Douglas H. Fisher, currently at Vanderbilt University.

COBWEB incrementally organizes observations into a classification tree. Each node in a classification tree represents a class (concept) and is labeled by a probabilistic concept that summarizes the attribute-value distributions of objects classified under the node. This classification tree can be used to predict missing attributes or the class of a new object.

Hence the correct option is (B).

69. Association rule learning is a method for discovering interesting relations between variables in large databases. It is intended to identify strong rules discovered in databases using some measures of interestingness. Based on the concept of strong rules, Rakesh Agrawal et al. introduced association rules for discovering regularities between products in large-scale transaction data recorded by point-of-sale (POS) systems in supermarkets. For example, the rule found in the sales data of a supermarket would indicate that if a customer buys onions and potatoes together, they are likely to also buy hamburger meat. Such information can be used as the basis for decisions about marketing activities such as, e.g., promotional pricing or product placements. In addition to the above example from market basket analysis association rules are employed today in many application areas including Web usage mining, intrusion detection, Continuous production, and bioinformatics. In contrast with sequence mining, association rule learning typically does not consider the order of items either within a transaction or across transactions.

Hence the correct option is (A).

70. JAD--->JAD (Joint Application Development) is a methodology that involves the client or end user in the design and development of an application, through a succession of collaborative workshops called JAD sessions

CASE Tools->Tools to automate many tasks of SDLC

Agile development--->Agile SDLC model is a combination of iterative and incremental process models with focus on process adaptability and customer satisfaction by rapid delivery of working software product. Agile Methods break the product into small incremental builds. These builds are provided in iterations.

Component based technology-->Reusable applications generally with one specific function. It is closely linked with idea of web services and service oriented architecture.

Hence the correct option is (B).

71. The Evolutionary Model model is preferred for software development when the requirements are not clear.
In a Waterfall model, each phase must be completed before the next phase can begin
Rapid Application Development uses minimal in favor of rapid prototype(functionally equivalent component of product)
Rational Unified Process divides the development process into four distinct phases: business modeling, analysis and design, implementation, testing, and deployment.
Hence the correct option is (C).

72. Programming language evaluation is no way related with cost of hardware.

Hence the correct option is (D).

73. a. Device controller   i. Extracts information from the controller register and store it in data buffer

b. Device driver   iii. Performs data transfer

c. Interrupt handler   iv. Processing of I/O request

d. Kernel I/O subsystem ii. I/O scheduling

Hence the correct option is (D).

74. Strategic value of data mining is time-stamping.Correct

Information collection is an expensive process in building an expert system.Correct

So, option (B) is correct.

75. An interface is a reference type in Java, it is similar to class, it is a collection of abstract methods. Interfaces are meant to define the **public** API of a type - and only that, not its implementation. An interface is implicitly abstract. You do not need to use the abstract keyword while declaring an interface.

Hence the correct option is (C).

76.

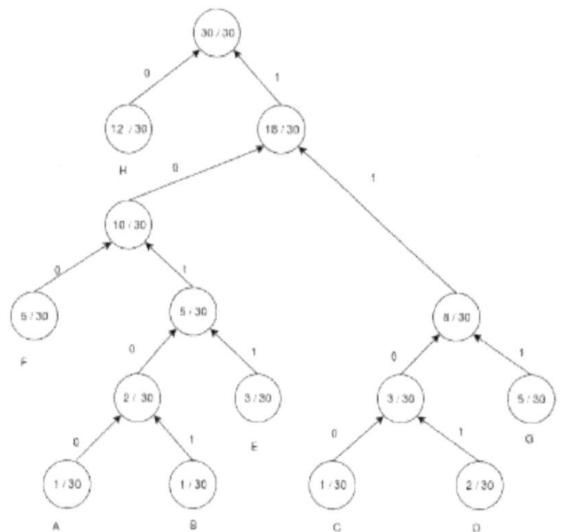

A – 10100 – 5 bits

B – 10101 – 5 bits

C – 1100 – 4 bits

D – 1101 – 4 bits

E – 1011 – 4 bits

F – 100 – 3 bits

G – 111 – 3 bits

H – 0 – 1 bit

average Huffman code size = $5 \times (1/30) + 5 \times (1/30) + 4 \times (2/30) + 4 \times (3/30) + 3 \times (5/30) + 3 \times (5/30) + 1 \times (12/30) = 76/30$.

Hence the correct option is (C).

77. Since number of allocation $=5$

which is m+n-1 (3+3-1) m, n are no. of rows and column it can not be Degenerate solution.

Also Total supply=Total demand=450

So solution is not infeasible , hence choice A, D are out.

for optimality we will check whether each $(C_{ij})'$ for non allocated cell is non negative

for this first we look for allocated cells

select the row and column with max allocation here we can take first row and assign $U_1=0$

then $V_1=16$ as $C_{11}=U_1+V_1$

Simialrly $U_2=-2$ as $C_{21}=U_2+V_1$

Simlarly $U_3=-4$ and $V_2=10$, $V_3=20$

now compute $(C_{ij})'$ for uncoccupied cell with $(C_{ij})'=C_{ij}-(U_i+V_j)$

For $C_{12}=20-(0+10) =10$, $C_{23}=18-(-2+20)=0$, $C_{31}=26-(-4+16)=14$, $C_{32}=24-(-4+10)=18$

which all are +ve and so solution is optimal and hence needs no improvement.

Hence the correct option is (B).

78. In computer programming, aliasing refers to the situation where the same memory location can be accessed using different names. For instance, if a function takes two pointers A and B which have the same value, then the name A aliases the name B.

Hence the correct option is (A).

79. a. Lambda calculus   -   Church, 1932

b. Lambda calculus as   -   Mecarthy, 1960
   programming language

c. Lazy evaluation   -   Wordsworth, 1970

d. Type classes   -   Haskel, 1990

Hence the correct option is (B).

80. ince file control block and the index block is already in memory we need not fetch them from disc.

We need to copy the new block to be added from disc (1 I/O operation). that's it.

Hence the correct option is (A).

81. Optical fiber works on the priciple of Total internal reflection

Total internal reflection is a phenomenon which occurs when a propagating wave strikes a medium boundary at an angle larger than a particular critical angle with respect to the normal to the surface.

if angle is equal or less then critical angle it will bend along or inside the surface respectively.

Hence the correct option is (C).

82. Since each two host need a cable so n(n-1)/2 cabels needed and n – 1 number of ports are required.

i.e. 10(10 – 1) / 2 = 5 $\times$ 9 = 45 cables.

9 number of ports are required for each device.

Hence the correct option is (C).

83. The throughput for pure ALOHA is $S = G \times e^{-2G}$, where G is the Load factor and take e = 2.71

The throughput is maximum , when G = 1/2 , which is S_{max} = 0.184

Transmission time of frame = 200 bits / 200 kbps = 1ms

Now, system as taken altogether produces 500 frames per sec i.e , 1/2 frame per ms which is load factor of transmission.

Now, as load factor G = 1/2 , then throughput is maximum for pure aloha.

Hence the correct option is (B).

84. The intersection of two regular languages is infinite is decidable. Whether a given context free language is regular is not decidable. Whether a given grammar is context free is decidable. Finiteness problem of regular language is decidable.

85. it is clearly mentioned that partial dependency exists which is against 2NF principle.

3 & 4 impossible coz 2nd normal form says about non-key dependency on something 1 is exact violation of 2nf so 1 may ensure the def'n of 2nf from it. b is in b/w no data about the attr. mentioned.

Hence the correct option is (A).

86. DML(Data Manipulation Language)-DML stands for data manipulation language.Examples of DDL commands:CREATE, DROP, ALTER, TRUNCATE, COMMENT, RENAME. It provides the facility of accessing data from a database.

Hence the correct option is (B).

87. "Either $-2 \leq x \leq -1$ or $1 \leq x \leq 2$".

i.e. Eiter x ≥ -2 or x ≤ -1 or $1 \leq x$ or x ≤ 2"

We have to find negation of above statement:

Negation of x ≥ -2 is x < 2. Negation of x ≤ -1 is x > -1.

Negation of 1 ≤ x is x < 1 Negation of x ≤ 2 is x > 2.

i.e. x < – 2 or 2 < x or – 1 < x < 1.

Hence the correct option is (A).

88. Let us take an example as R= {(10,1),(20,2)} and S={(2,30),(3,40)}

I) R⋈S= {(20, 2,30)}. So π A, B R⋈S = {(20,2)}

II) π B (S) ={(2),(3)}. So R⋈π B (S) = {(20,2)}

III) π A (R) X π B (S) ={10,20} X {2,3} ={(10,2),(10,3),(20,2),(20,3)}

R ∩ π A (R) X π B (S)={(20,2)}

IV) R X S = {(10,1,2,30),(10,1,3,40),(20,2,2,30),(20,2,3,40)}

π A, R.B R X S ={(10,2),(10,3),(20,2),(20,3)}

Hence the correct option is (D).

89. Does a given program ever produce an output - Undecidable

If L is CFL, Then L' is also CFL. - Undecidable

Given a CFG, G, L(G) = {empty} - Decidable

If L is a recursive language, then, is L' also recursive -Decidable.

90. p+[3-5] $\times$[xyz] = p+(3+4+5) $\times$(x+y+z)

Since, p has to be present as the first character of each string,

I. p443y -> matched

II. p6y -> not matched since 6 cannot used .

III. 3xyz -> not matched Strings must start with p.

IV. p35z -> matched

V. p353535x -> matched

VI. ppp5 -> not matched Strings must end with x, or y, or z.

Hence the correct option is (D).

91. A prototype typically simulates only a few aspects of, and may be completely different from, the final product.

Prototyping has several benefits: The software designer and implementer can get valuable feedback from the users early in the project.

here are many advantages to using prototyping in software development

Reduced time and costs: Prototyping can improve the quality of requirements and specifications provided to developers. Because changes cost exponentially more to implement as they are detected later in development, the early determination of what the user really wants can result in faster and less expensive software.

Improved and increased user involvement: Prototyping requires user involvement and allows them to see and interact with a prototype allowing them to provide better and more complete feedback and specifications. The presence of the prototype being examined by the user prevents many misunderstandings and miscommunications that occur when each side believe the other understands what they said. Since users know the better than anyone on the development team does, increased interaction can result in a final product that has greater tangible and intangible quality. The final product is more likely to satisfy the user's desire for look, feel and performance.

Hence the correct option is (B).

92. There are a number of software quality indicators that are based on the measurable design characteristics of a computer program. Design structural quality index (DSQI) is one such measure. The following values must be ascertained to compute the DSQI

S_1 = the total number of modules defined in the program architecture

S_2 = the number of modules whose correct function depends on the source of data input or that produces data to be used elsewhere {in general control modules (among others) would not be counted as part of S_2}

S_3 = the number of modules whose correct function depends on prior processing

Program structure: D_1, where D_1 is defined as follows:

If the architectural design was developed using a distinct method(e.g., data flow-oriented design or object oriented design), then D_1 = 1; otherwise D_1 = 0.

Module independence: $D_2 = 1 - (S_2/S_1)$

Module not dependent on prior processing: $D_3 = 1 - (S_3/S_1)$

Hence the correct option is (B).

93. Waterfall Model

Waterfall model does not have iteration or feedback path. Requirement Gathering, Design, Coding is there for waterfall model. But no risk analysis. Because once done ;we r not doing the iterative action. whatever Done is Done ;)

Hence the correct option is (B).

94. Accuracy: refers to the deviation of a measurement from a standard or true value of the quantity being measured.

Correctness: The degree to which a system is free from [defects] in its specification, design, and implementation.

Robustness: The degree to which a system continues to function(tolarates) in the presence of invalid inputs or stressful environmental conditions(Unexpected problems).

Reliability: The ability of a system to perform its requested functions under stated conditions whenever required - having a long mean time between failures.

Hence the correct option is (D).

95. The maximum number of cells possible (including both base cells and aggregate cells) in the data cube, C: $(p + 1)^n$.

Hence the correct option is (D).

96. FORTRAN I, II, and IV contain only static variables

All objects in Java are explicit heap-dynamic variables and are destroyed by 'garbage collection'

Languages such as APL, ALGOL 68, and LISP use implicit heap-dynamic variables.

Hence the correct option is (C).

97. Given:

The vertex set of G is {(i, j): 1 <= i <= 12, 1 <= j <= 12}.

There is an edge between (a, b) and (c, d) if |a − c| <= 1 and |b − d| <= 1.

There can be total 12 ✕12 possible vertices. The vertices are (1, 1), (1, 2) ....(1, 12) (2, 1), (2, 2), ...

The number of edges in this graph?

Number of edges is equal to number of pairs of vertices that satisfy

above conditions. For example, vertex pair {(1, 1), (1, 2)} satisfy above condition.

For (1, 1), there can be an edge to (1, 2), (2, 1), (2, 2). Note that there can be self-loop as mentioned in the question.

Same is count for (12, 12), (1, 12) and (12, 1)

For (1, 2), there can be an edge to (1, 1), (2, 1), (2, 2), (2, 3) (1, 3)

Same is count for (1, 3), (1, 4)....(1, 11), (12, 2), ...(12, 11)

For (2, 2), there can be an edge to (1, 1), (1, 2), (1, 3), (2, 1), (2, 3), (3, 1), (3, 2), (3, 3)

Same is count for remaining vertices.

For all pairs (i, j) there can total 8 vertices connected to them if i and j are not in {1, 12}

There are total 100 vertices without a 1 or 12. So total 800 edges.

For vertices with 1, total edges = (Edges where 1 is first part) +(Edges where 1 is second part and not first part) = (3 + 5 $\times$ 10 + 3) + (5 $\times$ 10) edges Same is count for vertices with 12.

Total number of edges:

= 800 + [(3 + 5 $\times$ 10 + 3) + 5 $\times$ 10] + [(3 + 5 $\times$ 10 + 3) + 5 $\times$ 10]

= 800 + 106 + 106

= 1012

Since graph is undirected, two edges from v_1 to v_2 and v_2 to v_1 should be counted as one.

So total number of undirected edges = 1012/2 = 506.

Hence the correct option is (C).

98. here Xm denotes variable X of calling function

and Ym denotes variable Y of calling function

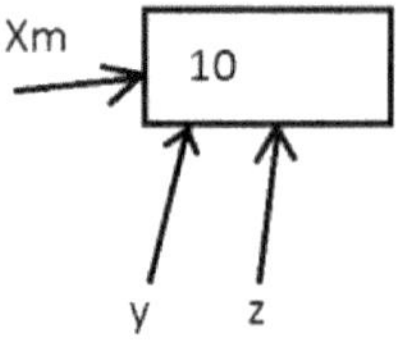

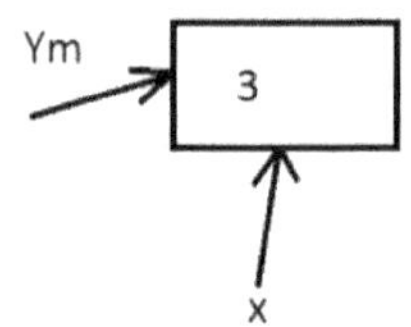

$$y = y + 4$$
$$y = 14$$
Now $Xm = 14$
$$z = x + y + z$$
$$z = 3 + 14 + 14$$
$$b/cx \rightarrow Ym$$
$$y \rightarrow Xm$$
$$z \rightarrow Xm$$
now $Xm = 31$
and $Ym = 3$

Hence the correct option is (B).

99. An OODBMS avoids the "impedance mismatch" problem. This is true - this is one of the stated goals of an OODBMS. An OODBMS avoids the "phantom" problem. False. Object databases have nothing to do with the phantom problem.
An OODBMS provides higher performance concurrency control than most relational databases. This is false. There's no reason to believe that the locking done in an OODBMS like ObjectStore is any more efficient than the locking done in a traditional RDBMS - in fact, it 's likely to be higher overhead because it is distributed and requires features like lock callback.
An OODBMS provides faster access to individual data objects once they have been read from
disk.
True Once an object has been read from disk in an OODBMS, the program can manipulate it as though it was a standard memory resident object.

Hence the correct option is (B).

100. V (G) = P + 1

Where P = Number of predicate nodes (node which has degree more than 1 i.e. conditional statemene)

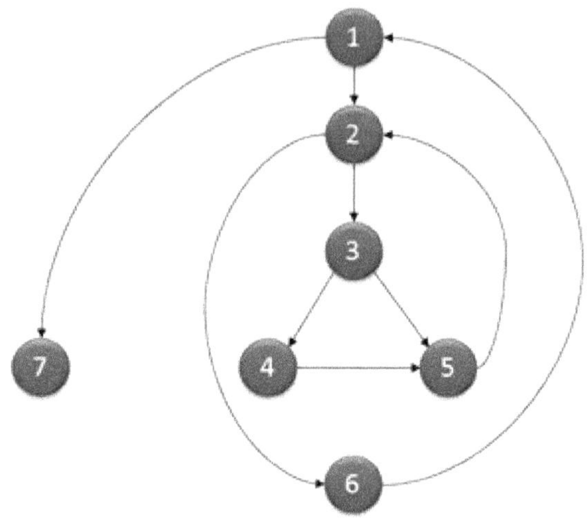

Hence the correct option is (A).

Q.1 How many solutions are there for the equation $x + y + z + u = 29$ subject to the constraints that $x \geq 1$, $y \geq 2$, $z \geq 3$ and $u \geq 0$?

A. 4,960 **B.** 2,600 **C.** 23,751 **D.** 8,855

Q.2 Consider the compound propositions as given below:
(a) $p \vee \sim(p \wedge q)$
(b) $(p \wedge \sim q) \vee \sim(p \wedge q)$
(c) $p \wedge (q \vee r)$
Which of the above propositions are tautologies?

A. (a) and (c) **B.** (b) and (c)
C. (a) and (b) **D.** only (a)

Q.3 Whichof the following refers to computing technologies in which the hardware and software components are distributed across a network?

A. Client and Server
B. User and System
C. User and File Server
D. User and Database Server

Q.4 The travelling salesman problem can be solved in

A. polynomial time using dynamic programming algorithm
B. polynomial time using branch-and-bound algorithm
C. exponential time using dynamic programming algorithm or branch-and-bound algorithm
D. polynomial time using backtracking algorithm

Q.5 Which of the following is asymptotically smaller?

A. $\lg(\lg^*n)$ **B.** $\lg^*(\lg n)$ **C.** $\lg(n!)$ **D.** $\lg^*(n!)$

Q.6 Method over-riding can be prevented by using final as a modifier at

A. the start of the class
B. the start of method declaration
C. the start of derived class
D. the start of the method declaration in the derived class

Q.7 Which of the following is not a correct statement?

A. Every class containing abstract method must be declared abstract.
B. Abstract class can directly be initiated with 'new' operator.
C. Abstract class can be initiated.
D. Abstract class does not contain any definition of implementation.

Q.8 Constructors have _____ return type.

A. void **B.** char **C.** int **D.** no

Q.9 An experimental file server is up for 75% of the time and down for 25% of the time due to bugs. How many times does this file server have to be replicated to give an availability of at least 99%?

A. 2 **B.** 4 **C.** 8 **D.** 16

Q.10 Consider the following statements:
(a) If primal (dual) problem has a finite optimal solution, then its dual (primal) problem has a finite optimal solution.
(b) If primal (dual) problem has an unbounded optimum solution, then its dual (primal) has no feasible solution at all.
(c) Both primal and dual problems may be infeasible.
Which of the statements are correct?

A. (a) and (b) only **B.** (a) and (c) only
C. (b) and (c) only **D.** (a), (b) and (c)

Q.11 In _____ method, the word is written to the block in both the cache and main memory, in parallel.

A. write through **B.** write back
C. write protected **D.** direct mapping

Q.12 In _______ allocation method for disk block allocation in a file system, insertion and deletion of blocks in a file is easy.

A. index **B.** linked
C. contiguous **D.** bit map

Q.13 A Unix file may be of the

A. regular file type
B. directory file type
C. device file type
D. Any one of the above

Q.14 The plain text message BAHI encrypted with RSA algorithm using $e = 3$, $d = 7$ and $n = 33$ and the characters of the message are encoded using the values 00 to 25 for letters A to Z. Suppose character by character encryption was implemented. Then, the cipher text message is

A. ABHI **B.** HAQC **C.** IHBA **D.** BHQC

Q.15 Consider the following statement.
(1) Path vector protocol is implemented using Border Gateway Protocol (BGP).
(2) Link state routing algorithm is implemented using Open shortest path first. (OSPF).
(3) Path vector protocol is same as Distance vector protocol.
(4) Routing algorithm is used to build the routing table at router.
Which of the following is false?

A. 1 and 2 only **B.** 2 and 3 only
C. 1 and 3 only **D.** 3 only

Q.16 How many bytes of data can be sent in 15 seconds over a serial link with baud rate of 9,600 in asynchronous mode with odd parity and two stop bits in the frame?

A. 10,000 bytes **B.** 12,000 bytes
C. 15,000 bytes **D.** 27,000 bytes

Q.17 The number of bits used for addressing in Gigabit Ethernet is

A. 32 **B.** 48 **C.** 64 **D.** 128

Q.18 Match the following:

(a) Line coding	(i) A technique to change analog signal to digital data
(b) Block coding	(ii) Provides synchronisation without increasing the number of bits
(c) Scrambling	(iii) A process of converting digital data to digital signal
(d) Pulse code modulation	(iv) Provides redundancy to ensure synchronisation and inherits error detection

A. (a) - (iv), (b) - (iii), (c) - (ii), (d) - (i)
B. (a) - (iii), (b) - (iv), (c) - (ii), (d) - (i)
C. (a) - (i), (b) - (iii), (c) - (ii), (d) - (iv)
D. (a) - (ii), (b) - (i), (c) - (iv), (d) - (iii)

Q.19 A message 'COMPUTERNETWORK' is encrypted (ignore quotes) using columnar transposition cipher with a key 'LAYER'. The encrypted message is:

A. CTTOEWMROPNRUEK
B. MROUEKCTTPNROEW
C. OEWPNRCTTUEKMRO
D. UEKPNRMROOEWCTT

Q.20 The global conceptual schema in a distributed database contains information about global relations. The condition that all the data of the global relation must be mapped into the fragments, i.e. it must not happen that a data item which belongs to a global relation does not belong to any fragment, is called

A. disjointness condition
B. completeness condition
C. reconstruction condition
D. aggregation condition

Q.21 Suppose database table T_1(P, R) currently has tuples {(10, 5), (15, 8), (25, 6)} and table T_2(A, C) currently has {(10, 6), (25, 3), (10, 5)}. Consider the following three relational algebra queries RA_1, RA_2 and RA_3:

$RA_1 : T_1 \bowtie T_1 \cdot P = T_2 \cdot A T_2$ where $\bowtie$ is natural join symbol

$RA_2 : T_1 \bowtie T_1 P = T_2 \cdot A T_2$ where $\bowtie$ is left outer join symbol

$RA_3 : T_1 \bowtie T_1 \cdot P = T_2 \cdot A$ and $T_1 \cdot R = T_2 \cdot C T_2$

The number of tuples in the resulting table of RA_1, RA_2 and RA_3 are given by:

A. 2, 4, 2   **B.** 2, 3, 2   **C.** 3, 3, 1   **D.** 3, 4, 1

Q.22 Consider the table R with attributes A, B and C. The functional dependencies that hold on R are : $A \rightarrow B, C \rightarrow AB$. Which of the following statements is/are true?

I. The decomposition of R into R_1(C, A) and R_2(A, B) is lossless.
II. The decomposition of R into R_1(A, B) and R_2(B, C) is lossy.

A. Only I
B. Only II
C. Both I and II
D. Neither I nor II

Q.23 Let A and B be sets in a finite universal set U. Given the following: $|A - B| |A \oplus B| |A| + |B|$ and $|A \cup B|$. Which of the following is in order of increasing size?

A. $|A - B| < |A \oplus B| < |A| + |B| < |A \cup B|$
B. $|A \oplus B| < |A - B| < |A \cup B| < |A| + |B|$
C. $|A \oplus B| < |A| + |B| < |A - B| < |A \cup B|$
D. $|A - B| < |A \oplus B| < |A \cup B| < |A| + |B|$

Q.24 Convert the octal number 0.4051 into its equivalent decimal number.

A. 0.5100098   **B.** 0.2096
C. 0.52   **D.** 0.4192

Q.25 Consider the recurrence relation:

$$T(n) = 8T\left(\frac{n}{2}\right) + Cn, \text{ if } n > 1$$
$$= b, \text{ if } n = 1$$

(Where b and c are constants)
The order of the algorithm corresponding to above recurrence relation is

A. n   **B.** n^2 **C.** n log n   **D.** n^3

Q.26 The Karnaugh map for a Boolean function is given as:

CD AB	C'D'	C'D	CD	CD'
A'B'	0	0	0	0
A'B	0	0	1	0
AB	1	1	1	1
AB'	0	1	1	1

The simplified Boolean equation for the above Karnaugh Map is

A. AB + CD + A`B + AD
B. AB + AC + AD + BCD
C. AB + AD + BC + ACD
D. AB + AC + BC + BCD

Q.27 In a resident-OS computer, which of the following systems must reside in the main memory under all situations?

A. Assembler   **B.** Linker
C. Loader   **D.** Compiler

Q.28 The regular expression corresponding to the language L, where L = {x ϵ {0, 1}*|x ends with 1 and does not contain substring 00}, is:

A. (1 + 01) * (10 + 01)   **B.** (1 + 01) * 01
C. (1 + 01) * (1 + 01)   **D.** (10 + 01) * 01

Q.29 Match the description of several parts of a classic optimising compiler in List - I with the names of those parts in List - II:

List - I	List - II
(a) A part of a compiler that is responsible for	(i)

recognising syntax	Optimizer
(b) A part of a compiler that takes as input a stream of characters and produces as output a stream of words along with their associated syntactic categories	(ii) Semantic analysis
(c) A part of a compiler that understands the meanings of variable names and other symbols and checks that they are used in way consistent with their definitions	(iii) Parser
(d) An IR-to-IR transformer that tries to improve the IR program in some way (Intermediate Representation)	(iv) Scanner

A. (a) - (iii), (b) - (iv), (c) - (ii), (d) - (i)
B. (a) - (iv), (b) - (iii), (c) - (ii), (d) - (i)
C. (a) - (ii), (b) - (iv), (c) - (i), (d) - (iii)
D. (a) - (ii), (b) - (iv), (c) - (iii), (d) - (i)

Q.30 Which of the following logic operations is performed by the following combinational circuit?

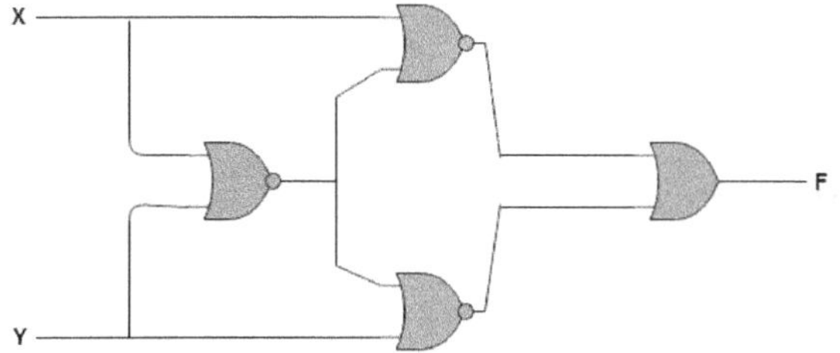

A. EXCLUSIVE-OR
B. EXCLUSIVE-NOR
C. NAND
D. NOR

Q.31 Which of the following in 8085 microprocessor performs HL = HL + HL?

A. DAD D   **B.** DAD H   **C.** DAD B   **D.** DAD SP

Q.32 Consider the following two statements:
(A) Business intelligence and data warehousing is used for forecasting and data mining.
(B) Business intelligence and data warehousing is used for analysis of large volumes of sales data.
Which of the following options is correct?

A. (A) is true, (B) is false.
B. Both (A) and (B) are true.
C. (A) is false, (B) is true.
D. Both (A) and (B) are false.

Q.33 Which of the following is a sequential circuit?
A. Multiplexer   **B.** Decoder
C. Counter   **D.** Full adder

Q.34 Which of the following in 8085 microprocessor performs HL = HL + DE?

A. DAD D   **B.** DAD H   **C.** DAD B   **D.** DAD SP

Q.35 Let f(n), g(n) and h(n) be functions defined for positive integers such that
f(n) = O(g(n)), g(n) ≠ O(f(n)), g(n) = O(h(n)) and h(n) = O(g(n))
Which of the following statements is false?

A. f(n) + g(n) = O(h(n) + h(n))
B. f(n) = O(h(n))
C. h(n) ≠ O(f(n))

D. f(n)h(n) ≠ O(g(n)h(n))

Q.36 Consider the following identities for regular expressions:
(a) (r + s)* = (s + r)*
(b) (r*)* = r*
(c) (r* s*)* = (r + s)*
Which of the above identities are true?

A. (a) and (b)   **B.** (b) and (c)
C. (c) and (a)   **D.** (a), (b) and (c)

Q.37 _________ system is market oriented and is used for data analysis by knowledge workers including managers, executives and analysts.

A. OLTP   **B.** OLAP
C. Data system   **D.** Market system

Q.38 Which of the following is not a lossy compression technique?

A. JPEG   **B.** MPEG
C. FFT   **D.** Arithmetic coding

Q.39 Forward chaining systems are _________ whereas backward chaining systems are _________.

A. data driven, data driven
B. goal driven, data driven
C. data driven, goal driven
D. goal driven, goal driven

Q.40 Consider the following graphs:

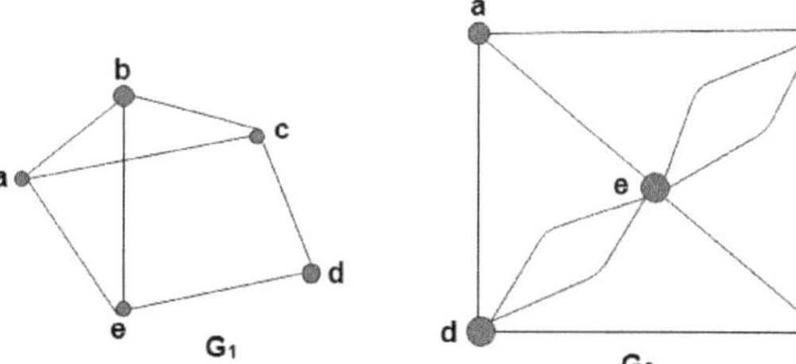

Which of the following is correct?

A. G₁ contains Euler circuit and G₂ does not contain Euler circuit.
B. G₁ does not contain Euler circuit and G₂ contains Euler circuit.
C. Both G₁ and G₂ do not contain Euler circuit.
D. Both G₁ and G₂ contain Euler circuit.

Q.41 Given the following prefix expression:

$$* + 3 + 3 \uparrow 3 + 3\,3\,3$$

What is the value of the prefix expression?

A. 2178   **B.** 2199   **C.** 2205   **D.** 2232

Q.42 Consider the following statements:
S_1: A queue can be implemented using two stacks.
S_2: A stack can be implemented using two queues.
Which of the following is correct?

A. S_1 is correct and S_2 is not correct.
B. S_1 is not correct and S_2 is correct.
C. Both S_1 and S_2 are correct.
D. Both S_1 and S_2 are incorrect.

Q.43 Which of the following is a correct statement?

A. Composition is a strong type of association between two classes with full ownership.

B. Composition is a strong type of association between two classes with partial ownership.

C. Composition is a weak type of association between two classes with partial ownership.

D. Composition is a weak type of association between two classes with strong ownership.

Q.44 Match each software term in List - I to its description in List - II:

List - I	List - II
I. Wizards	a. Forms that provide structure for a document
II. Templates	b. A series of commands grouped into a single command
III. Macro	c. A single program that incorporates most commonly used tools
IV. Integrated software	d. Step-by-step guides in application software
V. Software suite	e. A bundled group of software programs

A. I - d, II - a, III - b, IV - c, V - e
B. I - b, II - a, III - d, IV - c, V - e
C. I - d, II - e, III - b, IV - a, V - c
D. I - e, II - c, III - b, IV - a, V - d

Q.45 Consider the following justifications for commonly using the two-level CPU scheduling:
I. It is used when memory is too small to hold all the ready processes.
II. It is used because its performance is same as that of the FIFO.
III. It is used because it facilitates putting some set of processes into memory and a choice is made from that.
IV. It is used because it does not allow to adjust the set of in-core processes.
Which of the following is true?

A. I, III and IV
B. I and II
C. III and IV
D. I and III

Q.46 Which of the following statement(s) is/are true regarding 'nice' command of UNIX?
I. It is used to set or change the priority of a process.
II. A process' nice value can be set at the time of creation.
III. 'nice' takes a command line as an argument.

A. I, II **B.** II, III **C.** I, II, III **D.** I, III

Q.47 If the disk head is located initially at track 32, find the number of disk moves required with FCFS scheduling criteria if the disk queue of I/O blocks requests are:
98, 37, 14, 124, 65, 67

A. 320 **B.** 322 **C.** 321 **D.** 319

Q.48 Consider a discrete memoryless channel and assume that H(x) is the amount of information per symbol at the input of the channel; H(y) is the amount of information per symbol at the output of the channel; H(x|y) is the amount of uncertainty remaining on x knowing y; and I (x; y) is the information

transmission.
Which of the following does not define the channel capacity of a discrete memoryless channel?

A. max I (x; y) p(x)
B. max [H(y) - H(y|x)] p(x)
C. max [H(x) - H(x|y)] p(x)
D. max H(x|y) p(x)

Q.49 Consider the following page reference string:
1, 2, 3, 4, 2, 1, 5, 6, 2, 1, 2, 3, 7, 6, 3, 2, 1, 2, 3, 6
Which of the following options gives the correct number of page faults related to LRU, FIFO and optimal page replacement algorithms, respectively, assuming 05 page frames and all frames are initially empty?

A. 10, 14, 8 **B.** 8, 10, 7 **C.** 7, 10, 8 **D.** 7, 10, 7

Q.50 Which of the following correctly describes WOW32?
A. Win 32 API library for creating processes and threads
B. Special kind of file system to the NT name space
C. Kernel-mode objects accessible through Win 32 AP
D. Special execution environment used to run 16-bit windows applications on 32-bit machines

Q.51 Consider the following statements:
(a) Assignment problem can be used to minimise the cost.
(b) Assignment problem is a special case of transportation problem.
(c) Assignment problem requires that only one activity be assigned to each resource.
Which of the following options is correct?

A. (a) and (b) **B.** (a) and (c)
C. (b) and (c) **D.** (a), (b) and (c)

Q.52 With respect to a loop in the transportation table, which of the following is incorrect?

A. Every loop has an odd number of cells and at least five cells.
B. Closed loops may or may not be square in shape.
C. All the cells in the loop that have a plus or minus sign, except the starting cell, must be occupied cells.
D. Every loop has an even number of cells and at least four cells.

Q.53 Assume that we need to download text documents at the rate of 100 pages per minute. A page is an average of 24 lines with 80 characters in each line and each character requires 8 bits. The required bit rate of the channel is ____.

A. 1.636 Kbps **B.** 1.636 Mbps
C. 3.272 Mbps **D.** 25.6 Kbps

Q.54 Which of the following layers of OSI reference model is also called end-to-end layer?

A. Network layer **B.** Data layer
C. Session layer **D.** Transport layer

Q.55 ________ do not take their decisions on measurements or estimates of the current traffic and topology.

A. Static algorithms
B. Adaptive algorithms
C. Non-adaptive algorithms

D. Recursive algorithms

Q.56 Consider the following ORACLE relations:

One (x, y) = {<2, 5>, <1, 6>, <1, 6>, <1, 6>, <4, 8>, <4, 8>}

Two (x, y) = {<2, 55>, <1, 1>, <4, 4>, <1, 6>, <4, 8>, <4, 8>, <9, 9>, <1, 6>}

Consider the following two SQL queries SQ1 and SQ2 :

SQ_1: (SELECT * FROM One)

    EXCEPT

    (SELECT * FROM Two);

SQ_2: (SELECT * FROM One)

    EXCEPT ALL

    (SELECT * FROM Two);

For each of the SQL queries, what is the cardinality (number of rows) of the result obtained when applied to the instances above?

A. 2 and 1, respectively

B. 1 and 2, respectively

C. 2 and 2, respectively

D. 1 and 1, respectively

Q.57 Which of the following pairs is correctly matched in the context of database design?

List - I (Database term)	List - II (Definition)
I. Specialization	A. Result of taking the union of two or more disjoint (lower-level) entity sets to produce a higher-level entity set
II. Generalization	B. Express the number of entities to which another entity can be associated via a relationship set
III. Aggregation	C. Result of taking a subset of a higher-level entity set to form a lower-level entity set
IV. Mapping cardinalities	D. An abstraction in which relationship sets (along with their associated entity sets) are treated as higher-level entity sets, and can participate in relationships

A. I - D, II - A, III - B, IV - C

B. I - D, II - C, III - B, IV - A

C. I - C, II - D, III - A, IV - B

D. I - C, II - A, III - D, IV - B

Q.58 A frame buffer array is addressed in row major order for a monitor with pixel locations starting from (0,0) and ending with (100,100). What is address of the pixel (6,10)? Assume one bit storage per pixel and starting pixel location at 0.

A. 1016   **B.** 1006   **C.** 610   **D.** 616

Q.59 In propositional logic, if $(P \rightarrow Q) \wedge (R \rightarrow S)$ and $(P \vee R)$ are two premises such that Y is the premise:

$$(P \rightarrow Q) \wedge (R \rightarrow S)$$
$$P \vee R$$
$$Y$$

A. $P \vee R$ **B.** $P \vee S$ **C.** $Q \vee R$ **D.** $Q \vee S$

Q.60 The hexadecimal equivalent of the octal number 2357 is:

A. 2EE   **B.** 2FF   **C.** 4EF   **D.** 4FE

Q.61 Consider the method mcq ( ):

```
int mcq (boolean a, boolean b, boolean c, boolean d) {
int ans = 1;
if (a) {
ans = 2;
} else if (b) {
ans = 3;
} else if (c) {
if (d) {
ans = 4;
}
}
return ans;
}
If
```

M_1 = Number of tests to exhaustively test mcq ( );

M_2 = Minimum number of tests to achieve full statement coverage for mcq ( ); and

M_3 = Minimum number of tests to achieve full branch coverage for mcq ( );

Then (M_1, M_2, M_3) = _________

A. (16, 3, 5)   **B.** (8, 5, 3)   **C.** (8, 3, 5)   **D.** (16, 4, 4)

Q.62 Consider the following assembly language instructions:

```
mov al, 15
mov ah, 15
xor al, al
mov cl, 3
shr ax, cl
add al, 90H
adc ah, 0
```

What is the value in ax register after execution of above instructions?

A. 0270H   **B.** 0170H   **C.** 01E0H   **D.** 0370H

Q.63 Relocation is externally defined symbols is preferred by

A. linker   **B.** loader

C. compiler   **D.** assembler

Q.64 The transition function for the language L = {w|n_a (w) and n_b(w) are both odd} is given by:

$\delta (q_0, a) = q_1$; $\delta (q_0, b) = q_2$

$\delta (q_1, a) = q_0$; $\delta (q_1, b) = q_3$

$\delta (q_2, a) = q_3$; $\delta (q_2, b) = q_0$

$\delta (q_3, a) = q_2$; $\delta (q_3, b) = q_1$

The initial and final states of the automata are

A. q_0 and q_0, respectively

B. q_0 and q_1, respectively

C. q_0 and q_2, respectively

D. q_0 and q_3, respectively

Q.65 The language L = {$a^i b\ c^i$ | i >= 0} over the alphabet {a, b, c} is

A. a regular language

B. not a deterministic context free language but a context free language

C. recursive and a deterministic context free language

D. not recursive

Q.66 Match the following:

List - I	List - II
a. Controlled inverter	i. A circuit that can add 3 bits
b. Full adder	ii. A circuit that can add 2 binary numbers
c. Half adder	iii. A circuit that transmits a binary word or its 1's complement
d. Binary adder	iv. A logic circuit that adds 2 bits

A. a - iii, b - ii, c - iv, d - i
B. a - ii, b - iv, c - i, d - iii
C. a - iii, b - iv, c - i, d - ii
D. a - iii, b - i, c - iv, d - ii

Q.67 Match each software lifecycle model in List - I to its description in List - II:

List - I	List - II
I. Code-and-Fix	a. Assess risks at each step; do most critical action first
II. Evolutionary prototyping	b. Build an initial small requirement specifications, code it, then evolve the specifications and code as needed
III. Spiral	c. Build initial requirement specification for several releases, then design-and-code in sequence
IV. Staged delivery	d. Standard phases (requirements, design, code, test) in order
V. Waterfall	e. Write some code, debug it, repeat (i.e. ad-hoc)

A. I - e, II - b, III - a, IV - c, V - d
B. I - e, II - c, III - a, IV - b, V - d
C. I - d, II - a, III - b, IV - c, V - e
D. I - c, II - e, III - a, IV - b, V - d

Q.68 A server crashes on the average once in 30 days, i.e. the Mean Time Between Failures (MTBF) is 30 days. When this happens, it takes 12 hours to reboot it, i.e. the Mean Time to Repair (MTTR) is 12 hours. The availability of server with these reliability data values is approximately

A. 96.3%   **B.** 97.3%   **C.** 98.3%   **D.** 99.3%

Q.69 Which of the following 8085 microprocessor hardware interrupt has the lowest priority?

A. RST 6.5   **B.** RST 7.5   **C.** TRAP   **D.** INTR

Q.70 Software safety is quality assurance activity that focuses on hazards that

A. affect the reliability of a software component
B. may cause an entire system to fail
C. may result from user input errors
D. prevent profitable marketing of the final product

Q.71 Consider a disk with 16384 bytes per track having a rotation time of 16 msec and average seek time of 40 msec. What is the time (in msec) to read a block of 1024 bytes from this disk?

A. 57 sec   **B.** 49 sec   **C.** 48 sec   **D.** 17 sec

Q.72 If the histogram of an image is clustered towards origin on X-axis of a histogram plot, then it indicates that the image is ______.

A. dark   **B.** good contrast
C. bright   **D.** very low contrast

Q.73 ________ allows selection of the relevant information necessary for the data warehouse.

A. Top-down view
B. Data warehouse view
C. Data source view
D. Business query view

Q.74 Java uses threads to enable the entire environment to be ______.

A. symmetric   **B.** asymmetric
C. synchronous   **D.** asynchronous

Q.75 OSPF protocol is practical implementation of ___ protocol and uses ___ .

A. LSR and Bellman ford algorithm
B. LSR and Dijkstra's algorithm
C. DVR and Floyd Warshall algorithm
D. None of the above

Q.76 Consider a hash table of size m = 10000, and the hash function h(K) = floor (m(KA mod 1)) for $A = \left(\sqrt{(5)} - 1 \right) / 2$. The key 123456 is mapped to location ______.

A. 46   **B.** 41   **C.** 43   **D.** 48

Q.77 Which of the following statements is correct when a class grants friend status to another class?

A. The member functions of the class generating friendship can access the members of the friend class.
B. All member functions of the class granted friendship have unrestricted access to the members of the class granting the friendship.
C. Class friendship is reciprocal to each other.
D. There is no such concept.

Q.78 What does the following statement in 'C' declare?
int (*f) (**int** *) ;

A. A function that takes an integer pointer as argument and returns an integer.
B. A function that takes an integer as argument and returns an integer pointer.
C. A pointer to a function that takes an integer pointer as argument and returns an integer.
D. A function that takes an integer pointer as argument and returns a function pointer

Q.79 Given i = 0, j = 1, k = -1
x = 0.5, y = 0.0
What is the output of the following expression in C language?
x * y < i + j || k

A. -1   **B.** 0   **C.** 1   **D.** 2

Q.80 A multi-computer with 256 CPUs is organised as 16 ✕ 16 grid. What is the worst case delay (in hops) that a message might have to take?

A. 16   **B.** 15   **C.** 32   **D.** 30

D. $x_1 = 2, x_2 = 0, x_2 = 2$ and $Z = 10$

Q.81 Suppose that the time to do a null remote procedure call (RPC) (i.e. 0 data bytes) is 1.0 msec, with an additional 1.5 msec for every 1K of data. How long does it take to read 32K from the file server as 32 1K RPCs?

A. 49 msec   **B.** 80 msec
C. 48 msec   **D.** 100 msec

Q.82 Which module gives control of the CPU to the process selected by the short-term scheduler?

A. Dispatcher   **B.** Interrupt
C. Scheduler   **D.** Threading

Q.83 Suppose we want to download text documents at the rate of 100 pages per second. Assume that a page consists of an average of 24 lines with 80 characters in each line. What is the required bit rate of the channel?

A. 192 Kbps   **B.** 512 Kbps
C. 1.248 Mbps   **D.** 1.536 Mbps

Q.84 In a relational database model, NULL values cannot be used

A. to allow duplicate tuples in the table by filling the primary key column(s) with NULL

B. to avoid confusion with actual legitimate data values like 0 (zero) for integer columns and '' (the empty string) for string columns

C. to leave columns in a tuple marked as "unknown" when the actual value is unknown

D. to fill a column in a tuple when that column does not really 'exist' for that particular tuple

Q.85 Pipelining improves performance by

A. decreasing instruction latency
B. eliminating data hazards
C. exploiting instruction level parallelism
D. decreasing the cache miss rate

Q.86 ECL is the fastest of all logic families. High speed in ECL is possible because transistors are used in difference amplifier configuration, in which they are never driven into ____.

A. race condition   **B.** saturation
C. delay   **D.** high impedance

Q.87 Let $m = (313)_4$ and $n = (322)_4$. Find the base 4 expansion of $m + n$.

A. $(635)_4$ **B.** $(32312)_4$ **C.** $(21323)_4$ **D.** $(1301)_4$

Q.88 Consider the following LPP:
Min $Z = 2x_1 + x_2 + 3x_3$
Subject to:
$x_1 - 2x_2 + x_3 \geq 4$
$2x_1 + x_2 + x_3 \leq 8$
$x_1 - x_3 \geq 0$
$x_1, x_2, x_3 \geq 0$
The solution of this LPP using Dual Simplex Method is:

A. $x_1 = 0, x_2 = 0, x_3 = 3$ and $Z = 9$
B. $x_1 = 0, x_2 = 6, x_2 = 0$ and $Z = 6$
C. $x_1 = 4, x_2 = 0, x_2 = 0$ and $Z = 8$

Q.89 The contents of Register (B) and Accumulator (A) of 8085 microprocessor are 49H and 3AH respectively. The contents of A and the status of carry flag (CY) and sign flag (S) after executing SUB B instructions are

A. A = 0FH; CY = 1; S = 1
B. A = F0H; CY = 0; S = 0
C. A = F1H; CY = 1; S = 1
D. A = 1FH; CY = 1; S = 1

Q.90 The family of context sensitive languages is ________ under union and ________ under reversal.

A. closed, not closed
B. not closed, not closed
C. closed, closed
D. not closed, closed

Q.91 Which of the following logic expressions is incorrect?

A. $1 \oplus 0 = 1$ **B.** $1 \oplus 1 \oplus 1 = 1$
C. $1 \oplus 1 \oplus 0 = 1$ **D.** $1 \oplus 1 = 0$

Q.92 Match the software maintenance activities in List - I to its meaning in List - II.

List - I	List - II
I. Corrective	(a) Concerned with performing activities to reduce the software complexity thereby improving program understandability and increasing software maintainability
II. Adaptive	(b) Concerned with fixing errors that are observed when the software is in use
III. Perfective	(c) Concerned with the change in the software that takes place to make the software adaptable to new environment (both hardware and software)
IV. Preventive	(d) Concerned with the change in the software that take place to make the software adaptable to changing user requirements

A. I - (b), II - (d), III - (c), IV - (a)
B. I - (b), II - (c), III - (d), IV - (a)
C. I - (c), II - (b), III - (d), IV - (a)
D. I - (a), II - (d), III - (b), IV - (c)

Q.93 Match each application/software design concept in List - I to its definition in List - II.

List - I	List - II
I. Coupling	(a) Easy to visually inspect the design of the software and understand its purpose
II. Cohesion	(b) Easy to add functionality to a software without having to redesign it
III. Scalable	(c) Focus of a code upon a single goal
IV. Readable	(d) Reliance of a code module upon other code modules

A. I - (b), II - (a), III - (d), IV - (c)
B. I - (c), II - (d), III - (a), IV - (b)
C. I - (d), II - (c), III - (b), IV - (a)

D. I - (d), II - (a), III - (c), IV - (b)

Q.94 Which of the following sets represents five stages defined by Capability Maturity Model (CMM) in increasing the order of maturity?

A. Initial, Defined, Repeatable, Managed, Optimized
B. Initial, Repeatable, Defined, Managed, Optimized
C. Initial, Defined, Managed, Repeatable, Optimized
D. Initial, Repeatable, Managed, Defined, Optimized

Q.95 Quadrature Amplitude Modulation means changing both

A. frequency and phase of the carrier
B. frequency and amplitude of the carrier
C. amplitude and phase of the carrier
D. amplitude and wavelength of the carrier

Q.96 Which of the following statements is not correct?

A. HTML is not screen precise formatting language.
B. HTML does not specify a logic.
C. DHTML is used for developing highly interactive web pages.
D. HTML is a programming language.

Q.97 If there are n integers to sort, each integer has d digits, and each digit is in the set {1, 2, ..., k}, radix sort can sort the numbers in:

A. $O(d\ n\ k)$
B. $O(d\ n^k)$
C. $O(d+n)k)$
D. $O(d(n+k))$

Q.98 Match the following:

a. Prim's algorithm	i. $O(V^2E)$
b. Bellman-Ford algorithm	ii. $O(VE\ lg\ V)$
c. Floyd-Warshall algorithm	iii. $O(E\ lg\ V)$
d. Johnson's algorithm	iv. $O(V^3)$

(Where V is the set of nodes and E is the set of edges in the graph)

A. a - i, b - iii, c - iv, d - ii
B. a - i, b - iii, c - ii, d - iv
C. a - iii, b - i, c - iv, d - ii
D. a - iii, b - i, c - ii, d - iv

Q.99 Which of the following conditions does not hold good for a solution to a critical section problem?

A. No assumptions may be made about speed or the number of CPUs
B. No two processes may be simultaneously inside their critical sections
C. Processes running outside its critical section may block other processes
D. Processes do not wait forever to enter its critical section

Q.100 Which of the following is not a basic primitive of the Graphics Kernel System (GKS)?

A. POLYLINE
B. POLYDRAW
C. FILL AREA
D. POLYMARKER

// Smart Answer Sheet //

Correct Percentage of students who answered correctly.　　**Skipped** Percentage of students who skipped.

Q.	Ans.	Correct / Skipped	Q.	Ans.	Correct / Skipped	Q.	Ans.	Correct / Skipped	Q.	Ans.	Correct / Skipped	Q.	Ans.	Correct / Skipped
1	B	30.86 % / 13.58 %	17	B	29.63 % / 37.04 %	33	C	39.51 % / 41.97 %	49	B	43.21 % / 40.74 %	65	C	28.4 % / 34.56 %
2	D	28.4 % / 37.03 %	18	B	30.86 % / 40.74 %	34	A	32.1 % / 41.97 %	50	D	27.16 % / 41.98 %	66	D	37.04 % / 41.97 %
3	A	40.74 % / 32.1 %	19	C	38.27 % / 41.98 %	35	D	33.33 % / 41.98 %	51	D	37.04 % / 41.97 %	67	A	28.4 % / 37.03 %
4	C	33.33 % / 38.27 %	20	B	32.1 % / 43.21 %	36	D	33.33 % / 35.81 %	52	A	25.93 % / 41.97 %	68	C	34.57 % / 38.27 %
5	A	43.21 % / 35.8 %	21	D	18.52 % / 35.8 %	37	B	51.85 % / 41.98 %	53	D	27.16 % / 38.27 %	69	D	37.04 % / 44.44 %
6	B	33.33 % / 37.04 %	22	C	33.33 % / 41.98 %	38	D	35.8 % / 41.98 %	54	D	44.44 % / 40.75 %	70	B	37.04 % / 44.44 %
7	B	32.1 % / 39.5 %	23	D	23.46 % / 39.5 %	39	C	37.04 % / 40.74 %	55	C	35.8 % / 41.98 %	71	B	24.69 % / 45.68 %
8	D	43.21 % / 39.51 %	24	A	32.1 % / 41.97 %	40	C	24.69 % / 41.98 %	56	B	34.57 % / 40.74 %	72	A	29.63 % / 43.21 %
9	B	30.86 % / 43.21 %	25	D	27.16 % / 41.98 %	41	C	37.04 % / 43.21 %	57	D	23.46 % / 40.74 %	73	A	22.22 % / 44.45 %
10	D	33.33 % / 40.74 %	26	B	40.74 % / 41.98 %	42	C	30.86 % / 41.98 %	58	A	27.16 % / 41.98 %	74	D	27.16 % / 37.04 %
11	A	32.1 % / 40.74 %	27	C	39.51 % / 40.74 %	43	A	30.86 % / 43.21 %	59	D	35.8 % / 45.68 %	75	B	30.86 % / 41.98 %
12	B	23.46 % / 39.5 %	28	C	40.74 % / 41.98 %	44	A	32.1 % / 41.97 %	60	C	49.38 % / 43.21 %	76	B	29.63 % / 46.91 %
13	D	32.1 % / 39.5 %	29	A	28.4 % / 35.8 %	45	D	24.69 % / 40.74 %	61	A	8.64 % / 46.92 %	77	B	39.51 % / 44.44 %
14	B	32.1 % / 40.74 %	30	A	39.51 % / 40.74 %	46	C	30.86 % / 40.74 %	62	A	23.46 % / 43.21 %	78	A	19.75 % / 35.81 %
15	D	37.04 % / 40.74 %	31	B	38.27 % / 41.98 %	47	C	46.91 % / 41.98 %	63	A	22.22 % / 38.27 %	79	C	33.33 % / 45.68 %
16	B	38.27 % / 32.1 %	32	B	48.15 % / 39.5 %	48	D	19.75 % / 32.1 %	64	D	28.4 % / 41.97 %	80	D	14.81 % / 40.75 %

Q.	Ans.	Correct / Skipped	Q.	Ans.	Correct / Skipped	Q.	Ans.	Correct / Skipped	Q.	Ans.	Correct / Skipped	Q.	Ans.	Correct / Skipped
81	B	25.93 % / 44.44 %	85	C	34.57 % / 43.21 %	89	C	24.69 % / 46.91 %	93	C	38.27 % / 41.98 %	97	A	20.99 % / 39.5 %
82	A	40.74 % / 40.74 %	86	B	28.4 % / 44.44 %	90	C	35.8 % / 43.21 %	94	B	33.33 % / 43.21 %	98	C	43.21 % / 43.21 %
83	D	20.99 % / 44.44 %	87	D	28.4 % / 43.2 %	91	C	34.57 % / 44.44 %	95	C	30.86 % / 39.51 %	99	C	28.4 % / 43.2 %
84	A	30.86 % / 44.45 %	88	C	37.04 % / 44.44 %	92	B	35.8 % / 45.68 %	96	D	40.74 % / 44.45 %	100	B	27.16 % / 43.21 %

//Hints and Solutions//

1. $x \geq 1, y \geq 2, z \geq 3$
We have to subtract these constraints from the total number of choices:
i.e. $29 - (1 + 2 + 3 + 0) = 23$
$^{(23 + 4 - 1)}C_{23} = 2,600$
So, option (B) is correct.

2. $p \vee \sim(p \wedge q) = p + (pq)' = p + p' + q' = 1 + q' = 1$. This is a tautology.
$(p \wedge \sim q) \vee \sim(p \wedge q) = pq' + (pq)' = pq' + p' + q' = p' + q'$. This is not a tautology.
$p \wedge (q \vee r) = pq + pr$. This is not a tautology.
So, option (D) is correct.

3. Client-server technology has distribution of hardware and software components across a network.

Hence the correct option is (A).

4. The travelling salesman problem can be solved in exponential time using dynamic programming algorithm or branch-and-bound algorithm.
So, option (C) is correct.

5. The options are in the following order:
$\lg(\lg^*n) < \lg^*(\lg n) < \lg(n!) < \lg^*(n!)$
So, option (A) is correct.

6. Method over-riding can be prevented by using final as a modifier at the start of method declaration.
Option (B) is correct.

7.

- Every class containing abstract method must be declared abstract. (**Correct**)
- Abstract class can directly be initiated with 'new' operator. (No it can't be initiated directed by only 'new' operator. So, it is **incorrect.**)
- Abstract class can be initiated.(**Correct**)
- Abstract class does not contain any definition of implementation. (**Correct**)

So, option (B) is correct.

8. Constructors have no return type.

Option (D) is correct.

9. Let us check each option.
(a) If there are 2 replications, probability of failing both at the same time $= .25 \times .25 = .0625 = 6.25\%$
Availability $= 100 - 6.25 = 93\%$ (Not the answer)
(b) In case of 4 replications, probability of failing all at the same time $= (0.25)4 = 0.0039 = 0.39\%$
Availability $= 100 - 0.39 \sim 99\%$ (Hence the answer)
There's no need to check further as all options are more than 4.
So, option (B) is correct.

10. ● If primal (dual) problem has a finite optimal solution, then its dual (primal) problem has a finite optimal solution. (**Correct**)

● If primal (dual) problem has an unbounded optimum solution, then its dual (primal) has no feasible solution at all. (**Correct**)

● Both primal and dual problems may be infeasible. (**Correct**)
So, option (D) is correct.

11. In write through method, the word is written to the block in both the cache and main memory, in parallel.
In write back method, the word is written to the block in cache but actual update into the corresponding location in main memory only at specified intervals or under certain conditions.
In write protected cache policy, a word cannot be modified or deleted.
In direct mapping, block M of main memory maps into block M modulo n of the cache, where n is the total number of blocks in cache.
So, option (A) is correct.

12. In linked allocation method for disk block allocation in a file system, insertion and deletion of blocks in a file is easy.
Option (B) is correct.

13. A Unix file may be of the regular file, directory file or device file type.
Option (D) is correct.

14. $\rightarrow$RSA algorithm using e = 3, d = 7 and n = 33 and text message BAHI (using the values 00 to 25 $\rightarrow$A(00), B(01), C(02), ...)

For B $\rightarrow[m = c^d \bmod n]$

i.e. $m = 1^7 \bmod 33$

$m = 1 \bmod 33$

$m = 1 \quad \rightarrow$B

A $\rightarrow 0^7 \bmod 33$

$m = 0 \bmod 33$

$m = 0$ A

$m = 7^7 \bmod 33$

$m = 13 \quad \rightarrow$N

$m = 8^7 \bmod 33$

$m = 17 \quad \rightarrow$R

The message will be BANR (using the values 00 to 25 $\rightarrow$A(00), B(01), C(02), ...). No option is matching.

But if we use the values 01 to 26 A(01), B(02), C(03), ...

Then, B $\rightarrow[m = c^d \bmod n]$

i.e. $m = 2^7 \bmod 33$

$m = 8 \bmod 33$

$m = 8 \quad \rightarrow$H

A $\rightarrow 1^7 \bmod 33$

m = 1 mod 33

m = 1 →A

m = 8^7 mod 33

m = 17 →Q

m = 9^7 mod 33

m = 3 →C

The message will be HAQC.

So, option (B) is correct.

15. Statement first is true, Path vector protocol is implemented using Border Gateway Protocol (BGP).
Statement second is true, Link state routing algorithm is implemented using Open shortest path first. (OSPF).
Statement 3 is false, both Path vector protocol and distance vector routing are different.
Statement 4 is true.

Hence the correct option is (D).

16. Given that it is an asynchronous mode of transmission, then along with per byte, you have to send some extra bit like start, stop bit and parity bits,etc. (start and stop bit are compulsory)
1 bit for start bit, 8 bits for data, 1 bit for parity, 2 bits for stop bits
$$\frac{9600 \times 15}{(1+8+1+2)} \text{ bytes} = 12,000 \text{ bytes}$$

Hence the correct option is (B).

17. For addressing in Gigabit Ethernet, 48 bits are used.
So, option (B) is correct.

18. • Line coding is a process of converting digital data to digital signal.

• Block coding provides redundancy to ensure synchronisation and inherits error detection.

• Scrambling provides synchronisation without increasing number of bits.

• Pulse code modulation is a technique to change analog signal to digital data.
So, option (B) is correct.

19. According to columnar transposition cipher with key LAYER, there are 5 elements in a key; so there will be 5 columns in every row.

Write down the order in key alphabetically.

L A Y E R

3 1 5 2 4

C O M P U

T E R N E

T W O R K

Now, encode it in column-wise manner from column 1 to column 5 according to order defined by key.

The encrypted message will be OEWPNRCTTUEKMRO.

Hence the correct option is (C).

20. The condition that all the data of the global relation must be mapped into the fragments, i.e. it must not happen that a data item which belongs to a global relation does not belong to any fragment, is called completeness condition.
In distributed system, it is convenient that fragment to be disjoint, so that the replication of data can be controlled explicitly at the allocation level. This is called disjointness condition.To reconstruct any global relation from its fragment is called reconstruction condition.
The formation of number of fragments into a cluster is called aggregation condition.
So, option (B) is correct.

21. $RA_1 : T_1 \bowtie T_1, P = T_2 \cdot AT_2$ where $\bowtie$ is natural join symbol. It will result 3 tuples:

P = A	R	C
10	5	6
10	5	5
25	6	3

$RA_2 : T_1 \bowtie AT_1 \cdot P = T_2 \cdot AT_2$ where $\bowtie$ is left outer join symbol. It will result in 4 tuples.

P = A	R	C
10	5	6
10	5	5
15	8	Null
25	6	3

$RA_3 : T1 \bowtie T_1 \cdot P = T_2 A$ and $T_1 R = T_2 \cdot CT_2$, It will result in 1 tuple.

P = A	R = C
10	5

So, option (D) is correct.

22. Decomposition of R into $R_1(C, A)$ and $R_2(A, B)$ is lossless.
Because C →A, A →B, so C →AB can be derived and there is no loss.
Decomposition of R into $R_1(A, B)$ and $R_2(B, C)$ is lossy.
Because A →B, C →B are derived but we can't derive C →AB, so it is lossy.
So, option (C) is correct.

23. We will draw Venn diagram for all sets: $|A - B|, |A \oplus B|, |A| + |B|$ and $|A \cup B|$

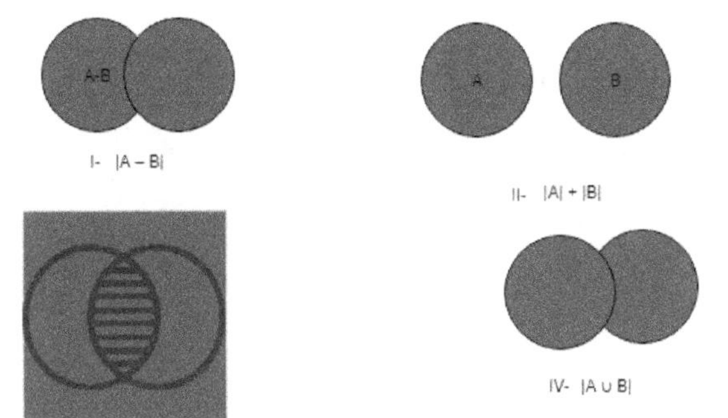

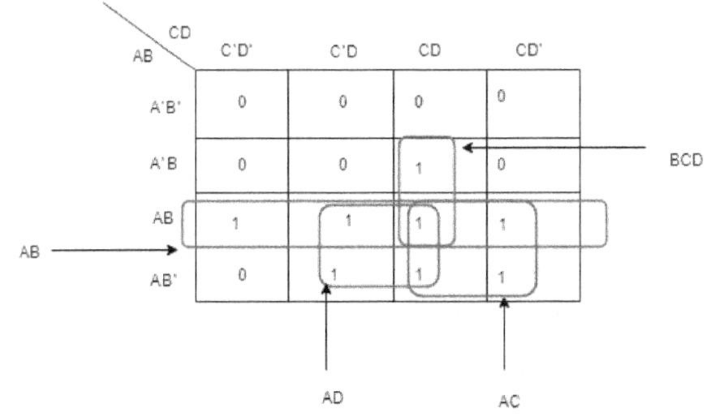

So, option (4) is correct.

Alternative way:

$$-|A - B| = |A| - |A \cap B|$$
$$|A \oplus B| = |A| + |B| - 2|A \cap B|$$
$$|A \cup B| = |A| + |B| - |A \cap B|$$

Therefore, $|A - B| < |A \oplus B| < |A \cup B| < |A| + |B|$

Hence the correct option is (D).

24. Convert 0.4051 into decimal in traditional way:

$$4 \times 8^{-1} + 0 \times 8^{-2} + 5 \times 8^{-3} + 1 \times 8^{-4}$$
$$= 0.5100098$$

Hence the correct option is (A).

25. We can use Master theorem to solve this recurrence relation:

$$T(n) = aT(n/2) + \Theta\left(n^k \log^p n\right)$$

In given question:

$$T(n) = 8T(n/2) + Cn$$

Here, $a = 8$ and $b = 2$ and $k = 1$ Clearly, $a > b^k$

So, $T(n) = \Theta\left(n^{\log_b a}\right)$

$$T(n) = \Theta\left(n^{\log_2 8}\right)$$

i.e. $T(n) = \Theta(n^3)$

So, option (D) is correct.

26.

By grouping, we will simply get:
AB + AC + AD + BCD
So, option (B) is correct.

27. Loader must reside in main memory because it is responsible for loading the process which is to be executed. If the loader is not in active memory, new processes cannot be loaded for further execution.

Hence the correct option is (C).

28. L = {x ∈ {0, 1}*|x ends with 1 and does not contain substring 00}:
(1 + 01) * (10 + 01)- This expression does not follow the condition mentioned above, i.e. it will contain 00 and can end with 0.
(1 + 01) * 01- It will always ends with 01.
(1 + 01) * (1 + 01)- It follows all the conditions mentioned.
(10 + 01) * 01- It will contain 00 as substring.
So, option (C) is correct.

29. Parser is a part of compiler and is responsible for syntax recognition.
Scanner (or tokenization) is used by lexical analyser.
In semantic analysis, consistency and definition of syntax is checked.
An optimiser is used improve the IR program.
So, option (A) is correct.

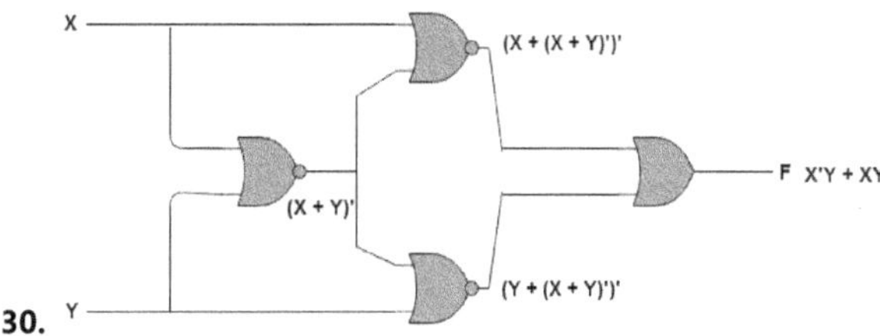

30.

F is EXCLUSIVE-OR between X and Y.

Hence the correct option is (A).

31. DAD will perform double addition (16 bit) between HL pair and any other pair of register.
Among HL, BC, DE and SP; B, H and D registers will be used first.
So, DAD H will perform HL = HL + HL;
DAD B will perform HL = HL + BC;
DAD D will perform HL = HL + DE;
SP is stack pointer and it is not a pair register, DAD SP will perform HL = HL + SP.
So, option (B) is correct.

32.

- Business intelligence and data warehousing is used for forecasting and data mining. (**Correct**)
- Business intelligence and data warehousing is used for analysis of large volumes of sales data. (**Correct**)

So, option (B) is correct.

33. Multiplexer, decoder and full adder are examples of combinational circuits.

Counter is a an example of sequential circuit.
So, option (C) is correct.

34. DAD will perform double addition (16 bit) between HL pair and any other pair of register. Among HL, BC, DE and SP; B, H and D register will be used first.

So, DAD H will perform HL = HL + HL;
DAD B will perform HL = HL + BC;
DAD D will perform HL = HL + DE;
SP is stack pointer and it is not a pair register, DAD SP will perform HL = HL + SP.
So, option (A) is correct.

35. We can verify as:

$$f \leq g \text{ but } g \neq f$$

Therefore, $f < g$

Also, $g = h$ as $g = O(h)$ and $h = O(g)$

Hence the correct option is (D).

36.

- (r + s)* will generate any strings containing r or s or both. We can draw DFA for (r + s)* and it is same as (s + r)*. It is a regular expression.

- (r*)* will generate any string containing r and its DFA can be drawn easily and it is same as r*. It is also a regular expression.

- (r* s*)* will generate any strings containing r or s or both. We can draw DFA for (r* s*)* and it is same as (r + s)*. It is a regular expression.

All the options are true. So, option (D) is correct.

37. OLAP (Online Application Program) system is market oriented and is used for data analysis by knowledge workers including managers, executives and analysts.
OLTP (online transaction processing) is a class of software programs capable of supporting transaction-oriented applications on the internet.
Data system is a term used to refer to an organised collection of symbols and processes that may be used to operate on such symbols.
A market system is the network of buyers, sellers and other actors that come together to trade in a given product or service.
So, option (B) is correct.

38. Lossy compression techniques are JPEG, MPEG and FFT, but arithmetic coding is an entropy coding used in lossless data compression.
So, option (D) is correct.

39. Forward chaining systems are data driven whereas backward chaining systems are goal driven.
So, option (C) is correct.

40. For a graph to be Euler graph, every vertex in the graph should have even degree.
In graph G_1, all the vertices have odd degrees. So, no Euler circuit is possible. Therefore, G_1 is not Euler graph.
Graph G_2 has vertices a, d and e. All these vertices have odd degrees as 3, 5, 3, respectively. So, no Euler circuit is possible. Hence, this graph is also not Euler graph.
So, option (C) is correct.

41. We have prefix expression:

$$* +3 + 3 \uparrow 3 + 333$$
$$= * +3 + 3 \uparrow 363$$
$$= * +3 + 37293$$
$$= * +37323$$
$$= x7353$$
$$= 2205$$

So, option (C) is correct.

42. A queue can be implemented using minimum two stacks.
A stack can be implemented using minimum two queues.
Both the statements are true.
So, option (C) is correct.

43.

- Composition is a strong type of association between two classes with full ownership. (Correct)

- Composition is a strong type of association between two classes with partial ownership. (Incorrect)

- Composition is a weak type of association between two classes with partial ownership. (Incorrect)

- Composition is a weak type of association between two classes with strong ownership. (Incorrect)

So, option (A) is correct.

44.

- Wizards are step-by-step guides in application software.

- Templates are forms that provide structure for a document.

- Macro is a series of commands grouped into a single command.

- Integrated software is a single program that incorporates most commonly used tools.

- Software suite is a bundled group of software programs.

So, option (A) is correct.

45. The two-level CPU scheduling is used when memory is too small to hold all the ready processes because it facilitates putting some set of processes into memory and a choice is made from that.

Hence the correct option is (D).

46. 'nice' command in Unix:

- It is used to set or change the priority of a process.
- It takes a command line as an argument.
- Its value can be set at the time of creation.

All the statements are correct.

So, option (C) is correct.

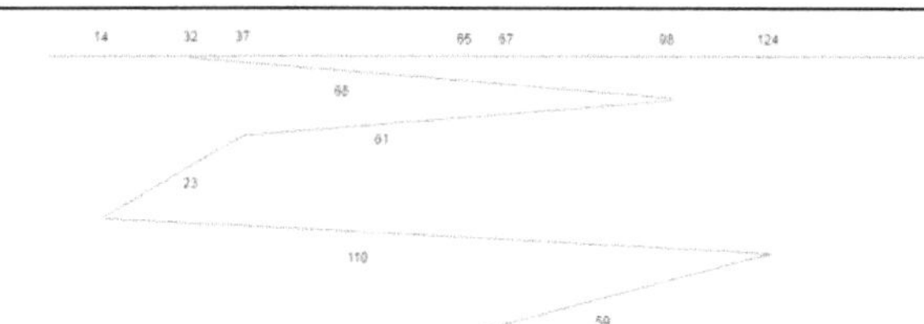

47.
Total disk movement = 66 + 61 + 23 + 110 + 59 + 2 = 321
So, option (C) is correct.

48. The channel capacity of a discrete memoryless channel is defined by:

C = max I(X; Y) p(x)

= max [H(Y) − H(Y |X)] p(x)

= max [H(X) − H(X| p(x)]

Hence the correct option is (D).

49. In LRU:

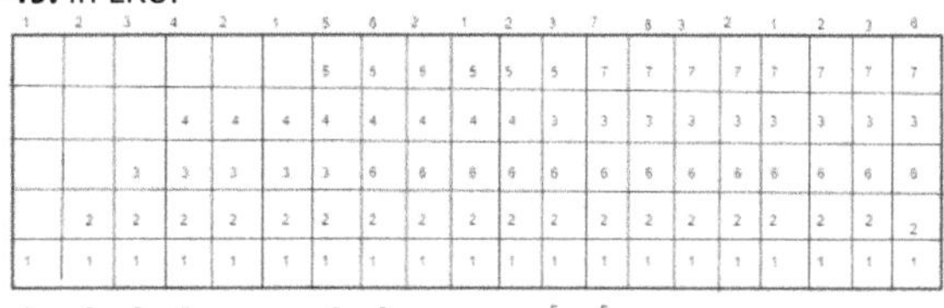

In FIFO:

In Optimal:

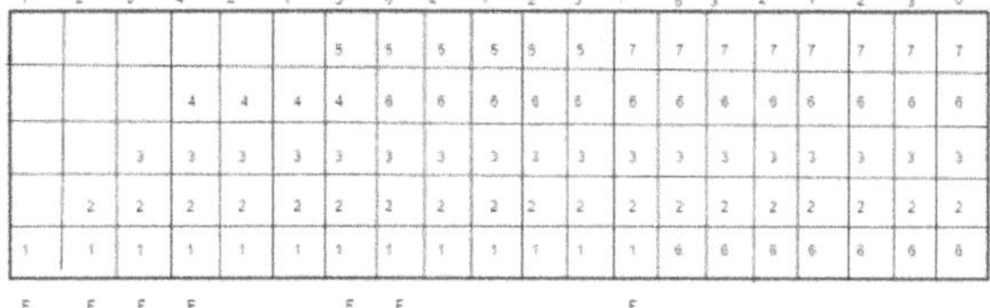

Respectively, there are 8, 10, 7 page faults.
So, option (B) is correct.

50. WOW32 is a special execution environment used to run 16-bit windows applications on 32-bit machines.
So, option (D) is correct.

51. Assignment problem is a special case of transportation problem. It requires that only one activity be assigned to each resource and it can be used to minimise the cost. All the statements are correct.

So, option (D) is correct.

52. 1. Every loop has an odd number of cells and at least five cells. (This is not necessary, so it is an incorrect statement.)
2. Closed loops may or may not be square in shape. (It is a correct statement.)
3. All the cells in the loop that have a plus or minus sign, except the starting cell, must be occupied cells. (It is a correct statement.)

4. Every loop has an even number of cells and at least four cells. (It is a correct statement.)
So, option (A) is correct.

53. There are 100 pages and each page contains 24 lines. Each line has 80 characters and each character weighs 8 bits. We have to download 100 pages per minute, i.e.

$$\frac{100\times24\times80\times8}{60} = 25.6 Kbps$$

So, option (D) is correct.

54. In OSI model, transport layer is responsible for end-to-end communication.
So, option (D) is correct.

55. Non-adoptive algorithms do not take their decisions on measurements or estimates of the current traffic and topology.
So, option (C) is correct.

56. SQ_1: (SELECT * FROM One)

EXCEPT

(SELECT * FROM Two);

It will result into single tuple (2, 5) because all duplicate tuples will be removed.

SQ_2: (SELECT * FROM One)

EXCEPT ALL

(SELECT * FROM Two);

It will result into 2 tuples < (2,5), (1.6) > because it will not remove duplicate.

So, option (B) is correct.

57.

- Specialization - Result of taking a subset of a higher-level entity set to form a lower-level entity set

- Generalization - Result of taking the union of two or more disjoint (lower-level) entity sets to produce a higher-level entity set

- Aggregation - An abstraction in which relationship sets (along with their associated entity sets) are treated as higher-level entity sets, and can participate in a relationship.

- Mapping cardinalities - Express the number of entities to which another entity can be associated via a relationship set

So, option (D) is correct.

58. Address of pixel (6,10) in row major order

= 0 + 1(6 - 0) +101 (10 - 0)

= 1016

(For pixel calculation address in row major order, use logic of how to find address of array element in column major order.)

Hence the correct option is (A).

59. Given that

$$(P \to Q) \land (R \to S)$$

$$(P \lor R)$$

Here, if P then Q and if R then S.

Now, $P \lor R$ means either Q is true or S is true.

So, Y will be $Q \lor S$

Hence the correct option is (D).

60. 2357 is given in octal.
So, its binary equivalent will be obtained by converting every number into 3-bit equivalent binary (010 011 101 111).
Now, to convert this octal number into its equivalent hexadecimal number, pair 4 bits of above binary number starting from MSB.
It will become (0100 1110 1111), which is equivalent to 4EF.
So, the answer is option (C).

61. int mcq (boolean a, boolean b, boolean c, boolean d)

{

1. int ans 1;

2. if (a)

3. {Answer = 2; }

4. elseif (b)

5. {Answer = 3;}

6. else if (c) {

7. if (d)

8. {Answer = 4;}

9. returns Answer;

} }

The total number of conditions is 4.

Hence, M_1 = Number of tests to exhaustively test mcq = 2 × 2 × 2 × 2 = 16 because each condition can be either true or false.

To cover all the statements, we need minimum 3 tests.

a b c and d cover statements 1, 2, 3 and 6.

T X X X (where X is true or false)

a b c d cover 1, 2, 4, 5, 6 statements, and

F T X X

The test case a b c d covers 1, 2, 4, 6, 7, 8, 9.

F F T T

So, full statement coverage requires minimum 3 test cases.

$\Rightarrow M_2 = 3$

The flow chart of above program is:

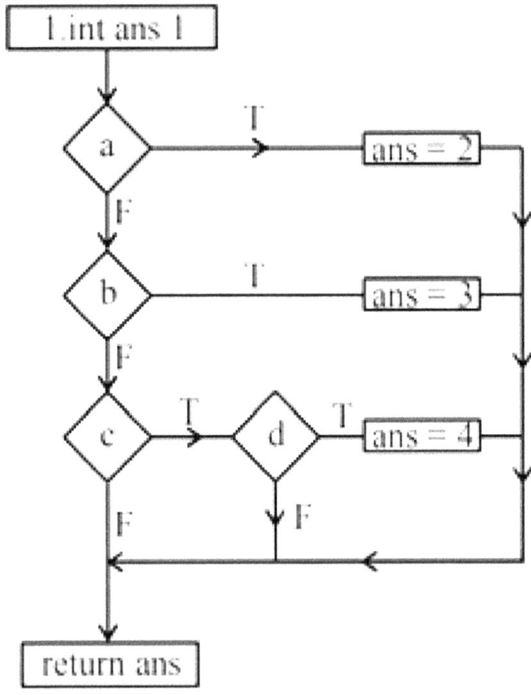

To cover all the branches, the minimum of test cases = 5

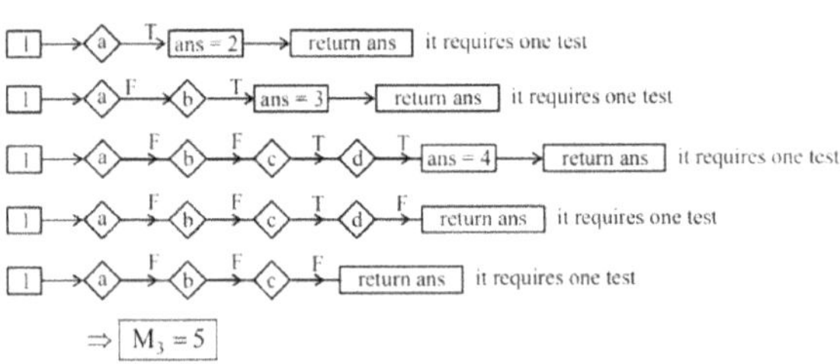

Hence the correct option is (A).

62. mov al, 15

It means move 15 to lower part of 'ax' register.

mov ah, 15

It means move 15 to higher part of 'ax' register.

The 'ax' register content looks like:

0000111100001111

xor al, al

It means 'XORing lower part of 'ax' register with its own content and storing result back in 'al'.

Now the 'ax' register content will be:

  00001111

  00001111

xor00000000

'ax' register content: 0000111100000000

move cl, 3

It means move 3 to lower part of 'cx' register.

The 'c' register content looks like:

0000000000000011

shr ax, cl

It will shift right and rotate content of 'ax' register.

The 'ax' register content looks like:

0000000111100000

add al, 90H

Add hexadecimal 90 to al:

 0000000111100000

  0000000010010000

+0000001001110000

adc ah, 0

It means addition with carry which does not affect 'ax' register.

So, content of ax register will be 0270H.

Hence the correct option is (A).

63. Relocation is the process of replacing symbolic references or names of libraries with actual usable addresses in memory before running a program. It is typically done by the linker during compilation (at compile time) although it can be done at run-time by a relocating loader.

Hence the correct option is (A).

64. Transition diagram for L = {w|n$_a$ (w) and n$_b$(w) are both odd}:

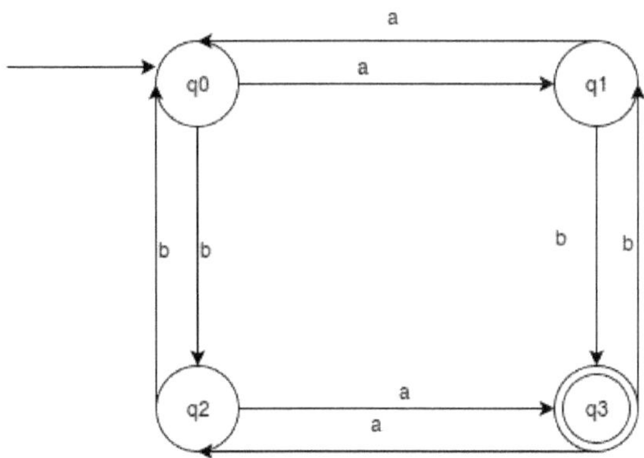

q$_3$ satisfies the condition - {w|n$_a$ (w) and n$_b$(w) are both odd}, so q$_3$ is the final state and all strings start from q$_0$, so q$_0$ is the final state.
So, option (D) is correct.

65. For a language to be recursive, it can be decided by a Turing machine. This means it will enter into the final state and reject the rest.
And for DCFL, it must decidable for a particular language whether the next character is going to be accepted or not.
So, option (C) is correct.

66. Controlled inverter is a circuit that transmits a binary word or its 1's complement.

Full adder is a circuit that can add 3 bits.
Half adder is a logic circuit that adds 2 bits.
Binary adder is a circuit that can add 2 binary numbers.
So, option (D) is correct.

67. In Code-and-Fix model write some code, debug it, repeat (i.e. ad-hoc)

In Evolutionary prototyping model build an initial small requirement specifications, code it, then "evolve" the specifications and code as needed.

In Spiral model is assess risks at each step; do most critical action first.

In Staged Delivery model build initial requirement specification for several releases, then design-and-code in sequence

In Waterfall model standard phases (requirements, design,code, test) in order.

Hence the correct option is (A).

68. MTBF = 30 days = 30 $\times$ 24 = 720 hour.

MTTR = 12 hour.

Availability(A) = MTBF / (MTBF + MTTR)

i.e. A = 720 / (720 + 12) = 0.9836 = 98.36%.

So, option (C) is correct.

69. 8085 microprocessor has 5 hardware interrupts. Named TRAP, RST 7.5, RST 6.5, RST 5.5 and INTR.

The above order is decreasing in priority.

So, option (D) is correct.

70. Software Quality Assurance (SQA) is a set of activities for ensuring quality in software engineering processes (that ultimately result in quality in software products).In developing products and services, quality assurance is any systematic process of checking to see whether a product or service being developed is meeting specified requirements.

Software Safety : Software System Safety optimizes system safety in the design, development, use, and maintenance of software systems and their integration with safety critical hardware systems in an operational environment.

Hence the correct option is (B).

71. Transfer time(TT) = (1024 bytes $\times$ 16 ms) / (16384 bytes)= 1 msec

Rotational latency = 16 msec / 2 = 8 msec

seek time = 40 msec.

total time = seek time + rotational latency + transfer time

= 40 + 8 + 1 = 49 msec

So, option (B) is correct.

72. Histogram is the graphical representation of the tonal distribution in a digital image.

• X axis represents the tonal variations

- Y axis represents the number of pixels
- Histogram for a very dark image will have most of its data points on the left side of the graph.
- Histogram for a very bright image will have most of its data points on the right side the graph.

Hence the correct option is (A).

73. Four views regarding the design of a data warehouse
Top-down view:
allows selection of the relevant information necessary for the data warehouse
Data source view:
exposes the information being captured, stored, and managed by operational systems
Data warehouse view:
consists of fact tables and dimension tables
Business query view:
sees the perspectives of data in the warehouse from the view of end-user.

Hence the correct option is (A).

74. Java uses threads to enable the entire environment to be asynchronous. Asynchronous threading is pre-emptive i.e. a thread once start executing a task it can hold it in mid, save the current state and start executing another task (context switching) according to priority and other specified criteria and threading.

So, option (D) is correct.

75. OSPF protocol is practical implementation of LSR (Link State Routing) category and uses Dijkstra's algorithm.

Hence the correct option is (B).

76. Given hash function: $h(K) = $ floor $\left(m(K \times A \bmod 1)\right)$

where $A = \left(\sqrt{(5)} - 1\right)/2$

$$h(= floor(10000 \times (123456 \times (\sqrt{5} - 1)/2)$$
$$123456) \bmod$$
$$= floor(10000 \times (76300.004115 \bmod 1)$$
$$= floor(10000 \times (.004115))$$
$$= 41.15$$
$$= 41$$

Hence the correct option is (B).

77.

- When a class grants friend status to another class then all member functions of the class granted friendship have unrestricted access to the members of the class granting the friendship.
- The member functions of the class generating friendship can access the members of the friend class.Incorrect statement.
- Class friendship is not reciprocal to each other.

So, option (B) is correct.

78. The steps to read complicated declarations :

1)Convert C declaration to postfix format and read from left to right.

2)To convert expression to postfix, start from innermost parenthesis, If innermost parenthesis is not present then start from declarations name and go right first. When first ending parenthesis encounters then go left. Once the whole parenthesis is parsed then come out from parenthesis.

3)Continue until complete declaration has been parsed.

At First, we convert the following given declaration into postfix:

int (* f) (int *)

Since there is no innermost bracket, so first we take declaration name f, so print "f" and then go to the right, since there is nothing to parse, so go to the left. There is * at the left side, so print "*".Come out of parenthesis. Hence postfix notation of given declaration can be written as follows:

f * (int *) int

Meaning: f is a pointer to function (which takes one argument of int pointer type) returning int

Hence the correct option is (A).

79. = x * y < i + j || k

= 0.5 * 0.0 < 0 + 1 || -1

= 0.0 < 0 + 1 || -1

= 0.0 < 1 || -1

= 1 || -1

= 1

Hence the correct option is (C).

80. We have 16 x 16 grid, There will be (M – 1) X (N – 1) hops for M X N grid.

In the given question M = N.

# of hops = (M – 1) X (M – 1)

= 2 X (M – 1)

= 2 X (16 – 1)

= 2 X 15

= 30 hops.

So, option (D) is correct.

81. According to given question

1K RPC takes – 1.5 X 32 + 1.0 = 49.0 msec

32 1K RPC will take:

1.5 X 32 + 1.0 X 32

= 80.0 msec

So, option (B) is correct.

82. There are three type of scheduler:

1. Short-term scheduler
2. Mid-term scheduler
3. Long-term scheduler

Dispatcher is responsible for handovering the control of CPU to the newly selected process by the Short-term scheduler.

So, option (A) is correct.

83. We have 100 pages, each page is having 24 line and in each line there are 80 character and each character is of 8 bits.

Now we have to calculate no of bits can be downloaded:

i.e.,

Downloading rate = 100 pages

= 100 pages $\times$ 24 line $\times$ 80 character $\times$ 8 bits

= 1536000 bits per second

i.e., 1.536 Mbps.

Hence the correct option is (D).

84. Relational Model represents how data is stored in Relational Databases. A relational database stores data in the form of relations (tables).
NULL Values: The value which is not known or unavailable is called NULL value. It is represented by blank space. e.g.; PHONE of STUDENT having ROLL_NO 4 is NULL.

Hence the correct option is (A).

85. Pipelining improves performance by exploiting instruction level parallelism.

For detailed information on pipelining Refer: Computer Organization and Architecture | Pipelining | Set 1 (Execution, Stages and Throughput)

So, option (C) is correct.

86. ECL is fastest among the three because the transistors are used in difference amplifier configuration, in which they are never driven into saturation and thereby the

storage time is eliminated.

The digital logic family which has the lowest propagation delay time is ECL (Lowest propagation delay time is possible in ECL because the transistors are used in

difference amplifier configuration, in which they are never driven into saturation and thereby the storage time is eliminated).

Non-saturated Logic: In Non-saturated Logic, the transistors are not driven into saturation.

(i) Schottky TTL

(ii) Emitter Coupled Logic (ECL)

Hence the correct option is (B).

87. We have m=(313)4 and n=(322)4 convert m and n into decimal:

$$m = 3 \times 4^2 + 1 \times 4^1 + 3 \times 4^0$$

$$m = 48 + 4 + 3$$

$$m = 55$$

Now $n = 3 \times 4^2 + 2 \times 4^1 + 2 \times 4^0$

$$n = 48 + 8 + 2$$

$$n = 58$$

$$m + n = 55 + 58$$

$$m + n = 113$$

Now we have to convert 113 in to base 4:

i.e. step $1 - 113\%4 = 1$
$113/4 = 28$
step $2 - 28\%4 = 0$
$28/4 = 7$
step $3 - 7\%4 = 3$
$7/4 = 1$
step $4 - 1\%4 = 1$
$1/4 - -> $ will not divide it in quant.
So we have to stop here.

The answer will be Residue from step 4 to step 1 inorder i.e. 1301. Answer-(1301)$_4$.

Hence the correct option is (D).

88. $x_1 = 4$, $x_2 = 0$, $x_2 = 0$ and $Z = 8$

Hence the correct option is (C).

89. (A) => 3AH => 00111010

(B) => 49H => 01001001

11110001

(A) => F1H

(CY) => 1

(S) => 1

The carry flag is set since the first operand is less than the second operand.

Since the result produces the negative result sign flag is set.

Hence the correct option is (C).

90. The family of context sensitive languages is closed under union and closed under reversal.

Hence the correct option is (C).

91. We know that x $\oplus$ y = x`y + xy`
So,

1. $1 \oplus 0 = 1`0 + 10` = 0 * 0 + 1 * 1 = 0 + 1 = 1$
2. $1 \oplus 1 \oplus 1 = (1 \oplus 1) \oplus 1 = (1`1 + 11`) \oplus 1 = (0) \oplus 1$
   $= 1`0 + 10` = 0 * 0 + 1 * 1 = 0 + 1 = 1$

3. $1 \oplus 1 \oplus 0 = 1 \oplus (1 \oplus 0) = 1 \oplus (1`0 + 10` = 0 * 0 + 1 * 1 = 0 + 1) = 1 \oplus 1 = 1`1 + 11` = 0$

4. $1 \oplus 1 = 1`1 + 11` = 0$

92.

- Corrective Concerned with fixing errors that are observed when the software is in use.

- Concerned with the change in the software that takes place to make the software adaptable to new environment (bothhardware and software).

- Perfective Concerned with the change in the software that takes place to make the software adaptable to changing user requirements.

- Preventive Concerned with performing activities to reduce the software complexity thereby improving program understandability and increasing software maintainability.

So, option (B) is correct.

93.

- Coupling is reliance of a code module upon other code modules.

- Cohesion is easy to visually inspect the design of the software and understand its purpose.

- Scalable is focus of a code upon a single goal.

- Readable is easy to add functionality to a software without having to redesign it.

So, option (C) is correct.

94. There are five levels defined along the continuum of the model and, according to the SEI: "Predictability, effectiveness, and control of an organization's software processes are believed to improve as the organization moves up these five levels. While not rigorous, the empirical evidence to date supports this belief".

1. Initial (chaotic, ad hoc, individual heroics) - the starting point for use of a new or undocumented repeat process.

2. Repeatable - the process is at least documented sufficiently such that repeating the same steps may be attempted.

3. Defined - the process is defined/confirmed as a standard business process.

4. Managed - the process is quantitatively managed in accordance with agreed-upon metrics.

5. Optimizing - process management includes deliberate process optimization/improvement.

Hence the correct option is (B).

95. Quadrature Amplitude Modulation means changing both amplitude and phase of the carrie.

So, option (C) is correct.

96.

- HTML is not screen precise formatting language.

- HTML does not specify a logic.Correct

- DHTML is used for developing highly interactive web pages.

- HTML is not a programming, it is hyper text markup language.

So, option (D) is correct.

97. Lets consider there are 'K' buckets (as given).

Now, for each digit you repeat the following:

1) place the digit of each number in the appropriate bin. - $\varnothing(n)$

2) append all the 'K' bins sequentially.

Thus, for a single digit, its $\varnothing(n+k)$,

For 'd' digits, its $\varnothing(d(n+k))$

Hence the correct option is (A).

98. a-iii   b- i   c- iv   d- ii

Hence the correct option is (C).

99. In Critical section problem:

No assumptions may be made about speeds or the number of CPUs.

No two processes may be simultaneously inside their critical sections.

Processes running outside its critical section can't block other processes getting enter into critical section.

Processes do not wait forever to enter its critical section.

So, option (C) is correct.

100. The basic primitive of the Graphics Kernel System (GKS):

- TEXT : It will draw string of character.

- CELL ARRAY: It will display a image composed of variety of colors.

- POLYLINE: It will draw a sequence of connected line segments.

- FILL AREA : It will specify a perticular area.

- POLYMARKER: It will mark the point with alike symbol.

- There is nothing like POLYDRAW in basic primitive of the Graphics Kernel System (GKS).

So, option (B) is correct.

Q.1 Which of the following properties must a Group G hold, in order to be an abelian group?
(a) The distributive property
(b) The commutative property
(c) The symmetric property

A. (a) and (b)

B. (b) and (c)

C. (c) only

D. All of these

Q.2 A bell-shaped membership function is specified by three parameters (a, b, c) as:

A. $\dfrac{1}{1+\left(\frac{x-c}{a}\right)^{b}}$

B. $\dfrac{1}{1+\left(\frac{x-c}{a}\right)^{2b}}$

C. $1+\left(\frac{x-c}{a}\right)^{b}$

D. $1+\left(\frac{x-c}{a}\right)^{2b}$

Q.3 The number of strings of length 4 that are generated by the regular expression (0⁺1⁺|2⁺3⁺)*, where | is an alternation character and {+, *} are quantification characters, is:

A. 08   **B.** 09   **C.** 10   **D.** 12

Q.4 Consider a hash table of size $m = 100$ and the hash function $h(k) = flogr\big(m(kA\,mod\,1)\big)$ for

$$A = \frac{(\sqrt{5}-1)}{2} = 0.618033$$

Compute the location to which the key $k = 123456$ is placed in hash table.

A. 77   **B.** 82   **C.** 88   **D.** 89

Q.5 Let f(n) and g(n) be asymptotically non-negative functions. Which of the following is correct?

A. θ (f(n) x g(n)) = min (f(n), g(n))

B. θ (f(n) x g(n)) = max (f(n), g(n))

C. θ (f(n) + g(n)) = min (f(n), g(n))

D. θ (f(n) + g(n)) = max (f(n), g(n))

Q.6 What is the value returned by the function f (given below) when n = 100?

```
int f (int n)
{ if (n = = 0) then return n;
else
return n + f(n - 2);
}
```

A. 2550   **B.** 2556   **C.** 5220   **D.** 5520

Q.7 When a method in a subclass has the same name and type signatures as a method in the superclass, then the method in the subclass _____ the method in the superclass.

A. overloads

B. friendships

C. inherits

D. overrides

Q.8 Which of the following statements concerning object-oriented databases is false?

A. Objects in an object-oriented database contain not only data but also methods for processing the data.

B. Object-oriented databases store computational instructions in the same place as data.

C. Object-oriented databases are more adept at handling structured (analytical) data than relational databases.

D. Object-oriented databases store more types of data than relational databases and access that data faster.

Q.9 In _______ disk scheduling algorithm, the disk head moves from one end to other end of the disk, serving the requests along the way. When the head reaches the other end, it immediately returns to the beginning of the disk without serving any requests on the return trip.

A. LOOK

B. SCAN

C. C-LOOK

D. C-SCAN

Q.10 Which of the following is incorrect for virtual memory?

A. Large programs can be written.

B. More I/O is required.

C. More addressable memory is available.

D. Faster and easy swapping of processes is possible.

Q.11 Consider the following four processes with the arrival time and length of CPU burst given in milliseconds:

Process	Arrival Time	Burst Time
P₁	0	8
P₂	1	4
P₃	2	9
P₄	3	5

The average waiting time (in milliseconds) for preemptive SJF scheduling algorithm is _________.

A. 6.5   **B.** 7.5   **C.** 6.75   **D.** 7.75

Q.12 A scheduling algorithm assigns priority proportional to the waiting time of a process. Every process starts with priority zero (lowest priority). The scheduler reevaluates the process priority for every 'T' time units and decides next process to be scheduled. If the process has no I/O operations and all arrive at time zero, then the scheduler implements which of the following criteria?

A. Priority Scheduling

B. Round Robin Scheduling

C. Shortest Job First

D. FCFS

Q.13 What is the function of the following unix command?
$ vi file1 file2

A. It edits file1 and stores the contents of file1 in file2.

B. Both files, i.e. file1 and file2 can be edited using 'ex' command to travel between the files.

C. Both files can be edited using 'mv' command to move between the files.

D. It edits file1 first, saves it and then edits file2.

Q.14 Station A uses 32 byte packets to transmit messages to station B using sliding window protocol. The round trip delay between A and B is 40 milliseconds and the bottleneck bandwidth on the path between A and B is 64 kbps. The optimal window size of A is

A. 10 packets   **B.** 20 packets
C. 30 packets   **D.** 40 packets

Q.15 The degeneracy does not occur in transportation problem at which of the following stages?
(m and n represent number of sources and destinations, respectively)
(a) While the values of dual variables u_i and v_j cannot be computed
(b) While obtaining an initial solution, we may have less than m + n -1 allocations
(c) At any stage while moving towards optimal solution, when two or more occupied cells with the same minimum allocation become unoccupied simultaneously
(d) At a stage when the number of +ve allocation is exactly m + n - 1

A. (a), (b) and (c)   **B.** (a), (c) and (d)
C. (a) and (d)   **D.** (a), (b), (c) and (d)

Q.16 Which of the following options with reference to UNIX operating system is not correct?

A. INT signal is sent by the terminal driver when one types and it is a request to terminate the current operation.

B. TERM is a request to terminate execution completely. The receiving process will clean up its state and exit.

C. QUIT is similar to TERM, except that it defaults to producing a core dump if not caught.

D. KILL is a blockable signal.

Q.17 The address of a class B host is to be split into subnets with a 6-bit subnet number. What is the maximum number of subnets and maximum number of hosts in each subnet?

A. 62 subnets and 1022 hosts
B. 64 subnets and 1024 hosts
C. 62 subnets and 254 hosts
D. 64 subnets and 256 hosts

Q.18 The IP address __________ is used by hosts when they are being booted.

A. 0.0.0.0   **B.** 1.0.0.0
C. 1.1.1.1   **D.** 255.255.255.255

Q.19 Which of the following protocols is used by email server to maintain a central repository that can be accessed from any machine?

A. POP3   **B.** IMAP   **C.** SMTP   **D.** DMSP

Q.20 Which of the following statements is/are false in the context of Relational DBMS?
I. Views in a database system are important because they help with access control by allowing users to see only a particular subset of the data in the database.
II. E-R diagrams are useful to logically model concepts.
III. An update anomaly is when it is not possible to store information unless some other, unrelated information is stored as well.
IV. SQL is a procedural language.

A. I and IV only   **B.** III and IV only
C. I, II and III only   **D.** II, III and IV only

Q.21 Let M and N be two entities in an E-R diagram with simple single-valued attributes. R_1 and R_2 are two relationships between M and N, whereas R_1 is one-to-many and R_2 is many-to-many. The minimum number of tables required to represent M, N, R_1 and R_2 in the relational model is _____.

A. 4   **B.** 6   **C.** 7   **D.** 3

Q.22 In RDBMS, the constraint that no key attribute (column) may be NULL is referred to as

A. referential integrity
B. multi-valued dependency
C. entity integrity
D. functional dependency

Q.23 The first order logic (FOL) statement $(R \lor Q) \land (P \neg Q)$ is equivalent to which of the following?

A. $R \lor \neg Q \land (P \lor \neg Q) \land (R \lor P$
B. $R \lor Q \land P \lor \neg Q \land \hat{R} \lor P$
C. $R \lor Q \land (P \lor \neg Q) \land (R \lor \neg P$
D. $R \lor Q \land (P \lor \neg Q) \land (\neg R \lor P$

Q.24 Find the Boolean product AB of the two matrices.

Let $A = \begin{bmatrix} 1 & 1 & 0 \\ 0 & 1 & 0 \\ 1 & 1 & 0 \\ 0 & 0 & 1 \end{bmatrix}$ and $B = \begin{bmatrix} 1 & 0 & 0 & 0 \\ 0 & 1 & 1 & 0 \\ 1 & 0 & 1 & 1 \end{bmatrix}$

A. $\begin{bmatrix} 1 & 1 & 1 & 0 \\ 0 & 1 & 1 & 0 \\ 1 & 1 & 1 & 0 \\ 1 & 0 & 1 & 1 \end{bmatrix}$ **B.** $\begin{bmatrix} 1 & 1 & 0 & 1 \\ 0 & 1 & 0 & 1 \\ 1 & 1 & 1 & 0 \\ 1 & 0 & 1 & 1 \end{bmatrix}$

C. $\begin{bmatrix} 1 & 1 & 0 & 1 \\ 0 & 1 & 1 & 0 \\ 1 & 1 & 1 & 0 \\ 1 & 0 & 1 & 1 \end{bmatrix}$ **D.** $\begin{bmatrix} 1 & 1 & 1 & 0 \\ 0 & 1 & 1 & 0 \\ 1 & 0 & 1 & 1 \\ 1 & 0 & 1 & 1 \end{bmatrix}$

Q.25 Consider the function f(x) = sin(x) in the interval [π/4, 7π/4]. The number and location(s) of the local minima of this function (respectively) are

A. One, at π/2
B. One, at 3π/2
C. Two, at π/2 and 3π/2
D. Two, at π/4 and 3π/2

Q.26 Consider the following program segment for a hypothetical CPU having three user registers Rl, R2 and R3.

Instruction	Operation	Instruction Size [in word]
MOV RI,5000;	RI × Memory[5000]	2
MOV R2,(R1);	R2 × Memory[(RI)]	1
ADD R2,R3;	R2 × R2 + R3	1

| MOV 6000, R2; | Memory[6000] × R2 | 2 |
| HALT; | Machine halts | 1 |

Let the clock cycles required for various operations be as follows:

Register to/from memory transfer:	3 clock cycles
ADD with both operands in register:	1 clock cycle
Instruction fetch and decode:	2 clock cycles per word

The total number of clock cycles required to execute the program is

A. 29   **B.** 24
C. 23   **D.** 20

Q.27 The _________ transfers the executable image of a C++ program from hard disk to main memory.

A. compiler   **B.** linker
C. debugger   **D.** loader

Q.28 The regular grammar for the language L = {$a^n b^m$ | n + m is even} is given by:

A.
$$S \to S_1 \mid S_2$$
$$S_1 \to aS_1 \mid A_1$$
$$A_1 \to bA_1 \mid \lambda$$
$$S_2 \to aaS_2 \mid A_2$$
$$A_2 \to bA_2 \mid \lambda$$

B.
$$S \to S_1 \mid S_2$$
$$S_1 \to aS_1 \mid aA_1$$
$$S_2 \to aaS_2 \mid A_2$$
$$A_1 \to bA_1 \mid \lambda$$
$$A_2 \to bA_2 \mid \lambda$$

C.
$$S \to S_1 \mid S_2$$
$$S_1 \to aaa\ S_1 \mid aA_1$$
$$S_2 \to aaS_2 \mid A_2$$
$$A_1 \to bA_1 \mid \lambda$$
$$A_2 \to bA_2 \mid \lambda$$

D.
$$S \to S_1 \mid S_2$$
$$S_1 \to aaS_1 \mid A_1$$
$$S_2 \to aaS_2 \mid aA_2$$
$$A_1 \to bbA_1 \mid \lambda$$
$$A_2 \to bbA_2 \mid \lambda$$

Q.29 There are exactly _________ different finite automata with three states x, y and z over the alphabet {a, b}, where x is always the start state.

A. 64   **B.** 56   **C.** 1024   **D.** 5832

Q.30 Consider a standard Circular Queue 'q' implementation (which has the same condition for Queue Full and Queue Empty) whose size is 11 and the elements of the queue are q[0], q[1], q[2], .., q[10]. The front and rear pointers are initialised to point at q[2] . In which position will the ninth element be added?

A. q[0]   **B.** q[1]   **C.** q[9]   **D.** q[10]

Q.31 The IEEE-754 double-precision format to represent floating point numbers, has a length of ____ bits.

A. 16   **B.** 32   **C.** 48   **D.** 64

Q.32 Which of the following is a characteristic of an MIS?

A. Provides guidance in identifying problems, finding and evaluating alternative solutions, and selecting or comparing alternatives
B. Draws on diverse yet predictable data resources to aggregate and summarize data
C. High volume, data capture focus
D. Has as its goal, the efficiency of data movement and processing and interfacing different TPS

Q.33 A software program that infers and manipulates existing knowledge in order to generate new knowledge is known as

A. data dictionary
B. reference mechanism
C. inference engine
D. control strategy

Q.34 Software engineering is an engineering discipline that is concerned with

A. how computer systems work
B. theories and methods that underlie computers and software systems
C. all aspects of software production
D. all aspects of computer-based systems development, including hardware, software and process engineering

Q.35 In a network of LANs connected by bridges, packets are sent from one LAN to another through intermediate bridges. Since more than one path may exist between two LANs, packets may have to be routed through multiple bridges. Why is the spanning tree algorithm used for bridge-routing?

A. For getting the shortest path routing between LANs
B. For avoiding loops in the routing paths
C. For fault tolerance
D. For minimising collisions

Q.36 Which of the following sequence of steps is taken in designing a fuzzy logic machine?

A. Fuzzification → Rule evaluation → Defuzzification
B. Fuzzification → Defuzzification → Rule evaluation
C. Rule evaluation → Fuzzification → Defuzzification
D. Rule evaluation → Defuzzification → Fuzzification

Q.37 As compared to rental and leasing methods to acquire computer systems for a Management Information System (MIS), purchase method has which of the following advantages?

A. It has high level of flexibility.
B. It does not require cash up-front.
C. It is a business investment.
D. It has little risk of obsolescence.

Q.38 The array of integers 'array' is given as shown below: What is the output of the following JAVA statements?
```
int [ ] p = new int [10];
int [ ] q = new int [10];
for (int k = 0; k < 10; k++)
p [k] = array [k];
q = p;
p [4] = 20;
System.out.println (array [4] + ':' + q [4]);
```
A. 20:20   **B.** 18:18   **C.** 18:20   **D.** 20:18

Q.39 What is the probability that a randomly selected bit string of length 10 is a palindrome?

A. 1/64   **B.** 1/32   **C.** 1/8   **D.** 1/4

Q.40 Consider the given graph:

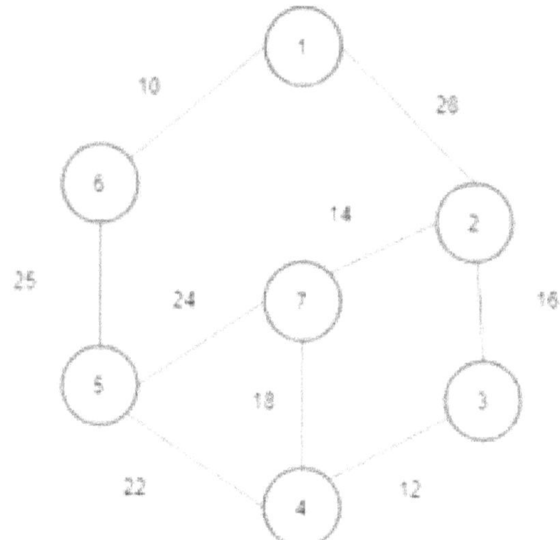

Its minimum cost spanning tree is __________.

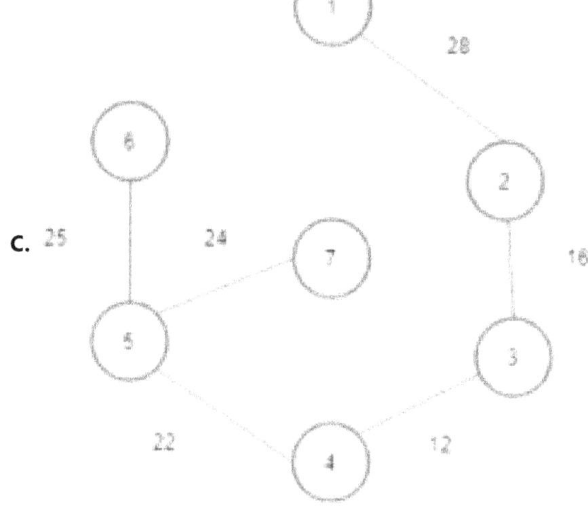

C.

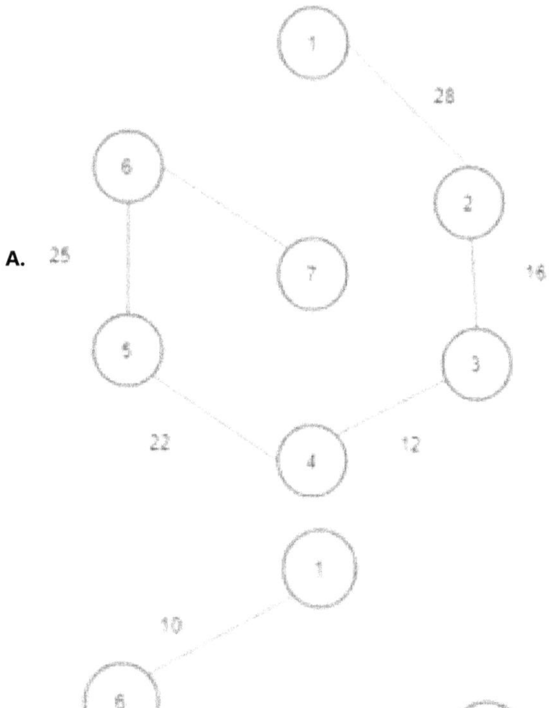

A.

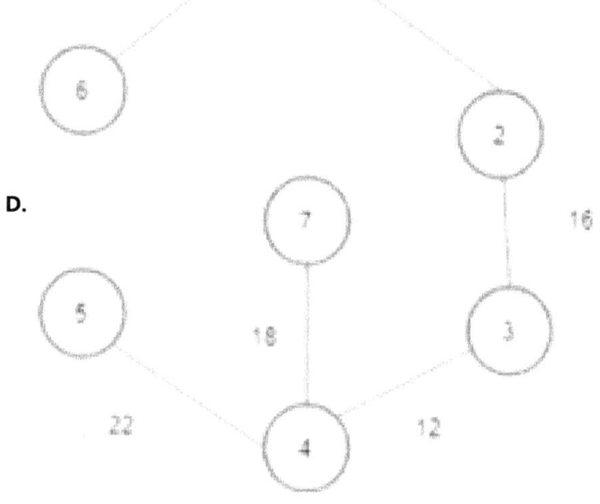

D.

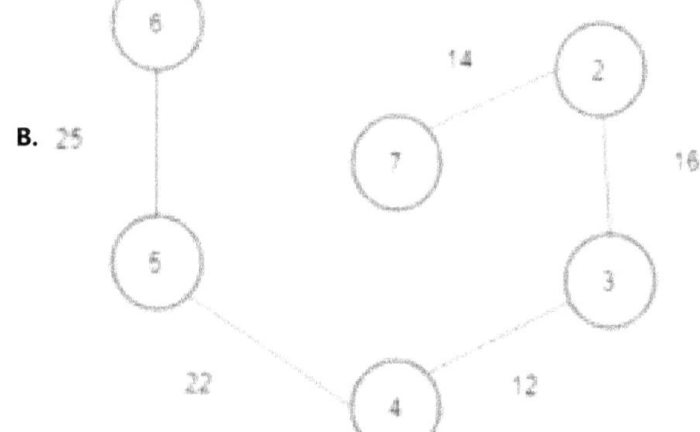

B.

Q.41 Which of the following statements is incorrect?

A. The grammar $S \rightarrow aS \ |aSbS| \ \epsilon$, where S is the only non-terminal symbol, and ϵ is the null string, is ambiguous.

B. An unambiguous grammar has same left most and right most derivation.

C. An ambiguous grammar can never be LR(k) for any k.

D. Recursive descent parser is a top-down parser.

Q.42 Consider the following binary search tree:

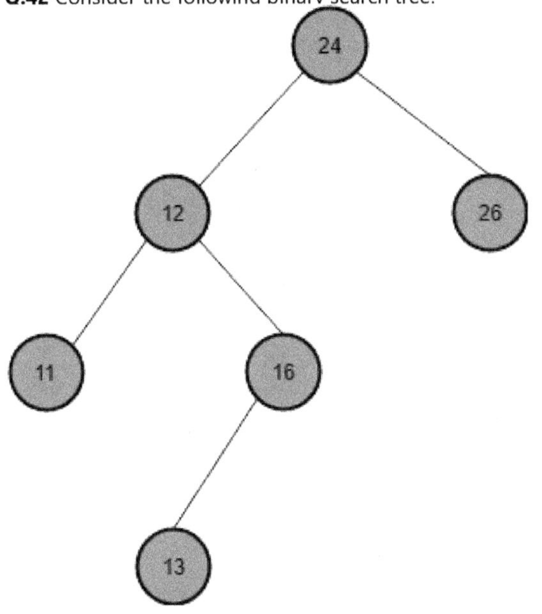

If we remove the root node, which of the nodes from the left subtree will be the new root?

A. 11   **B.** 12   **C.** 13   **D.** 16

Q.43 Consider a system which has 'n' number of processes and 'm' number of resource types. The time complexity of the safety algorithm, which checks whether a system is in safe state or not, is of the order of:

A. $O(mn)$ **B.** $O(m^2n^2)$ **C.** $O(m^2n)$ **D.** $O(mn^2)$

Q.44 In ______, the bodies of the two loops are merged together to form a single loop provided that they do not make any references to each other.

A. loop unrolling   **B.** strength reduction
C. loop concatenation   **D.** loop jamming

Q.45 Which of the following is not typically a benefit of dynamic linking?
I. Reduction in overall program execution time
II. Reduction in overall space consumption in memory
III. Reduction in overall space consumption on disk
IV. Reduction in the cost of software updates

A. I and IV   **B.** I only   **C.** II and III   **D.** IV only

Q.46 Implicit return type of a class constructor is

A. not of class type itself
B. class type itself
C. a destructor of class type
D. a destructor not of class type

Q.47 Suppose there are six files F1, F2, F3, F4, F5, F6 with corresponding sizes 150 KB, 225 KB, 75 KB, 60 KB, 275 KB and 65 KB respectively. The files are to be stored on a sequential device in such a way that optimizes access time. In what order should the files be stored ?

A. F5, F2, F1, F3, F6, F4
B. F4, F6, F3, F1, F2, F5
C. F1, F2, F3, F4, F5, F6

D. F6, F5, F4, F3, F2, F1

Q.48 The general configuration of the microprogrammed control unit is given below:

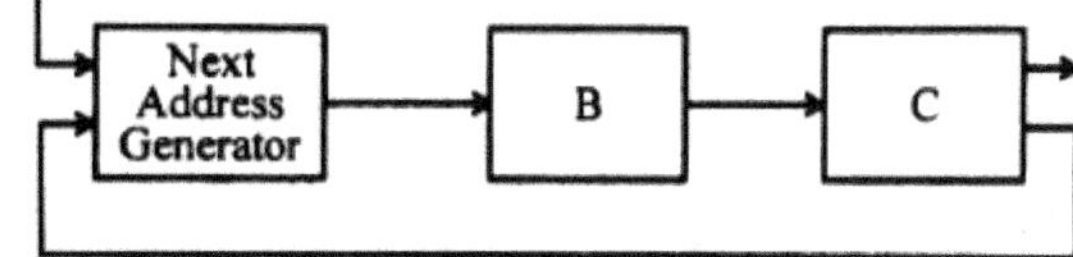

What are blocks B and C in the diagram, respectively?

A. Block address register and cache memory
B. Control address register and control memory
C. Branch register and cache memory
D. Control address register and random access memory

Q.49 Simplified Boolean equation for the following truth table is:

X	Y	Z	F
0	0	0	0
0	0	1	1
0	1	0	0
0	1	1	1
1	0	0	1
1	0	1	0
1	1	0	1
1	1	1	0

A. $F = yz' + y'z$ **B.** $F = xy' + x'y$
C. $F = x'z + xz'$ **D.** $F = x'z + xz' + xyz$

Q.50 Distributed operating systems consist of

A. loosely coupled OS software on a loosely coupled hardware
B. loosely coupled OS software on a tightly coupled hardware
C. Tightly coupled OS software on a loosely coupled hardware
D. Tightly coupled OS software on a tightly coupled hardware

Q.51 Consider the following program:

```
void main()
{
char S = "GRADEUPCS/IT";
printf ("%c", *(S+2));
printf ("%c", *(S+7));
}
```

What is the output of the above program:

A. RP   **B.** AC   **C.** RC   **D.** AP

Q.52 Suppose there are n stations in a slotted LAN. Each station attempts to transmit with a probability P in each time slot. The probability that only one station transmits in a given slot is ______.

A. $nP(1 - P)^{n-1}$ **B.** nP

C. $P(1 - P)^{n-1}$ **D.** $n^P(1 - P)^{n-1}$

Q.53 Which of the given operations can be performed over a Linked List-

1. Searching
2. Insertion
3. Sorting
4. Merging
5. Concatenation

A. only 1, 2, and 4   **B.** only 1,2,3 and 4

C. only 1,2,3 and 5   **D.** All of the given

Q.54 Match the following Layers and Protocols for a user browsing with SSL:

a. Application of layer	i. TCP
b. Transport layer	ii. IP
c. Network layer	iii. PPP
d. Datalink layer	iv. HTTP

A. a - iv, b - i, c - ii, d - iii

B. a - iii, b - ii, c - i, d - iv

C. a - ii, b - iii, c - iv, d - i

D. a - iii, b - i, c - iv, d - ii

Q.55 Which of the following statements are true?
(a) The fragmentation fields in the base header section of IPv4 have moved to the fragmentation extension header in IPv6.
(b) The authentication extension header is new in IPv6.
(c) The record route option is not implemented in IPv6.

A. (a) and (b)   **B.** (b) and (c)

C. (a) and (c)   **D.** (a), (b) and (c)

Q.56 Which of the following wireless technologies, used in IoT, consumes the least amount of power?

A. Zigbee   **B.** Bluetooth

C. Wi-Fi   **D.** GSM/CDMA

Q.57 If there are N people in the world and are using secret key encryption/decryption for privacy purpose, then the number of secret keys that will be required is:

A. n   **B.** (n - 1)   **C.** $\frac{n(n-1)}{2}$ **D.** $\frac{n(n+1)}{2}$

Q.58 Consider the following two commands C_1 and C_2 on the relation R from an SQL database:

C_1 : drop table R;

C_2 : delete from R;

Which of the following statements is true?

I. Both C_1 and C_2 delete the schema for R.

II. C_2 retains relation R, but deletes all tuples in R.

III. C_1 deletes not only all tuples of R, but also the schema for R.

A. I only   **B.** I and II

C. II and III   **D.** I, II and III

Q.59 Which of the following statements is true?

D_1: The decomposition of the schema R(A, B, C) into R_1(A, B) and R_2(A, C) is always lossless.

D_2: The decomposition of the schema R(A, B, C, D, E) having AD $\rightarrow$B, C $\rightarrow$DE, B $\rightarrow$AE and AE $\rightarrow$C, into R_1 (A, B, D) and R_2 (A, C, D, E) is lossless.

A. Both D_1 and D_2 **B.** Neither D_1 nor D_2

C. Only D_1 **D.** Only D_2

Q.60 In distributed databases, location transparency allows for database users, programmers and administrators to treat the data as if it is at one location. An SQL query with location transparency needs to specify

A. inheritances   **B.** fragments

C. locations   **D.** local formats

Q.61 Let P and Q be two propositions, $\neg(P \leftrightarrow Q)$ is equivalent to:

(I) $P \leftrightarrow Q$

(II) $\neg P \leftrightarrow Q$

(III) $\neg P \leftrightarrow \neg Q$

(IV) $Q \rightarrow P$

A. (I) and (II)   **B.** (II) and (III)

C. (III) and (IV)   **D.** None of the above

Q.62 The Boolean function with the Karnaugh map is:

CD \ AB	00	01	11	10
00	0	1	1	0
01	0	1	1	1
11	1	1	1	1
10	0	1	1	0

A. (A + C).D + B   **B.** (A + B).C + D

C. (A + D).C + B   **D.** (A + C).B + D

Q.63 Which of the following propositional logic formulas is true when exactly two of p, q and r are true?

A. $((p \rightarrow q) \wedge r) \vee (p \wedge q \wedge \sim r)$

B. $(\sim (p \rightarrow q) \wedge r) \vee (p \wedge q \wedge \sim r)$

C. $((p \rightarrow q) \wedge r) \vee (p \wedge q \wedge \sim r)$

D. $(\sim (p \rightarrow q) \wedge r) \wedge (p \wedge q \wedge \sim r)$

Q.64 An index register in a digital computer is used for

A. address modification

B. indirect addressing

C. storing one of the operands

D. pointing to the stack address

Q.65 To execute all loops at their boundaries and within their operational bounds, is an example of

A. black box testing

B. alpha testing

C. recovery testing

D. white box testing

Q.66 Given the following two statements:

S_1: If L_1 and L_2 are recursively enumerable languages over Σ, then $L_1 \cup L_2$ and $L_2 \cap L_2$ are also recursively enumerable.

S_2: The set of recursively enumerable languages is countable.

Which of the following statements is true?

A. S_1 is correct and S_2 is not correct.

B. S_1 is not correct and S_2 is correct.

C. Both S_1 and S_1 are not correct.

D. Both S_1 and S_2 are correct.

Q.67 Tthe following two languages are given:

$L_1 = \{a^n b a^n | n > 0\}$

$L_2 = \{a^n b \, a^n b^{n+1} | n > 0\}$

Which of the following statements is correct?

A. L_1 is context free language and L_2 is not context free language.

B. L_1 is not context free language and L_2 is context free language.

C. Both L_1 and L_2 are context free languages.

D. Both L_1 and L_2 are not context free languages.

Q.68 Consider the following grammar.

$$S \to Ax/By$$
$$A \to By/Cw$$
$$B \to x/Bw$$
$$C \to y$$

Which of the following expressions describes the same set of strings as the grammar?

A. xw*y + xw*yx + ywx

B. xwy + xw*xyx + ywx

C. xw*y + xwxyx + ywx

D. xwxy + xww*y + ywx

Q.69 The simplified form of a Boolean equation (AB' + AB'C + AC) (A'C' + B') is:

A. AB'   **B.** AB'C   **C.** A'B   **D.** ABC

Q.70 How does randomized hill-climbing choose the next move each time?

A. It generates a random move from the moveset, and accepts this move.

B. It generates a random move from the whole state space, and accepts this move.

C. It generates a random move from the moveset, and accepts this move only if this move improves the evaluation function.

D. It generates a random move from the whole state space, and accepts this move only if this move improves the evaluation function.

Q.71 Which of the following is not one of three software product aspects addressed by McCall's software quality factors?

A. Ability to undergo change

B. Adaptability to new environments

C. Operational characteristics

D. Production costs and scheduling

Q.72 Which of the following statement(s) is/are true with respect to software architecture?

S_1: Coupling is a measure of how well the things grouped together in a module belong together logically.

S_2: Cohesion is a measure of the degree of interaction between software modules.

S_3: If coupling is low and cohesion is high, then it is easier to change one module without affecting others.

A. S_1 and S_2

B. Only S_3

C. S_1, S_2 and S_3

D. Only S_1

Q.73 Which of the following statements is incorrect for Parallel Virtual Machine (PVM)?

A. The PVM communication model provides asynchronous blocking send, asynchronous blocking receive, and non-blocking receive function.

B. Message buffers are allocated dynamically.

C. The PVM communication model assumes that any task can send a message to any other PVM task and that there is no limit to the size or number of such messages.

D. In PVM model, the message order is not preserved.

Q.74 Given the following statements:

(A) To implement Abstract Data Type (ADT), a programming language require a syntactic unit to encapsulate type definition.

(B) To implement ADT, a programming language requires some primitive operations that are built in the language processor.

(C) C++, Ada, Java 5.0, C#2005 provide support for parameterised ADT.

Which of the following options is correct?

A. (A), (B) and (C) are false.

B. (A) and (B) are true; (C) is false.

C. (A) is true; (B) and (C) are false.

D. (A), (B) and (C) are true.

Q.75 Match the following:

List - I	List - II
(a) Intelligence	(i) Contextual, tacit, transfer needs learning
(b) Knowledge	(ii) Scattered facts, easily transferable
(c) Information	(iii) Judgmental
(d) Data	(iv) Codifiable, endorsed with relevance and purpose

	(a)	(b)	(c)	(d)
(1)	(iii)	(iv)	(i)	(ii)

(2)	(iii)	(iv)	(ii)	(i)
(3)	(iv)	(iii)	(i)	(ii)
(4)	(iv)	(iii)	(ii)	(i)

A. (1) **B.** (2) **C.** (3) **D.** (4)

Q.76 Which of the following HTML codes affects the vertical alignment of the table content?

A. <td style = 'vertical-align : middle'>Text Here</td>

B. <td valign = 'centre'>Text Here</td>

C. <td style = 'text-align : centre'>Text Here</td>

D. <td align = 'middle'>Text Here</td>

Q.77 The number of strings of length 4 that are generated by the regular expression $(0|\in)1+2*(3|\in)$, where | is an alternation character, {+, *} are quantification characters, and $\in$ is the null string, is:

A. 08 **B.** 10 **C.** 11 **D.** 12

Q.78 Consider the following operations performed on a stack of size 5:
Push(a); Pop(); Push(b); Push(c); Pop();
Push(d); Pop(); Pop(); Push(e);
Which of the following statements is correct?

A. Underflow occurs

B. Stack operations performed smoothly

C. Overflow occurs

D. None of the above

Q.79 Which of the following is not an inherent application of stack?

A. Implementation of recursion

B. Evaluation of a postfix expression

C. Job scheduling

D. Reverse a string

Q.80 It is possible to define a class within a class termed as nested class. There are _____ types of nested classes.

A. 2 **B.** 3 **C.** 4 **D.** 5

Q.81 Which of the following statements is correct?
(1) Every class containing abstract method must not be declared abstract.
(2) Abstract class cannot be directly initiated with 'new' operator.
(3) Abstract class cannot be initiated.
(4) Abstract class contains definition of implementation.

A. (1) **B.** (2)

C. (2) and (3) **D.** All of the above

Q.82 Two atomic operations permissible on semaphores are ________ and ________.

A. wait, stop **B.** wait, hold

C. hold, signal **D.** wait, signal

Q.83 Which of the following represents one of the disadvantages of user level threads compared to Kernel level threads?

A. If a user level thread of a process executes a system call, all threads in that process are blocked.

B. Scheduling is application dependent.

C. Thread switching doesn't require kernel mode privileges.

D. The library procedures invoked for thread management in user level threads are local procedures.

Q.84 The maximum size of the data that the application layer can pass on to the TCP layer below is ___.

A. 2^{16} bytes

B. 2^{16} bytes + TCP header length

C. 2^{16} bytes - TCP header length

D. 2^{15} bytes

Q.85 Which of the following routing techniques is/are used in distributed systems?
(a) Fixed Routing
(b) Virtual Routing
(c) Dynamic Routing

A. (a) only **B.** (a) and (b)

C. (c) only **D.** (a), (b) and (c)

Q.86 Consider the following database table having A, B, C and D as its four attributes and four possible candidate keys (I, II, III and IV) for this table:

A	B	C	D
a1	b1	c1	d1
a2	b3	c3	d1
a1	b2	c1	d2

I : (B)
II : (B, C)
III : (A, D)
IV : (C, D)
If different symbols stand for different values in the table (e.g., d_1 is definitely not equal to d_2), then which of the above could not be the candidate key for the database table?

A. I and III only **B.** III and IV only

C. II only **D.** I only

Q.87 Consider the following ORACLE relations:
R (A, B, C) = {<1, 2, 3>, <1, 2, 0>, <1, 3, 1>, <6, 2, 3>, <1, 4, 2>, <3, 1, 4>}
S (B, C, D) = {<2, 3, 7>, <1, 4, 5>, <1, 2, 3>, <2, 3, 4>, <3, 1, 4>}
Consider the following two SQL queries SQ_1 and SQ_2:
SQ_1: SELECT R·B, AVG (S·B)
FROM R, S
WHERE R·A = S·C AND S·D < 7 GROUP BY R·B;
SQ_2: SELECT DISTINCT S·B, MIN (S·C)
FROM S
GROUP BY S·B
HAVING COUNT (DISTINCT S·D) > 1;

If M is the number of tuples returned by SQ_1 and N is the number of tuples returned by SQ_2, then

A. M = 4, N = 2
B. M = 5, N = 3
C. M = 2, N = 2
D. M = 3, N = 3

Q.88 Semi-join strategies are techniques for query processing in distributed database system.
Which of the following is a semi-join technique?

A. Only the joining attributes are sent from one site to another and then all of the rows are returned.

B. All of the attributes are sent from one site to another and then only the required rows are returned.

C. Only the joining attributes are sent from one site to another and then only the required rows are returned.

D. All of the above

Q.89 Let P, Q, R and S be propositions.

Assume that the equivalences $P \Leftrightarrow (Q \vee \neg Q)$ and $Q \Leftrightarrow R$ hold.

Then, the truth value of the formula $(P \wedge Q) \Rightarrow ((P \wedge R) \vee S)$ is always

A. true
B. false
C. same as truth table of Q
D. same as truth table of S

Q.90 The output of the following combinational circuit is F.

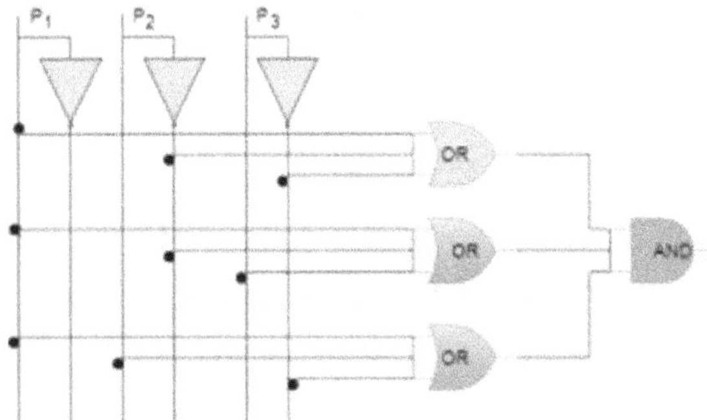

The value of F is:

A. $P_1 + P'_2 P_3$
B. $P_1 + P'_2 P'_3$
C. $P_1 + P_2 P'_3$
D. $P'_1 + P_2 P_3$

Q.91 Consider the two class classification task that consists of the following points:
Class C_1: [-1, -1], [-1, 1], [1, -1]
Class C_2: [1,1]
The decision boundary between the two classes C_1 and C_2 using single perception is given by:

A. $x_1 - x_2 - 0.5 = 0$
B. $-x_1 + x_2 - 0.5 = 0$
C. $0.5(x_1 + x_2) - 1.5 = 0$
D. $x_1 + x_2 - 0.5 = 0$

Q.92 An unsorted array is given. The array has this property that every element in array is at most k distance from its position in sorted array where k is a positive integer smaller than size of array. Which sorting algorithm can be easily modified for sorting this array and what is the obtainable time complexity?

A. Insertion sort with time complexity O(kn)
B. Heap sort with time complexity O(n Log k)
C. Quick sort with time complexity O(k Log k)
D. Merge sort with time complexity O(k Log k)

Q.93 Consider the following two statements:
S_1: { 0^{2n} | n >= l} is a regular language.
S_2: { $0^m\ 0^n\ 0^{(m + n)}$ | m >= 1 and n >= 2} is a regular language.
Which of the following statements is correct?

A. Only S_1 is correct.
B. Only S_2 is correct.
C. Both S_1 and S_2 are correct.
D. Neither S_1 nor S_2 is correct.

Q.94 The prototyping model of software development is

A. a reasonable approach when requirements are well-defined

B. a useful approach when a customer cannot define requirements clearly

C. the best approach to use for projects with large development teams

D. a risky model that rarely produces a meaningful product

Q.95 A company maintains records of sales made by its salespersons and pays them commission based on each individual's total sales made in a year. This data is maintained in a table with following schema:
salesinfo = (salespersonid, totalsales, commission)
In a certain year, due to better business results, the company decides to further reward its salespersons by enhancing the commission paid to them as per the following formula:
If commission < = 50000, enhance it by 2%
If 50000 < commission < = 100000, enhance it by 4%
If commission > 100000, enhance it by 6%
The IT staff has written three different SQL scripts to calculate enhancement for each slab, each of these scripts is to run as a separate transaction as follows:
T1
Update salesinfo
Set commission = commission * 1.02
Where commission < = 50000;
T2
Update salesinfo
Set commission = commission * 1.04
Where commission > 50000 and commission is < = 100000;
T3
Update salesinfo
Set commission = commission * 1.06
Where commission > 100000;

Which of the following options of running these transactions will update the commission of all salespersons correctly?

A. Execute T1, followed by T2, followed by T3
B. Execute T2, followed by T3; T1 running concurrently throughout
C. Execute T3 followed by T2; T1 running concurrently throughout

D. Execute T3, followed by T2, followed by T1

Q.96 The symmetric difference of two sets S_1 and S_2 is defined as:

$S_1 \ominus S_2$ = {x|x $\in S_1$ or x $\in S_2$, but x is not in both S_1 and S_2}

The nor of two languages is defined as:

nor (L_1, L_2) = {w|w | $\in L_1$ and w | $\in L_1$}.

Which of the following is correct?

A. The family of regular languages is closed under symmetric difference but not closed under nor.

B. The family of regular languages is closed under nor but not closed under symmetric difference.

C. The family of regular languages are closed under both symmetric difference and nor.

D. The family of regular languages are not closed under both symmetric difference and nor.

Q.97 Which of the following is not true about comparison based sorting algorithms?

A. The minimum possible time complexity of a comparison based sorting algorithm is O(n log n) for a random input array.

B. Any comparison based sorting algorithm can be made stable by using position as a criteria when two elements are compared.

C. Counting sort is not a comparison based sorting algorithm.

D. Heap sort is not a comparison based sorting algorithm.

Q.98 Which of the following is correct?

A. Java applets can not be written in any programming language.

B. An applet is not a small program.

C. An applet can run on its own.

D. Applets are embedded in another applications.

Q.99 Consider the following relation:

Works (emp_name, company_name, salary)

Here, emp_name is primary key.

Consider the following SQL query:

```
Select emp_name
From Works T
where salary>(select avg (salary)
        from Works S
        where T.company_name=
        S. Company_name)
```

The above query is for-

A. finding the highest paid employee who earns more than the average salary of all employees of his company

B. finding the highest paid employee who earns more than the average salary of all the employees of all the companies

C. finding all employees who earn more than the average salary of all employees of all the companies

D. finding all employees who earn more than the average salary of all employees of their company

Q.100 'If X, then Y unless Z' is represented by which of the following formulas in propositional logic?

A. $(x \wedge y) \to \neg z$

B. $(x \wedge \neg z) \to Y$

C. $x \to (Y \wedge \neg Z)$

D. $Y \to (X \wedge \neg Z)$

// Smart Answer Sheet //

Correct — Percentage of students who answered correctly. **Skipped** — Percentage of students who skipped.

Q.	Ans.	Correct / Skipped
1	D	39.47 % / 14.48 %
2	B	42.11 % / 38.15 %
3	C	31.58 % / 43.42 %
4	C	27.63 % / 43.42 %
5	D	32.89 % / 40.79 %
6	A	26.32 % / 40.79 %
7	D	34.21 % / 43.42 %
8	C	26.32 % / 43.42 %
9	D	34.21 % / 40.79 %
10	B	43.42 % / 43.42 %
11	A	38.16 % / 38.16 %
12	B	28.95 % / 43.42 %
13	B	36.84 % / 43.42 %
14	A	27.63 % / 48.69 %
15	C	26.32 % / 44.73 %
16	D	30.26 % / 46.06 %
17	A	32.89 % / 43.43 %
18	A	34.21 % / 44.74 %
19	B	36.84 % / 44.74 %
20	D	19.74 % / 38.15 %
21	D	36.84 % / 47.37 %
22	C	28.95 % / 40.79 %
23	B	27.63 % / 43.42 %
24	A	31.58 % / 44.74 %
25	D	25.0 % / 48.68 %
26	B	31.58 % / 50.0 %
27	D	34.21 % / 44.74 %
28	D	22.37 % / 40.79 %
29	D	23.68 % / 46.06 %
30	A	25.0 % / 43.42 %
31	D	25.0 % / 36.84 %
32	B	26.32 % / 44.73 %
33	C	43.42 % / 44.74 %
34	C	23.68 % / 42.11 %
35	B	30.26 % / 42.11 %
36	A	34.21 % / 42.11 %
37	C	34.21 % / 46.05 %
38	C	27.63 % / 48.69 %
39	B	39.47 % / 44.74 %
40	B	42.11 % / 47.36 %
41	B	34.21 % / 39.47 %
42	D	38.16 % / 44.73 %
43	D	23.68 % / 42.11 %
44	D	30.26 % / 44.74 %
45	B	17.11 % / 42.1 %
46	B	43.42 % / 46.05 %
47	B	44.74 % / 47.37 %
48	B	27.63 % / 44.74 %
49	C	26.32 % / 46.05 %
50	C	34.21 % / 44.74 %
51	B	28.95 % / 46.05 %
52	A	30.26 % / 46.06 %
53	D	36.84 % / 43.42 %
54	A	44.74 % / 46.05 %
55	D	34.21 % / 46.05 %
56	B	35.53 % / 46.05 %
57	C	44.74 % / 46.05 %
58	C	35.53 % / 44.73 %
59	D	21.05 % / 42.11 %
60	B	35.53 % / 44.73 %
61	A	17.11 % / 47.36 %
62	A	30.26 % / 48.69 %
63	B	21.05 % / 44.74 %
64	A	19.74 % / 46.05 %
65	D	27.63 % / 44.74 %
66	D	32.89 % / 47.37 %
67	A	32.89 % / 44.74 %
68	C	28.95 % / 48.68 %
69	A	26.32 % / 35.52 %
70	C	38.16 % / 43.42 %
71	D	31.58 % / 42.1 %
72	B	26.32 % / 46.05 %
73	D	19.74 % / 44.73 %
74	D	35.53 % / 44.73 %
75	B	25.0 % / 43.42 %
76	A	34.21 % / 46.05 %
77	D	21.05 % / 42.11 %
78	B	46.05 % / 44.74 %
79	C	40.79 % / 44.74 %
80	A	34.21 % / 46.05 %

Q.	Ans.	Correct / Skipped	Q.	Ans.	Correct / Skipped	Q.	Ans.	Correct / Skipped	Q.	Ans.	Correct / Skipped	Q.	Ans.	Correct / Skipped
81	C	30.26 % / 46.06 %	85	A	18.42 % / 43.42 %	89	A	27.63 % / 50.0 %	93	C	30.26 % / 46.06 %	97	D	23.68 % / 42.11 %
82	D	35.53 % / 40.79 %	86	C	23.68 % / 48.69 %	90	B	38.16 % / 47.37 %	94	B	38.16 % / 43.42 %	98	D	30.26 % / 44.74 %
83	A	28.95 % / 44.73 %	87	A	23.68 % / 50.0 %	91	D	21.05 % / 44.74 %	95	D	19.74 % / 44.73 %	99	D	26.32 % / 44.73 %
84	A	23.68 % / 46.06 %	88	C	25.0 % / 39.47 %	92	B	38.16 % / 46.05 %	96	C	34.21 % / 46.05 %	100	B	25.0 % / 43.42 %

//Hints and Solutions//

1. An abelian group, also called a commutative group, is a group in which the result of applying the group operation to two group elements does not depend on the order in which they are written. Since the group is given, so all the other properties are inclusive. So, option (D) is correct.

2. $\dfrac{1}{1+\left(\frac{x-c}{a}\right)^{2b}}$ is the bell-shaped membership function by three parameters (a, b, c).
So, option (B) is correct.

3. Possible strings of length 4 are:
0001, 0111, 0011, 0101, 0123, 2323, 2333, 2223, 2233, 2301
Total 10 strings are possible.
So, option (C) is correct.

4. h(k) = floor(m(kA mod 1))

M = 100; k = 123456

h(k) = floor(100(123456 ✕ 0.618033 mod 1))

h(k) = floor(100(76189.882048 mod 1))

h(k) = floor(100 ✕ 0.882048)

h(k) = floor(88.2048)

h(k) = 88

So, option (C) is correct.

5. f(n) ≤ f(n) x g(n) and g(n) ≤ f(n) x g(n)

Hence, max(f(n), g(n)) ∈ O(f(n) x g(n))

If f(n) or g(n) = 0, then f(n) x g(n) ≤ max (f(n), g(n))

Hence, max(f(n), g(n)) ∈ Ω (f(n) x g(n))

So, max (f(n), g(n)) ∈ Θ (f(n) x g(n))

f(n) ≤ f(n) + g(n) and g(n) ≤ f(n) + g(n)

Hence, max (f(n), g(n)) ∈ O(f(n) + g(n))

f(n) + g(n) ≤ 2 x max (f(n), g(n))

Hence, max (f(n), g(n)) ∈ Ω (f(n) + g(n))

Hence, we get that max(f(n), g(n)) ∈ Θ(f(n) + g(n))

Hence the correct answer is option (D).

6. We have the function:

int f (int n)

{ if (n = = 0) then return n;

else

return n + f(n - 2);

}

We have to find output for n = 100, i.e.

<>int f(100)

{ if (n = = 0) then return n; //failure//

else

return 100 + f(98)

{ if (n = = 0) then return n; //failure//

else

return 98 + f(96)

{ if (n = = 0) then return n; //failure//

else

return 96 + f(94).......................f(0); // It will be an AP series of 100, 98, 96, ..., 0//;

};

};

}

Sum of series when we know first and last term and number of terms:

$$S_n = \frac{n}{2} \times (\text{first term} + \text{last term})$$
$$= \frac{51}{2} \times (100 + 0)$$
$$= 51 \times 50$$
$$= 2550$$

Hence the correct answer is option (A).

7.

- When a method in a subclass has the same name and type signatures as a method in the superclass, then the method in the subclass overrides the method in the superclass.

- **Overloading** allows different methods to have same name, but different signatures where signature can differ by number of input parameters or type of input parameters or both. Overloading is related to compile time (or static) polymorphism..

- A friend class can access private and protected members of other class in which it is declared as friend.

- The capability of a class to derive properties and characteristics from another class is called inheritance.

So, option (D) is correct.

8. Objects in an object-oriented database contain not only data but also methods for processing the data. (Correct)

Object-oriented databases store computational instructions in the same place as data. (Correct)

Object-oriented databases are more adept at handling structured (analytical) data than relational databases. (Incorrect)

Object-oriented databases store more types of data than relational databases and access that data faster. (Correct)
So, option (C) is the correct answer.

9. • **C-SCAN:** In C-SCAN disk scheduling algorithm, the disk head serves the request from one end to other end but when it reaches to other end, it immediately returns to the starting of the disk without serving any request.

● **SCAN:** In SCAN algorithm, the disk arm moves into a particular direction and services the requests coming in its path and after reaching the end of disk, it reverses its direction and again services the request arriving in its path.

● **LOOK:** It is similar to the SCAN disk scheduling algorithm except the difference that the disk arm in spite of going to the end of the disk goes only to the last request to be serviced in front of the head and then reverses its direction from there only.

● **C-LOOK:** C-LOOK is similar to C-SCAN disk scheduling algorithm. In C-LOOK, the disk arm inspite of going to the end goes only to the last request to be serviced in front of the head and then from there goes to the other end's last request.
So option (D) is correct.

10. We can write large programs when we have memory extension.
There is less I/O requirement in case of virtual memory.
More addressable memory is available with virtual memory
Faster and easy swapping of processes with the help of page replacement policy is possible in virtual memory.
So, option (B) is correct.

11. First we will make Gantt chart of the given process, then we will calculate turn around time and waiting time of individual process.

P1	P2	P4	P1	P3
0	1	5	10	17	26

Process id	CT	TAT	WT
P1	17	16	9
P2	5	4	0
P3	26	24	15
P4	10	7	2

Now, we have to calculate average waiting time for the schedule:

Average waiting time = wt(P_1 + P_2 + P_3 + P_4)/number of processes

Or, $\dfrac{9+0+15+2}{4}$

$= \dfrac{26}{4}$

$= 6.5$ milliseconds
So, option (A) is correct.

12. A scheduling algorithm assigns priority proportional to the waiting time of a process. Every process starts with priority zero (lowest priority). The scheduler reevaluates the process priority for every 'T' time units and decides next process to be scheduled. If the process have no I/O operations and all arrive at time zero, then the scheduler implements **Round Robin Scheduling** criteria.
Round Robin is a CPU scheduling algorithm where each process is assigned a fixed time slot in a cyclic way.
● A fixed time is allotted to each process, called quantum, for execution.

● Once a process is executed for given time period that process is preempted and other process executes for given time period.
● Context switching is used to save states of preempted processes.
So, option (B) is correct.

13. By command $ vi file1 file2: //vi two (or more) files at the same time
Both files, i.e. file1 and file2 can be edited using 'ex' command to travel between the files. //ex commands enable you to switch between multiple files.
So, option (B) is correct.

14. Round trip propagation delay $= 40ms$

Frame size $= 32 \times 8$ bits

Bottleneck bandwidth $= 64$ kbps

Total data $= 40ms \times 64kbps$

i.e. (40×64) bits

$= \dfrac{40 \times 64}{8}$ bytes

$= 320$ bytes

Packet size is 32 bytes.

Number of packets $= \dfrac{\text{Total Data}}{\text{Packet Size}}$

$= \dfrac{320B}{32B}$

$= 10$ packets
So, option (A) is correct.

15. 1. Degeneracy does not occur in transportation problem when the values of dual variables u_i and v_j cannot be computed.
2. Degeneracy does not occur in transportation problem when the number of positive allocation is exactly m + n - 1.
3. Degeneracy occurs when obtaining an initial solution, we may have less than m + n - 1 allocations.
4. At any stage while moving towards optimal solution, when two or more occupied cells with the same minimum allocation become unoccupied simultaneously, then degeneracy will occur.
So, option (C) is correct.

16. In UNIX operating system:
● INT signal is sent by the terminal driver when one types and it is a request to terminate the current operation. (Correct)
● TERM is a request to terminate execution completely. The receiving process will clean up its state and exit. (Correct)
● QUIT is similar to TERM, except that it defaults to producing a core dump if not caught. (Correct)
● KILL is not a blockable signal. (Incorrect)
So, option (D) is correct.

17. Maximum number of subnets = 2^6 - 2 = 62
Note that 2 is subtracted from 2^6. The RFC 950 specification reserves the subnet values consisting of all zeros (see above) and all ones (broadcast), reducing the number of available subnets by two.
Maximum number of hosts = 2^{10} - 2 = 1022
So, option (A) is correct.

18. The IP address 0.0.0.0 is usually being booted and is mainly used by the host.
The IP address is the identity of any computer like the IMEI

number in mobile phones.
Every software detects the IP address and it is done by a detection method.
A boot is the system of computing device that software can easily use.
So, option (A) is the correct answer.

19. POP3 is post office protocol Version 3. POP is a protocol which listens on port 110 and is responsible for accessing the mail service on a client machine. POP3 works in two modes such as Delete Mode and Keep Mode.

IMAP is Internet Messaged Access Protocol which is used by email server to maintain a central repository that can be accessed from any machine.

SMTP is simple mail transfer protocol.

DMSP is distributed mail service protocol.
So, option (B) is correct.

20. Views in a database system are important because they help with access control by allowing users to see only a particular subset of the data in the database. (Correct)

E-R diagrams are useful to logically model concepts. (Incorrect)

An update anomaly is when it is not possible to store information unless some other, unrelated information is stored as well. (Incorrect)

SQL is a procedural language. (Incorrect)
So, option (D) is correct.

21. Strong entities E_1 and E_2 are represented as separate tables. In addition to that many-to-many relationships(R_2) must be converted as separate table by having primary keys of E_1 and E_2 as foreign keys.
One-to-many relationship (R_1) must be transferred to 'many' side table (i.e. E_2) by having primary key of one side (E_1) as foreign key (this way we need not make a separate table for R_1).
Let relation schema be $E_1(a_1, a_2)$ and $E_2(b_1, b_2)$.
So, option (D) is correct.

22. In RDBMS, the constraint that no key attribute (column) may be NULL is referred to as entity integrity.

Referential integrity states that table relationships must always be consistent.

Multi-valued dependency is a full constraint between two sets of attributes in a relation.

Functional dependency is a relationship that exists when one attribute uniquely determines another attribute.
So, option (C) is correct.

23. The first order logic (FOL) statement $R \vee Q \wedge (P \vee \neg Q$ is $PR + \neg QR + PQ$ is equivalent to:
Option 1-
$R \vee \neg Q \wedge P \vee \neg Q \wedge (R \vee P$ is $(R + \neg Q)(P + \neg Q)(R + P)$, i.e.
$RP + R\neg Q + P\neg Q$ is not equivalent to $PR + \neg QR + PQ$
Option 2-

$R \vee Q \wedge (P \vee \neg Q) \wedge (R \vee P$ is $(R + Q)(P + \neg Q)(P + R)$,
ie. $PR + \neg QR + PQ$ is exactly same.
Option 3-
$R \vee Q \wedge (P \vee \neg Q) \wedge (R \vee \neg P$ is $(R + Q)(P + \neg Q)(R + \neg P)$, i.e.
$PR + \neg QR + R(P \to Q)$ is not equivalent to $PR + \neg QR + PQ$
Option 4-
$R \vee Q \wedge (P \vee \neg Q) \wedge (\neg R \vee P$ is $(R + Q)(P + \neg Q)(\neg R + P)$, i.e.
$PR + PQ + P(Q \to R)$ is not equivalent to $PR + \neg QR + PQ$
So, option (B) is correct.

24. Here we have to follow two basics:
1. Matrix multiplication rule- For multiplication of two matrices, column in first matrix must be equal to rows in second matrix.
2. We have to find Boolean product of two matrices, so we must know Boolean product, i.e.

A	B	F
0	0	0
0	1	0
1	0	0
1	1	1

No we have $A = \begin{bmatrix} 1 & 1 & 0 \\ 0 & 1 & 0 \\ 1 & 1 & 0 \\ 0 & 0 & 1 \end{bmatrix}$

And, $B = \begin{bmatrix} 1 & 0 & 0 & 0 \\ 0 & 1 & 1 & 0 \\ 1 & 0 & 1 & 1 \end{bmatrix}$

Now, the product AB

$$\begin{bmatrix} 1\cdot1+1\cdot & 1\cdot0+1\cdot & 1\cdot0+1\cdot & 1\cdot0+1\cdot \\ 0+0\cdot1 & 1+0\cdot0 & 1+0\cdot1 & 0+0\cdot1 \\ 0\cdot1+1\cdot & 0\cdot0+1\cdot & 0\cdot0+1\cdot & 0\cdot0+1\cdot \\ 0+0\cdot1 & 1+0\cdot0 & 1+0\cdot1 & 0+0\cdot1 \\ 1\cdot1+1\cdot & 1\cdot0+1\cdot & 1\cdot0+1\cdot & 1\cdot0+1\cdot \\ 0+0\cdot1 & 1+0\cdot0 & 1+0\cdot1 & 0+0\cdot1 \\ 0\cdot1+0\cdot & 0\cdot0+0\cdot & 0\cdot0+0\cdot & 0\cdot0+0\cdot \\ 0+1\cdot1 & 1+1\cdot0 & 1+1\cdot1 & 0+1\cdot1 \end{bmatrix}$$

$$AB = \begin{bmatrix} 1 & 1 & 1 & 0 \\ 0 & 1 & 1 & 0 \\ 1 & 1 & 1 & 0 \\ 1 & 0 & 1 & 1 \end{bmatrix}$$

So, option (A) is correct.

25. $f'(s) = \cos x = 0$ gives roots $\dfrac{\pi}{2}$ and $\dfrac{3\pi}{2}$ which lie between the domain given in the question, i.e. $\left[\dfrac{\pi}{4}, \dfrac{7\pi}{4}\right]$

$f''(x) = -(\sin x)$ at $\dfrac{\pi}{2}$; It gives $-1 < 0.$ It means that it is local maxima and at $\dfrac{3\pi}{2}$, it gives $1 > 0,$ which is local minima.

since at $\dfrac{\pi}{2}$ it is local maxima, so, before it, graph is strictly increasing. Thus, $\dfrac{\pi}{4}$ is also local minima.

Therefore, there are two local minima $\dfrac{\pi}{4}$ and $\dfrac{3\pi}{2}$

Hence the correct answer is option (D).

26. The clock cycles are per block; if an instruction size is 2, then it requires twice the number of clock cycles.

Instruction number	Size	Number of clock cycles
1	2	3 x 1 + 2 x 2
2	1	1 x 3 + 2
3	1(add only)	2 + 3
4	2	3 x 1 + 2 x 2
5	1	2(Fetch and Decode)
	Total	24

So, option (B) is correct.

27. The loader transfers the executable image of a C++ program from hard disk to main memory.
Debugger is a computer program that is used to test and debug other programs (target program).
Compiler is a software which converts a program written in high level language (source language) to low level language (object/target/machine language).

Linker takes object files, links them with each other and with any library files that you specify, and produces an executable output file.
So, option (D) is correct.

28. For n + m to be even, n and m should be even or n and m should be odd.

$S \rightarrow S_1 \mid S_2$

$S_1 \rightarrow aaS_1 \mid A_1$ (As A_1 derives even number of b's, so without any problem, S_1 derives even number of a's.)

$S_2 \rightarrow aaS_2 \mid aA_2$ (As A_2 derives odd number of b's, so aA_2 will have even number of a's and b's.)

$A_1 \rightarrow bbA_1 \mid \lambda$ (This derives even number of b's.)

$A_2 \rightarrow bbA_2 \mid \lambda$ (This derives odd number of b's.)

Hence the correct answer is option (D).

29. Let x be the number of states and y be the number of symbols.
So, x = 3 and y = 2
Number of different automata = $2^x \times x^{xy} = 2^3 \times 3^{3 \times 2}$
= $2^3 \times 3^6$
= 5832
Option (D) is correct.

30. In Standard Implementation of Circular Queue,

For enqueue, we increment the REAR pointer and then insert an element.

For dequeue, we increment the FRONT and then remove the element at that position.

For empty check, when FRONT == REAR, we declare queue as empty.

Initially the Queue is empty, so FRONT and REAR point to same index

Increment the REAR and insert at that position - 1st Element inserted

Increment the REAR and insert at that position - 2nd Element inserted

Continue in this manner and insert 9th element

Hence the correct answer is option (A).

31. The IEEE-754 double-precision format to represent floating point numbers, has a length of 64 bits.
1 bit is for sign, 11 bit is for exponent and rest 52 is for fraction.
So, option (D) is correct.

32. A characteristic of an Management Information System (MIS) is that it draws on diverse yet predictable data resources to aggregate and summarize data.
Other characteristics of MIS are as follows:
- Management-oriented
- Management-directed integrated
- Common data flows
- Heavy planning-element
- Sub-system concept
- Common database
- User friendly/Flexibility
- Information as a resource
- Provides guidance in identifying problems, finding and evaluating alternative solutions, and selecting or comparing alternatives (these are characteristics of decision support system (DSS))
- High volume, data capture focus, efficiency of data movement, processing and interfacing different TPS (these are the characteristics of transaction processing system (TPS))
So, option (B) is correct.

33. A software program that infers and manipulates existing knowledge in order to generate new knowledge is known as inference engine.

A data dictionary is a collection of descriptions of the data objects or items in a data model for the benefit of programmers and others who need to refer to them.

Control strategies are specific action plans for bringing a process back into control.

Reference is what relates words to the world of objects on whose condition the truth of sentences hinges and it is natural to wonder what sorts of relations underlie the reference relation-to wonder, i.e. what constitutes the mechanism of reference.
So, option (C) is correct.

34. Software engineering is an engineering discipline that is concerned with all aspects of software production. Software engineering is an engineering branch associated with development of software product using well-defined scientific principles, methods and procedures. The outcome of software engineering is an efficient and reliable software product.
Option (C) is correct.

35. The spanning tree algorithm is used for bridge-routing to avoid loops in the routing paths.

Hence the correct answer is option (B).

36. first fuzzication then some rule(inference) then based on these rules defuzzication(conversion into crispy set) is performed.

Hence the correct answer is option (A).

37. Purcahsing a line will not yield better reliability or flexibiliy than leased one.

Hence the correct answer is option (C).

38. If the base type of an array is int, it is referred to as an "array of ints." An array with base type String is referred to as an "array of Strings." However, an array is not, properly speaking, a list of integers or strings or other values.

Hence the correct answer is option (C).

39. we have to select 10 bits and with every bit we have two choice either 0 or 1 so the total no of 10 length bit strings are 2^{10}

now in palindrome if we chose first 5 bits then our job is done as next 5 are fixed (first 5 in reverse order)

0 or 1 0 or 1 0 or 1 0 or1 0 or 1 fixed fixed fixed fixed fixed

So, for five bits can be chosen in 25 (for every bit either 0 or 1).

Probability = $2^5/2^{10}$ = $1/2^5$ = 1/ 32

Hence the correct answer is option (B).

40. The minimum cost tree is:

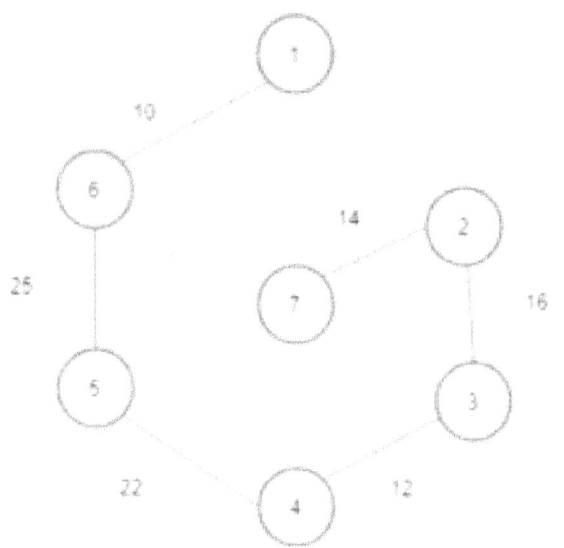

Hence the correct answer is option (B).

41. An unambiguous grammar has same left most and right most derivation.

Hence the correct answer is option (B).

42. In computer science, binary search trees, sometimes called ordered or sorted binary trees, are a particular type of container: data structures that store "items" in memory.

Hence the correct answer is option (D).

43. The below part introduces (n $^*m$) time complexity

for $I = 1$ to N do $//* n$ times

if $($ (not FINISH[i]) and

NEED i $<=$ WORK) then // $^*m$ times, if it's an array search but it is also nested in a repeat loop. If that loop can run, in worst case, n times, then the procedure has $O(n^*n^*m)$ time complexity.

WORK = WORK + ALLOCATION_i; / / also O(m) Operation, vectors addition

So, the code that executes in the for loop has $O(m + m)$ time complexity.

Of course, $O(m + m) = O(m)$ and the final complexity is $O(n^*n^*m)$

Hence the correct answer is option (D).

44. Let us examine each option:

A) Loop unrolling: The number of jumps can be reduced by replicating the body of the loop if the number of iterations is found to be constant (that is, the number of iterations is known at compile time).

If body of loop is big, unrolling is not favorable.

B) Strength reduction: Replacing an expensive operation with an equivalent cheaper operation is called strength reduction. For example, the * operator can be replaced by a lower strength operator +.

In computer science, loop fusion (or loop jamming) is a compiler optimization and loop transformation which replaces multiple loops with a single one. It is possible when two loops iterate over the same range and do not reference each other's data.

Loop fusion does not always improve run-time speed. On some architectures, two loops may actually perform better than one loop because, for example, there is increased data locality within each loop. In these cases, a single loop may be transformed into two, which is called loop fission.

Hence the correct answer is option (D).

45. In computing, a dynamic linker is the part of an operating system that loads and links the shared libraries needed by an executable when it is executed (at "run time"), by copying the content of libraries from persistent storage to RAM, and filling jump tables and relocating pointers.

Hence the correct answer is option (B).

46. The implicit return type of a class' constructor is the class type itself. It is the constructor's job to initialise the internal state of an object so that the code creating an instance will have a fully initialised, usable object immediately.

Hence the correct answer is option (B).

47. For access time optimization sort the files in incresing order of file size.

Hence the correct answer is option (B).

48. A microprogrammed control unit is a relatively simple logic circuit that is capable of (1) sequencing through microinstructions and (2) generating control signals to execute each microinstruction. The concept of microprogram is similar to computer program.

Hence the correct answer is option (B).

49. In mathematics and mathematical logic, Boolean algebra is the branch of algebra in which the values of the variables are the truth values true and false, usually denoted 1 and 0 respectively.

Hence the correct answer is option (C).

50. A Distributed operating system is usually defined as running on more loosely coupled hardware . There is one single OS, the goal of Distributed system is to make the collection of machines behave more like a single machine. So that means there is tightly coupled OS running on a loosely coupled hardware

Hence the correct answer is option (C).

51. With S+2 'A' will be accessed and with S+7 'C' will be accessed as S is pointing to 'G'.

Hence the correct answer is option (B).

52. P(X) = Probability that station X attempts to transmit = P

P (-X) = Probability that station X does not transmit = 1-P

Required is: Probability that only one station transmits = y

Y = (A₁, -A₂, -A₃...... -Aₙ) + (-A₁, A₂, A₃.......-Aₙ) + (-A₁, -A₂, A₃.....-Aₙ) + ... + (-A₁, -A₂, -A₃......Aₙ)

$= (p*(1-p)*(1-p)*\ldots\ldots (1-p) + (1-p)*p*(1-p)\ldots\ldots(1-p) + \ldots\ldots\ldots$

$= p*(1-p)^{(n-1)} + p*(1-p)^{n-1} + \ldots\ldots\ldots\ldots\ldots\ldots\ldots\ldots\ldots\ldots\ldots + p*(1-p)^{(n-1)}$

$= n*p*(1-p)^{(n-1)}$

Hence the correct answer is option (A).

53. All of the given operations can be performed over a Linked List-

1.   Searching
2.   Insertion
3.   Sorting
4.   Merging
5.   Concatenation

Hence the correct option is (D).

54. a - iv, b - i, c - ii, d - iii

Hence the correct option is (A).

55. The fragmentation fields in the base header section of IPv4 have moved to the fragmentation extension header in IPv6:

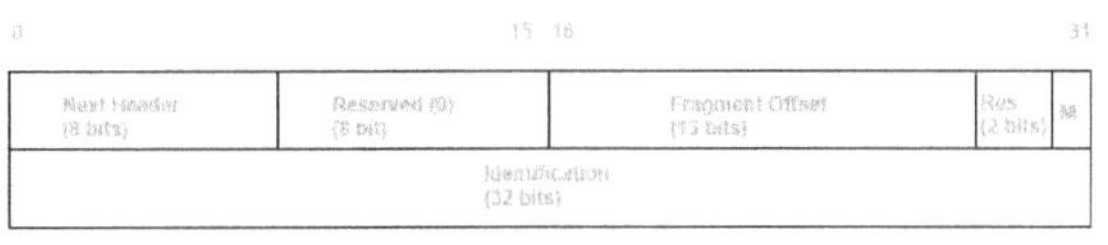

So, given statement is correct.

Authentication header (protocol 51) is identical in both IPv4 and IPv6, but authentication extension header is new in IPv6. So, given statement is correct.

In the IPv6 specifications [IPv6], no record route function is defined, and the record route function for IPv4 is less flexible and has scalability problems. So, given statement is correct.

Hence, option (D) is correct.

56. For instance, the technology is used in many speaker systems. Bluetooth Low Energy uses less power than standard Bluetooth and is used in hardware such as fitness trackers, smart watches and other connected devices in order to wirelessly transmit data without heavily compromising the battery power in a user's phone.Feb 26, 2015.

Hence the correct option is (B).

57. Answer is $\dfrac{n(n-1)}{2}$, since every two user have own secret key encryption and decryption.

Hence the correct option is (C).

58. Drop command remove all tuples of the relation as well as schema also.

Delete command in sql removes tuples from the relation but retain the schema of table in database.

Hence the correct option is (C).

59. Only D_2. Since AD is key and it present in both the tables .

Not D_1.

Since in D_1 fd's not given...

If we take B -> A and C->A then it is lossy since no common attributes contain key from one of the table.

Hence the correct answer is option (D).

60. In SQL query with location transparency the end user must specify the database fragment name but does not need to specify where those fragments are located.

Fragmentation transparency is the highest level of transparency. The end user or programmer does not need to know that a database is partitioned. Therefore, neither fragment names nor fragment locations are specified prior to data access.

Local mapping transparency exists when the end user or programmer must specify both the fragment names and their locations.

Hence the correct answer is option (B).

61. $\neg(P \leftrightarrow Q)$ is equivalent to (I) and (II).

Hence the correct answer is option (A).

62. In mathematics and logic, a Boolean function is a function of the form $f: B^k \to B$, where B = {0, 1} is a Boolean domain and k is a non-negative integer called the arity of the function.

Hence the correct answer is option (A).

63. Draw the truth table of three variables and output will be 1 (true) only when exactly two variables are 1 (true) else output will be 0 (false).

Therefore,

p	q	r	Output (f)
0	0	0	0
0	0	1	0
0	1	0	0
0	1	1	1
1	0	0	0
1	0	1	1
1	1	0	1
1	1	1	0

$$f = (\sim p \wedge q \wedge r) \vee (p \wedge \sim q \wedge r) \vee (p \wedge q \wedge \sim r)$$

$$f = \{(\sim p \wedge q) \vee (p \wedge \sim q)\} \wedge r \vee (p \wedge q \wedge \sim r)$$
$$f = \{(p \oplus q)\} \wedge r \vee (p \wedge q \wedge \sim r)$$
$$f = \{\sim (p \to q)\} \wedge r \vee (p \wedge q \wedge \sim r)$$

Hence the correct answer is option (B).

64. An index register in a computer's CPU is a processor register used for modifying operand addresses during the run of a program, typically for doing vector/array operations.

Hence the correct answer is option (A).

65. WHITE BOX TESTING (also known as Clear Box Testing, Open Box Testing, Glass Box Testing, Transparent Box Testing, Code-Based Testing or Structural Testing) is a software testing method in which the internal structure/design/implementation of the item being tested is known to the tester.

Hence the correct answer is option (D).

66. Both S_1 and S_2 are correct.

Hence the correct answer is option (D).

67. L_1 is context free language and L_2 is not context free language.

Hence the correct answer is option (A).

68. Grammar is
$$S \to Ax \mid By$$
$$A \to By \mid Cw$$
$$B \to x \mid Bw$$
$$C \to y$$
Now observe that what strings these productions are generating

$C \to y$ is generating only y.

$B \to x \mid B_w$ is generating x, xw, xww, xwww, ... That is xw^*.

$A \to By \mid Cw$ is generating $xw^*y + yw$.

$S \to Ax \mid By$ is generating $(xw^*y + yv)x + xw^*y$

That is regular expression for given grammar.

Hence the correct answer is option (C).

69. $A \cdot AB'$
$$(AB' + AB' + AC)(A'C + B')$$
$$(AB' + AC)(A'C' + B')$$
$$AB'A'C' + AB'B' + ACA'C' + ACB'$$
$$AB'B' + ACB' = AB'(C + 1) = AB'$$

Hence the correct answer is option (A).

70. Randomized Hill Climbing: Sample p points randomly in the neighborhood of the currently best solution; determine the best solution of the n sampled points. If it is better than the current solution, make it the new current solution and continue the search; otherwise, terminate returning the current solution.

Hence the correct answer is option (C).

71. McCall's 3 software quality factors:

1>Ability to undergo change

2>Adaptiability to new environments

3>Operational characteristics

but Production costs and scheduling is not the aspect of quality factor.

So, option (D) is correct.

72. If coupling is low and cohesion is high, then it is easier to change one module without affecting others.

Hence the correct answer is option (B).

73. Parallel Virtual Machine (PVM) is a software tool for parallel networking of computers. It is designed to allow a network of heterogeneous Unix and/or Windows machines to be used as a single distributed parallel processor.

Hence the correct answer is option (D).

74. (A), (B) and (C) are true.

Hence the correct answer is option (D).

75. (2)- (iii) (iv) (ii) (i)

Hence the correct answer is option (B).

76. <td style = 'vertical-align : middle'>Text Here</td>

Hence the correct answer is option (A).

77. The number of strings of length 4=12

Hence the correct answer is option (D).

78. Given stack size = 5

Operation	Stack contents
push(a)	a
pop()	-
push(b)	b
push(c)	b,c
pop()	b
push(d)	b,d
pop()	b
pop()	-
push(e)	e

Hence the correct answer is option (B).

79. Job scheduling is commonly done via queue data structure .

Implementation of recursion :since for each function call stack is used to store its activation record.

Evaluation of a postfix expression : perfect example for stack data structure application push until operator not found.

Reverse a string : simple example for reverse any string : push all then pop all.

Hence the correct answer is option (C).

80. A nested class is a member of its enclosing class. Non-static nested classes (inner classes) have access to other members of the enclosing class, even if they are declared private. Static nested classes do not have access to other members of the enclosing class.

Hence the correct answer is option (A).

81.

- Abstract class cannot be directly initiated with 'new' operator.
- Abstract class cannot be initiated.

Hence the correct answer is option (C).

82. Two atomic operations permissible on semaphores are wait and signal.

Hence the correct answer is option (D).

83. In general, user-level threads can be implemented using one of four models. All models maps user-level threads to kernel-level threads. A kernel thread is similar to a process in a non-threaded (single-threaded) system. The kernel thread is the unit of execution that is scheduled by the kernel to execute on the CPU.

Hence the correct answer is option (A).

84. The Internet protocol suite is the conceptual model and set of communications protocols used in the Internet and similar computer networks. It is commonly known as TCP/IP because the foundational protocols in the suite are the Transmission Control Protocol and the Internet Protocol.

Hence the correct answer is option (A).

85. Fixed routing refers to router-provided networking services. These services use routers (devices used to link networks) fixed over a network link to provide different data paths for fast and reliable transmission. Fixed routing is not used for real-time processing. This term is also known as static routing.

Hence the correct answer is option (A).

86. II only could not be the candidate key for the database table

Hence the correct answer is option (C).

87. M = 4, N = 2

Hence the correct answer is option (A).

88. Only the joining attributes are sent from one site to another and then only the required rows are returned.

Hence the correct answer is option (C).

89. $P \Leftrightarrow (Q \vee \neg Q)$ "P should be true because RHS will be TRUE always "

$Q \Leftrightarrow R$ "when Q is true R is true" and "when Q is false R is false "

$$(P \wedge Q) \Rightarrow ((P \wedge R) \vee S)$$

there can be only 2 cases (value of S doesn't matter)

1) $P =$ True, $Q =$ True and $R =$ True

$$(T \wedge T) \Rightarrow ((T \wedge T) \vee S)$$

so this case is True

2) $P =$ True, $Q = R =$ False

$$(T \wedge F) \Rightarrow ((P \wedge R) \vee S)$$

In case implication if the premises is false then whole statement is true
this case is also true
The given expression is True in both the cases.
Hence the correct answer is option (A).

90. The value of $F = P_1 + P'_2 P'_3$

Hence the correct answer is option (B).

91. The decision boundary between the two classes C_1 and C_2 using single perception is given by: $x_1 + x_2 - 0.5 = 0$

Hence the correct answer is option (D).

92. Heap sort with time complexity O(n Log k)

Hence the correct answer is option (D).

93. Both S_1 and S_2 are correct.

Lets consider both the statements separately to find the correct option.

$S_1 : \{0^{2n} \mid n \geq 1 |\}$

Applying the values of n,

$\rightarrow S_1 = 00, 0000, 000000, \ldots\ldots$ The behaviour shown by the output is regular and hence, the language is a regular language.

$S_2 : \{ 0^m \, 1^n \, 0^{m+n} \mid m \geq 1 \text{ and } n \geq 1| \}$

Applying the values of m and n,

$S_2 = 0100, 00110000, 000111000000, \ldots\ldots$

Here the values of m and n are kept same so they are showing the output in symmetry but if we use the different values of m and n then the output will display a behaviour which is not regular. Therefore, confirmed is that S_1 is a regular language.

Hence the correct answer is option (C).

94. The Prototyping Model is a systems development method (SDM) in which a prototype (an early approximation of a final system or product) is built, tested, and then reworked as necessary until an acceptable prototype is finally achieved from which the complete system or product can now be developed.

Hence the correct answer is option (B).

95. Execute T3, followed by T2, followed by T1

Hence the correct answer is option (D).

96. The family of regular languages are closed under both symmetric difference and nor.

Hence the correct answer is option (C).

97. Heap sort is not a comparison based sorting algorithm.

Hence the correct answer is option (D).

98. In computing, an applet is any small application that performs one specific task that runs within the scope of a dedicated widget engine or a larger program, often as a plug-in.[1] The term is frequently used to refer to a Java applet, a program written in the Java programming language that is designed to be placed on a web page. Applets are typical examples of transient and auxiliary applications that don't monopolize the user's attention. Applets are not full-featured application programs, and are intended to be easily accessible.

Hence the correct answer is option (D).

99. finding all employees who earn more than the average salary of all employees of their company.

Hence the correct answer is option (D).

100. Implication " P implies Q'' i.e., $(p \to Q)$, where P is Premise and Q is Conclusion, can be equivalently expressed in many ways. And the two equivalent expression relevant to the question are as follows:

1. "If P then Q''

2. " Q unless $\neg P''$

Both of these are equivalent to the propositional formula $(P \to Q)$

Now compare "If X then Y unless Z'' with $"Q$ unless $\neg P''$, here $(\neg P = Z)$ so $(P = \neg Z)$ and $(Q = Y)$

Compare with "if P then Q'', here $(P = X), (Q = Y)$

So we get premise $P = X$ and $\neg Z$, conclusion $Q = Y$

Equivalent propositional formula $(X \wedge \neg Z) \to Y$

PS: Someone messaged me that i have taken "If X then $(Y$ unless Z)" in above explanation and how to know if we take "(If X then Y) unless Z'' or "If X then $(Y$ unless Z)". So let me show that both way gives the same answer.

"If X then Y) unless $Z'' \equiv (X \to Y)$ unless Z

$\equiv \neg Z \to (X \to Y)$

$\equiv \neg Z \to (\neg X \vee Y)$

$\equiv Z \vee \neg X \vee Y$

$\equiv \neg(X \wedge \neg Z) \vee Y$

$\equiv (X \wedge \neg Z) \to Y$

Hence the correct answer is option (B).

Q.1 Which of the following is incorrect about Array-

A. Array is Linear Data Structure

B. Array is Homogeneous Data Structure

C. Array is Dynamic Data Structure

D. Array follows contiguous memory allocation

Q.2 Let s be a sorted array of n integers. Let t(n) denote the time taken for the most efficient algorithm to determine if there are two elements with sum less than1000 in s. Which of the following statements is true?

A. t (n) is 0(1)

B. n ≤t(n) ≤ n log$_2$ n

C. n log$_2$ n ≤ t(n) <(n/2)

D. t(n) =(n/2)

Q.3 How many fibres are required by a unidirectional and bidirectional ring respectively, to support their working traffic?

A. 1 and 1   **B.** 2 and 1   **C.** 2 and 2   **D.** 1 and 2

Q.4 Find odd one out related to transmission media cables?

A. Basic rate ISDN can transmit data at a rate of 512 kilobits per second on an existing local telephone line.

B. A T1 line is a dedicated telephone connection of 24 channels.

C. A T1 channel can be configured to carry either voice or data traffic.

D. Cable modems provide high-speed transmission over cable TV lines and are shared by many users.

Q.5 What does a metric of 16 hops represent when using RIP?

A. Number of hops to the destination

B. Destination unreachable

C. Number of routers

D. Bandwidth

Q.6 If the 8085 adds 87H and 79H, specify the contents of the accumulator and the status of the S, Z, and CY flag?

A. 10H; S =1, Z = 0, CY = 1

B. 01H; S =0, Z = 0, CY = 1

C. 00H; S =0, Z = 1, CY = 1

D. 11H; S =1, Z = 1, CY = 0

Q.7 If the stack pointer is initialized with (4FEB) H, then after execution of Push operation in 8085 microprocessor, the Stack Pointer shall be

A. 4FEA   **B.** 4FEC   **C.** 4FE9   **D.** 4FED

Q.8 If an input and output port can have the same 8-bit address how does the 8085 differentiate between the ports?

A. The input port requires the WR and the output port requires the RD signal

B. The input port requires the RD and the output port requires the WR signal

C. The input port and output port requires low I/O

D. None of the above

Q.9 Consider the grammar given below

Assume that + and . have the same but least precedence, * and / have the next higher precedence but the same precedence and finally ^ has the highest precedence. Assume + and . associate to the left like * and / and that ^ associates to the right. Choose the correct statement with respect to relations for the ordered pairs (^,^) , (-,-) , (+,+) , (*,*) in the operator precedence table constructed for the grammar

A. all <   **B.** all >   **C.** <,>,=,<   **D.** <,>,>,>

Q.10 If A →αβ$_1$ | αβ$_2$ are two A-productions and the input begins with a non-empty string derived from a. Then in such a situation _____ is preferable

A. Left factoring

B. Eliminating of Left recursion

C. Eliminating of ambiguity

D. None of the above

Q.11 Which of the following conversion is not possible (algorithmically)?

A. regular grammar to context-free grammar

B. nondeterministic FSA to deterministic FSA

C. nondeterministic PDA to deterministic PDA

D. nondeterministic TM to deterministic TM

Q.12 A layer-4 firewall (a device that can look at all protocol headers up to the transport layer) CANNOT

A. block entire HTTP traffic during 9:00 PM and 5:00 AM

B. block all ICMP traffic

C. stop incoming traffic from a specific IP address but allow outgoing traffic to the same IP address

D. block TCP traffic from a specific user on a multi-user system during 9:00 PM and 5:00 AM

Q.13 Match the following:

Column I	Column II
p) time sharing	(1) Program first executed when a computer is turned on
q) process	(2) Part of an operating system that communicates with the user
r) bootstrap	(3) Technique that allows multiprocessing on a computer with a single CPU
s) shell	(4) Activity of executing a program

Which of the following correctly matched with pqrs respectively:

A. (4), (1), (2), (3)   **B.** (3), (4), (1), (2)

C. (2), (3), (4), (1)   **D.** (1), (4), (2), (3)

Q.14 In Priority Scheduling a priority number is associated with each process. The CPU is allocated to the process with the highest priority. The problem of starvation is resolved by which of the following?

A. Terminating the process.

B. Aging

C. Mutual Exclusion

D. Semaphore

Q.15 Which of the following does not support for Page-Stealer process?

A. It is a kernel process that makes room for the incoming pages

B. It is created by the Kernel at the system initialization and invokes it throughout the lifetime of the system.

C. Kernel locks a region when a process faults on a page in the region, so that page stealer cannot steal the page, which is being faulted in.

D. All are correct.

Q.16 If you type 'cat prog.c' at a UNIX command prompt, which of the following sequences of system calls would be invoked?

A. The shell calls fork(); the child process calls exec() and the parent calls wait()

B. The shell calls fork(); the child calls wait() and the parent calls exec()

C. The shell calls exec() and then wait() and then fork()

D. The shell calls wait() then fork(), creating a child which calls exec()

Q.17 Which of these describe the activity of a contract review?

A. Evaluation of the target market

B. Evaluation of the development risks

C. Evaluation of the weather during the software development.

D. Evaluation of the staff's personal background

Q.18 Insufficient identification is a

A. Technology-related problem

B. Process-related problem

C. People-related problem

D. Product-related problem

Q.19 Five nines of reliability refers to

A. Five software engineering practices that must be in place and assessed at level 9 in order to ensure reliability

B. A product that is operational 99.999% of the time

C. A product that fails one time in 10,000 days

D. A product which fails only five times in 99,999 days

Q.20 Which of the following is not a static testing tool?

A. Static analyzers

B. Code inspectors

C. Output comparators

D. Standard enforces

Q.21 $S \rightarrow A \mid B$

$A \rightarrow a \mid b$

$B \rightarrow b \mid c$

The grammar is

A. LL(1)

B. LR(1)

C. Both (a) and (b)

D. None of these

Q.22 Select the options due to which credit theft is impossible with smart card

I. Key to unlock encrypted information required

II. No physical signature on the card

III. There is no external account number on the card

IV. Smart cards can be used with only acquainted merchants

A. Only I and II

B. Only II and III

C. Only I and III

D. Only I and IV

Q.23 Match the following:

Column I	Column II
p) FAT12	(i) 1996 (Windows 95 OSR2)
q) FAT16	(ii) 1977 (Microsoft Disk BASIC)
r) FAT32	(iii) 1988 (MS-DOS 4.0)

Which of the following correctly matched with pqr respectively:

A. (iii), (i), (ii)

B. (iii), (ii), (i)

C. (ii), (iii), (i)

D. (i), (iii), (ii)

Q.24 Which macro sends an output message to the debug window of compiler:

A. COUT

B. FOUT

C. TRACE

D. Display

Q.25 In windows 95 which tool is used to kill errant hidden processes?

A. Task Manager

B. Process Manager

C. PVIEW

D. Explorer

Q.26 Which question corresponds best to the following query?

SELECT CID, CDUR - 1,' = PRICE' FROM COURSES ORDER BY 2

A. Select three columns from the COURSES table, of which the third one has a constant value, i.e. " = PRICE". Leave an empty line after every second line.

B. Select two columns from the COURSES table, the second one gets as title " = PRICE".Sort the data according to the second column, in ascending order.

C. Select three columns from the COURSES table, of which the third one has a constant value i.e. " = PRICE". Sort the data according to the second column, in ascending order.

D. Select two columns from the COURSES table, of which the second one has a constant value, i.e. " = PRICE". Sort the data according to the second column, in ascending order.

Q.27 A modification to the database expressed in terms of a view must be translated to the –

A. Actual relation in the conceptual model of the database

B. Queries in the actual database

C. Relations of all the views of that database

D. Need not be translated and the view of a database accommodates the modification

Q.28 If $D_1, D_2 ..... D_n$ are domains in relational model then the relation is a table which is a subset of ---

A. $\{ D_1, D_2 ..... D_n\}$

B. $D_1 \times D_2 \times .... D_n$

C. $D_1 \cup D_2 \cup .....D_n$

D. Maximum $\{ D_1, D_2 ..... D_n\}$

Q.29 If the in order and pre order traversal of a binary tree are DBFEGHAC and ABDEFGHC respectively then, the post order traversal of that tree is

A. DFGABCHE

B. FHDGEBCA

C. DFHGEBCA

D. CGHFEDBA

Q.30 "n" elements of a queue are to be reversed using another queue. The number of "ADD" and "REMOVE" required to do so is,

A. 2n

B. 4n

C. n

D. the task cannot be done

Q.31 Prim's algorithm is a method available for finding out the minimum cost of a spanning tree. Its time complexity is given by:

A. $O(n \times n)$ B. $O(n \log n)$

C. $O(n)$ D. $O(1)$

Q.32 Maximum number of children in a node in a B-tree of order "m" is:

A. m   B. m/2-1   C. m/2+1   D. m/2

Q.33 A has one share in a lottery in which there is 1 prize & 2 blanks; B has three shares in a lottery in which there are 3 prizes & 6 blanks: compare the probability of A's success to that of B's success as

A. 7:16   B. 16:7   C. 6:14   D. 14:6

Q.34 The following 'C' code : -

```
# include < stdio.h >
main ( )
{ file * FP ;
FP = fopen ( " trial " , " r " );
}
```

FP points to :-

A. First character in the file

B. A structure which contains a ' char ' pointer to the first character in the file.

C. Name of the file.

D. None.

Q.35 Consider different activities related to email.

m_1: Send an email from a mail client to a mail server

m_2: Download an email from mailbox server to a mail client

m_3: Checking email in a web browser

Which is the application level protocol used in each activity?

A. m_1: HTTP m_2: SMTP m_3: POP

B. m_1: SMTP m_2 : FTP m_3 : HTTP

C. m_1: SMTP m_2: POP m_3: HTTP

D. m_1: POP m_2: SMTP m_3: IMAP

Q.36 The distance between two stations M and N is L kilometers. All frames are K bits long. The propagation delay per kilometer is t seconds. Let R bits/second be the channel capacity. Assuming that processing delay is negligible, the minimum number of bits for the sequence number field in a frame for maximum utilization, when the sliding window protocol is used, is:

A. $\left\lceil \log_2 \frac{2LtR+2K}{K} \right\rceil$ B. $\left\lceil \log_2 \frac{2LtR}{K} \right\rceil$

C. $\left\lceil \log_2 \frac{2LtR+K}{2K} \right\rceil$ D. $\left\lceil \log_2 \frac{2LtR+K}{K} \right\rceil$

Q.37 How many characters per second (7 bits + 1 parity) can be transmitted over a 2400 bps line if the transfer is synchronous (1 start and 1 stop bit)?

A. 300   B. 240   C. 250   D. 275

Q.38 What is true about private constructor?

A. Private constructor ensures only one instance of a class exist at any point of time

B. Private constructor ensures multiple instances of a class exist at any point of time

C. Private constructor eases the instantiation of a class

D. Private constructor allows creating objects in other classes

Q.39 What happens when an exception is not caught?

A. Code in the catch block is generated.

B. An error occurs.

C. The program is aborted.

D. The program executes normally.

Q.40 _____ is the abstraction process of introducing new characters to an existing class of objects to create one or more new classes of objects.

A. Specialization   B. Generalization

C. Abstraction   D. Aggregation

Q.41 What will be the result of the following addition? $(3BCA.5078)16 + (9EBD.97F3)16 + (5FB.E2C)16$

A. $(E082.CB2C)16$ B. $(14916.9241)16$

C. $(E083.CB2B)16$ D. $(E916.9241)16$

Q.42 Assertion (A): A digital multiplexer can also be used to implement combinational logic function

Reason (R): In a combinational circuit, the current output depends on the previous outputs also

A. Both A and R are individually true and R is the correct explanation of A

B. Both A and R are individually true, but R is not the correct explanation of A

C. A is true, but R is false

D. A is false, but R is true

Q.43 In the RSA public key cryptosystem, the private and public keys are (e, n) and (d, n) respectively, where n = p + -q and p and q are large primes. Besides, n is public and p and q are private. Let M be an integer such that $0<M<n$ and $\phi(n)=(p-1)(q-1)$ Now consider the following equations.

I. $M^r = M^e \bmod n$

II. $M=(M^r)^d M = (M^1)^d \bmod n$

II. ed = I mod n

III. ed = I mod $\emptyset(n)$

IV. $Mr = M^e \bmod (n)$

$M=(M^r)^d \bmod \emptyset(n)$

Which of the above equations correctly represent RSA crypto system?

A. I and II   B. I and IV

C. II and IV   D. III and IV

Q.44 Assume that there are 32 input-output storing units, 32 functions to select and 16 data routes to select. Assume control memory of 16384. How many encoded bits are required assuming that there is a next address field at the microinstructions? Two MUX are used one at input and one at output for a set of 8 registers.

A. 26   **B.** 27   **C.** 28   **D.** 29

Q.45 Match the following categories with respect to 8085 instructions:

Column I	Column II
p) Data transfer instruction	(i) CALL
q) Arithmetic Instruction	(ii) CMP
r) Logical Instruction	(iii) STA
s) Branch Instruction	(iv) DCR

Which of the following correctly matched with pqrs respectively:

A. (ii), (iii), (iv), (i)   **B.** (iii), (ii), (i), (iv)
C. (i), (iii), (ii), (iv)   **D.** (iii), (iv), (ii), (i)

Q.46 Find odd one out:

A. ANAR   **B.** PCHL   **C.** ORAR   **D.** CMA

Q.47 The PCI bus is the important bus found in all the new Pentium systems because
I.It has plug and play characteristicsII.It has ability to function with a 64 bit data busIII.Any Microprocessor can be interfaced to it with PCI controller or bridge

A. Only I and II   **B.** Only II and III
C. Only I and III   **D.** All of the above

Q.48 A single register to clear the lower four bits of the accumulator in 8085 assembly language is?

A. XRI 0FH   **B.** ANI F0H
C. XRI F0H   **D.** ANI 0FH

Q.49 The part of a database management system which ensures that the data remains in a consistent state is,

A. Authorization and integrity manager
B. Buffer manager
C. Transaction manager
D. File manager

Q.50 Which of the following are factors in deciding on database distribution strategies?

I.Organizational forces

II.Frequency of data access

III.Reliability needs

A. Only I and II   **B.** Only II and III
C. Only I and III   **D.** All of the above

Q.51 One way to generate, store and forward messages for completed transactions to be broadcast across a network is through the use of

A. Stored procedures   **B.** Triggers
C. Functions   **D.** SQL statements

Q.52 Evaluate these two SQL statements and determine what is true about them?

I.SELECT last_name, salary , hire_date
FROM EMPLOYEES
ORDER BY salary DESC;

II.SELECT last_name, salary, hire_date
FROM EMPLOYEES
ORDER BY 2 DESC;

A. The two statements produce identical results.
B. The second statement returns a syntax error.
C. There is no need to specify DESC because the results are sorted in descending order by default.
D. The two statements can be made to produce identical results by adding a column alias for the salary column in the second SQL statement.

Q.53 Which syntax turns an existing constraint on?

A. ALTER TABLE table_name
ENABLE constraint_name;
B. ALTER TABLE table_name
STATUS = ENABLE CONSTRAINT constraint_name;
C. ALTER TABLE table_name
ENABLE CONSTRAINT constraint_name;
D. ALTER TABLE table_name
STATUS ENABLE CONSTRAINT constraint_name;

Q.54 What is the type of Oracle backup in which all uncommitted changes have been removed from the data files?

A. Full backup   **B.** Consistent backup
C. Inconsistent backup   **D.** Differential backup

Q.55 For implementing priority queue which data structure is best regarding the time complexities of enqueue and dequeue operations in priority queue :

A. Array   **B.** Binary Search Tree
C. AVL Tree   **D.** Heap Tree

Q.56 When a C/SDK program in message handling begins, it immediately registers at least one window class using.

A. Register class ( ) API function and a RGSCLASS data structure
B. Register class ( ) API function and a WNDCLASS data structure
C. Window Register class ( ) API function and a RGSCLASS data structure
D. Window Register class ( ) API function and a WNDCLASS data structure

Q.57 For window message components, which one is not correct.?

A. Window message has an unsigned integer containing the actual message.
B. LPARAM is a 4-byte parameter
C. WPARAM is a 32-Bits parameter in win 32.
D. WPARAM contains additional data, required to handle the message

Q.58 What is/are false about UNIX operating system?

(i) Unix consider all files to be a continuous sequence of characters.

(ii) Unix treat physical devices as if they are files & hence programs can access devices with same syntax as files.

(iii) Unix is multi user, multi-programmed but not time scheduled operating system.

(iv) Programs written using UNIX can not be run on a variety of architecture.

A. (i), (ii), (iv) **B.** (ii), (iii), (iv)
C. (iii), (iv) **D.** (ii), (iv)

Q.59 Given

LPP max z = $6x_1 + 4x_2$

Subject to $x_1 + 2x_2 < 720$

$2x_1 + x_2 < 780$

$x_1 < 320$

$x_1, x_2, x_3 > 0$

The optional value of objective function will be

A. 2550 **B.** 2560
C. 2540 **D.** None of these

Q.60 The number of distinct Boolean expression of 4 variables is

A. 16 **B.** 256 **C.** 1024 **D.** 65536

Q.61 While opening a TCP connection, the initial sequence number is to be derived using a time-of-day (ToD) clock that keeps running even when the host is down. The low order 32 bits of the counter of the ToD clock is to be used for the initial sequence numbers. The clock counters increments once per millisecond. The maximum packet lifetime is given to be 64s. Which one of the choices given below is closest to the minimum permissible rate at which sequence numbers used for packets of a connection can increase?

A. 0.015/s **B.** 0.064/s **C.** 0.135/s **D.** 0.327/s

Q.62 A push down automation has

A. Infinite set of pushdown symbols
B. Only one special pushdown symbol
C. Finite set of input symbols
D. all of these

Q.63 In TM, the tape has k-tuple of tape symbol, where k is,

A. Number of tracks
B. Number of alphabets
C. Set of tape symbols
D. None of these

Q.64 The given language

L = { $a^m b^m$: m positive} is,

A. Regular **B.** Not regular
C. unpredictable **D.** None of these

Q.65 The Breadth - first search Tree are used in,

A. Banking **B.** Defense
C. Law **D.** All of these

Q.66 Which of the following parser is more powerful and expensive?

A. Simple LR **B.** Look ahead LR
C. Canonical LR **D.** None of these

Q.67 Which of the following is not the required condition for binary search algorithm?

A. The list must be sorted

B. there should be the direct access to the middle element in any sublist

C. There must be mechanism to delete and/or insert elements in list

D. none of above

Q.68 A BCNF is

A. Loss less join and dependency preserving
B. Loss less join and not dependency preserving
C. Not loss less join and dependency preserving
D. None of these

Q.69 Functional dependencies are generalization of

A. Key dependencies
B. Relational dependencies
C. Database dependencies
D. Functional dependencies

Q.70 If $(30)_x$ in base x number system is equal to $(17)_y$ in base y number system, the possible values of x and y are

A. 5, 9 **B.** 5, 8 **C.** 6, 8 **D.** 13, 9

Q.71 The greatest negative number which can be stored in a 8 – bit register using 2's complement arithmetic is

A. – 256 **B.** – 255 **C.** – 127 **D.** – 128

Q.72 ________protocol is typically used for error reposing.

A. DNS **B.** ICMP **C.** POP-3 **D.** IMPC

Q.73 When processing on output in XML, "new line" symbols are

A. Copied into output "as is", i.e. "CR + LF" for window, CR for macintosh, LF for Unix.
B. Converted to single CR symbol
C. Converted to single LF symbol
D. Discarded

Q.74 How can you open a link in a new browser window?

A. < a hrsf = "url" new>
B. < a href = "url" target = "-blank" >
C. <a href = "url" target = "new">
D. None of these

Q.75 Using which tag we insert a Java script in HTML page?

A. < save script type = "text/javescript" > </javascript>
B. < script type = "text/javascript"> </jscript>
C. <Jscript type = "text/javascript"> </jscript>
D. <HTML script type = "text/javascript"> </HTML script>

Q.76 Which of the following aggregate methods does not work if hiring and lay off are possible?

A. The linear rule
B. Simulation
C. The management coefficients model
D. The transportation method.

Q.77 (i) DPSH with eight phases will enable the bit rate to be tripled over the corresponding two phase modulation.

(ii) The diameter of a single mode fiber is generally greater than the diameter of a multi mode fiber.

Which of the following option is correct w.r.t the above statement?

A. (i) – T (ii) – F
B. (i) – F (ii) –F
C. (i)–F (ii) – T
D. (i) – T (ii) – T

Q.78 If the .... Bit in X.25 standard is set to 1, it means that there is more than one packet.

A. Q
B. D
C. M
D. P

Q.79 Match the following

(1) Time domain reflectometry   (i) transmission

(2) Frequency hopping and spread   (ii) A technique that detects cable
spectrum techniques are involved in   breaks bad taps or loose connectors

(3) 10 base 2   (iii) Multiplexing

(4) Sharing of communication channel.   (iv) thin ethernet

Which of the following option is correct for the given match-ups?

A. (1) – (ii) (2) – (i) (3) – (iv) (4) – (iii)
B. (1) – (i) (2) – (ii) (3) – (iv) (4) – (iii)
C. (1) – (iii) (2) – (ii) (3) – (i) (4) – (iv)
D. (1) – (iv) (2) – (i) (3) – (iii) (4) – (ii)

Q.80 What is the maximum burst length on a 155.52 Mbps ATM ABR connection whose PCR value 200,000 and whose L value is 25 msec?

A. 13
B. 12
C. 14
D. 15

Q.81 What is the maximum value till a 5 stage ripple counter can count:

A. 25
B. 29
C. 31
D. 45

Q.82 Consider the following CFG

$$S \rightarrow OB \qquad S \rightarrow bA$$
$$B \rightarrow b \qquad A \rightarrow a$$
$$B \rightarrow bS \qquad A \rightarrow aS$$
$$B \rightarrow aBB \qquad A \rightarrow bAA$$

Consider the following derivation

$$S \Rightarrow aB$$
$$\Rightarrow aaBB$$
$$\Rightarrow aabb$$
$$\Rightarrow aabsb$$
$$\Rightarrow aabb \; Ab$$
$$\Rightarrow aabbab$$

A. A leftmost derivation
B. A rightmost derivation
C. Both leftmost and rightmost derivation
D. Neither leftmost nor rightmost derivation

Q.83 Which of the following regular expression identity is true

A. $r(*) = r*$
B. $(r* s*)* = (r + s)*$
C. $(r + s)* = r* + s*$
D. $r*s* = r* + s*$

Q.84 Which of the following is the correct way to declare a multidimensional array in Java?

A. int[] arr;
B. int arr;
C. int[][]arr;
D. int arr;

Q.85 A self relocating program is one which

A. Cannot be made to execute in any area of storage other than the one designated for it at the time of its coding or translation.

B. Consists of a program and relevant information for its relocation.

C. Can itself perform the relocation of its address-sensitive portions

D. All of the above

Q.86 Arrange the following steps of structured design methodology in the correct order

(i) First level factoring

(ii) Restate the problem as a data flow diagram

(iii) Identify the input and output data elements

(iv) Factoring of input, output and transform branches.

A. (ii)-(iii)-(iv)-(i)
B. (ii)-(iii)-(i)-(iv)
C. (ii)-(iv)-(iii)-(i)
D. (i)-(ii)-(iii)-(iv)

Q.87 Which of the following options is true for the given statement?

(i) On line data capture is preferable to batch data entry because it reduces human effort in entering data.

(ii) Prototyping motivates the end user and required his active participation.

A. (i) T (ii) F
B. (i) F (ii) T
C. (i) F (ii) F
D. (i) T (ii) T

Q.88 Software metrics cannot be applied in

A. Cost and size estimation techniques.
B. Controlling software development projects
C. Prediction of quality levels
D. None of these

Q.89 Representation of list in PROLOG is

A. {2, 4, 8, 10, 12}
B. [2, 4, 8, 10, 12], ["jack", "jill", "jane 1"]
C. [2, 4, 8, 10, 12]
D. {"jack", "jill", "jane 1"}

Q.90 Which of the following is a control structure in PROLOG?

A. p:-a, b, c;
p:-d, e, f;
B. p:-a; b; c;
p:-d; e; f;
C. p:-a, b, c;
p:-d, e, f;
D. None of these

Q.91 __________ is the number of arguments in a predicate form.

A. Atom
B. Arity
C. Parameter
D. Clause

Q.92 Which of the following is not a graphic standard?

A. MHEG
B. PREMO
C. OAD
D. Acrobat

Q.93 Arrange the following steps of animation in the correct sequence.

(i) Object definitions

(ii) Generation of in-between frames

(iii) Storyboard layout

(iv) Keyframe specifications

A. (iii), (i), (iv), (ii)
B. (iii), (iv), (ii), (i)
C. (i), (ii), (iii), (iv)
D. (iv), (ii), (i), (iii)

C. Only 2 and 3
D. 1, 2 and 3

Q.94 _________ allow object motion characteristics to be specified as part of the object definitions

A. Key frame systems
B. Parameterized systems
C. Scripting systems
D. None of these

Q.95 Which of the following statement is true?

A. Macro definition can not appear within other macro definition in assembly language programs
B. Overlaying is used to run a program which is longer than the address space of computer.
C. Mutual memory can be used to accommodate a program which is longer than the address space of computer.
D. It is not possible to write interrupt service routines in a high level language.

Q.96 In anomaly detection, to detect anomalous login time for a user we use,

A. Monitoring system calls commands
B. Linux based commands
C. Monitoring shell commands
D. Monitoring kernel commands

Q.97 main( )
{int x = 4, y = 0, z;while(x > = 0){if (x = = y)break;elseprintf("\n %d%d", x, y);x- -;y++;}}What will be the output of the given program

A. 3 1
4 0
B. 4 0
3 1
C. 1 3
0 4
D. 3 3
4 0

Q.98 _________ and ___________ are the two advantages of high level programming language

A. Readability, Robustness
B. Portability, Robustness
C. Readability, Portability
D. None of these

Q.99 Which of the following options is correct for the given statements?
(i) A PROLOG program does not involve a number of facts and rules(ii) PROLOG is known for its in-built depth first search engine and for its case in qui ck prototyping. (iii) A matching in PROLOG is performed argument to argument only.

A. Only (i) is correct
B. Only (ii) is correct
C. (i) and (ii) both are correct
D. All are correct

Q.100 Which of the following subtraction operations results in F_{16}?

(1) $(BA)_{16} - (AB)_{16}$
(2) $(BC)_{16} - (CB)_{16}$
(3) $(CB)_{16} - (BC)_{16}$

Select the correct answer using the code given below:

A. Only 1 and 2
B. Only 1 and 3

// Smart Answer Sheet //

Correct Percentage of students who answered correctly. **Skipped** Percentage of students who skipped.

Q.	Ans.	Correct / Skipped	Q.	Ans.	Correct / Skipped	Q.	Ans.	Correct / Skipped	Q.	Ans.	Correct / Skipped	Q.	Ans.	Correct / Skipped
1	C	23.5 % / 47.48 %	17	A	15.83 % / 47.48 %	33	A	10.07 % / 50.36 %	49	C	16.31 % / 54.19 %	65	D	30.46 % / 52.99 %
2	A	25.18 % / 37.65 %	18	B	16.31 % / 56.35 %	34	D	12.71 % / 24.46 %	50	D	16.31 % / 56.35 %	66	C	27.58 % / 52.76 %
3	D	15.11 % / 51.8 %	19	B	18.23 % / 55.15 %	35	C	19.42 % / 57.8 %	51	B	23.5 % / 50.6 %	67	C	23.26 % / 51.56 %
4	A	14.39 % / 43.4 %	20	C	30.7 % / 21.1 %	36	D	16.55 % / 48.92 %	52	A	17.99 % / 43.16 %	68	B	15.35 % / 54.19 %
5	B	12.71 % / 56.11 %	21	D	12.95 % / 40.05 %	37	A	16.07 % / 49.64 %	53	C	29.02 % / 38.85 %	69	A	14.63 % / 53.24 %
6	C	19.42 % / 56.12 %	22	C	20.14 % / 35.5 %	38	A	7.91 % / 57.08 %	54	B	15.11 % / 55.15 %	70	B	11.27 % / 59.95 %
7	D	10.07 % / 53.96 %	23	C	16.31 % / 57.07 %	39	C	19.66 % / 49.4 %	55	D	17.51 % / 51.55 %	71	D	11.99 % / 59.23 %
8	B	19.18 % / 58.04 %	24	C	30.22 % / 15.82 %	40	A	11.51 % / 54.44 %	56	B	20.86 % / 52.28 %	72	B	29.5 % / 22.3 %
9	D	9.35 % / 60.19 %	25	C	12.95 % / 55.64 %	41	C	21.82 % / 59.0 %	57	D	11.75 % / 59.95 %	73	C	17.75 % / 41.0 %
10	A	14.39 % / 55.87 %	26	C	14.39 % / 60.43 %	42	C	20.86 % / 34.3 %	58	C	10.79 % / 58.51 %	74	B	17.51 % / 52.75 %
11	C	17.75 % / 52.75 %	27	A	10.79 % / 55.16 %	43	B	16.55 % / 57.55 %	59	B	18.94 % / 55.64 %	75	B	23.5 % / 53.72 %
12	A	19.42 % / 48.69 %	28	B	23.02 % / 28.78 %	44	D	6.95 % / 44.37 %	60	D	16.07 % / 46.28 %	76	D	12.71 % / 53.72 %
13	B	26.14 % / 53.96 %	29	C	21.1 % / 58.76 %	45	D	13.43 % / 55.63 %	61	A	20.86 % / 48.44 %	77	A	16.55 % / 57.07 %
14	B	23.5 % / 34.77 %	30	D	15.35 % / 33.81 %	46	B	17.03 % / 40.52 %	62	C	21.34 % / 50.6 %	78	C	22.78 % / 53.48 %
15	D	21.82 % / 56.84 %	31	A	11.03 % / 47.96 %	47	D	18.94 % / 56.36 %	63	A	17.99 % / 52.03 %	79	A	15.83 % / 57.55 %
16	A	15.35 % / 49.16 %	32	A	12.95 % / 44.6 %	48	B	16.31 % / 50.36 %	64	B	16.79 % / 42.92 %	80	B	22.06 % / 48.92 %

Q.	Ans.	Correct		Q.	Ans.	Correct		Q.	Ans.	Correct		Q.	Ans.	Correct		Q.	Ans.	Correct
		Skipped				Skipped				Skipped				Skipped				Skipped
81	C	22.3 %		85	C	14.87 %		89	B	22.3 %		93	A	15.83 %		97	B	33.09 %
		42.69 %				54.67 %				58.04 %				58.27 %				47.49 %
82	D	8.87 %		86	B	17.27 %		90	A	9.83 %		94	B	23.26 %		98	C	23.26 %
		41.73 %				54.43 %				57.08 %				47.48 %				50.84 %
83	B	18.71 %		87	C	8.87 %		91	B	8.63 %		95	B	17.51 %		99	B	15.83 %
		43.16 %				57.08 %				54.92 %				47.24 %				56.59 %
84	C	16.55 %		88	D	7.67 %		92	C	15.11 %		96	C	16.07 %		100	B	23.26 %
		55.39 %				51.08 %				55.87 %				52.28 %				55.4 %

//Hints and Solutions//

1. Only option C is incorrect as Array is Static data structure.

Hence the correct option is (C).

2. Array will be sorted in ascending order. if there are two elements with sum less than 1000 means there are two elements with the sum value less than 1000 or not. If we sort the array in descending order we have to check the last two elements. So in both ascending and descending it is not dependent on n, thus the complexity is O(1).

Hence the correct option is (A).

3. SONET rings can be classified by the routing principle and the SONET overhead used for triggering protection switching. A ring is called a unidirectional ring if bidirectional working signals follow opposite physical routes around a ring , while bidirectional working signals in a bidirectional ring follow the same route. Due to this routing principle, a unidirectional and a bidirectional ring, require one and two fibers respectively, to support their working traffic.

Hence the correct option is (D).

4. Each ISDN line is made up of separate 64-Kbps "channels" for sending and receiving calls, plus a channel that is used primarily for signaling.

Hence the correct option is (A).

5. Routing Information Protocol is a distance vector routing protocol that uses hop count as its metric. The maximum hop count is 15. 16 hops are considered unreachable. RIP updates are broadcast every 30 seconds by default. RIP has an administrative distance of 120.

Hence the correct option is (B).

6. The sum of 87H and 79H =100H.

Therefore, the accumulator will have 00H, and the flags will be S =0, Z = 1, CY = 1

Hence the correct option is (C).

7. If the stack pointer is initialized with (4FEB) H, then after execution of push operation in 8085 microprocessor, stack pointer shall be 4FED.

Hence the correct option is (D).

8. The 8085 differentiates between the input and output ports of the same address by the control signal. The input port requires the RD and the output port requires the WR signal.

Hence the correct option is (B).

9. Relations for the ordered pairs $(\wedge,\wedge),(-,-) , (+,+), (*,*)$ in the operator precedence table constructed for the grammar will be $<,>,>,>$ as exponent is of right associative to itself and $+ , - , *$ and $/$ are left associative.

Hence the correct option is (D).

10. Left factoring is a grammar transformation that is useful for production of grammar suitable for predictive parsing. In given situation, we do not know whether to expand A to $\alpha\ \beta_1$ or $\alpha\ \beta_2$

However, we may defer the decision by expanding A to $\alpha A'$. Then after seeing the input derived from α, we expand A' to β_1 or β_2 i.e. left factored, the original productions becomes

$A \rightarrow \alpha A'$

$A \rightarrow \beta_1|\beta_1$

11. It is not possible to convert nondeterministic PDA to deterministic PDA.

Hence the correct option is (C).

12. Since it is a layer 4 firewall it cannot block application layer protocol like HTTP.

Hence the correct option is (A).

13. p) time sharing technique that allows multiprocessing on a computer with a single CPU
q) process activity of executing a program
r) bootstrap program first executed when a computer is turned on
s) shell part of an operating system that communicates with the user.

Hence the correct option is (B).

14. Aging resolves or avoids the problem of starvation.

Hence the correct option is (B).

15. Option (1), (2) and (3) all are correct.

Page-Stealer process is the Kernel process that makes room for the incoming pages, by swapping the memory pages that are not the part of the working set of a process.

It is created by the Kernel at the system initialization and invokes it throughout the lifetime of the system. Kernel locks a region when a process faults on a page in the region, so that page stealer cannot steal the page, which is being faulted in.

Hence the correct option is (D).

16. The shell calls fork(); the child process calls exec() and the parent calls wait(). The shell is just another process that can take a string as standard input, look for the program referenced by the string, and then run this program. Unless the program is put in the background, the shell will wait until the program has finished.

Hence the correct option is (A).

17. Evaluation of the target market is an activity of a contract review.

Hence the correct option is (A).

18. Insufficient identification is a process-related problem. Unidentified, partially identified, and unplanned risks pose a threat to the success of a software project. You need to intensively identify risks and evolve a risk management plan such that the project is completed successfully, on time.

Hence the correct option is (B).

19. Five nines of reliability refer to a product that is operational 99.999% of the time.

Hence the correct option is (B).

20. Static analyzers ;A static analyzer operates from a pre-computed database of descriptive information derived from the source text of the program. Code inspectors: A code inspector does a simple job of enforcing standards in a uniform way for many programs. These can be single statement or multiple statement rules.Output comparators :These are used in dynamic testing-both single-module and multiple-module varieties to check that predicted and actual outputs are equivalent.Standard enforces :This tool is like a code inspector. The main distribution is that a full-blown static analyzer looks at whole programs, whereas a standard enforcer looks at only single statements.

Hence the correct option is (C).

21. The grammar is ambiguous because the string 'b' has two parse tree as shown below

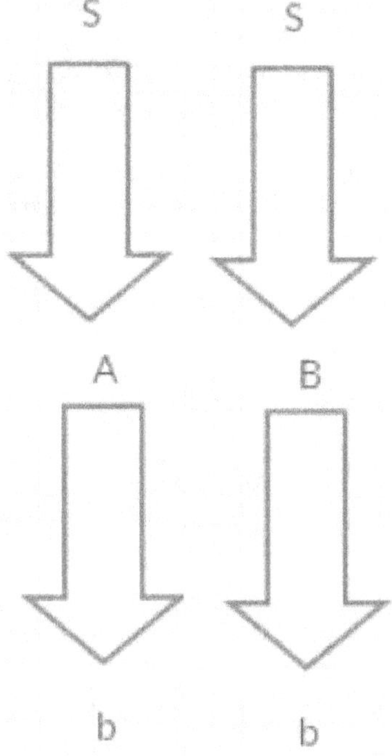

22. Credit theft is impossible with smart card as key to unlock encrypted information is required and also due to the absence of external account number on the card.

Hence the correct option is (C).

23. FAT12 is a12-bit version developed by Microsoft in1977 for Microsoft Disk BA SIC

FAT16 is a 16-bit version introduced in July 1988 for MS-DOS 4.0

FAT32 is a 32-bit version introduced in August 1996 for Windows 95 OSR2

Hence the correct option is (C).

24. TRACE macro sends an output message to the debug window of compiler. User can also see the trace messages without the debugger running using DebugView.

Hence the correct option is (C).

25. PVIEW is used to kill errant hidden processes in windows95. With PView, user can modify status of processes running on the system. As a result the entire system's processes can be stopped and potentially halt.

Hence the correct option is (C).

26. Select three columns from the COURSES table, of which the third one has a constant value, i.e. " = PRICE". Sort the data according to the second column, in ascending order.

Hence the correct option is (C).

27. It must be translated to the actual relation in the conceptual model of the database.

Hence the correct option is (A).

28. Because it may have the values from all the domains.

Hence the correct option is (B).

29. In order traversal is left->root->right and pre order is root->left-> right so it can used to find the post order traversal. first check the node in preorder and then find the root in in order, check left and right nodes and create a tree and then find the post order.

Hence the correct option is (C).

30. The queue can not be reversed as it is based on the concept of FIFO.

Hence the correct option is (D).

31. The time complexity of Prim's Algorithm is O(n $\times$ n).

Hence the correct option is (A).

32. If a B-tree is created with order m then the node may have max. of m hildren and then it splits into two and middle child becomes the root.

Hence the correct option is (A).

33. A can draw a ticket in $^{3}C_1 = 3$ ways.

Number of cases in which A can get a prize is 1.

Probability of A's success $= 1/3$

B can draw a ticket in $^{9}C_3$ ways $= 9.8.7/3.2.1 = 84$ ways.

Number of ways in which B gets all blanks $= ^{6}C_3 = 6.5.4/32.1 = 20$

Number of ways of getting a prize $= 84 - 20 = 64$

Thus the probability of B's success $= 9\dfrac{64}{84} = \dfrac{16}{21}$

So,

A's probability of success: B's probability of success $= \dfrac{1}{3} \times \dfrac{16}{21}$.

Hence the correct option is (A).

34. Here P represents file pointer. It points to the structure, in which char pointer exists which points to the first character of file.

Hence the correct option is (D).

35. Sending an email will be done through user agent and message transfer agent by SMTP, downloading an email from mail box is done through POP, checking email in a web browser is done through HTTP.

Hence the correct option is (C).

36. Total propagation delay = Lt sec.

Roundtrip time = 2 ✕ Lt = 2 Lt sec.

Number of bits transmitted in roundtrip = 2 LtR bits

Number of frames = (Tansmission Time + 2 ✕ Propagation Time)/Transmission Time

Number of frames = (K/R + 2Lt) / (K/R)

= 2LtR/K + 1 = (2LtR + K)/ K

Bits required for the sequence number field:

$$\left\lceil \log_2 \frac{2LtR+K}{K} \right\rceil$$

Hence the correct option is (D).

37. Start and stop bits are not needed in synchronous transfer of data, so it is 2400/ 8 =300.

Hence the correct option is (A).

38. Object of private constructor can only be created within class. Private constructor is used in singleton pattern.

Hence the correct option is (A).

39. When an exception is not caught, the program is aborted. Whenever an exception is generated (in the code which is placed in the 'try' block), it is thrown using a 'throw' statement in the 'try' block which is caught by the 'catch' block where it is handled appropriately.

Hence the correct option is (C).

40. Abstraction is simplification mechanism used to hide superfluous details of a set of objects. It allows one to concentrate on the properties that are of interest to the application. Generalization is the abstraction process of viewing sets of objects as a single general class by concentrating on the general characteristics of the constituent sets while suppressing or ignoring their difference. Specialization is the abstraction process of introducing new characteristics to an existing class of objects to create one or more new classes of objects.

Hence the correct option is (A).

41. Addition in hexadecimal number system is same as other number system. Since hexadecimal number, upto 15(F) are defined, a carry will be generated if addition is larger than F. Another way is to convert the hexadecimal numbers into equivalent binary numbers and then add the numbers.

Hence the correct option is (C).

42. A digital multiplexer can also be used to implement combinational logic function -**True**
In a combinational circuit, the current output depends on the previous outputs also -**False**

Hence the correct option is (C).

43. In RSA public key cryptography a public key provide for everyone but they have their separate private key.

According to formula of public key cryptography

I. M' = M^e mod, M = (M)^d mod n

IV M' = M^e mod φ(n), M = (M')^d mod φ(n)

represent RSA cryptosystem.

Hence the correct option is (B).

44. 32 functions need 5 bit encoding in control memory microinstruction to enable selection of one of the function.

16 data routes need 4 bit encoding in control memory microinstruction to enable selection of one of the data route. 32 − 2 − 8 = 22 independent storing units. Number of control signals, 22 ✕ 2 = 44. Two control signals are needed for two MUXs. Total number of control signals 46 signals for storing input-output register. Since 44 > 25, 6 bit encoding is required in control memory microinstruction to enable selection of one of the unit. 16384 (= 214) addresses are there in control memory. 14-bits are thus required from next-address field in the control memory. Therefore, for all the 4 fields the control memory need (5 + 4 + 6 + 14) encoding bits in each microinstruction.

Hence the correct option is (D).

45. Categories of 8085 instructions that manipulate data:

· STA is a data transfer instruction

· DCR is a arithmetic Instruction

· CMP is a logical Instruction

· CALL is a branch Instruction

Hence the correct option is (D).

46. ANAR - logical group instructions for 8085- AND accumulator with register
• PCHL - unconditional branch instructions. PCHL instruction exchange the contents of the program counter with the contents of the H and L registers.• ORAR - logical group instructions for 8085- OR accumulator with register• CMA - logical group instructions for 8085- Complement the Accumulator

Hence the correct option is (B).

47. The PCI bus is found in all the new Pentium systems as it has plug and play characteristics, has the ability to function with a 64 bit data bus and any microprocessor can be interfaced to it with PCI controller or bridge.

Hence the correct option is (D).

48. ANI stands for "Logical AND with Accumulator Using Immediate Data". This ANDs the accumulator with immediate. F leaves the high nibble whatever it is, 0 clears the lower nibble.

Hence the correct option is (B).

49. A transaction manager is the part of an application that is responsible for coordinating transactions across one or more resources. Transaction managers are responsible for ensuring that resources are not left in an inconsistent state, if there is a system failure and the application crashes.

Hence the correct option is (C).

50. Organizational forces, frequency of data access, need for growth and expansion, technological capabilities and need for reliable service are the factors for deciding on database distribution strategies.

Hence the correct option is (D).

51. For real-time requirements, store and forward messages for each completed transaction can be broadcast across the network informing all nodes to update data as soon as possible, without forcing a confirmation to the originating node before the database at the originating node is updated. One way to generate such messages is by using triggers. A trigger can be stored at each local database so that when a piece of replicated data is updated, the trigger executes corresponding update commands against remote database replicas.

Hence the correct option is (B).

52. These two statements produce identical results, because it is possible even to use numbers to indicate the column position where Oracle should order the output from a statement.

Hence the correct option is (A).

53. ALTER TABLE statement with ENABLE CONSTRAINT keyword is correct answer to enable an existing constraint.

Hence the correct option is (C).

54. A consistent backup is one in which the files being backed up contain all changes up to the same system change number. This means that the files in the backup contain all the data taken from a same point in time. Unlike an inconsistent backup, a consistent whole database backup does not require recovery after it is restored. An inconsistent backup is a backup of one or more database files that user make while the database is open or after the database has shut down abnormally.

Hence the correct option is (B).

55. In the priority queue, elements can be inserted in any order but the dequeue is always done in sorted order.

Heap is generally preferred for priority queue implementation because heaps provide better performance compared to arrays or linked lists. In a Binary Heap, getHighestPriority() can be implemented in O(1) time, insert() can be implemented in O(Logn) time and deleteHighestPriority() can also be implemented in O(Logn) time.

Hence, the correct option is (D).

56. WNDCLASS data structure include a pointer to a class() function for handling the window's message.

Hence the correct option is (B).

57. WPARAM is of 32 Bits in win-32 & is not used in handling the message.

Hence the correct option is (D).

58. Unix is also a time shared OS & programs using UNIX can be run on variety of architecture as it assumes to have no knowledge of architectures.

Hence the correct option is (C).

59.

Basic	x_1	x_2	s_1	s_2	s_3	Solution	Ratio
z_1	0	2	1	0	−1	400	200
s_2	0	1	0	1	−2	140	140 →
s_3	1	0	0	0	1	320	
z	0	−4	0	0	6	320	

Entering variable = x_2, Leaving variable s_2.

Basic	x_1	x_2	s_1	s_2	s_3	Solution	Ratio
s_3	0	0	1/3	2/3	1	40	
s_2	0	1	2/3	−1/3	0	220	
s_1	1	0	−1/3	2/3	0	280	
z	0	0	2/3	8/3	0	2560	

Hence the correct option is (B).

60. The number of distinct Boolean expression of n variable is 2^{2n}. Thus

$$2^{24} = 2^{16} = 65536$$

Hence D. is correct answer.

61. The maximum packet lifetime is given to be 64 seconds in the question.

Thus, a sequence number increments after every 64 seconds.

So, minimum permissible rate = 1 / 64 = 0.015 per second.

Hence the correct option is (A).

62. A pushdown automation consists of

i. a finite non empty set of states denoted by Q,

ii. a finite non empty set of input symbols denoted by Σ,

iii. a finite non empty set of pushdown symbols denoted by Γ,

iv. a special state called the initial state denoted by q_0,

v. a special pushdown symbol called the initial symbol on the pushdown store denoted by Z_0.

Hence the correct option is (C).

63. In a multiple track TM, a single tape is assumed to be divided into several tracks. Now the tape alphabet is required to consist of k-tuples of tape symbols, k being the number of tracks. Hence the only difference between the standard TM and the TM with multiple tracks is the set of tape symbols.

Hence the correct option is (A).

64. Suppose L is regular. Then, there exists a finite state automation M which accepts L. Suppose M has K states. Let w = $a^k b^k$.

Then |w| > k.

By the pumping Lemma w = xyz where y is not empty and w_2 = xy^2z is also accepted by M. If y consists of only a' s or only b's, then w_2 will not have the same number of a's as b's. If y contains both a's and b's, then w_2 will have a's following b's. In either case w_2 does not belong to L, which is a contradiction. Thus L is not regular.

Hence the correct option is (B).

65. Breadth first search are heuristic technique used in medicine, law, biology and chemistry etc.

Hence the correct option is (D).

66. 1. Simple LR (SLR for short), is the easiest to implement, but the least powerful of the three. It may fail to produce a parsing table for certain grammars on which the other methods succeed.

2. Canonical LR is the most powerful and the most expensive.

3. Look ahead LR (LALR for short), is intermediate in power and cost between the other two. The LALR method will work on most programming-language grammars and,with some effort, can be implemented efficiently.

Hence the correct option is (C).

67. Deletion and insertion of elements is not required in binary search.

Hence the correct option is (C).

68. Dependency preserving is not condition for BCNF.

Hence the correct option is (B).

69. In key dependencies as in Functional dependencies there is the dependency of keys.

Hence the correct option is (A).

70. 3x= y+7

3x-y= 7

By substituting options, we get x= 5, y=8 satisfies the above equation.

Hence the correct option is (B).

71. 128 greatest negative number which can be stored in a 8 – bit register using 2's complement arithmetic.

72. ICMP is the **I**nternet **C**ontrol **M**essage **P**rotocol. It is an **application layer protocol**. It is used by hosts, routers, & gateways to communicate network layer information to each other. The most typical use of ICMP is for error reporting.

Hence the correct option is (B).

73. For processing an output in XML, "new line" symbol are first converted to single LF symbol.

Hence the correct option is (C).

74. If you want to open a link in a new browser then it will be opened with <a href = "url" target ="-blank"> syntax.

Hence the correct option is (B).

75. <Script type = "text/javascript"> </jscript> using this tag , we insert a javascript in HTTH page. In all project this can be used.

Hence the correct option is (B).

76. The transportation method does not work if hiring and layoff is possible. This is an aggregate method.

Hence the correct option is (D).

77. Eight phase digital transmission implies 23 bits/second. Hence, the bit rate can be tripled over corresponding two phase modulation.Multi mode fiber allows more than one ray of light at a moment. It is generally greater in diameter than a single mode fiber.

Hence the correct option is (A).

78. If the M bit in X.25 standard is set to 1, it means that there is more than one packet. The M-bit or More Data indicates whether this particular packet is carrying the total intended message or whether there is more data to follow as part of this transmission.

Hence the correct option is (C).

79. Multiplexing is sharing of communication channel. Multiplexing involves multiple signals or streams of information on a carrier at the same time in the form of a single, complex signal. 10Base2 cabling is also popularly known as thin Ethernet.It supports transmission up to a maximum distance of 20 mts. Such Cables are cheaper and used for smaller lowcost LAN's.Frequency hopping and spread spectrum techniques are involved in transmission.Spread Spectrum is the wide range of frequencies during transmission.Time Domain Reflectometry is a technique that detects cable breaks, bad taps or loose connectors. The TDR measures the time it takes for the signal to travel down the cable and reflect back. The TDR then converts this time to distance and displays the information as a waveform and/or distance reading.

Hence the correct option is (A).

80. Use the formula $N = \dfrac{1+L}{(T-8)}$

Here $T = 5\mu$ sec
$L = 25\mu sec$ and
$D = 2.73\mu sec$
Putting the values and solving,
we get $N = 12.01$ which round down to 12 cells.
Hence the correct option is (B).

81. A binary ripple counter can count up to the binary value represented by n bits:

$\Rightarrow 2^n-1$

$\Rightarrow 2^5-1$

$\Rightarrow 31$

Hence the correct option is (C).

82. Given derivation is neither leftmost nor rightmost derivation because this is not restricted for left-right recursion/replacement.

Hence the correct option is (D).

83. $(r*s*)* = (r + s)* = (r* + s*)*$

This is the one of the identity from the 12 identities of regular grammar.

Hence the correct option is (B).

84. The syntax to declare multidimensional array in java is either int[][] arr; or int arr[][];

Hence the correct option is (C).

85. A self relocating program is one which can itself perform the relocation of its address-sensitive portions.

Hence the correct option is (C).

86. The basic principle behind the structured design methodology in problem partitioning

the four major steps are

1. Restate the problem

2. Identify the input and output

3. First level factoring

4. Factoring of input, output and transform branches.

Hence the correct option is (B).

87. None of the given statements are true.

Hence the correct option is (C).

88. Areas of application of software metrics are :

1. Prediction of quality levels for software in terms of reliability

2. Cost and size estimation techniques

3. Controlling software development projects through measurement.

Hence the correct option is (D).

89. Lists in PROLOG constitute elements separated by commas and enclosed within square brackets. The elements could comprise of any data type.eg – [2, 4, 8, 10, 12] and ['jack', 'jill', 'jane' 1]

Hence the correct option is (B).

90. p:-a, b, c

p:-d, e, f ,

This represents the control structure in PROLOG. Given representation means that p is true if either (a and b and c) is true or (d and e and f) is true the comma implies an AND.

Hence the correct option is (A).

91. Arity is the number of arguments in a predicate form. It is represented by a/n placed after the predicate name. n is the number of arguments for instance the predicate relishes/2 takes two arguments.

Hence the correct option is (B).

92. Some of the important standards for providing structure to multimedia applications are–

1. MHEG

2. PREMO

3. ODA

4. Acrobat

5. Hytime

6. SGML

Hence the correct option is (C).

93. The steps involved in the animation are-

(i) Storyboard layout

(ii) Object definitions

(iii) Keyframe specifications

(iv) Generation of in-between frames

Hence the correct option is (A).

94. Parameterized systems allow object motion characteristics to be specified as part of the object definitions. The adjustable parameters control such object characteristics as degrees of freedom, motion limitations and allowable shape changes.

Hence the correct option is (B).

95. All (1), (3) and (4) are false. The difference between (2) and (3) is vital.

80386 processor has 32 bit address capacity (32 pins for address) hence it its capable of accessing 232 = 22 ⨉ 230 = 4GB = 4096 MB of main memory. Present day computers have atmost 32 MB RAM. The address space of 386 processor is 4GB and hence virtual memory can be atmost 4 GB. If a program is of 5 GB, we have to use only overlying technique.

Hence the correct option is (B).

96. Monitoring shell commands is an example of anomaly detection. Monitoring shell commands is used to detect anomalous commands for a given user or detecting an anomalous login time for a user.

Hence the correct option is (C).

97. Option (2) gives the correct O/P for the program.

Hence the correct option is (B).

98. Readability – Programs written in high level languages are more readable than assembly and machine language. Portability – Programs could be run on different machines with little or no change.

Hence the correct option is (C).

99. A PROLOG program comprises a description of the problem using a number of facts and rules. Matching in PROLOG is performed predicate to predicate and argument to argument.

Hence the correct option is (B).

100. The following subtraction operations result in F_{16}:

(i) $(BA)_{16} - (AB)_{16} = (F)_{16}$

(ii) $(BC)_{16} - (CB)_{16} =$ will give negative 15

(iii) $(CB)_{16} - (BC)_{16} = (F)_{16}$

Hence, the correct option is (B).

Q.1 Given a hash table T with 25 slots that stores 2000 elements, the load factor α for T is__________.

A. 80   **B.** 50   **C.** 40   **D.** 30

Q.2 Consider the hashing function h(k)=k mod 7. The number of collisions with linear probing for the insertion of the following keys 29, 36, 16, 30.

A. 2   **B.** 3   **C.** 4   **D.** 1

Q.3 Solve the following Recurrence Relation:

T(n) = 1 if n=1

T(n)= T(n/2) + c else

A. $O(n^3)$ **B.** $O(\log n)$ **C.** $O(n)$ **D.** $O(n^2)$

Q.4 A bulb in a staircase has two switches, one switch being at the ground floor and the other one at the first floor. The bulb can be turned ON and also can be turned OFF by any one of the switches irrespective of the state of the other switch. The logic of switching of the bulb resembles

A. AND gate   **B.** OR gate
C. XOR gate   **D.** NAND gate

Q.5 Consider the following graph

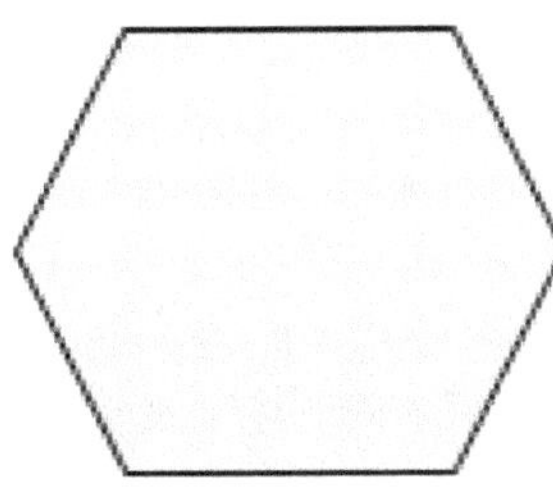

What is the total number of spanning tree for the above graph?

A. 5   **B.** 6   **C.** 12   **D.** 11

Q.6 Which of the following are regular sets?

I. $\{a^n b^{2m} \mid n \geq 0, m \geq 0\}$

II. $\{a^n b^m \mid n = 2m\}$

III. $\{a^n b^m \mid n \neq m\}$

IV. $\{xcy \mid x,y \in \{a,b\}^*\}$

A. I and IV only   **B.** I and III only
C. I only   **D.** IV only

Q.7 Total number of ordering possible with elements 12, 10, 8, 5, 3, 2, 1, 13, 7, 9, 18 such that it satisfied max heap property

________.

A. 15600   **B.** 19200   **C.** 1800   **D.** 17600

Q.8 Consider a linked list L which has 'n' nodes in it. Now consider an algorithm on the linked list which identifies whether a cycle exists or not in the linked list. If cycle is present , then it also finds the initial node of the cycle. What is the time complexity of the best algorithm for this problem ?

A. $O(n^2)$ **B.** $O(n^3)$

C. $O(n\log n)$ **D.** $O(n)$

Q.9 Which one of the following is TRUE about the interior gateway routing protocols – Routing Information Protocol (RIP) and Open Shortest Path First (OSPF)?

A. RILP uses distance vector routing and OSPF uses link state routing

B. OSPF uses distance vector routing and RIP uses link state routing

C. Both RIP and OSPF use link state routing

D. Both RIP and OSPF use distance vector routing

Q.10 Consider socket API on a Linux machine that supports connected UDP sockets. A connected UDP socket is a UDP socket on which connect function has already been called. Which of the following statements is/are CORRECT?

I. A connected UDP socket can be used to communicate with multiple peers simultaneously.

II. A process can successfully call connect function again for an already connected UDP socket.

A. I only   **B.** II only
C. Both I and II   **D.** Neither I nor IIs

Q.11 In C programming, which of the following is not used as a token separator during lexical analysis?

A. White space   **B.** Comment
C. Semicolon   **D.** None of these

Q.12 Match List-I (Dynamic algorithm) with List-II (Average case running time) and select the correct answer using the codes given below the lists:

List – I (Dynamic algorithm)	List – II (Average case running time)
A. Matrix chain multiplication	1. $O(mn)$
B. Travelling salesman problem	2. $O(n^3)$
C. 0/1 knapsack	3. $O(n^n)$
D. Fibonacci series	4. $O(n)$

A. A-1 B-3 C-2 D-4   **B.** A-1 B-3 C-3 D-2
C. A-2 B-3 C-3 D-2   **D.** A-2 B-3 C-1 D-4

Q.13 Consider the following undirected graph with 8 nodes .

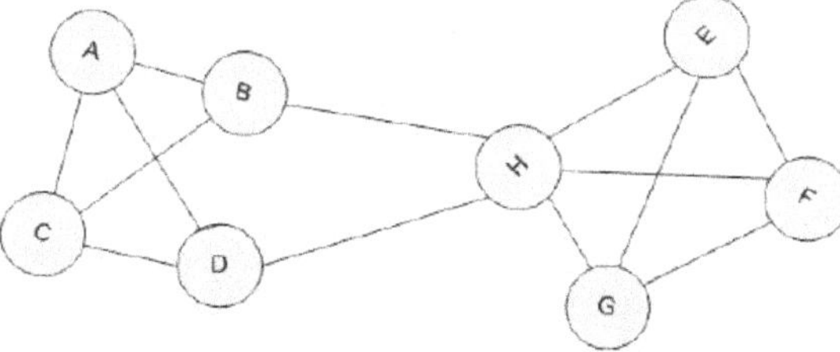

Now consider the following traversals made on the graph :

I. ABCDHEFG

II. ACBDHFGE

III. ADBCHGFE

IV. HBDEGACF

Which of the above traversals are valid Breadth First traversals ?

A. Only I and II **B.** Only II and III
C. Only I and III **D.** All are valid

Q.14 main ()
```
main ()
{
if (fork() >=0 )
{
printf("*");
if(fork() == 0)
{
printf("*");
}
}
else
{
// do nothing
}
printf("*");
}
```
A. 7 **B.** 8 **C.** 9 **D.** 10

Q.15 A priority queue is implemented as a Max-Heap. Initially, it has 5 elements. The level-order traversal of the heap is: 10, 8, 5, 3, 2. Two new elements 1 and 7 are inserted into the heap in that order. The level-order traversal of the heap after the insertion of the elements is:

A. 10, 8, 7, 3, 2, 1, 5 **B.** 10, 8, 7, 2, 3, 1, 5
C. 10, 8, 7, 1, 2, 3, 5 **D.** 10, 8, 7, 5, 3, 2, 1

Q.16 What is the size of the 'total length' field in IPv 4 datagram?
A. 4 bits **B.** 8 bits **C.** 16 bits **D.** 32 bits

Q.17 If a processor has 32-bit virtual address, 28-bit physical address, 2 kb pages. How many bits are required for the virtual, physical page number ?
A. 17, 21 **B.** 21,17 **C.** 6, 10 **D.** None

Q.18 The octal value of hexadecimal number AB123 is
A. $(2540443)_8$ **B.** $(2540423)_8$
C. $(2530443)_8$ **D.** $(2440407)_8$

Q.19 Consider the following grammar.

$S \rightarrow S * E$
$S \rightarrow E$
$E \rightarrow F + E$
$E \rightarrow F$
$F \rightarrow id$

Consider the following LR(0) items corresponding to the grammar above.

(i) $S \rightarrow S *.E$
(ii) $E \rightarrow F. +E$
(iii) $E \rightarrow F +.E$

Given the items above, which two of them will appear in the same set in the canonical sets-of-items for the grammar?

A. (i) and (ii) **B.** (ii) and (iii)

C. (i) and (iii) **D.** None of the above

Q.20 We have used distance vector routing algorithm for the following graph. Routing tables for Q, S, U are shown below. They came to router R. Delays measured from router R to Q, S, U are 6, 4,8.

Q: (3, 0, 3, 5, 10, 5)W
S: (10, 9, 3, 0, 12, 5)
U: (5, 6, 4, 3, 7,0)
Find the distance vector for router R

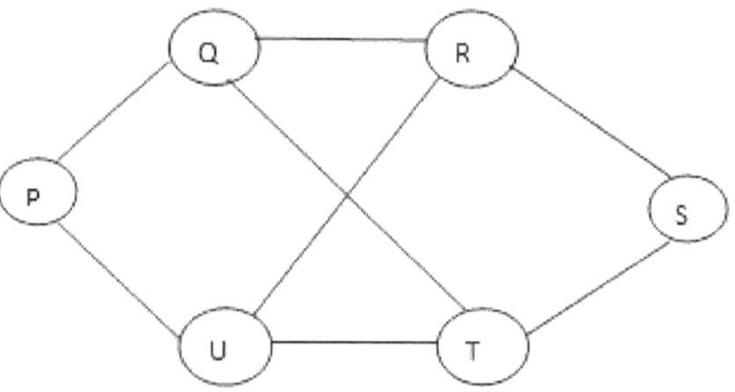

A. (9, 7, 0, 11, 16, 8) **B.** (8, 7, 0, 11, 16, 9)
C. (9, 6, 0, 11,4, 8) **D.** (9, 6, 0,11 ,16 ,9)

Q.21 Which of the following describes a handle (as applicable to LR-parsing) appropriately?

A. It is the position in a sentential form where the next shift or reduce operation will occur

B. It is a non-terminal whose production will be used for reduction in the next step

C. It is a production that may be used for reduction in a future step along with a position in the sentential form where the next sh1ft or reduce operation will occur

D. It is the production p that will be used for reduction in the next step along with a position in the sentential form where the right hand side of the production may be found

Q.22 How many of the following is true about UDP?
A) Reliable
B) Connection less
C) It uses acknowledgement
D) It uses checksum
A. A) and C) **B.** B) and D)
C. B) and A) **D.** A) and D)

Q.23 Match List-I with List-II and select the correct answer using the codes given below the lists:

List – I	List – II
A. Quick sort	1. Greedy algorithm
B. Longest common subsequence	2. Divide and conquer
C. Kruskal's algorithm	3. Dynamic programming
D. Shortest distance from a given node to every node	

A. A-2 B-3 C-1 D-3 **B.** A-2 B-1 C-3 D-2
C. A-2 B-3 C-1 D-1 **D.** A-2 B-1 C-2 D-1

Q.24 Consider the following process table with Arrival time and Burst time (All time in ms).

Process	Arrival Time	Burs time
P_1	1	2
P_2	6	4
P_3	4	10
P_4	5	6

Average waiting time of these processes by using SRTF scheduling is _______ (ms). (Upto 1 decimal place)

A. 3 **B.** 4.5 **C.** 4 **D.** 3.5

Q.25 Which of the following is incorrect regarding internet control message protocol (ICMP)?

A. When something unexpected occurs in routers these kind of events are reported by the ICMP.

B. ICMP and BOOTP protocols are equivalent in their usage.

C. Each ICMP message type is encapsulated in a IP packet.

D. ICMP is also used to test the connectivity.

Q.26 The Fiber Distributed Data Interface uses:

A. single mode fibers and LEDs

B. multimode fibers and LEDs

C. multimode fibers and LEDs

D. multimode fibers and ILDs

Q.27 Which of the following services is not provided by wireless access point in 802.11 WLAN?

A. Association **B.** Dis aasociation

C. Error correction **D.** Integration

Q.28 What is the size (in terms of bits) of Header length field in IPV4 header?

A. 2 **B.** 4 **C.** 8 **D.** 16

Q.29 A canonical set of items is given below

$$S \to L > R \quad Q \to R$$

On input symbol < the set has

A. A shift-reduce conflict and a reduce-reduce conflict.

B. A shift-reduce conflict but not a reduce-reduce conflict.

C. A reduce-reduce conflict but not a shift-reduce conflict.

D. Neither a shift-reduce nor a reduce-reduce conflict.

Q.30 Consider the following grammar G

$$S \to F \mid H$$
$$F \to p \mid c$$
$$H \to d \mid c$$

where S,F, and Hare non-terminal symbols , p, d, and care terminal symbols. Which of the following statement (s) is/are correct?

S_1. LL(1) can parse al strings that are generated using grammar G

S_2. LR(1) can parse all strings that are generated using grammar G

A. Only S_1 **B.** Only S_2

C. Both S_1 and S_2 **D.** Neither S_1 nor S_2

Q.31 The post order traversal of a binary search tree is

7, 12, 11, 15, 14, 13, 20, 22, 25, 24, 21, 17

Then the preorder traversal of this tree is:

A. 17, 13, 11, 12, 7, 14, 15, 21, 20, 24, 22, 25

B. 17, 13, 11, 7, 12, 15, 14, 21, 20, 24, 25, 22

C. 17, 13, 11, 7, 12, 14, 21, 15, 20, 24, 22, 25

D. 17, 13, 11, 7, 12, 14, 15, 21, 20, 24, 22, 25

Q.32 What is the value printed by the following C program?

```c
#include < stdio.h >
int f(int * a, int n)
{
if (n < = 0)return 0;
else if(*a % 2 = = 0) return * a + f(a + 1, n – 1);
else return * a – f(a + 1, n – 1);
}
int main ( )
{
int a[ ] = {12, 7, 13, 4, 11, 6};
printf ("%d", f(a,6));
return 0;
}
```

A. -9 **B.** 5 **C.** 15 **D.** 19

Q.33 The mechanism involves in direct searching is:

A. Binary Search **B.** Linear Search

C. Tree Search **D.** Hashing

Q.34 Which of the following algorithm design techniques is used in strassen's algorithm?

A. Dynamic Programming

B. Backtracking

C. Divide and Conquer

D. Greedy Method

Q.35 Consider the following flow control diagram over transport layer:

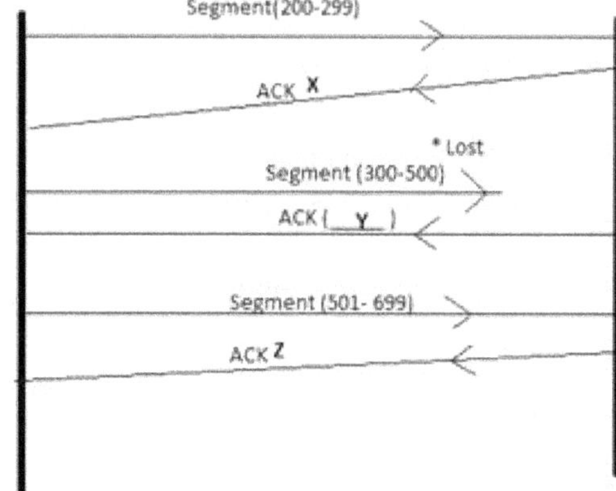

What is the value of X+ Y- Z _______

A. 300 **B.** 400 **C.** 600 **D.** 200

Q.36 The Mobile Application Protocol (MAP) typically runs on top of which protocol?

A. The Mobile Application Protocol (MAP) typically runs on top of which protocol?

B. SMTP (Simple Mail Transfer Protocol)

C. SS7 (Signalling System 7)

D. HTTP (Hyper Text Transfer Protocol)

Q.37 The maximum payload of a TCP segment is:

A. 65,535 **B.** 65,515 **C.** 65,495 **D.** 65,475

Q.38 F's complemented of $(2BFD)_{hex}$ in decimal is___.

A. D405 **B.** D400 **C.** D401 **D.** D402

Q.39 Quicksort is run on an input size of 1000 and the time taken is 100 ms in worst case. Find the time taken to execute the same code in same conditions when the input size is 128 and best case is considered _________ (in microseconds)?

A. 89.6 **B.** 18.2 **C.** 78.2 **D.** 65.3

Q.40 Encoding or scrambling data for transmission across a network is known as:A stack can be implemented using two queues. Let the queues be q_1, q_2 and the stack be s.

The operations push and pop are implemented in the following way:

push(s, x):

a. enqueue x to q_2.

b. P

c. Q

pop(s):

dequeue from q_1

The best possible option for P and Q are respectively:

A. dequeue each element from q_1 and enqueue to q_2, dequeue each element from q_2 and enqueue to q_1

B. dequeue each element from q_2 and enqueue to q_1, dequeue each element from q_1 and enqueue to q_2

C. dequeue each element from q_1 and enqueue to q_2, no operation

D. dequeue each element from q_2 and enqueue to q_1, no operation

Q.41 Suppose, a digitized voice channel is made by digitizing 8 kHz bandwidth analog voice signal. It is required to sample the signal at twice the highest frequency (two samples per hertz). What is the bit rate required, if it is assumed that each sample requires 8 bits?

A. 32 kbps **B.** 64 kbps **C.** 128 kbps **D.** 256 kbps

Q.42 Which one of the following devices reduce collision domain to zero

A. Repeater **B.** Hub **C.** Bridge **D.** Switch

Q.43 Consider an arbitrary set of CPU-bound processes with unequal CPU burst lengths submitted at the same time to a computer system. Which one of the following process scheduling algorithms would minimize the average waiting time in the ready queue?

A. Shortest remaining time first

B. Round-robin with time quantum less than the shortest CPU burst

C. Uniform random

D. Highest priority first with priority proportional to CPU burst length

Q.44 An array of 25 distinct elements is to be sorted using quicksort. Assume that the pivot element is chosen uniformly at random. The probability that the pivot element gets placed in the worst possible location in the first round of partitioning (rounded off to 2 decimal places) is _______.

A. 0.2 **B.** 0.23 **C.** 0.08 **D.** 1.3

Q.45 CPU scheduling is a process which allows one process to use the CPU while the execution of another process is on hold(waiting time) due to unavailability of any resource like I/O etc, thereby making full use of CPU. Thus the task of CPU is to maximize its UTILISATION. What among the following is not true to achieve that

A. Max throughput

B. Min waiting time

C. Max turnaround time

D. Min response time

Q.46 Consider the C program

```
Main()
{
int x = 10;
x = x + y + z;
}
```

How many tokens are identified by lexical analyzer?

A. 18 **B.** 20 **C.** 23 **D.** 26

Q.47 Consider the following processes, with the arrival time and the length of the CPU burst given in milliseconds. The scheduling algorithm used is preemptive shortest remaining time first.

Process	Arrival Time	Burst Time
P1	0	10
P2	3	6
P3	7	1
P4	8	3

The average turnaround time of these processes is ____ milliseconds.

A. 3.45 **B.** 5.34 **C.** 8.25 **D.** 9.34

Q.48 Consider the following SDT.

$E \rightarrow E+T$ {E.x=E.x $\times$ T.x}

$E \rightarrow T$ {E.x=T.x}

$T \rightarrow T \times F$ {T.x=T.x-F.x}

$T \rightarrow F$ {T.x=F.x-1}

$F \rightarrow id$ {F.x=5}

If bottom up parsing uses S-attributed definition then what is the value of attribute evaluated at root E for an input string " id+id*id "?

A. -4 **B.** -6 **C.** -8 **D.** -9

Q.49 When compared with analog cellular systems, an advantage of digital TDMA cellular system is that:

A. it is less complicated

B. it requires less of computer memory

C. it conserves spectrum bandwidth

D. it costs less

Q.50 Match the following:

List-I

a. Application layer

b. Transport layer

c. Network layer

d. Data link layer

List-II

1. TCP

2. HDLC

3. HTTP

4. BGP

A. a-2 b-1 c-4 d-3   **B.** a-3 b-4 c-1 d-2

C. a-3 b-1 c-4 d-2   **D.** a-2 b-4 c-1 d-3

Q.51 X.25 protocol consists of:

A. Physical an Frame levels

B. Frame and Packet levels

C. Physical, Frame and Packet levels

D. None of the above

Q.52 Device on one network can communicate with devices on another network via a

A. Hub/Switch   **B.** Utility server

C. File server   **D.** Gateway

Q.53 "Telnet" is used to ______

A. Connect to a remote computer

B. Copy the files without viewing them

C. Display the web pages on browser

D. None of these

Q.54 Consider the following keys that are hashed into the hash table in the order given using the hash function $h(i) = (2i + 5)$ mod 11.

12, 44, 13, 88, 23, 94, 11, 39, 20, 16, 5.

Assume hash table has locations from 0 to 10. If hash table uses chaining to handle the collisions, how many locations are left without hashing any element into it?

A. 1   **B.** 3   **C.** 5   **D.** 7

Q.55 Mobile IP provides two basic functions.

A. Route discovery and registration

B. Agent discovery and registration

C. IP binding and registration

D. None of the above

Q.56 GSM/CDMA system:

A. are limited to very low speed data

B. require no local loop wires

C. are predominantly used for voice

D. all of the above

Q.57 In case of Bus/Tree topology signal balancing issue is overcome by

A. Modulation   **B.** Polling

C. Segmentation   **D.** Strong transmitter

Q.58 X.25 is ______ Network.

A. Connection Oriented Network

B. Connection Less Network

C. Either Connection Oriented or Connection Less

D. Neither Connection Oriented nor Connection Less

Q.59 What is the purpose of the PSH flag in the TCP header?

A. Typically used to indicate end of message

B. Typically used to indicate beginning of message

C. Typically used to push the message

D. Typically used to indicate stop the message

Q.60 Medium term scheduler is

A. used to control the degree of multiprogramming

B. used to swap processes between secondary storage and main memory and is done periodically to ensure high CPU utilisation and low page fault rate

C. used to allocate CPU to a process

D. None of these

Q.61 A system has three processes P_1, P_2, P_3 and three resources R_1, R_2, R_3. There are two instances of R_1, one instance of R_2 and three instances of R_3. P_1 holds an instance of R_1 and an R_3 and is requesting an R_2. P_2 holds an R_1 and an R_2 and is requesting an instance of R_3. P_3 holds an instance of R_3 and is requesting an R_2. Write 0 if above scenario leads to deadlock or write 1, if deadlock does not exist.

A. 1   **B.** 2   **C.** 3   **D.** 4

Q.62 A sequential access file has 15 bytes record. Assume that the first record is numbered as 1, than what will be the logical location at which first byte of sixth record will be stored ______

A. 75   **B.** 76   **C.** 77   **D.** 78

Q.63 Consider allocation of memory to a new process. Assume that none of the existing holes in the memory will exactly fit the process's memory requirement. Hence, a new hole of smaller size will be created if allocation is made of the existing holes. Which one of the following statements is TRUE?

A. The hole created by the best fit is never larger than the hole created by first fit

B. The hole created by the best fit is always larger than the hole created by next fit

C. The hole created by the next fit is never larger than the hole created by best fit

D. The hole created by worst fit is always larger than the hole created by first fit

Q.64 The language L = {$0^i 2 1^i$| i ≥ 0} over the alphabet {0,1,2} is :

A. not recursive

B. is recursive and is a deterministic CFL

C. is a regular language.

D. is not a deterministic CFL but a CFL.

Q.65 Data Encryption Techniques are particularly used for ______.

A. protecting data in Data Communication System.
B. reduce Storage Space Requirement.
C. enhances Data Integrity.
D. decreases Data Integrity.

Q.66 Both hosts and routers are TCP/IP protocol software. However, routers do not use protocol from all layers. The layer for which protocol software is not needed by a router is

A. Layer – 5 (Application)
B. Layer – 1 (Physical)
C. Layer – 3 (Internet)
D. Layer – 2 (Network Interface)

Q.67 While unit testing a module, it is found that for a set of test data, maximum 90% of the code alone were tested with a probability of success 0.9. The reliability of the module is

A. atleast greater than 0.9
B. equal to 0.9
C. atmost 0.81
D. atleast 1/0.81

Q.68 For the transmission of the signal, Blue-tooth wireless technology uses

A. time division multiplexing
B. frequency division multiplexing
C. time division duplex
D. frequency division duplex

Q.69 The greatest negative number which can be stored in computer that has 8-bit work length and uses 2's complement arithmetic is

A. - 256 **B.** - 255 **C.** -128 **D.** -127

Q.70 Match the following:

List - I
i. Ethernet
ii. Token Ring
iii. Cut-through switch
iv. Spanning tree

List - II
A. Deterministic
B. Utilize the full wire speed
C. Prevent looping
D. Checking valid address.

A. i – d, ii – a, iii – b, iv – c
B. i – a, ii – d, iii – b, iv – c
C. i – d, ii – d, iii – c, iv – b
D. i – d, ii – c, iii – b, iv – a

Q.71 Identify the IP address from the following:

A. 300.215-3173 **B.** 302.215@417.5
C. 202.50.20.148 **D.** 202-50-20-148

Q.72 The acronym FTP stands for

A. File Transfer Protocol
B. Fast Transfer Protocol
C. File Tracking Protocol
D. File Transfer Procedure

Q.73 Match the following:

List – I
a. Physical layer
b. Datalink layer
c. Network layer
d. Transport layer
e. Application layer

List – II
i. Allow resources to network access
ii. Move packets from one destination to other
iii. Process to process message delivery
iv. Transmission of bit stream
v. Formation of frames

A. a-iv b-v c-ii d-iii e-i **B.** a-v b-iv c-i d-ii e-iii
C. a-i b-iii c-ii d-v e-iv **D.** a-I b-ii c-iv d-iii e-v

Q.74 Match List-I with List-II and select the correct answer using the codes given below the lists:

List-I
P. Retransmission Timer
Q. Persistent Timer
R. Time Wait Timer
S. Keep Alive Timer

List-II
1) Used to deal with zero window size deadlock situation
2) Used to prevent long idle connection.
3) Used to retransmit lost segments.
4) Used for TCP connection termination

A. P-1 Q-2 R-3 S-4 **B.** P-2 Q-1 R-4 S-3
C. P-3 Q-1 R-4 S-2 **D.** P-3 Q-4 R-1 S-2

Q.75 Consider the following code for inorder traversal of a binary tree.

```
Void traversal (node *root)
{
if (root ==0)
{
Print f("empty tree");
}
else
{
itraversal (root  left);
printf("%d\n", root  data);
liraversal (root right);
}
}
```

Which of the following is true about above snippet of code.

A. It prints inorder traversal and then prints "empty tree" infinite times.
B. It prints only inorder traversal of tree
C. It prints inorder traversal also prints "empty tree" 2N times

("N" is number of total nodes in tree).

D. It prints inorder traversal of tree and also prints "empty tree" (N+1) times, where N is the total number of nodes in tree.

Q.76 Match the following port numbers with their uses:

List – I

(a) 23

(b) 25

(c) 80

(d) 119

List – II

(i) World wide web

(ii) Remote Login

(iii) USENET news

(iv) E-mail

A. (a)-(iv) (b)- (i) (c)-(ii) (d)- (iii)

B. (a)- (ii) (b)- (i) (c)- (iv) (d)- (iii)

C. (a)- (ii) (b)- (iv) (c)- (iii) (d)- (i)

D. (a)- (ii) (b)-(iv) (c)- (i) (d)-(iii)

Q.77 Which are the two modes of IP security?

A. Transport and certificate

B. Transport and tunnel

C. Certificate and tunnel

D. Preshared and transport

Q.78 If there is a process of size 4MB. Given that number of pages is 512 K and page table entry is 8 bytes. Then Optimal page size so that wastage is minimum is _____KB.

A. 7　　　**B.** 8　　　**C.** 9　　　**D.** 10

Q.79 Match the following with respect to the Mobile Computing Architecture.

List - I

a. Downlink control

b. Radio communication data rate

c. The average duration of user's stay in cell

d. FDDI bandwidth

List - II

1. 100 Mbps

2. Residency latency (RL)

3. Sending data from a BS to MD

4. 2-Mbps

A. a-2 b-1 c-4 d-3　　　**B.** a-3 b-4 c-2 d-1

C. a-4 b-1 c-2 d-1　　　**D.** a-4 b-3 c-1 d-2

Q.80 Consider a system having segmented paging where segment is divided into 8K pages and each page has 2K entries. Memory is byte addressable. Segment number can be specified with 15 bits. The physical address space is 512KB and page table entry size is 8 bits. Then calculate the difference between the logical address and physical address bits?

A. 17　　　**B.** 18　　　**C.** 19　　　**D.** 20

Q.81 Consider the following 3 processes with the length of cpu burst time(in milliseconds). All processes arriving at the same time in order P1, P2, P3

Process	Brust time
P1	24
P2	3
P3	3

If Round Robin Scheduling is used with time quantum of 1 Unit then average waiting time will be,

A. 6.5ms　　　**B.** 5.66ms　　　**C.** 7ms　　　**D.** 8ms

Q.82 Which of the following protocols is an application layer protocol that establishes, manages and terminates multimedia sessions?

A. Session Maintenance Protocol

B. Real-time Streaming Protocol

C. Real-time Transport Control Protocol

D. Session Initiation Protocol

Q.83 Convey effect is not observed in-

1-FCFS

2-SJF

3-SRTF

A. Only in 1　　　**B.** Only in 1 & 2

C. Only in 3　　　**D.** Only in 2 & 3

Q.84 Consider a system implementing inverted page table concept. If physical address is 32 bit wide and page size is 16 KB. System is having a process to 48 bit wide that is virtual address is 48 bit wide. Then the size of Inverted page entry (in bytes) if inverted page table is of 2 MB.

A. 1 Byte　　　**B.** 2 Byte　　　**C.** 4 Byte　　　**D.** 8 Byte

Q.85 If $(32)_5 = (X4)_y$, then the possible value of X and Y respectively:

(X and Y are positive numbers)

A. 12, 3　　　**B.** 13,1　　　**C.** 1,13　　　**D.** 3,12

Q.86 Consider the following equation:

$(X)_6 = (235)_6 + (231)_6$

The 6's complement of X will be________.

A. 50　　　**B.** 65　　　**C.** 70　　　**D.** 75

Q.87 Consider the equation $(84)_x = (66)_y$ with the base system x & y both unknown, then the possible value of x & y is -

A. 4,6　　　**B.** 7,8

C. 4,5　　　**D.** None of the Above

Q.88 What is the equivalent CFL for the following CFG ?

S -> 0S1 / ∈

A. {x | x is a palindrome }

B. {x | x = 0n1n for n >= 0}

C. {x | x = 0n1n for n > 0}

D. {x | x = 0n1n for n > 1}

Q.89 A system uses FIFO policy for page replacement. It has 4 page frames with no pages loaded to begin with. The system first accesses 100 distinct pages in some order and then

accesses the same 100 pages but now in the reverse order. How many page faults will occur?

A. 196 **B.** 192 **C.** 197 **D.** 195

Q.90 Which of the following statement is true regarding the languages?

A. Membership is decidable for RE languages.

B. Finiteness property is decidable for recursive language.

C. Emptiness property is decidable for context free languages.

D. Equivalence of 2 languages is decidable in context sensitive languages.

Q.91 Consider the following problems

A) L is a context sensitive language (CSL), complement of L is of same type.

B) Let L1 and L2 is CSL, intersection of L1 and L2 is empty or not.

C) Finiteness problem in CFGs.

D) Emptiness problem for CFGs

Number of problems that are decidable is ____.

A. 1 **B.** 2 **C.** 3 **D.** 4

Q.92 consider the following statements

Statement 1- If S_1 and S_2 are countable sets, then union of S_1 and S_2 is countable.

Statement 2- The cartesian product or union of finite countable sets may or may not be countable.

Statement 3- The set of all languages that are not recursively enumerable is uncountable.

Number of statements that are correct is ______.

A. 1 **B.** 2

C. 3 **D.** None of the above

Q.93 In indirect communication between Processes P and Q what do the two process have in common or what do they share

A. there is another process R to handle and pass on the message between P and Q

B. there is another machine between the two process to help communication

C. there is a mailbox to help communication between P and Q

D. None of these

Q.94 If a software company wants to have computer network consisting of 96 hosts, then what is the best possible mask that the network administrator should choose.

A. 255.255.255.126 **B.** 255.255.255.127

C. 255.255.255.128 **D.** 255.255.255.129

Q.95 Given two binary strings with binary value 10011100 and 1010101 and some operation is performed on them and output according to it is -71. Code for ADD operation is 1, for SUB 2, for AND 3 and XOR for 4. Give the integer code for correct operation. Assuming unsigned numbers.

A. 1 **B.** 2 **C.** 3 **D.** 4

Q.96 A computer system contains a main memory of 32 K size wth 16 bit words. It also has a 4 K word cache divided into 4

slot sets with 64 words per slot. Assume that the cache is initially empty. The processor fetches words from 0, 1, 2, ...4351 in that order repeatedly 10 times. Assume a LRU policy for block replacement. How many miss operations will occur?

A. 244 **B.** 248 **C.** 322 **D.** 168

Q.97 The time delay for four segment pipeline is t_1 = 50ns, t_2 = 45 ns, t_3 = 95ns, t_4 = 30ns. The interface register delay time is t_r = 5ns. The time to add 100 pairs of numbers in the pipeline is 10.3μs. The time is reduced to half of the total time what should be done in the pipeline to achieve this.

A. Divide t_3 into two segment of 50 and 45.

B. Divide t_3 into three segment of 30, 30 and 35

C. Divide t_1 into two segment of 25 and 25

D. This cannot be achieved

Q.98 Given the following information:

• TLB hit rate 95%, TLB access time is 1 cycle.

• cache hit rate 90 %, cache access time is 1 cycle.

• When TLB and cache both get miss; page fault rate is 1%

• The TLB access and acache access are sequential.

• Access to main memory required 75 cycles

• Access to hard drive requires 50,000 cycles.

Compute the average memory access latencies when the cache is physically addresses (in cycles).

A. 2.45 **B.** 9.35 **C.** 15.75 **D.** 18.25

Q.99 Check sum used along with each packet computes the sum of the data, where data is treated as a sequence of

A. Integer **B.** Character

C. Real numbers **D.** Bits

Q.100 Consider the following processors P_1, P_2 and P_3 having pipeline register latencies 1, 2 and 3 respectively.

P_1 : Four stage pipeline with stage latencies 1 ns, 2 ns, 3 ns, 4 ns

P_2 : Three stage pipeline with stage latencies 0.5 ns, 1.5 ns, 3 ns.

P_3 : Two stage pipeline with stage latencies 0.4 ns and 1.4 ns.

Which processor have highest cycle clock time?

A. P_1 **B.** P_2

C. P_3 **D.** Both P_2 and P_1

// Smart Answer Sheet //

Correct Percentage of students who answered correctly. **Skipped** Percentage of students who skipped.

Q.	Ans.	Correct / Skipped	Q.	Ans.	Correct / Skipped	Q.	Ans.	Correct / Skipped	Q.	Ans.	Correct / Skipped	Q.	Ans.	Correct / Skipped
1	A	86.71 % / 0.0 %	17	B	84.02 % / 0.0 %	33	D	81.39 % / 0.0 %	49	C	90.0 % / 0.0 %	65	A	80.66 % / 0.0 %
2	B	89.08 % / 0.0 %	18	C	78.44 % / 0.0 %	34	C	87.64 % / 0.0 %	50	C	77.37 % / 0.0 %	66	A	83.35 % / 0.0 %
3	B	84.92 % / 0.0 %	19	D	87.1 % / 0.0 %	35	A	80.93 % / 0.0 %	51	C	87.79 % / 0.0 %	67	C	76.03 % / 0.0 %
4	C	81.9 % / 0.0 %	20	C	88.84 % / 0.0 %	36	C	87.47 % / 0.0 %	52	D	87.18 % / 0.0 %	68	C	87.55 % / 0.0 %
5	B	86.85 % / 0.0 %	21	D	81.07 % / 0.0 %	37	C	83.58 % / 0.0 %	53	A	89.09 % / 0.0 %	69	C	85.2 % / 0.0 %
6	A	87.81 % / 0.0 %	22	B	84.79 % / 0.0 %	38	D	87.59 % / 0.0 %	54	C	87.63 % / 0.0 %	70	D	83.68 % / 0.0 %
7	B	85.12 % / 0.0 %	23	C	76.9 % / 0.0 %	39	A	82.81 % / 0.0 %	55	B	80.88 % / 0.0 %	71	C	86.74 % / 0.0 %
8	D	77.83 % / 0.0 %	24	D	89.44 % / 0.0 %	40	A	80.13 % / 0.0 %	56	D	89.35 % / 0.0 %	72	A	85.89 % / 0.0 %
9	A	82.08 % / 0.0 %	25	B	86.75 % / 0.0 %	41	C	81.6 % / 0.0 %	57	C	80.74 % / 0.0 %	73	A	87.78 % / 0.0 %
10	B	78.56 % / 0.0 %	26	B	78.08 % / 0.0 %	42	D	79.61 % / 0.0 %	58	A	84.06 % / 0.0 %	74	C	81.95 % / 0.0 %
11	D	87.39 % / 0.0 %	27	C	89.14 % / 0.0 %	43	A	89.14 % / 0.0 %	59	C	82.17 % / 0.0 %	75	D	81.96 % / 0.0 %
12	D	79.54 % / 0.0 %	28	B	79.35 % / 0.0 %	44	C	78.06 % / 0.0 %	60	B	77.21 % / 0.0 %	76	D	86.72 % / 0.0 %
13	D	82.04 % / 0.0 %	29	D	76.73 % / 0.0 %	45	C	80.2 % / 0.0 %	61	A	80.1 % / 0.0 %	77	B	88.54 % / 0.0 %
14	B	80.51 % / 0.0 %	30	D	87.81 % / 0.0 %	46	A	86.46 % / 0.0 %	62	A	82.89 % / 0.0 %	78	B	79.47 % / 0.0 %
15	A	77.79 % / 0.0 %	31	D	88.5 % / 0.0 %	47	C	80.76 % / 0.0 %	63	A	76.52 % / 0.0 %	79	B	78.9 % / 0.0 %
16	C	85.43 % / 0.0 %	32	C	84.2 % / 0.0 %	48	A	83.27 % / 0.0 %	64	B	88.42 % / 0.0 %	80	D	80.31 % / 0.0 %

Q.	Ans.	Correct	Skipped
81	B	86.77 %	0.0 %
82	D	83.47 %	0.0 %
83	D	82.25 %	0.0 %
84	D	76.1 %	0.0 %

Q.	Ans.	Correct	Skipped
85	C	81.4 %	0.0 %
86	A	86.8 %	0.0 %
87	D	80.91 %	0.0 %
88	C	85.01 %	0.0 %

Q.	Ans.	Correct	Skipped
89	A	89.63 %	0.0 %
90	C	84.32 %	0.0 %
91	C	76.62 %	0.0 %
92	B	80.49 %	0.0 %

Q.	Ans.	Correct	Skipped
93	C	80.76 %	0.0 %
94	C	87.52 %	0.0 %
95	A	80.75 %	0.0 %
96	B	81.67 %	0.0 %

Q.	Ans.	Correct	Skipped
97	A	84.81 %	0.0 %
98	C	77.28 %	0.0 %
99	D	88.65 %	0.0 %
100	D	76.31 %	0.0 %

//Hints and Solutions//

1. Load factor = (no. of elements) / (no. of table slots) = 2000/25 = 80

A hash table (hash map) is a data structure used to implement an associative array, a structure that can map keys to values. A hash table uses a hash function to compute an index into an array of buckets or slots, from which the desired value can be found.

Ideally, the hash function will assign each key to a unique bucket, but it is possible that two keys will generate an identical hash causing both keys to point to the same bucket. Instead, most hash table designs assume that hash collisions—different keys that are assigned by the hash function to the same bucket—will occur and must be accommodated in some way.

In a well-dimensioned hash table, the average cost (number of instructions) for each lookup is independent of the number of elements stored in the table. Many hash table designs also allow arbitrary insertions and deletions of key-value pairs, at (amortized) constant average cost per operation.

Hence the correct option is (A).

2. Total number of collisions is 3.

Hence the correct option is (B).

3. $T(n) = T\left(\dfrac{n}{2}\right) + C$

$T\left(\dfrac{n}{2^2}\right) + C + C$

$= T\left(\dfrac{n}{2^3}\right) + C + C + C$

$= T\left(\dfrac{n}{2^k}\right) + C \times C$

$\dfrac{X}{2^k} = 1$

log n = k

= T(1) + log n × C

T(n) = log n

Hence the correct option is (B).

4. Let switches = p_1, p_2

p_1	p_2	$Z_{(o/p)}$
OFF	OFF	OFF
OFF	ON	ON
ON	OFF	ON
ON	ON	OFF

It is clear from the above Truth Table that a XOR gate is implemented.

5. The spanning tree of this graph will have 5 edges and we have different permutations to have it. If we remove one vertex at a time, we can have all possible spanning trees. As there are 6 vertices, hence 6 spanning tree.

Hence the correct option is (B).

6. The sets which can be represented by regular expressions are called regular sets.

So,

{xcy | x,y $\in$ {a,b}*} = (a+b)* c (a+b)* is a regular

{$a^n b^{2m}$ | n ≥ 0, m ≥ 0} = a* (bb)* is also regular

I and IV lanugages have no dependency, so regular

But II and III languages have dependency, so not regular.

Hence the correct option is (A).

7. max heap will be a full binary tree

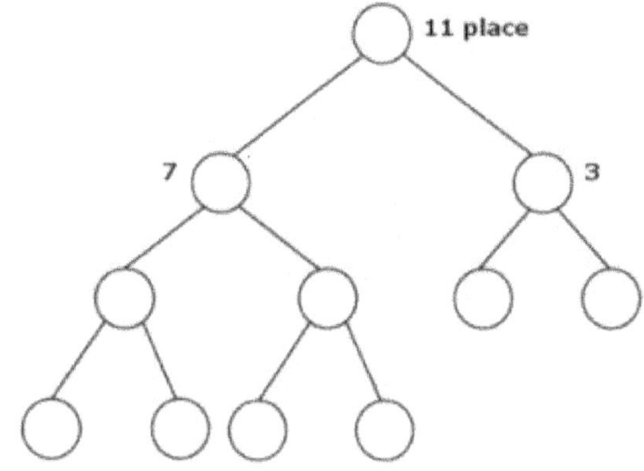

Total 7 elements are there

Number of ordering possible $= \dfrac{11!}{11 \times 7 \times 3 \times 3 \times 3} = 19200$

Hence the correct option is (B).

8. To find a cycle , one for loop is required whose time will be O(n)

Now to find the initial point of cycle , we store the addresses of all nodes into another array , and then run a loop again . The address which is repeated for the first time will be the first node of cycle.

Hence overall O(n).

Hence the correct option is (D).

9. RIP Uses Distance Vector Routing and OSPF uses Link State Routing.

Hence the correct option is (A).

10. A process with a connected UDP socket can call connect again for that socket for one of two reasons:

(1) To specify a new IP address and port.

(2) To unconnect the socket.

Hence the correct option is (B).

11. A) int x => two tokens int x

B) in/*comment*/t => two tokens in,t

C) int;=> Two tokens int and ;

White spaces, comments and semicolons are used as token separators in C programming.

Hence the correct option is (D).

12. A) Matrix chain multiplication : $O(n^3)$

B) Travelling salesman problem : $O(n^n)$

C) 0/1 knapsack : $O(mn)$

D) Fibonacci series : $O(n)$

Hence the correct option is (D).

13. All are valid traversals. We can verify using queue as a data structure.

Hence the correct option is (D).

14. fork() returns PID of newly created child to parent and ZERO to child process. That's why both parent (P) and child (C1) will execute first if block. So 2 times * will be printed.

Then second fork will be executed by both processes P and C1 and they will be created 2 more processes C2 and C3.

P and C1 will not enter second if block. So they will come out of if block and then finally prints last printf. So 2 times again.

C2 and C3 will execute second if block. So 2 times × is printed.

And both will also print last printf. So 2 more times again.

Total number of times × is printed is 8.

Hence the correct option is (B).

15. Initial max-heap is after inserting 1

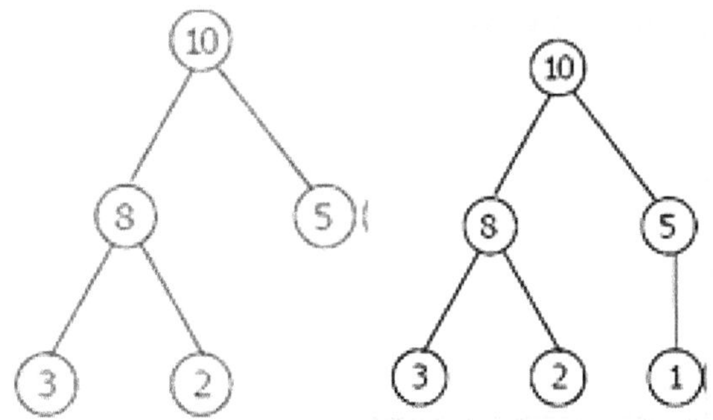

Heapification is not required as it satisfies max-heap property

After inserting 7

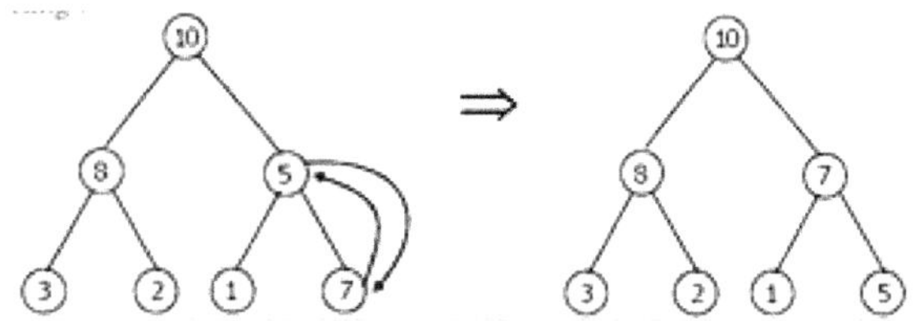

Hence level order traversal is 10, 8, 7, 3, 2, 1, 5.

Hence the correct option is (A).

16. In the original design of IPv4, an IP address was divided into two parts: the network identifier was the most significant (highest order) octet of the address, and the host identifier was the rest of the address .The Total Length field is the total length of the IPv4 datagram in bytes. Using this field and the IHL field can indicate where the data portion of the datagram starts, and its length. Because this is a 16-bit field, the maximum size of an IPv4 datagram (including header) is 65,535 bytes.

Hence the correct option is (C).

17. Page size is $2kb = 2^{11}$ b,

Hence page offset and frame offset both take 11 bits each.

32 bit virtual address

Page number - 21 bits	Page offset - 11 bits

28 bits physical address

Frame number -17 bits	Frame offset - 11 bits

Hence the correct option is (B).

18. A B 1 2 3

1010 1011 0001 0010 0011

010 101 011 000 100 100 011

2 5 3 0 4 4 3

19. If we look at the LR(0) items given,

In (i) "." is after *, that means it has just processed * input.

In (ii) "." is after F, it has just processed F.

In (iii) "." is after +, it has just processed +.

So none of these belong to the same canonical set of item. Because "." comes either before all alphabet or just after the alphabet has just processed.

Hence the correct option is (D).

20. Routing table for R will be:

P→R –Q-P = (6+3)=9, R – S –P=(4+10)=14, R-U-P=(8+5)=13 →9.

Q→R-Q =6, R-S-Q=(9+4)=13, R-U-Q =(8+4)=12 →6.

R →0

S →R-S= 4, R-Q-S=(6+5)=11, R-U-S =(8+3) =11.

T→R-Q-T=(6+ 10)=16., R-S-T =(4+12)=16, R-U-T=(8+7)=15 →15.

U→8

Hence the correct option is (C).

21. If we have a cfg G then the derivation S →A → w means A →w is production to be used where w is reduced to A. 'w' is called the handle. In an LR parser we will have a reduce state for A →w.

Case (A): the handle does not arise for a shift operation.

Case (B): A handle is a string of characters in the RHS of a rule, it is not the LHS of a rule

Case (C): the handle only enters for reduce operations.

Hence the correct option is (D).

22. UDP is connection less protocol, It is a unreliable protocol, It do not uses acknowledgement, It uses checksum for error detection.

Hence the correct option is (B).

23. A : Quick sort uses divide and conquer.

B : Longest common subsequence uses dynamic programming.

C : Kruskal's algorithm is greedy algorithm.

D : Shortest distance from a given node to every node is greedy algorithm.

Hence the correct option is (C).

24.

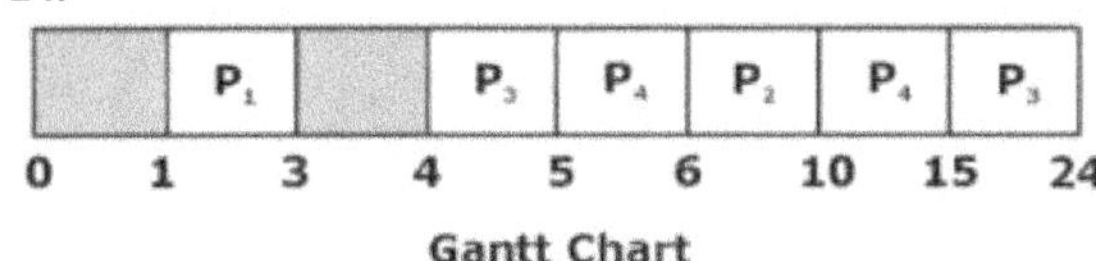

Gantt Chart

Process	Waiting Time
P₁	0
P₂	0
P₃	10
P₄	4

$$Average\ Waiting\ Time = \frac{0+0+10+4}{4} = \frac{14}{4} = 3.5$$

Hence the correct option is (D).

25. ICMP and BOOTP protocols are equivalent in their usage. All other statements are true.

ICMP is error reporting protocol used when something unexpected occurs in routers, used to test connectivity while BOOTP is IP protocol network it task is to automatically assign an IP address to network devices from configuration server.

Hence the correct option is (B).

26. Light sources differ for single-mode and multi-mode in FDDI. Single mode uses laser light and multimode uses LED light.

Hence the correct option is (B).

27. The IEEE 802.11 defines a set of services that provides the functionality needed to let the LLC layer send and receive MSDUs (MAC Service Data Units). The services includes the following: Authentication, deauthentication, privacy, MSDU delivery, association, disassociation, distribution, integration and reassociation.

Hence the correct option is (C).

28. IPV4 is the 4th version of internet protocol it helps in routing internet traffic. It's header has length of 4bits which is equivalent to number of 32 bit words.

Hence the correct answer is option (B).

29. On input symbol ' < ' which is not present in the given canonical set of items. Hence it is neither a shift-reduce nor a reduce-reduce conflict on symbol '<'. Thus D is the correct option.

Hence the correct option is (D).

30. The given grammar is ambiguous as there are two possible leftmost derivations for string "c".

First Leftmost Derivation

S → F

F → c

Second Leftmost Derivation

S → H

H → c

An Ambiguous grammar can neither be LL (1) nor LR (1) , so the Result is Neither S_1 nor S_2

Hence the correct option is (D).

31. We know that in order of BST is increasing order:

Inorder: 7, 11, 12, 13, 14, 15, 17, 20, 21, 22, 24, 25

Post order: 7, 12, 11, 15, 14, 13, 20, 22, 25, 24, 21, 17.

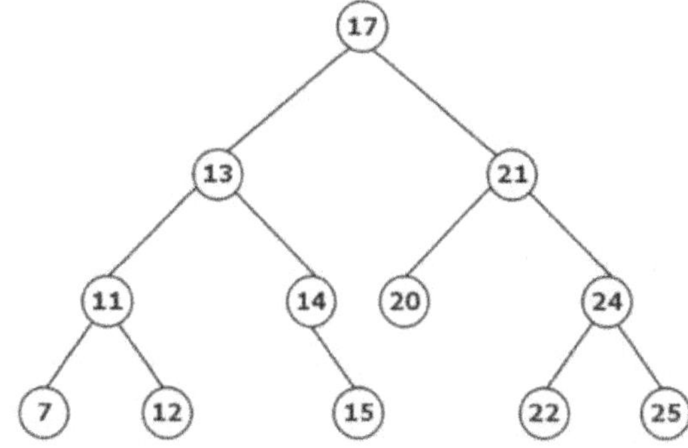

So, Pre-order: 17, 13, 11, 7, 12, 14, 15, 21, 20, 24, 22, 25

Hence the correct option is (D).

32. f() is a recursive function which adds f(a+1, n-1) to *a if *a is even. If *a is odd then f() subtracts f(a+1, n-1) from *a. See below recursion tree for execution of f(a, 6).

f (add(12), 6) /*Since 12 is first element. A contains address of 12 * /

|

|

12 + f(add(7), 5) /* since 7 is the next element, a+1 contains address of 7 * /

|

|

7 – f (add(13), 4)

|

|

13 – f(add(4), 3)

|

|

4 + f (add(11), 2)

|

|

11 – f (add (6), 1)

|

|

6 + 0

So, the final returned value is 12 + (7 – (13 – (4 +(11 – (6 + 0))))) = 15

Hence the correct option is (C).

33. Hashing is one way to enable security during the process of message transmission when the message is intended for a particular recipient only.

Hence the correct option is (D).

34. Strassen's algorithm is implemented by using Divide and Conquer and its recurrence equation is T(n) = $7T\left(\frac{n}{2}\right) + O(n^2)$

It takes Time Complexity = $O(n^{2.81})$.

Hence the correct option is (C).

35. The segment with Sequence no(200-299) will be accepted and ACk will be generated with sequence no 300.

Segment with sequence no 300 to 500 will be lost in the network so same ACK will be generated. Hence, Value of Y will be 300.

Segment with sequence no(501-699) will be accepted but Ack will always be inorder.

Hence, value of Z will be 300.

Hence the correct option is (A).

36. The MAP typically runs on top of SS7 (Signaling System 7).

Hence the correct option is (C).

37. 65535 (ip packet max)-20(ip header)-20(tcp header)

Hence option c is the correct answer.

38. F F F F

- 2 B F D

____

D 4 0 2

Therefore, F's complement of $(2BFD)_{hex}$= $(D402)_{hex}$

Hence the correct option is (D).

39. Time complexity of Quicksort in worst case = $O(n^2)$ = $c.n^2$ = 100ms

So, c = $100/1000^2$ = 10^{-4}

Time complexity of Quicksort in best case = O(nlog n) = c.nlog n = $10^{-4} \times 128 \times \log_2 128$

= 89.6 microseconds

Hence the correct option is (A).

40. This method moves every new element to first of q_1 so that it is LIFO. It does so using q_2. First it enqueues to q_2 and one by one dequeues from q_1 to q_2 and the reverse it so that new element moves to front of q_1. Thus dequeue from q_1 is similar to popping.

Hence the correct option is (A).

41. The bit rate can be calculated as:

No. of samples $\times$ bandwidth $\times$ bits required by each sample

2 $\times$ 8000 $\times$ 8=128000=128 kbps

Hence the correct option is (C).

42. Switch reduces collision domain to zero.

Hence the correct option is (D).

43. SRTF is pre-emptive SJF which produces less average waiting time.

Hence the correct option is (A).

44. Given an array of 25 distinct elements, and pivot element is chosen uniformly randomly. So, there are only 2 worst case positionin the pivot element is either first (or) last.

Therefore, required probability is,

= 2/25

= 0.08

Hence the correct option is (C).

45. Turnaround time – amount of time to execute a particular process.

Hence the correct option is (C).

46. Y and z are not declared in the program and declaration error is produced by only semantic analyzer.

Lexical analyzer job is to group the characters into a token.

Main ( )

{

int x = 10 ;

x = x + y + z ;

}

tokens are identified by lexical analyzer = 18

Hence the correct option is (A).

47.

Process	Arrival Time	Burst Time	CT	TAT
P1	0	10	20	20
P2	3	6	10	7
P3	7	1	8	1
P4	8	3	13	5

Now Create Gantt chart.

P1	P2	P3	P4	P5	P1
0-3	3-7	7-8	8-10	10-13	13-20

thereafter we calculate TAT of every process.

Turn Around Time(TAT) = Completion Time(CT) − Arrival Time(AT)

TAT for P_1 = 20 − 0 = 20

TAT for P_2 = 10 − 3 = 7

TAT for P_3 = 8 - 7 = 1

TAT for P_4 = 13 − 8 = 5

Average TAT = (20 + 7 + 1 + 5)/4 = 8.25

Hence the correct option is (C).

48. Input string "id+id*id"

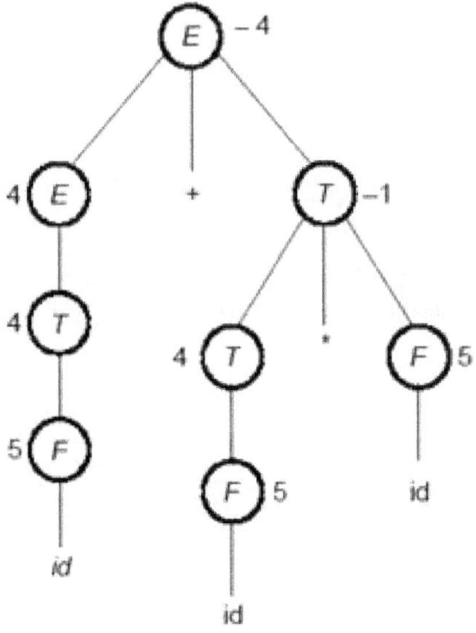

The value -4 is computed at root E. (bottom up parsing uses " Reverse of RMD").

Hence the correct option is (A).

49. When compared with analog cellular systems, an advantage of digital TDMA cellular system is that it conserves spectrum bandwidth.

Hence the correct option is (C).

50. The Hypertext Transfer Protocol (HTTP) is a most extensively used application layer protocol. Http provides us with weightless protocol so that pages that uses HTML language can be retrieved easily from the web.

The transport layer has duty of establishing an impermanent relationship between 2 application programs and proving them data as requested by them. TCP is used in it for those connections in which stable connection is needed between hosts.

The data link layer is layer 2 of networking. The HDLC protocols used in data link layer are set of rules which are been used for sending data among networks.

In network layer Border Gateway Protocol (BGP) is used for the purpose of interchanging routing and reachability details within autonomous system on the web.

Hence the correct option is (C).

51. X.25 is an ITU-T standard **protocol** suite for packet switched wide area network (WAN) communication. An **X.25** WAN consists of packet-switching exchange. And this work at physical layer.

Hence the correct option is (C).

52. The gateway is a device used to connect networks using different protocols. Gateways operate at the network layer of the OSI model. In order to communicate with a host on another network, an IP host must be configured with a route to the destination network. If a configuration route is not found, the host uses the gateway (default IP router) to transmit the traffic to the destination host. The default t gateway is where the IP sends packets that are destined for remote networks. If no default gateway is specified, communication is limited to the local network. Gateways receive data from a network using one type of protocol stack, removes that protocol stack and repackages it with the protocol stack that the other network can use.

Hence the correct option is (D).

53. Telnet is used to connect to a remote computer and search the library's holding.

Hence the correct option is (A).

54.

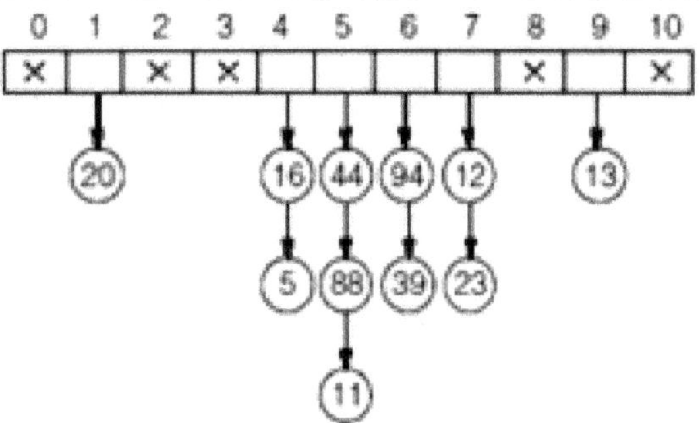

h(key) = (2×key+5)mod 11.

Total 5 locations left without mapping an element.

Hence the correct option is (C).

55. Mobile IP gives two essential capacities: specialist revelation and enrollment. During discovery of agent, home specialists and foreign agents may promote their accessibility on each connection for which they give benefit. A recently available mobile node can send a requesting on the connection to learn if any planned operators are available. At the point when the mobile node is far from home, it enrolls its care-of address with its home operator during the registration stage. It depends on its technique used for connection, the mobile node will enlist either specifically with its home agent, or through a remote agent that advances the registration to the home agent.

56. GSM: GSM (Global System for Mobile Communications), is a standard developed by the European Telecommunications Standards Institute (ETSI) to describe the protocols for second-generation (2G) digital cellular networks used by mobile phones.

CDMA: Code division multiple access (CDMA) is a channel access method used by various radio communication technology.

These technologies used for full duplex. So all option are correct.

Hence the correct option is (D).

57. Because of signal balancing issue is overcome by segment the networks, use the amplifier or repeater between segments.

Hence the correct option is (C).

58. An X.25 network provides a means by which one X.25 DTE (a Terminal or Host of some kind) can exchange data with one or more other X.25 Host, on the other side of the network. Data is carried within individual packets – X.25 is often referred to as a Packet Switching Protocol.X.25 to better meet the requirements of Connection Oriented Network Service (CONS). Public X.25 networks were not required to make use of NSAP addressing, By contrast, X.25 is a Connection-Oriented protocol: the routing information used by the network is carried only in the packets used to establish the connection; thereafter addressing information is not required. This does, however, mean that the X.25 network switching nodes need be aware of each connection, unlike IP routers.

Hence the correct option is (A).

59. PSH flag in the TCP header is typically used to indicate stop the message.

Hence the correct option is (C).

60. By definition the Medium term scheduler is used to swap the processes between secondary storage and main memory to ensure high CPU utilization.

Hence the correct option is (B).

61.

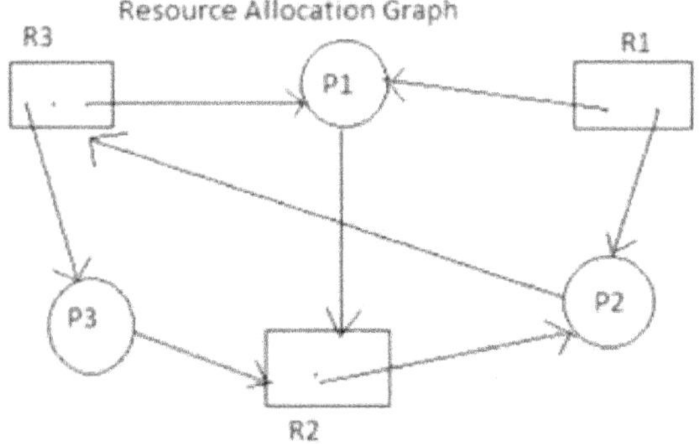

First P_2 can be assigned with an instance of R_3, and hence after execution P_2 will release all its resources. All the process needs can be satisfied. Hence deadlock does not exist in this scenario.

Hence the correct option is (A).

62. Here, Record Size= 15 Byte

For 1st record, bytes will be numbered from 0 to 14, for the second record it will be numbered from 15 to 29, and so on. In this manner, the first byte of the sixth record will be at byte positioned at 75.

Hence the correct option is (A).

63. Let us consider a new process required 120 kb memory and existing holes in the memory are 200, 300, 150 kb as shown in the diagram in the same order.

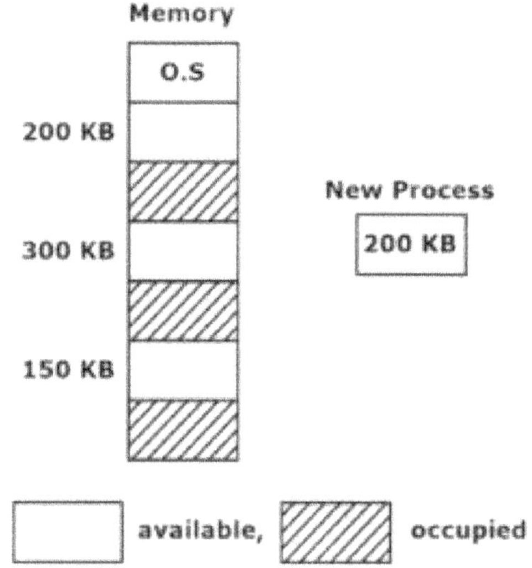

Now, when we allocate, this new process a memory using different algorithms, it would be like given below

Algorithm Allocated partition size of new tube

First Fit 200 KB 80 KB

Best Fit 150 KB 30 KB

Worst Fit 300 KB 180 KB

Next Fit 300 KB 180 KB

Hence the correct option is (A).

64. $L=\{0^i 21^i \mid i \geq 0\}$ has only one comparison that can be done using a DPDA. Hence, its DCFL.

Context free languages are a proper subset of Recursive Languages.

∴ it is recursive too.

Hence the correct option is (B).

65. Data Encryption Techniques are used for protecting data in communication system.

Hence the correct option is (A).

66. The features that stood out during the research, which led to making the TCP/IP reference model were:

• Support for a flexible architecture. Adding more machines to a network was easy.

• The network was robust, and connections remained intact until the source and destination machines were functioning.

The overall idea was to allow one application on one computer to talk to(send data packets) another application running on different computer.

Hence the correct option is (A).

67. Reliability of the module is probability of software failure in a particular time and in a particular environment . probability for 90 % of the code to have success maximum = 0.9.

Suppose there are 2 blocks so we consider the probability of success for both 1st and 2nd block to be 0.9

So, reliability module = 0.9 $\times$ 0.9

= 0.82

Hence the correct option is (C).

68. Time division duplex also and commonly used in short as TDD represent the duplex communication links where uplink is isolated from downlink by the allotment of various schedule openings in a similar frequency band. It is a transmission plot that permits uneven stream for uplink and downlink information transmission. Clients are designated schedule openings for uplink and downlink transmission.

Hence the correct option is (C).

69. The largest negative number is 1000 0000 = -128.

Hence the correct option is (C).

70. Ethernet checking a valid address or not. And token ring prevent looping in system.

Hence the correct option is (D).

71. The correct format to write IP address is that each sets of digits should have dots in between.

Hence the correct option is (C).

72. FTP stands for file transfer protocol as it is used for transferring file over internet from one computer to another.

Hence the correct option is (A).

73. 1.Physical layer:- Transmission and reception of raw bit streams over a physical medium.

2.Data Link Layer:- Reliable transmission of data frames between two nodes connected by a Physical layer.

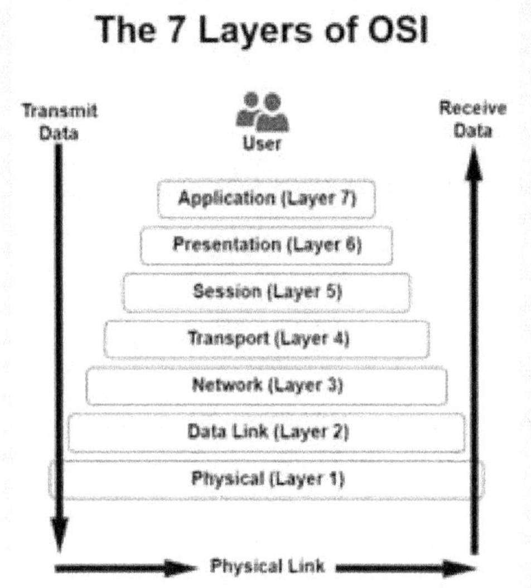

3. Network Layer: - Structuring and managing a multi-node network, including addressing, routing and traffic control.

4.Transport Layer: - Reliable transmission of data segments between points on a network, including segmentation, acknowledgement and multiplexing.

5.Application Layer:- High-level APIs, including resource sharing, remote file access.

Hence the correct option is (A).

74. • Retransmission Timer is used to retransmit last segments, when either packet lost or ACK lost.

• Persistent Timer is used to deal with a zero-window size deadlock situation.

• Keep alive time is used to prevent long idle connection between two TCP's.

• TCP Time Wait Timer is used during TCP connection termination.

Hence the correct option is (C).

75. "Empty tree" will be printed (N+1) times in addition to inorder traversal. It is so because, if root is zero, the control has to return, but it instead just prints "empty tree" (N+1) times, because for a binary tree with N nodes, there are (N+1) empty nodes.

Hence the correct option is (D).

76. There are various port no. which is we use but here we discussed few of them . Basically port number we used to establish the connection between sever and client.

" A port is identified for each address and protocol by a 16-bit number, commonly known as the port number."

23-remote login
25-E-mail
80-World wide web
119-USENET news

Hence the correct option is (D).

77. For enforcing IP security we need a host to host transport mode and also in a network tunneling mode.

Hence the correct option is (B).

78. Virtual address space (VAS) = 4 MB = 2^{22} bytes

Page table entry (PTE) = 8 bytes.

We know that,

Optimal page size = $\sqrt{2}$ × VAS × PTE = $\sqrt{2}$ × 2^{22} × 2^3 = $\sqrt{2^{26}}$ = 2^{13} bytes = 8 KB

Hence the correct option is (B).

79. Downlink control is used for sending data from BS to MD. Radio communication data rate is 2-Mbps. The average duration of user's stay in cell is RL. FDDI bandwidth is 100-Mbps.

Hence the correct option is (B).

80. Logical address, LA = s + d where s is segment no. bits and d is segment size.

= s + p1 + d1

= 15 + log(8K) + frame/page size

= 15 + 13 + log(2K)

= 15 + 13 + 11

= 39 bits.

Physical address, PA = frame no. bits + d1

= f + 11

= $\log_2(512K/2K)$ + 11

= 8 + 11

= 19 bits.

Difference, LA - PA = 20.

Hence the correct option is (D).

81.

P1	P2	P3	P1	P2	P3	P1	P2	P3	P1	
0	1	2	3	4	5	6	7	8	9	30

Average waiting time=(2+2+2)+(1+2+2)+(2+2+2) / 3= 17/3 =5.66ms

Hence the correct option is (B).

82. The protocol explain the message that is transfer in between the Clint and the Server which govern establishment, termination and other essential elements of a call . SIP basically use for communication and transferring the data. The most effective tool of SIP are in Internet telephony for voice and video calls.

SIP is an application layer protocol designed to be independent of the underlying transport layer. It is a text-based protocol, incorporating many elements of the Hypertext Transfer Protocol (HTTP) and the Simple Mail Transfer Protocol (SMTP).

Hence the correct option is (D).

83. basically, convey effect occur in FCFS scheduling algorithm.

SJF, SRTF --> No Convoy Effect.

Hence the correct option is (D).

84. According to ,

Physical address = 32 bit, page size = 16 KB, size of inverted page table = 2 MB

We know that,

Size of inverted page table = number of frames * size of inverted Page table entry

Where number of frames = size of memory/page size = $2^{32}/2^{14}$ = 2^{18}

So, size of inverted page table entry = size of inverted page table / number of frames

= 2^{21} / 2^{18} = 8 Bytes

Hence the correct option is (D).

85. 3 (times) 5^1 + 2 (times) 5^0 = X (times) Y^1 + 4 (times) Y^0

15 + 2 = XY + 4

XY = 13

Then possible combinations are X= 13 and Y =1 or X=1 and Y = 13.

But X = 13 and Y = 1 is not possible because no digit can be greater than its base here 3>1.

X = 1 and Y = 13 is correct answer.

Hence the correct option is (C).

86. $(X)_6$= $(235)_6$+ $(231)_6$=$(510)_6$
So, 6 complement of X will be 5's complement $+1$.
Hence, Answer is 50.

Hence correct answer is option (A).

87. All the answers are incorrect as if a number is given in base X, then the digits of that number has to be in the range [0,X-1]. So, here as (84)x is given, that means x has to be greater than 8, otherwise the number cannot exist in that base. Similarly for (66)y, y should be greater than 6, otherwise it is impossible. Hence, with the condition x>8 and y>6, the correct minimum value for pair (x,y) is (10,13).

Hence correct answer is option (D).

88. {x | x = $0^n 1^n$ for n >= 0}

Above given options represent the following-

A) S do not produce 010 which is palindrome

B) Correct

C) It do not have null string

D) This also don't have null string

Hence correct answer is option (C).

89. Initially all pages are bring in physical memory and all are different, so that all time page fault occur.

So, 100 page faults after that in reverse order pages required.

So we see that 4 pages at last already in memory.

So there is no page fault for these.

So only 100 – 4 = 96 page faults occur.

Total page faults = 100 + 96 = 196

Hence the correct answer is option (A).

90. Membership states that w ϵ L(G) iff there exist an derivation of w using production. So membership property is valid for all except RE languages.

Finiteness property states that L(M) is finite iff there is no cycle in directed path between final and initial states and is valid only for regular and context free languages.

Emptiness property states that L(M)=empty iff there is no directed path to reach final states and is valid for context free language so statement C is true.

Equivalence of 2 languages is valid only for regular languages.

Hence the correct answer is option (C).

91. All the above problems are decidable except the 2) one.

Hence answer will be 3.

92. All the statements are correct except 2 because the cartesian product or union of finite countable sets is countable.

Hence correct answer is option (B).

93. Mailbox sharing

P_1 and P_2 share mailbox A

P_1 sends P_2 receives.

Hence the correct answer is option (C).

94. We should choose class 'C' network as we require only 96.

96 hosts, so it would require.

Minimum of 7 bits for host id.

For providing 96 hosts.

Mask is 255.255.255.128

Hence correct answer is option (C).

95. 2's complement of 10011100 is 01100100 then added to the minuend i.e 01100100+01010101= 10111001 since no carry taking its 2's complement 01000111 which will be negative thus answer -01000111 => -71.

Hence the correct answer is option (A).

96. Cache holds 64b blocks without replacement.

CPU fetches words from 0 to 4351 (Total 4352 words)

Number of blocks required .

1st time = 68 miss operations (initially cache was empty)

For 2nd time reference, the available blocks in cache are 64. But the misses (B_0, B_1, B_2 and B_3) lead to subsequent misses of (B_{16} to B_{19}), (B_{32} to B_{35}) and (B_{64} to B_{67}) with LRU policy. The same processes repeated 9 times.

total = 68+9×(4+4+4+4+4)

= 248

Hence the correct answer is option (B).

97. Divide segment t_3 into two segments of 50 + 5 = 55

and 45 + 5 = 50 ns. This makes t_p = 55 ns; k = 5

(k + n – 1) tp = (5 + 99) 55 = 5,720 ns = 5.72 µs

Hence the correct answer is option (A).

98. 0.95 0.9(1+1) TLB hit, cache hit

+0.950.1(1+1+75) TLB hit, cache miss

+0.0050.9(1+75+1+75)TLB miss ,cache hit

+0.050.10.99(1+75+1+75) TLB miss, cache miss, no page fault.

+0.050.10.01(1+75+1+75+ 50000) TLB miss, cache miss, page fault

 15.75 cycles

Hence the correct answer is option (C).

99. Check sum is the mistake identifying system when information is dealt with as a succession of character. Equality is the component utilized when information is dealt with as a succession of bits.

Hence, the correct option is (D).

100. P_1: Cycle clock time= Max(1,2,3,4)+1

= 4 + 1 = 5 ns

P_2: Max(0.5,1.5,3)+2=3+2=5 ns

P_3: Max(0.4,1.4)+3

= 1.4+3

= 4.4 ns

Hence the correct answer is option (D).

Q.1 Which 3 layers does a router have?

A. Network Layer, Data Link Layer, Physical Layer

B. Network Layer, Data Link Layer, Transport Layer

C. Network Layer, Data Link Layer, Application Layer

D. Transport Layer, Data Link Layer, Application Layer

Q.2 For the 8-bit word 00111001, the check bits stored with it would be 0111. Suppose, when the word is read from memory, the check bits are calculated to be 1101. What is the data word that was read from memory?

A. 10011001 **B.** 00011001

C. 00111000 **D.** 11000110

Q.3 In a typical mobile phone system with hexagonal cells, it is forbidden to reuse a frequency band in adjacent cells. If 840 frequencies are available, how many can be used in a given cell?

A. 280 **B.** 210 **C.** 140 **D.** 120

Q.4 Using and in the RSA algorithm, what is the value of cipher text for a plain text if $p=3$, $q=11$, $d=7$, $e=3$, $M=5$, $C=??$

A. 13 **B.** 21 **C.** 26 **D.** 8

Q.5 A message "COMPUTER NETWORK" encrypted (ignore quotes) using columnar transposition cipher with a key "LAYER". The encrypted message is :

A. CTTOEWMROPNRUEK

B. MROUEKCTTPNROEW

C. OEWPNRCTTUEKMRO

D. UEKPNRMROOEWCTT

Q.6 Which technology is sometime referred to as wireless cable?

A. MMDS **B.** ATM **C.** LMDS **D.** CDMA

Q.7 An analog signal has a bit rate of 6000 bps and a baud rate of 2000 baud. How many data elements are carried by each signal elements?

A. 0.336 bits baud

B. 3 bits baud

C. 120,00,000 bits baud

D. None of the above

Q.8 The device which connects dissimilar LANs of different topologies using different sets of communication protocols so that information can flow from one to another is called :

A. Router **B.** Bridge **C.** Gateway **D.** Switch

Q.9 Race-around condition occurs in

A. Multiplexer **B.** ROM

C. Flip-flops **D.** Application

Q.10 Given the CIDR representation 100.1.2.35 / 20 . Find the range of IP Addresses in the CIDR block.

A. [100.1.0.0 , 100.1.0.255]

B. [100.1.0.0 , 100.1.15.255]

C. [100.1.2.0 , 100.1.15.255]

D. [100.1.2.0 , 100.1.2.255]

Q.11 The technique of temporarily delaying outgoing acknowledgements so that they can be hooked onto the next outgoing data frame is known as :

A. Bit stuffing **B.** Piggy backing

C. Pipeline **D.** Broadcasting

Q.12 The decimal number for the BCD code $(100001110100)_{BCD}$ is ______.

A. 674 **B.** 874 **C.** 557 **D.** 987

Q.13 Which of the following TCP/IP Internet protocol is diskless machine uses to obtain its IP address from a server?

A. RARP **B.** RIP **C.** ARP **D.** X.25

Q.14 Suppose that someone starts with a chain letter. Each person who receives the letter is asked to send it on to 4 other people. Some people do this, while some do not send any letter. How many people have seen the letter, including the first person, if no one receives more than one letter and if the chain letter ends after there have been 100 people who read it but did not send it out? Also find how many people sent out the letter?

A. 22 **B.** 11 **C.** 33 **D.** 44

Q.15 The bit rate of a signal is 3000 bps. If each signal unit carries 6 bits, the baud rate of the signal is ______.

A. 500 baud/sec **B.** 1000 baud/sec

C. 3000 baud/sec **D.** 18000 baud/sec

Q.16 Match the following:

List – I

a. Physical layer

b. Datalink layer

c. Network layer

d. Transport layer

e. Application layer

List – II

i. Allow resources to network access

ii. Move packets from one destination to other

iii. Process to process message delivery

iv. Transmission of bit stream

v. Formation of frames

A. iv, v, ii, iii, i **B.** v, iv, i, ii, iii

C. i, iii, ii, v, iv **D.** i, ii, iv, iii, v

Q.17 The unlicensed National Information Infrastructure band operates at the ______ frequency.

A. 2.4 GHz **B.** 5 GHz **C.** 33 MHz **D.** 15 MHz

Q.18 Which transmission technique guarantees that data packets will be received by the receiver in the same order in which they were sent by the sender?

A. Broadcasting

B. Unicasting

C. Packet Switching

D. Circuit Switching

Q.19 In order that a code is 't' error correcting, the minimum Hamming distance should be:

A. t　　**B.** 2t - 1　　**C.** 2t　　**D.** 2t + 1

Q.20 Consider a very large network of 10000 routers. Two host A and B are connected with this network. Host A sends data to host B and after some unit of time host A receives ICMP time exceeded message for the same data packet. The maximum number of routers that can be travelled by packets when message reaches back to host A is _______.

A. 509　　**B.** 601　　**C.** 312　　**D.** 522

Q.21 The GSM network is divided into the following three major systems:

A. SS, BSS, OSS

B. BSS, BSC, MSC

C. CELL, BSC, OSS

D. SS, CELL, MSC

Q.22 Four channels are multiplexed using TDM. If each channel sends 100 bytes/second and we multiplex 1 byte per channel, then the bit rate for the link is ....bps

A. 400　　**B.** 800　　**C.** 1600　　**D.** 3200

Q.23 Which of the following IP address class is a multicast address?

A. Class A　　**B.** Class B　　**C.** Class C　　**D.** Class D

Q.24 Network that use different technologies can be connected by using

A. Packets　　**B.** Switches　　**C.** Bridges　　**D.** Routers

Q.25 Given grammar

S -> aAS {print 3}

S -> a {print 1}

A -> SbA {print 3}

A -> SS {print 2}

A -> ba {print 2}

For generating aabbaa what will be the output printed?

A. 13213　　**B.** 12313　　**C.** 31213　　**D.** 12123

Q.26 To employ multi-access in GSM, users are given different:

A. time slots

B. bandpass filters

C. handsets

D. frequency bands

Q.27 The period of a signal is 10 ms.What is the frequency in Hertz?

A. 10　　**B.** 100　　**C.** 1000　　**D.** 10000

Q.28 In a classful addressing, first four bits in Class A IP address is:

A. 0001　　**B.** 1100　　**C.** 1011　　**D.** 1110

Q.29 Decryption and encryption of data are the responsibility of which of the following layer?

A. Physical layer

B. Data link layer

C. Presentation layer

D. Session layer

Q.30 AES is a round cipher based on the Rijndal Algorithm that uses a 128-bit block of data. AES has three different configurations. _____ rounds with a key size of 128 bits, _____ rounds with a key size of 192 bits and _____ rounds with a key size of 256 bits.

A. 5, 7, 15

B. 10, 12, 14

C. 5, 6, 7

D. 20, 12, 14

Q.31 Which of the following is not associated with the session layer?

A. Dialogue control

B. Token management

C. Semantics of the information transmitted

D. Synchronization

Q.32 In classful addressing, an IP address 123.23.156.4 belongs to _____ class format.

A. A　　**B.** B　　**C.** C　　**D.** D

Q.33 What is the maximum sequence number in selective repeat sliding window protocol used in a computer network if sender window size is 4 ?

A. 4　　**B.** 7　　**C.** 18　　**D.** 16

Q.34 Which of the following are Data Link Layer standard?

1. Ethernet

2. HSSI

3. Frame Relay

4. 10 – Base T

5. Token Ring

A. 1, 2, 3

B. 1, 3, 5

C. 1, 3, 4, 5

D. 1, 2, 3, 4, 5

Q.35 The minimal expression of $F(w,x,y,z) = \sum(0,4,6,7,8,9,15)$ is

A. xy+wx'y'+wy'z

B. xy'+wx'y'+wy'z'

C. xyz+wx'y'+w'y'z'+w'xy

D. none of these

Q.36 Which of the following control fields in TCP header is used to specify whether the sender has no more data to transmit?

A. FIN　　**B.** RST　　**C.** SYN　　**D.** PSH

Q.37 Count the number of literals in the following expression :

F = AB' + BC' + CD' + DE'

A. 6　　**B.** 7　　**C.** 8　　**D.** 9

Q.38 Usually information security in a network is achieved by:

A. Layering

B. Cryptography

C. Grade of service

D. None of the above

Q.39 Page Shift Keying (PSK) Method is used to modulate digital signal at 9600 bps using 16 level. Find the line signals and speed (i.e.) modulation rate).

A. 2400 bauds

B. 1200 bauds

C. 4800 bauds

D. 9600 bauds

Q.40 If in an error detection and correction code a message

M : "You are good students" is stored as

C' : Youare areyou aregood goodare goodstudents studentsgood.

What is the space required to store M' in general? (assume that 'n' is the length of M)

A. 2n

B. 3n

C. 4n

D. less than 4n

Q.41 Match the following:

List - I

i. Ethernet

ii. Token Ring

iii. Cut-through switch

iv. Spanning tree

List - II

A. Deterministic

B. Utilize the full wire speed

C. Prevent looping

D. Checking valid address.

A. d, a, b, c   **B.** a, d, b, c   **C.** d, a, c, b   **D.** d, c, b, a

Q.42 In a binary Hamming code, the number of check digits is r then number of message digits is equal to:

A. $2^r - 1$ **B.** $2^r - r - 1$ **C.** $2^r - r + 1$ **D.** $2^r + r - 1$

Q.43 Which provides an interface to the TCP/IP suit protocols in Windows95 and Windows NT?

A. FTP Active-X Control

B. TCP/IP Active-X Control

C. Calinsock Active-X Control

D. HTML Active-X Control

Q.44 Encoding or scrambling data for transmission across a network is known as:

A. Protection

B. Detection

C. Encryption

D. Decryption

Q.45 In 16-bit 2's complement representation, the decimal number −28 is:

A. 1111 1111 0001 1100

B. 0000 0000 1110 0100

C. 1111 1111 1110 0100

D. 1000 0000 1110 0100

Q.46 Match the Following Lists:

List-I

a. Call Control

b. A-bis

c. BSMAP

d. CDMA

List-II

i. Interface betweenProtocol Basse T-ansceiver Station (BTS) and Base Control Station (BCS)

ii. Speed Spectrum

iii. Connection man-agement

iv. Works between Mobile Switching Centre (MSC) and Base Station Subsystem (BSS)

A. iii, iv, i, ii

B. iii, i, iv, ii

C. i, ii, iii, iv

D. iv, iii, ii, i

Q.47 Which layer of OSI reference model uses the ICMP (Internet Control Message Protocol)?

A. Transport layer

B. Data link layer

C. Network layer

D. Application layer

Q.48 The throughput of pure ALOHA is given by:

A. $S = G$

B. $S = e^{2G}$

C. $S = Ge^{2G}$

D. $S = Ge^{-2G}$

Q.49 In which Routing Method do all the routers have a common database?

A. Distance vector

B. Link state

C. Link vector

D. Dijkestra method

Q.50 4-bit 2's complement representation of a decimal number is 1000. The number is___

A. -2   **B.** -6   **C.** -1   **D.** -8

Q.51 Coaxial cables are categorized by Radio Government rating are adapted for specialized functions. Category RG-59 with impedance 75 Ω used for:

A. Cable TV

B. Ethernet

C. Thin Ethernet

D. Thick Ethernet

Q.52 Which of the following fields in IPv 4 datagram is not related to fragmentation?

A. Type of service

B. Fragment offset

C. Flags

D. Identification

Q.53 Check sum used along with each packet computes the sum of the data, where data is treated as a sequence of:

A. Integer

B. Character

C. Real numbers

D. Bits

Q.54 Which of the following algorithm is not a broadcast routing algorithm?

A. Flooding

B. Multidimensional Routing

C. Reverse Path Forwarding

D. All of the above

Q.55 Infrared signals can be used for short range communication in a closed area using _______ propagation.

A. ground

B. sky

C. line of sight

D. space

Q.56 Find the solution for the following instance of post correspondence problem

$$\binom{abab}{ababaaa} \cdot \binom{aaabbb}{bb} \cdot \binom{aab}{baab} \cdot \binom{ba}{baa} \cdot \binom{ab}{ba} \cdot \binom{aa}{a}$$

A. ababaaabbbaabbaababaa

B. ababababababbbbbababababa

C. aaabbbbababababbaaabbab

D. abaabbabaabbabaabbaba

Q.57 Using RSA algorithm, what is the value of cipher text C, if the plain text M = 5 and p = 3, q = 11 & d = 7?

A. 33   **B.** 5   **C.** 25   **D.** 26

Q.58 Match the following:

List-I

a. Application layer

b. Transport layer

c. Network layer

d. Data link layer

List-II

1. TCP

2. HDLC

3. HTTP

4. BGP

A. 2, 1, 4, 3   **B.** 3, 4, 1, 2   **C.** 3, 1, 4, 2   **D.** 2, 4, 1, 3

Q.59 The single stage network is also called:

A. one sided network

B. two sided network

C. recirculating network

D. pipeline network

Q.60 Another name of IEEE 802.11 a is ___________.

A. Wi-Max   **B.** Fast Ethernet

C. Wi-Fi   **D.** 802.11 g

Q.61 Main aim of software engineering is to produce:

A. program

B. software

C. budget

D. software within budget in the given schedule

Q.62 Which process model is also called as classic life cycle model?

A. Waterfall model   **B.** RAD model

C. Prototyping model   **D.** Incremental model

Q.63 Which one from the following is highly associated activity of project planning?

A. Keep track of the project progress.

B. Compare actual and planned progress and costs

C. Identify the activities, milestones and deliverable produced by a project.

D. Both (B) and (C)

Q.64 Which one of the following is not a/an image/graphic file format?

A. PNG   **B.** GIF   **C.** BMP   **D.** GUI

Q.65 Which of the following operating system is better for implementing client-server network?

A. Windows 95   **B.** Windows 98

C. Windows 2000   **D.** All of these

Q.66 The design issue of Datalink Layer in OSI Reference Model is:

A. Framing

B. Representation of bits

C. Synchronization of bits

D. Connection control

Q.67 In which circuit switching, delivery of data is delayed because data must be stored and retrieved from RAM?

A. Space division   **B.** Time division

C. Virtual   **D.** Packet

Q.68 Which of the following in not a congestion policy at network layer?

A. Flow Control Policy

B. Packet Discard Policy

C. Packet Lifetime Management Policy

D. Routing Algorithm

Q.69 Device on one network can communicate with devices on another network via :

A. Hub/Switch   **B.** Utility server

C. File server   **D.** Gateway

Q.70 How many distinct stages are there in DES algorithm which is parameterized by a 56-bit key?

A. 16   **B.** 17   **C.** 18   **D.** 19

Q.71 Which of the following is/are restriction(s) in classless addressing?

A. The number of addresses needs to be a power of 2.

B. The mask needs to be included in the address to define the block.

C. The starting address must be divisible by the number of addresses in the block.

D. All o f above.

Q.72 Consider the following grammar:

$$S \rightarrow ABa/aAb/aC$$
$$A \rightarrow aB/\in$$
$$B \rightarrow bA/e$$
$$C \rightarrow a/b$$

Identify the grammar after eliminating null productions:

A.
$$S \rightarrow ABa/aAb/aC$$
$$A \rightarrow aB/a$$
$$B \rightarrow bA/b$$
$$C \rightarrow a/b$$

B.
$$S \rightarrow ABa/aAb/aC/a/ab$$
$$A \rightarrow aB/a$$
$$B \rightarrow bA/b$$
$$C \rightarrow a/b$$

C.
$$S \rightarrow ABa/aAb/aC/Ba/Aa$$
$$A \rightarrow aB/a$$
$$B \rightarrow bA/b$$
$$C \rightarrow a/b$$

D.
$$S \rightarrow ABa/aAb/aC/a/ab/Ba/Aa$$
$$A \rightarrow aB/a$$
$$B \rightarrow bA/b$$
$$C \rightarrow a/b$$

Q.73 The iconic feature of the RISC machine among the following are:

A. Reduced number of addressing modes

B. Increased memory size

C. Having a branch delay slot

D. All of the mentioned

Q.74 Using Booth's Algorithm for multiplication, the multiplier -57 will be recoded as

A. 0 -1 0 0 1 0 0 -1

B. 1 1 0 0 0 1 1 1

C. 0 -1 0 0 1 0 0 0

D. 0 1 0 0 -1 0 0 1

Q.75 What is the average access time(in msec) for transferring 512 bytes of data in a system with following specifications.

average seek time=6 msec

disk rotation = 3000 rotation per minute (RPM)

data transfer speed = 40 KB/second

controller overhead = 0.2 msec

A. 28.5 **B.** 28.6 **C.** 28.7 **D.** 228.8

Q.76 What will be the efficiency (in percentage) of the pipeline if 5 stages pipelined with the respective delay of 20,30,40,50,60?

A. 65 % **B.** 66 % **C.** 67 % **D.** 68 %

Q.77 Which of the following is not true about RISC?

A. It is a type of microprocessor that has a limited number of instructions

B. Instructions cannot be completed in one machine cycle.

C. It uses hardwire control unit

D. It is used for real time application

Q.78 Why More than one words are put in one block in order to exploit?

A. Spatial locality **B.** Temporal locality

C. More misses **D.** None of the above

Q.79 Consider the following problems:

1. Membership problems for CFGs.

2. Finiteness problem for FSAs.

3. Ambiguity problem for CFGs.

4. Equivalence problem for FSAs.

Which one of the above problems is undecidable?

A. Only 4 **B.** 1 and 3

C. Only 3 **D.** 2, 1, and 4

Q.80 Identify Regular Language from the following

A. $L = \{ww^R xw, x \in (a + b) +\}$

B. $L = \{xww^R w, x \in (a + b) *\}$

C. $L = \{wxww, x \in (a + b)^+\}$

D. $L = \{w_1 w_2 x \, |w_1 = w_2, w_1, w_2 \in (a + b)^+, x \in (a + b)^{'}\}$

Q.81 Consider a DFA with 1000000000000000000000000000 states over the input alphabet consisting of all the Greek alphabet letters.

What can you say about it ?

A. It is not possible that it accepts the empty string

B. It is not possible that it accepts only the empty string

C. It is not possible that it accepts strings of length only 1

D. It is possible that it accepts all strings over the input alphabet

Q.82 Consider the following statements :

S_1: All regular languages are linear.

S_2: All linear grammar are regular.

S_3: Some DCFL's are also regular.

S_4: All regular are DCFL.

A. S_1, S_2 and S_3 are true

B. S_1, S_2 and S_4 are true

C. S_1, S_3 and S_4 are true

D. S_2, S_3 and S_4 are true

Q.83 Let < M > be the encoding of a Turing machine as a string over $\sum = \{0,1\}$ Let L= $\{< M > M$ is a Turing machine that accepts a string of length 2014}. Then, L is:

A. decidable and recursively enumerable

B. undecidable and recursively enumerable

C. undecidable and not recursively enumerable

D. decidable but not recursively enumerable

Q.84 Consider the following statements.

(a) TCP is connection-oriented protocol and UDP is connectionless protocol.

(b) SMTP work on Port no 27 and POP work on port no

(c) FTP is stateless protocol while HTTP is state-ful protocol.

(d) FTP is OUT OF BAND protocol while HTTP is IN BAND protocol.

The number of correct statement is ________?

A. Only (a) and (d) **B.** Only (b) and (c)

C. All of the above **D.** None of the above

Q.85 In a room one person access home server from tab, another person from android mobile, one from PC, another one from laptop. The network they are using is a type of:

A. LAN **B.** MAN **C.** WAN **D.** PAN

Q.86 Which of the following is NOT true?

A. BGP is an Intra Domain Protocol

B. FIP is a Path vector Routing Algorithm

C. OSPF is a distance Vector Routing Algorithm

D. All of these

Q.87 Which of the following correctly describe the "telnet"?

A. It provides remote access to servers and networking devices.

B. It transfers web pages from webservers to cllients

C. It transfers email messages and attachments

D. None of these

Q.88 A link has a transmission speed of bits/sec. It uses data packets of size 1000 bytes each. Assume that the acknowledgement has negligible transmission delay , and its propagation delay is same as data propagation delay. Also assume that the processing delays at nodes are negligible. The efficiency of stop and wait protocol in this setup is exactly 25%. The value of one way propagation delay (in milliseconds) is

__________.

A. 11 **B.** 12 **C.** 13 **D.** 14

Q.89 SRS consists of:

A. problem statement   **B.** product design

C. Both A and B   **D.** Neither A nor B

Q.90 Which layer manages and synchronises conversations between two different applications:

A. Application layer   **B.** Presentation layer

C. Session layer   **D.** None of above

Q.91 TCP/IP was included by a _______ operating system.

A. UNIX   **B.** DARPAN

C. ACP   **D.** NCP

Q.92 Which one of the following tests is not a black box testing.

A. Unit testing   **B.** Functional testing

C. System testing   **D.** Acceptance testing

Q.93 Identify the true statements

I. Maintaining connection semantics between two directly connected nodes is done by network layer.

II. Recovering lost packet between two directly connected nodes is done by transport layer.

III. Recovering lost packets between two nodes separated by multiple hops is done by data link control.

IV. Arbitration is done between multiple nodes attached to a single medium to resolve conflicts.

A. Only I and IV   **B.** Only I and II

C. Only III and IV   **D.** Only II and III

Q.94 Consider the following transition table from PDA.

δ	$\Sigma\varepsilon$		
	a	b	ε
→ q_0	$(q_0,\ \varepsilon/a)$	$(q_1,\ a/\varepsilon)$	$(q_0,\ \varepsilon/z_0)$
q_1	–	$(q_1,\ a/\varepsilon)$	$(q_1,\ z_0/\varepsilon)$

$PD(Q, \Sigma, \delta, \Gamma, q_0, z_0, \phi)$ Where $Q = (q_0, q_1)$ and $\delta \times \Sigma, \times \Gamma, \rightarrow Q \times \Gamma$

[Example: In above table $\delta(q_0, a) = (q_0, \varepsilon/a)$ is same as $\delta(q_0, a, \varepsilon) = (q_0, a)$]

Consider the following languages. $L_1 = \{a^n b^m \mid m, n \geq 0\}$

$L_2 = \{a^n b^n \mid n \geq 1\}$

$L_3 = \{a^m b^n \mid m > n\}$

$L_4 = \{a^m b^n \mid m < n\}$

How many of the above language L_1, L_2, L_3 and L_4 are subset of the language L where L is the language accepted y the given PDA?

A. 1   **B.** 37

C. 3   **D.** None of the above

Q.95 What are the main building blocks of all XML documents?

A. Entity References, Namespace

B. Elements, Attributes

C. Comments, Character Data

D. Processing Instructions, CDATA sections.

Q.96 In Prim's algorithm , we use decrease key operation. What is the time complexity of this decrease key operation in case of Prim's Algorithm :

A. O(n)   **B.** O(nlog n)

C. O(log n)   **D.** O(n²)

Q.97 Consider following three statements from the program to move the last node of linked list to front of the linked list.

1) p-->next = null;

2) s1-->next = s;

3) s = s1;

where s points to the first node, s1 points to the last node and p points to the previous node(2nd last node). which order of these three statements will provide the exact functionality to move last node to front.

A. 1 2 3   **B.** 2 3 1

C. 2 1 3   **D.** all of the above

Q.98 More than one binary search tree can be drawn if following is given:

A. Only pre-order

B. Only post order

C. Only in order

D. Both pre-order and post order

Q.99 Match the following data structures and their applications?

List-I

1) Stack

2) Queue

3) Linked list

4) Trees

List-II

p. Serving request of singled shared resource

q. Implementing other data structures

r. Recursive function

s. Implementing algorithms

A. s, q, p, r   **B.** r, p, s, q   **C.** r, s, q, p   **D.** r, p, q, s

Q.100 Which of the following defines the referencing environment.

A. The set of binding in effect at a given point in a program.

B. The textual region of the program where a binding is active.

C. Both (a) and (b)

D. Neither (a) nor (b)

// Smart Answer Sheet //

Correct — Percentage of students who answered correctly. **Skipped** — Percentage of students who skipped.

Q.	Ans.	Correct / Skipped	Q.	Ans.	Correct / Skipped	Q.	Ans.	Correct / Skipped	Q.	Ans.	Correct / Skipped	Q.	Ans.	Correct / Skipped
1	A	82.58 % / 0.0 %	17	B	78.88 % / 0.0 %	33	B	89.22 % / 0.0 %	49	B	78.69 % / 0.0 %	65	C	78.87 % / 0.0 %
2	B	89.46 % / 0.0 %	18	D	78.83 % / 0.0 %	34	B	82.36 % / 0.0 %	50	D	81.94 % / 0.0 %	66	A	86.24 % / 0.0 %
3	A	85.59 % / 0.0 %	19	D	82.92 % / 0.0 %	35	C	84.39 % / 0.0 %	51	A	76.43 % / 0.0 %	67	B	85.66 % / 0.0 %
4	C	86.66 % / 0.0 %	20	A	84.07 % / 0.0 %	36	A	88.68 % / 0.0 %	52	A	78.74 % / 0.0 %	68	A	86.87 % / 0.0 %
5	A	83.28 % / 0.0 %	21	A	85.52 % / 0.0 %	37	A	83.28 % / 0.0 %	53	D	83.56 % / 0.0 %	69	D	89.33 % / 0.0 %
6	A	88.14 % / 0.0 %	22	D	83.07 % / 0.0 %	38	B	80.61 % / 0.0 %	54	D	79.5 % / 0.0 %	70	D	77.88 % / 0.0 %
7	B	88.55 % / 0.0 %	23	D	76.78 % / 0.0 %	39	A	79.7 % / 0.0 %	55	C	87.4 % / 0.0 %	71	D	81.14 % / 0.0 %
8	C	88.69 % / 0.0 %	24	D	81.34 % / 0.0 %	40	D	78.49 % / 0.0 %	56	A	81.27 % / 0.0 %	72	D	80.31 % / 0.0 %
9	C	82.46 % / 0.0 %	25	B	80.55 % / 0.0 %	41	D	77.22 % / 0.0 %	57	D	85.57 % / 0.0 %	73	C	85.36 % / 0.0 %
10	B	88.92 % / 0.0 %	26	B	89.13 % / 0.0 %	42	B	77.36 % / 0.0 %	58	C	87.75 % / 0.0 %	74	A	85.45 % / 0.0 %
11	B	87.93 % / 0.0 %	27	B	86.43 % / 0.0 %	43	C	81.06 % / 0.0 %	59	C	87.49 % / 0.0 %	75	C	76.57 % / 0.0 %
12	B	87.79 % / 0.0 %	28	A	79.1 % / 0.0 %	44	C	86.51 % / 0.0 %	60	C	89.35 % / 0.0 %	76	C	80.53 % / 0.0 %
13	A	78.26 % / 0.0 %	29	C	81.08 % / 0.0 %	45	C	76.97 % / 0.0 %	61	D	77.7 % / 0.0 %	77	B	79.52 % / 0.0 %
14	C	84.44 % / 0.0 %	30	B	89.98 % / 0.0 %	46	B	89.69 % / 0.0 %	62	A	78.87 % / 0.0 %	78	A	87.99 % / 0.0 %
15	A	79.45 % / 0.0 %	31	C	76.89 % / 0.0 %	47	C	85.53 % / 0.0 %	63	C	79.9 % / 0.0 %	79	C	89.67 % / 0.0 %
16	A	83.06 % / 0.0 %	32	A	80.83 % / 0.0 %	48	D	83.14 % / 0.0 %	64	D	80.32 % / 0.0 %	80	B	81.29 % / 0.0 %

Q.	Ans.	Correct / Skipped
81	D	84.46 % / 0.0 %
82	C	84.85 % / 0.0 %
83	B	86.48 % / 0.0 %
84	A	88.99 % / 0.0 %

Q.	Ans.	Correct / Skipped
85	A	78.9 % / 0.0 %
86	D	85.73 % / 0.0 %
87	A	80.17 % / 0.0 %
88	B	88.8 % / 0.0 %

Q.	Ans.	Correct / Skipped
89	C	79.83 % / 0.0 %
90	C	83.84 % / 0.0 %
91	A	89.43 % / 0.0 %
92	A	77.34 % / 0.0 %

Q.	Ans.	Correct / Skipped
93	D	89.07 % / 0.0 %
94	A	81.93 % / 0.0 %
95	B	78.16 % / 0.0 %
96	C	87.99 % / 0.0 %

Q.	Ans.	Correct / Skipped
97	D	83.84 % / 0.0 %
98	C	84.62 % / 0.0 %
99	D	77.04 % / 0.0 %
100	A	85.12 % / 0.0 %

//Hints and Solutions//

1. Router is a networking device which accepts networking packets and reads the address and does the routing. Router has only 3 layers:

- Network Layer
- Data link layer (Ethernet Layer)
- Physical Layer

Hence correct answer is option (A).

2.

- We are initially provided with a 8bit word which is 00111001

Digit 8 = 0

Digit 7=0

Digit 6 = 1

Digit 5 = 1

Digit 4 = 1

Digit 3 = 0

Digit 2 = 0

Digit 1 = 1

We have calculated it's parity which is 01111 which are written as p8p4p2p1

Bit number:

12	11	10	9	8	7	6	5	4	3	2
0	0	1	1	0	1	0	0	1	1	1

The string is encoded as by writing given word with parity bits so it is

d8d7d6d5p8d4d3d2p4d1p2p1.

001101001111.

Check bit at the end side is 1101

c1 = 1

c2 = 0

c4 = 1

c8 = 1

Now do XOR of 1101 with 0111 which gives string 1010 and after converting it to decimal we get 10. Here only tenth bit is converted so by flipping it we get 00011001.

Hence the correct answer is option (B).

3. Each cell has six neighbours because its hexagonal. If the central cell uses frequency group A, its six neighbours can use B, C, B, C, B, and C respectively

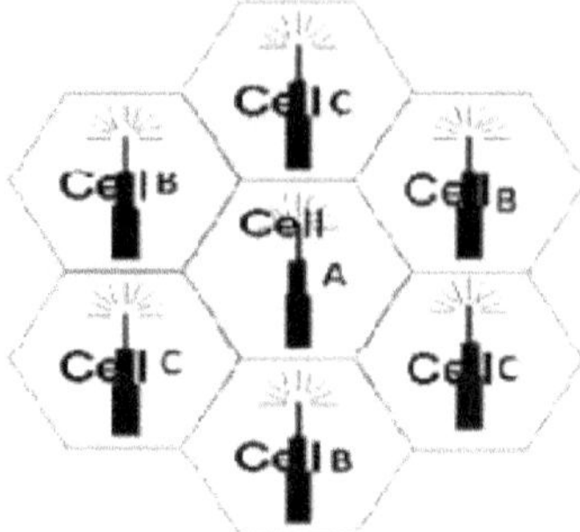

you saw in the diagram we have use only three unique cell to communicate to each other .

So, we have 840 frequency are available for total hexagon ;

But we need only three cell so required frequency

840/3 = =280

Hence the correct answer is option (A).

4. we have p=3,q=11. n=(p $\times$ q) = (3 $\times$ 11)=33

m=(p-1) $\times$(q-1) = (2 $\times$ 10)=20

Find a small odd integer e, that is relatively prime to m.

If e=3, then GCD(3,20)=1. e should be small and prime and so we let e=3.

d is given, d=7.

Public key = (e,n). (Values of e and n are known).

To encrypt a message, we apply the public key to the function

E(s) = s^e(mod n),

where **s is the given message** and e and n represent the public key integer pair. In the above question, the plain text M = 5. Plain text needs to be encrypted using the above formula.

E(s) = s^e(mod n)

=5^3(mod 33)

= 125 (mod 33)

= 26

As a result, the encrypted message **E(s) = 26**. This is what gets transmitted.

Hence the correct answer is option (C).

5. For the above question we need to perform transposition cipher

C	O	M	P	U
T	E	R	N	E
T	W	O	R	K

Layer is of 5 length therefore computer network is been written in 5 columns horizontally

CTTOEWMROPNRUEK.

Hence the correct answer is option (A).

6. MMDS stands for multipoint multichannel distribution system. MMDS is a broadband wireless technology.

Hence the correct answer is option (A).

7. It is the easy way. In the simple language 2000 bauds or elements in one sec are send by the analog signal. So 6000 bits are transmitted in one second.. Therefore, 6000/2000 = 3 bits/baud is transmitted.

Hence the correct answer is option (B).

8. A gateway is a network node that connects two networks using different protocols together. While a bridge is used to join two similar types of networks, a gateway is used to join two dissimilar networks.

Hence the correct answer is option (C).

9. Race-around condition occurs in J-K Flip-Flop.

10. Given CIDR representation is 100.1.2.35 / 20.

It suggests-

• 20 bits are used for the identification of network.

• Remaining 12 bits are used for the identification of hosts in the network.

Given CIDR IP Address may be represented as-

01100100.00000001.00000010.00100011 / 20

So,

• First IP Address = 01100100.00000001.00000000.00000000 = 100.1.0.0

• Last IP Address = 01100100.00000001.00001111.11111111 = 100.1.15.255

Thus, Range of IP Addresses = [100.1.0.0 , 100.1.15.255]

Hence the correct answer is option (B).

11. Piggybacking basically points out to a method with sole purpose of getting unauthorized free network access, it can lead to reduction in speed of data transfer for other user of the network.

Hence the correct answer is option (B).

12. BCD code is 4 weighted code i.e in which each decimal digit is represented with4-bit binary format.

$(874)_{10} \rightarrow (1000\ 0111\ 0100)_2$

13. ARP is used to get MAC address and RARP is used to get IP address.

Hence the correct answer is option (A).

14. No. of receivers=4×No. of senders+1(Initial person doesn't have a sender)

x+100=4x+1

3x=99

x=33

Hence the correct answer is option (C).

15. Band rate = $\dfrac{3000}{6}$

= 500 band sec.

Hence the correct answer is option (A).

16. 1.Physical layer:- Transmission and reception of raw bit streams over a physical medium.

2.Data Link Layer:- Reliable transmission of data frames between two nodes connected by a Physical layer.

The 7 Layers of OSI

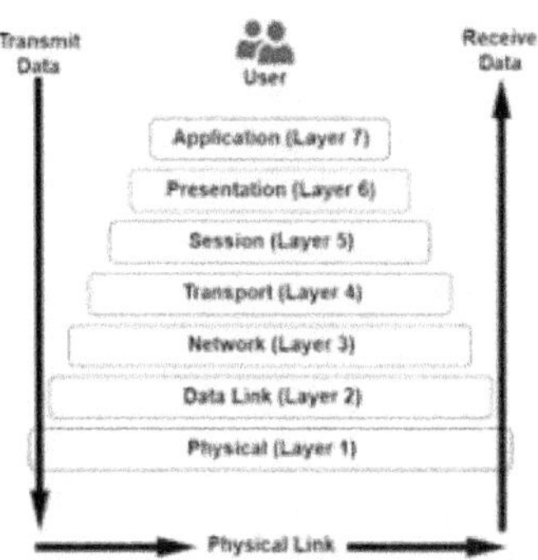

3. Network Layer: - Structuring and managing a multi-node network, including addressing, routing and traffic control.

4.Transport Layer: - Reliable transmission of data segments between points on a network, including segmentation, acknowledgement and multiplexing.

5.Application Layer:- High-level APIs, including resource sharing, remote file access.

Hence the correct answer is option (A).

17. The Unlicensed National Information Infrastructure (U-NII) radio band is part of the radio frequency spectrum used by IEEE-802.11a devices and by many wireless ISPs. It operates over four ranges:

U-NII Low (U-NII-1): 5.150-5.250 GHz. Originally limited to indoor use only. Regulations required use of an integrated antenna, with power limited to 50 mW. Rules changed in 2014 to permit outdoor operation, maximum fixed power 1 watt, maximum fixed EIRP 4 watts (+36 dBm) point-to-multipoint, 200 watts (+53 dBm) point-to-point. However, strict out-of-band emission rules limit practical point-to-point power to lower levels.

U-NII Mid (U-NII-2A): 5.250-5.350 GHz. Both outdoor and indoor use, subject to Dynamic Frequency Selection (DFS, or radar avoidance). Regulations allow for a user-installable antenna. Power limited to 250 mW

U-NII-2B: 5.350-5.470 GHz. Currently 120MHz of spectrum not allocated by the FCC for unlicensed use.

U-NII Worldwide (U-NII-2C / U-NII-2e): 5.470-5.725 GHz. Both outdoor and indoor use, subject to Dynamic Frequency Selection (DFS, or radar avoidance). Power limited to 250 mW. This spectrum was added by the FCC in 2003 to "align the frequency bands used by U-NII devices in the United States with bands in other parts of the world". The FCC currently has an interim limitation on operations on channels which overlap the 5600 - 5650 MHz band.

U-NII Upper (U-NII-3): 5.725 to 5.850 GHz. Sometimes referred to as U-NII / ISM due to overlap with the ISM band. Regulations allow for a user-installable antenna. Power limited to 1W.

Hence the correct answer is option (B).

18. Circuit switching refers to a methodology in which the data packets received by the receiver are in the exact same order as they were been dispatched by the sender as the path is established and packets are traveling in the same sequence.

Hence the correct answer is option (D).

19. Thus a code with **minimum Hamming distance** d between its codewords can detect at most d-1 errors and can correct ⌊(d-1)/2⌋ errors. So for t error correcting we need 2t+1.

Hence the correct answer is option (D).

20. ICMP message sends time exceeded message when TTL value becomes zero. TTL uses 8-bit in IP header which can travel maximum of 255 routers.

Total routers travelled = 255 (packet going forward) + 254 (ICMP time exceeded message coming back) = 509

Hence the correct answer is option (A).

21. The GSM network is divided into 3 major system SS, BSS, OSS.

BSS: Base Station System,

SS: Switching System:

OSS: OSS define as Operation and Support System. The switching system (SS) is responsible for performing call processing and subscriber-related functions.

BSS: BSS define as All radio-related function are performed in the BSS, which consists of base station controllers (BSCs) and the base transceiver stations (BTSs).

Hence the correct answer is option (A).

22. Firstly we understand the working of Multiplexer using TDM.

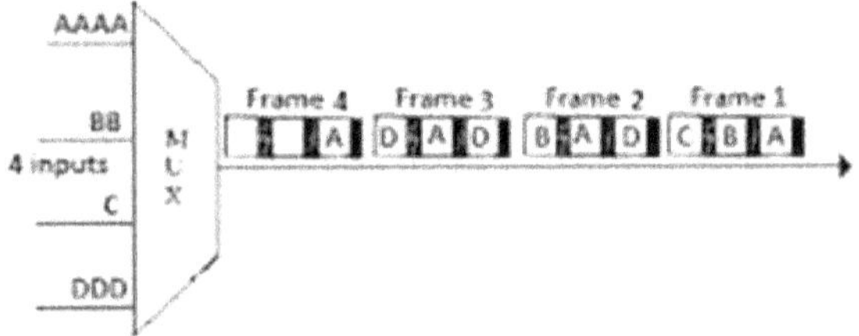

Each frame contain 1 byte from each channel; { 1 Byte = 8 Bit}

we have 4 channels

Then ,the size of each frame is

1 × 4= 4 bytes = =~ 32 bits.

Each channel is sending 100 bytes/second

A frame carries 1 byte from each channel,

The frame rate must be 100 frames per second. {its given}

Then the total rate is = 32 × 100 = 3200 bits/second

Hence the correct answer is option (D).

23. In Class D IP address 1st 4 bit are been fixed to 1110 which gives class D range which is from 224.0.0.0 to 239.255.255.255. Class D is also set for multicasting. In multicasting there is no need to take out host address from IP address.

Hence the correct answer is option (D).

24. A **network packet** is a formatted unit of data carried by a packet-switched network. When data is formatted into packets, and packet switching is employed, the bandwidth of the communication medium can be better shared among users than with circuit switching. Computer communications links that do not support packets, such as traditional point-to-point telecommunications links, simply transmit data as a bit stream.

A **network switch** (also called switching hub, bridging hub, officially MAC bridge) is a computer networking device that connects devices together on a computer network by using packet switching to receive, process, and forward data to the destination device.

Bridges only forward packets between networks that are destined for the other network. Term used by Novell to denote a computer that accepts packets at the network layer and forward them to another network.

A **router** is a networking device that forwards data packets between computer networks. Routers perform the traffic directing functions on the Internet. A data packet is typically forwarded from one router to another router through the networks that constitute an internet work until it reaches its destination node.

Hence the correct answer is option (D).

25. Parse tree is as follows

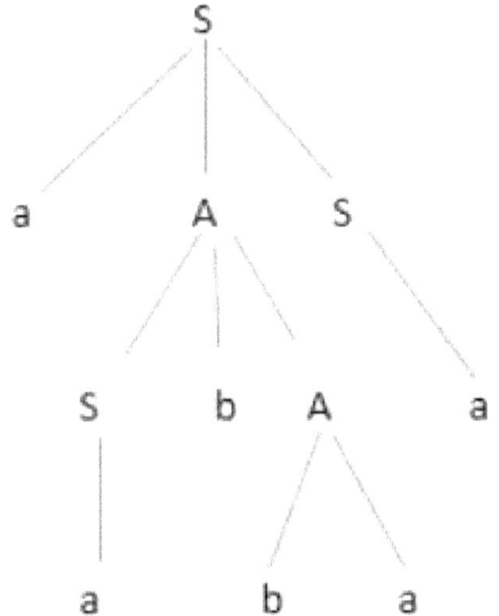

26. For multiple access in GSM, users have different band pass filters. GSM (Global System for Mobile communications) is an open, digital cellular technology used for transmitting mobile voice and data services. GSM differs from first generation wireless

systems in that it uses digital technology and Time Division Multiple Access (TDMA) transmission methods.

Hence the correct answer is option (B).

27. According to the formula : 1/period= frequency. We can see the arrangements between period and the frequency. So Placing the values in the formula : $1/(10 \times 10^{-3}) = 100$.

Hence the correct answer is option (B).

28. In class A, the first bit of the first octet is always set to 0 (zero).

ok let's a take an example

00000001.00000001.00000001.00000001.

Hence the correct answer is option (A).

29. The presentation layer is responsible for the delivery and formatting of information to the application layer for further processing or display. It relieves the application layer of concern regarding syntactical differences in data representation within the end-user systems. An example of a presentation service would be the conversion of an EBCDIC-coded text computer file to an ASCII-coded file.

The presentation layer is the lowest layer at which application programmers consider data structure and presentation, instead of simply sending data in the form of datagram or packets between hosts. This layer deals with issues of string representation - whether they use the Pascal method (an integer length field followed by the specified amount of bytes) or the C/C++ method. The idea is that the application layer should be able to point at the data to be moved, and the presentation layer will deal with the rest.

Hence the correct answer is option (C).

30. In AES number of rounds is variable and depends on the length of the key. AES uses 10 rounds for 128-bit keys, 12 rounds for 192-bit keys and 14 rounds for 256-bit keys. Each of these rounds uses a different 128-bit round key, which is calculated from the original AES key.

Hence the correct answer is option (B).

31. Session Layer In the seven-layer OSI model of computer networking, the session layer is layer 5.The session layer provides the mechanism for opening, closing and managing a session between end-user application processes,

Communication sessions consist of requests and responses that occur between applications. Session-layer services are commonly used in application environments that make use of remote procedure calls.

Hence the correct answer is option (C).

32. Only class A format has the above IP address as Class A has it's first octet in range of (0-127)

(128- 191) is the range for class B which obviously doesn't satisfy the above condition and for Class C range is between 192 and 223 and for Class D range is between 224 and 239. So as we can see only option fit's in the above IP address.

Class A range is 0-126 only. 127 is not there in Class A range. Class B range starts from 128. IP starting with 127 reserved for different testing purposes i.e. 127.0.0.1 is loop back which can't be be given/used for others purposes.

Hence the correct answer is option (A).

33. Selective Reject (or Selective Repeat) protocol is one of the automatic repeat-request (ARQ) techniques used for communications.

In SR protocol the window size of the receiver and sender must be (N + 1)/2, where N is the maximum sequence number.

If N is the maximum available sequence numbers then, the window size of both sender and receiver must be N/2.

Here n = 4,

So Maximum window size is 8.

The maximum sequence number will be 7, as sequence number starts from 0.

Hence the correct answer is option (B).

34. HSSI means High-Speed Serial Interface, and this work at Physical layer. and 10 base t is a physical media, twisted wire resides in physical layer.

Hence the correct answer is option (B).

35. For given SOP, we can draw k-map as

0	1	3	2
1			
1 4	5	1 7	1 6
12	13	1 15	14
1 8	1 9	11	10

Hence, from the above k-map, we can find the minimal expression as xyz+wx'y'+w'y'z'+w'xy

So the correct option is (C).

36. FIN in TCP determines when to shut down the connection under scenario when sender has nothing to send.

Hence the correct answer is option (A).

37. Un-complemented and complemented variables are counted as two different literals.

Hence the above expression has 6 literals.

Hence the correct answer is option (A).

38. Cryptography involves creating written or generated codes that allows information to be kept secret. **Cryptography** converts data into a format that is unreadable.

Hence the correct answer is option (B).

39. Phase-shift keying (PSK) is a digital modulation process which conveys data by changing (modulating) the phase of a reference signal (the carrier wave). The modulation occurs by varying the sine and cosine inputs at a precise time. It is widely used for wireless LANs, RFID and Bluetooth communication.

Modulation	Baud Rate	Bit Rate
4-PSK	N	2N
8-PSK	N	3N
16-PSK	N	4N

According to the table given above, for a 16-PSK, given the baud rate N, the bit rate would be 4N. Here bps is provides which is 9600. In order to calculate the baud rate we have to divide bps/4, because the signal level is 16. So the answer would be 9600/4 = **2400 baud**.

Hence the correct answer is option (A).

40. the space required is 4n-4 ... if one word treated as 1 size. so given M is the size of 4. so space required for store c is 4 ✕4-4=12. if M is the size of 5 then space for C is 4 ✕5-4=16 because we can generate n-1pair of M (size of m is n).. so after counting of each pair with their opposite is 4n-4.

So. answer to this question is option d, (less than 4n).

Hence the correct answer is option (D).

41. Ethernet checking a valid address or not. And token ring prevent looping in system.

Hence the correct answer is option (D).

42. Hamming codes belong to a class of binary codes, they aim for achieving maximum possible rate for their code. In it for each integer r(r ≥ 2) there would always be code with it's code block length $n = 2^r - 1$ and the size of the message would be $2^r - r - 1$.

Hence the correct answer is option (B).

43. Calinsock Active-X Control is helpful in providing interface to the TCP/IP suit protocol. Windows Socket Api(WSA) defines how windows network should access network utilities Like TCP/IP.

Hence the correct answer is option (C).

44. In order to transfer data securely encryption is effective way to do that. In encryption process, information to be transferred is encoded securely so that only authorized parties can access it. To decrypt information authorized party should have secret key or password. The data when unencrypted is known a plain text while encrypted test is called as cipher text.

In Encryption information is encrypted packet-by-packet basis. There are two types of Encryption: asymmetric encryption (public key) and symmetric encryption (private key). In symmetric encryption same key is used to encrypt and decrypt data in order to keep the key secret. In asymmetric one key is used for encoding and other key is used for decoding.

Hence the correct answer is option (C).

45. +28 ⇒ 0000 0000 0001 1100

−28 ⇒ 1111 1111 1110 0100 (2's complement form)

Hence the correct answer is option (C).

46. Call control is a procedure that is utilized as a part of broadcast communications systems to screen and keep up associations once they have been built up.

The A-bis interface comprises of the A3 and Ab segments. The important parts of the BCS/BTS interface definition for a CDMA framework are: 1. Support of client activity connection to a frame selector function (A3) 2. Support of Paging Channel informing, Access Channel informing, Radio capacities and Broadcast framework data capacities (Ab)

BSMAP also known as The Base station Management Application Part, underpins all Radio Re-source Management and Facility Management techniques between the MSC and the BS. or, on the other hand to a cell(s) inside the BS.

CDMA also known Code-Division Multiple Access, is a computerized cell innovation that utilized spread range procedures.

Hence the correct answer is option (B).

47. Internet Control Message Protocol (ICMP and (ICMPv6)

Is part of the Internet layer and uses the IP datagram delivery facility to sends its messages. ICMP sends messages that perform control, error reporting, and informational functions for TCP/IP. The following figure is the ICMP header format.

Hence the correct answer is option (C).

48. For all loads, throughput is...

$S = GP_0$ where P_0 = Probability that a packet does not suffer a collision

The probability that k frames generated during a given frame time is given by poisson distribution.

$P[k] = (G^k e^{-G})/k!$

So probability of zero frames i.e. k=0

$P_0 = (G^0 e^{-G})/0! = e^{-G}$

If an interval is 2 frame time long, the mean no. of frames generated is 2G

Probability that no other frames is transmitted during vurnerable period is,

$P0 = e^{-2G}$

So, throughput,

$$S = GP_0 = Ge^{-2G}$$

Hence the correct answer is option (D).

49. Routing is the process of selecting a path for traffic in a network, or between or across multiple networks. Routing is performed for many types of networks, including circuit-switched networks, such as the public switched telephone network (PSTN), computer networks, such as the Internet, as well as in networks used in public and private transportation, such as the system of streets, roads, and highways in national infrastructure.

Link-state routing protocols are one of the two main classes of routing protocols used in packet switching networks for computer communications, the other being distance-vector routing protocols. Examples of link-state routing protocols include Open Shortest Path First (OSPF) and intermediate system to intermediate system (IS-IS).

Hence the correct answer is option (B).

50. 1000

MSB is 1 so, -ve number.

Take 2's complement for magnitude.

```
0111
+   1
______  = -8
1000
```

51. Coaxial cable are categorized by radio Government rating are adopted for specialized functions. Category RG-59 with impedance 75 Ohm is used for cable TV.

Number of the people seen the letter

$$= \frac{100 \times 4 - 1}{4 - 1} = \frac{399}{3} = 133$$

Number of the people send out the letter

= 133 − 100 = 33

Hence the correct answer is option (A).

52. IPv 4 datagram fragmentation :-Different Networks may have different maximum transmission unit (MTU), for example due to differences in LAN technology. When one network wants to transmit datagrams to a network with a smaller MTU, the routers on path may fragment and reassemble datagrams.

Hence the correct answer is option (A).

53. Check sum is the mistake identifying system when information is dealt with as a succession of character. Equality is the component utilized when information is dealt with as a succession of bits.

Hence the correct answer is option (D).

54. The packets in broadcast are not directed and sent by the switches on any system.

Communicate directing should be possible in two ways:

A switch makes an information bundle and afterward sends it to each host one by one. For this situation, the switch makes various duplicates of single information packets with various addresses. All packets are sent as unicast but since they are sent to all, it recreates as though switch is broadcasting.

Flooding is least difficult strategy bundle sending or packet forwarding. When a packet is received, at that time the switches send it to every one of the interfaces aside from the one on which it was received.

Hence the correct answer is option (D).

55. Infrared radiation, or simply infrared or IR, is electromagnetic radiation (EMR) with longer wavelengths than those of visible light, and is therefore invisible, although it is sometimes loosely called infrared light. It extends from the nominal red edge of the visible spectrum at 700 nanometres (frequency 430 THz), to 1 mm (300 GHz) (although people can see infrared up to at least 1050 nm in experiments). Most of the thermal radiation emitted by objects near room temperature is infrared. Like all EMR, IR carries radiant energy, and behaves both like a wave and like its quantum particle, the photon.

Hence the correct answer is option (C).

56. The solution for this instance
$$i_1 = 1 \quad i_2 = 2 \quad i_3 = 3 \quad i_4 = 4 \quad i_5 = 5 \quad i_6 = 5$$
is $i_7 = 6$

The solution for this instance is = ababaaabbbaabbaababaa

Hence the correct answer is option (A).

57. $n = pq = 3.11 = 33, \ p = (p-1)(q-1)$

= 2.10 = 20

$$ed = mod\varnothing; 7e = 1 mod 20;$$
7e-1=mod20; 7e-1=20; 7e=21; e=3

c = memod n = c = 5^3 mod33 = 26

Find the least odd value of e that is prime as compared to m

The encrypted message e is 26 which is been transmitted.

Hence the correct answer is option (D).

58. The Hypertext Transfer Protocol (HTTP) is a most extensively used application layer protocol. Http provides us with weightless protocol so that pages that uses HTML language can be retrieved easily from the web.

The transport layer has duty of establishing an impermanent relationship between 2 application programs and proving them data as requested by them. TCP is used in it for those connections in which stable connection is needed between hosts.

The data link layer is layer 2 of networking. The HDLC protocols used in data link layer are set of rules which are been used for sending data among networks.

In network layer Border Gateway Protocol (BGP) is used for the purpose of interchanging routing and reachability details within autonomous system on the web.

Hence the correct answer is option (C).

59. Single-stage networks A single-stage network is a switching network with N input selectors (IS) and N output selectors

The single-stage network is also called a recirculating network. Data items may have to recirculate through the single stage several times before reaching their final destinations.

Hence the correct answer is option (C).

60. IEEE 802.11 standards provide the bases for Wi-Fi networks.

Hence the correct answer is option (C).

61. Software engineering is the systematic approach to the development, operation, maintenance and retirement of software. Software Engineering is the application of science and

mathematics by which the capabilities of computer equipment are made useful to man via computer programs, procedures, and associated documentations.

Hence the correct answer is option (D).

62. The waterfall model is a process designed to move in a sequence this is a popular model used in software development where the progress is seen as going slowly and gradually downwards (like one waterfall) through the stages of idea to maintenance.

The waterfall model is also known as the classical life cycle model, the stages of developing a software moves linearly and in sequence from feasibility study to requirement analysis and designing, coding, testing, integration, implementation, and maintenance. So this model is also called as the Linear Sequential Model.

Hence the correct answer is option (A).

63. The option 1 is keeping the track of the project, that comes later when the project is up and running, it's not a part associated with project planning. Similarly the option B is a comparison that can only be made in the later phase of the project. So the answer is 3rd option which has parts when it comes to planning.

Hence the correct answer is option (C).

64. GUI (graphical user interface) is a user interface that includes graphical elements, such as windows, icons and buttons. It is used by windows to make it user friendly while dos uses command line interface. GUI is a program interface that takes advantage of the computer's graphics capabilities to make the program easier to use.

Hence the correct answer is option (D).

65. Windows 2000 provides peer to peer computing for each computer which is in a network i.e it is a better implementation of client-server network.

Hence the correct answer is option (C).

66. Representation of bits and Synchronization of bit are related to Physical Layer. Connection control is related to Transport Layer.

Hence the correct answer is option (A).

67. Circuit switching is a method of implementing a telecommunications network in which two network nodes establish a dedicated communications channel (circuit) through the network before the nodes may communicate. The circuit guarantees the full bandwidth of the channel and remains connected for the duration of the communication session. The circuit functions as if the nodes were physically connected as with an electrical circuit.

Hence the correct answer is option (B).

68. A Flow control Policy. It is present at transport layer and not in network layer.

Network layer policies are given as follows:

1) Virtual circuits versus datagram inside the subnet

2) Packet sequencing and administration strategy

3) Packet dispose of strategy

4) Routing calculation

5) Packet lifetime administration

Hence the correct answer is option (A).

69. The gateway is a device used to connect networks using different protocols. Gateways operate at the network layer of the OSI model. In order to communicate with a host on another network, an IP host must be configured with a route to the destination network. If a configuration route is not found, the host uses the gateway (default IP router) to transmit the traffic to the destination host. The default t gateway is where the IP sends packets that are destined for remote networks. If no default gateway is specified, communication is limited to the local network. Gateways receive data from a network using one type of protocol stack, removes that protocol stack and repackages it with the protocol stack that the other network can use.

Hence the correct answer is option (D).

70. In Data Encryption Standard, the simple text, in this case it's the password, will be encrypted in block of 64 bits, yielding 64 bits of cipher text. The algorithm which is parameterized by 56 bit key has 19 distinct stages.

Hence the correct answer is option (D).

71. Classless Inter-Domain Routing (CIDR) is a method for allocating IP addresses and IP routing. The Internet Engineering Task Force introduced CIDR in 1993 to replace the previous addressing architecture of classful network design in the Internet. Its goal was to slow the growth of routing tables on routers across the Internet, and to help slow the rapid exhaustion of IPv4 addresses.

Hence the correct answer is option (D).

72. Null-able variables are : $\{A, B\}$
Hence putting them null and generating new productions will give null free grammar.
The correct grammar after eliminating all null productions are :
$$S \rightarrow ABa/aAb/aC/a/ab/Ba/Aa$$
$$A \rightarrow aB/a$$
$$B \rightarrow bA/b$$
$$C \rightarrow a/b$$
Hence correct answer is option (D).

73. A branch delay slot is an instruction space immediately following a jump or branch. When a branch instruction is involved, the location of the following delay slot instruction in the pipeline may be called a branch delay slot. Branch delay slots are found mainly in older RISC architectures and DSP architectures.

Hence correct answer is option (C).

74. 2's complement of -57 is 11000111 (8 bit representation).

Append 0 at the LSB = 110001110

start from right end taking pairs of two symbols which are encoded as :

$00 \rightarrow 0$

$01 \rightarrow +1$

$10 \rightarrow -1$

$11 \rightarrow 0$

Hence correct answer is option (A).

75. we know that,

Average access time(T_{avg}) = T_s+T+$T_{data\_transfer}$+$T_{controller\_overhead}$

Now, since 3000 Rotation à 60 $\times 10^3$ msec

So 1 rotation à 60 $\times 10^3/3000$ =20 msec

T_r =1/2 $\times$ rotational delay =10 msec

Again since 40 KB can be transfer in 10^3 msec

So 512 Byte can be transfer(T_t)= 512 $\times 10^3/40 \times 2^{10}$ =12.5 msec

Now,

Average access time (T_{avg}) = T_s+T+$T_{data\_transfer}$+$T_{controller\_overhead}$ = 6+10+12.5+0.2 =28.7 msec

Hence correct answer is option (C).

76. Pipeline with 5 stages
$$K = 5$$
$$\text{Max delay} = 60$$
$$\Rightarrow \eta(efficiency) = \frac{5}{k} = \frac{200}{60}$$
$$\Rightarrow \eta = 3.33$$
$$\Rightarrow \eta = \frac{5}{k}$$
$$\Rightarrow \eta = \frac{2.83}{5}$$
$$\Rightarrow \eta = 0.666$$
$$\Rightarrow \eta = 0.67$$
$$67\% \text{ efficiency.}$$

Hence correct answer is option (C).

77. RISC is hardwired and Instruction take single clock cycle to get executed.

Hence correct answer is option (B).

78. Spatial locality is the one which is to exploit.

Hence correct answer is option (A).

79. Ambiguity is not an operation and hence its decidability is not fixed. The CFG is never closed under such operation.

Hence correct answer is option (C).

80. (a) L = {ww^{R}x $|$ w, x $\in$ (a + b)$^+$} is not regular

(b) L = {xww^R $|$ w, x $\in$ (a + b)*} is regular = (a + b)*

(c) L = {wxw $|$ w, x $\in$ (a + b)$^+$} is not regular

(d) L = {w₁w₂x $|$ w₁ = w₂, w₁, w₂, $\in$(a+b)₊, x $\in$(a + b)*} is not regular

Hence correct answer is option (B).

81. We can say about it :-

a) It is possible when the first state itself is a final state.

b) It is possible when only the first state is final state and there are no incoming transitions in it.

c) It is also possible when the second state is final state , and it has only one incoming transition from state 1.

d) This is also possible by making first state as final state and a single loop with all the Greek alphabets on it. Rest unusable transitions on all other states.

Hence correct answer is option (D).

82. Consider the Chomsky Hierarchy

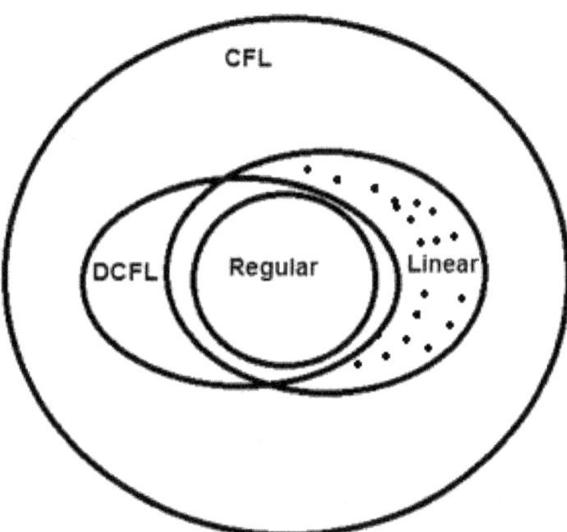

So , now we can answer the statements.

S_1 : All regular languages are linear , true because regular is a subset of linear.

S_2 : All linear grammar are regular , false because the dotted region in above diagram shows linear grammars which are not regular.

S_3 : Some DCFL's are also regular, true because regular is a subset of DCFl .

S_4 : All regular are DCFL , true because regular is a subset of DCFl.

Hence correct answer is option (C).

83. The language accepted by the Turing machine is recursively enumerable. If is undecidable as the turing machine may halt or it may loop for the strings whose length is not equal to 2014.

Hence correct answer is option (B).

84. Statement a is true.

Statement b is false SMTP work on port no 25 while POP works on port no 110.

Statement c is false FTP is stateful protocol because in FTP server keep some information about sender. HTTP is stateless protocol, server do not keep any information about sender.

Statement d is true, in FTP we have two connections. One for commands and other for data.

Hence correct answer is option (A).

85. This is example of Local area network.

Hence correct answer is option (A).

86. Intra Domain Routing Protocols

A- RIP : Routing Information Protocols (D.V.R. Algorothm).

B- OSPF : Open Shortest Path First (Link State Routing Algorithm).

Inter domain protocols

A- BGP : Border Gateway Protocol (Path Vector Routing Algorithm).

Hence correct answer is option (D).

87. Telnet provides remote access to servers and networking devices.

Hence correct answer is option (A).

88. $B = 10^6$ bits/s

Packet size=1000 bytes=8000 bits

Link utilization=25%

Transmission Time(TT)= $\dfrac{packet\ size}{Bandwidth} = \dfrac{8000}{10^6} = 8 \times 10^{-3}$

As we know, LU= $\dfrac{TT}{TT+2PT} \times 100$

$$\Rightarrow 25 = \dfrac{TT}{TT+2PT} \times 100$$

$$\Rightarrow 25(TT + 2PT) = 100TT$$

$$\Rightarrow TT + 2PT = 4TT$$

$$\Rightarrow PT = \dfrac{3TT}{2} = \dfrac{3}{2} \times 8 \times 10^{-3} = 12 \times 10^{-3}$$

=12 milliseconds

Hence correct answer is option (B).

89. SRS consists of both problem statement and product design.

Hence correct answer is option (C).

90. Session layer manages and synchronises conversations between two different applications. It also controls logging on and off, user identification, billing and session management.

Hence correct answer is option (C).

91. TCP/IP was included by a version of UNIX operating system.

Hence correct answer is option (A).

92. Unit testing is white box testing applied only for a small unit of code no larger than a class (Low Level Design).

Functional testing can be applied for whole product (High Level Design).

System and acceptance testing applied for whole product (Requirements analysis).

Hence correct answer is option (A).

93. The correct statement are :

1. Recovering lost packet between two directly connected nodes is done by data link layer.

2. Recovering lost packet between two nodes separated by multiple hops is done by transport layer.

Hence correct answer is option (D).

94.

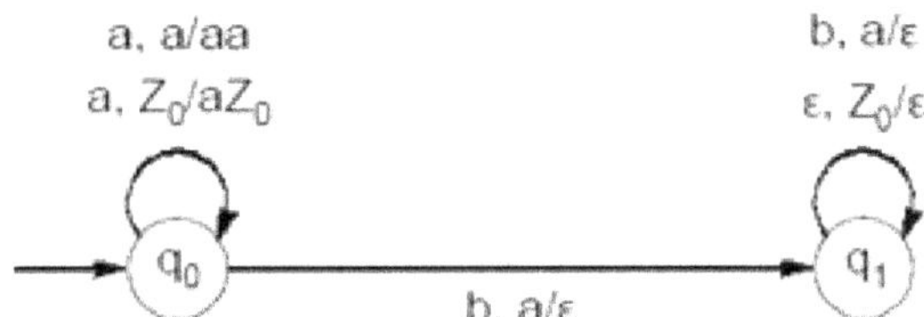

It accepts $L = \{a^n b^n \mid n \geq 1\}$ and $L = L_2$
Only L_2 is the subset of L

Hence correct answer is option (A).

95. Building blocks of XML documents are Elements, Tags, Attributes, Entities, PCDATA and CDATA.

Hence correct answer is option (B).

96. In Prim's algorithm , heap of vertices are created and decrease key operation is performed on the heap elements which takes O(log n) time. Decrease key operation is performed to change the value of distance in every iteration.

Hence correct answer is option (C).

97. All above sequences will result in correct functionality. Order of statement 2 and 3 can't be swapped, rest we can have statement 1 anywhere in the sequence.

Hence correct answer is option (D).

98. if only in order is given then more than one binary search tree can be drawn because for each binary search tree ascending order of node value will be in order. So, if only pre-order or only post order or both is given then one can draw unique binary search tree.

Hence correct answer is option (C).

99. Correct order is :

1. Stack r. Recursive function

2. Queue p. Serving request of singled shared resource

3. Linked list q. Implementing other data structures

4. Trees s. Implementing algorithms

Hence correct answer is option (D).

100. "Referencing environment" is the set of binding in effect at a given point in a program.

"Scope" is the textual region of the program where a binding is active.

Hence correct answer is option (A).

Q.1 If x is an array of interger, then the value of & x[i] is same as
A. & x[i-1] + size of (int)
B. x + size of (int) * i
C. x+i
D. None of these

Q.2 If S is an array of 80 characters, then the value assigned to S through the statement scanf ("%s",S) with input 12345 would be
A. "12345"
B. nothing since 12345 is an integer
C. S is an illegal name for string
D. %s cannot be used for reading in values of S

Q.3 Size of the array need not be specified, when
A. Initialization is a part of definition
B. It is a declaratrion
C. It is a formal parameter
D. All of these

Q.4 A one dimensional array A has indices 1....75. Each element is a string and takes up three memory words. The array is stored starting at location 1120 decimal. The starting address of A [49] is
A. 1167   **B.** 1164   **C.** 1264   **D.** 1169

Q.5 Minimum number of interchange needed to convert the array 89,19,40,14,17,12,10,2,5,7,11,6,9,70, into a heap with the maximum element at the root is
A. 0   **B.** 1   **C.** 2   **D.** 3

Q.6 The program fragment
int i = 263 ;
putchar (i) ;
prints
A. 263
B. ASCII equivalent of 263
C. rings the bell
D. garbage

Q.7 The value of ab if ab & 0 x 3f equals 0 x 27 is
A. 047   **B.** 0 x 0 f   **C.** 0 x f3   **D.** 0 x 27

Q.8 Consider following program fragment
if (a > b)
printf("a> b") ;
else
printf ("else part") ;
printf ("a< = b") a <= b
will be printed if
A. a>b   **B.** a<b
C. a=b   **D.** All of these

Q.9 If a file is opened in r+ mode then
A. reading is possible
B. writing is possible
C. both (a) & (b)
D. all the above comments are true

Q.10 The default parameter passing mechanism is
A. call by value   **B.** call by reference
C. call by value result   **D.** none of above

Q.11 If y is of integer type then the expression
$3 \times (y - 8) / 9$ and $(y - 8) / 9 \times 3$
A. must yield the same value
B. must yield different values
C. may or may not yield the same value
D. none of these

Q.12 The following code fragment
int x, y =2, z, a;
x = (y* = 2) + (z = a = y)
printf ("%d" , x);
A. prints 8
B. prints 6
C. prints 6 or 8 depending on the compiler implementation
D. is syntactically wrong

Q.13 Process control block does not contain:
A. Process ID   **B.** Registers
C. Bootstrap Program   **D.** Program Counter

Q.14 WIFI operates at
A. Network layer   **B.** Data link layer
C. Transport layer   **D.** Application layer

Q.15 The expression 5-2-3*5-2 will evaluate to 18, if - is left associative and
A. * has precedence over *
B. * has precedence over -
C. - has precedence over *
D. - has precedence over -

Q.16 Which of the folllowing best expresses **"Coercion"**
A. Takes place across an assignment operator
B. Takes place if an operator has operands of different data types
C. Means casting
D. Both (a) & (b)

Q.17 Prior to using a pointer variable it should be
A. Declared
B. Initialized
C. Both declared and initalized
D. None of these

Q.18 The scaling factor that is use in header extension length field of routing extension header in IPv6 data packet is
A. 6 **B.** 7 **C.** 8 **D.** 9

Q.19 Peep-hole optimization is a form of
A. loop optimization
B. local optimization
C. constant folding
D. data flow analysis

Q.20 Which one of the following is the tightest upper bound that represents the time complexity of inserting an object into a binary search tree of n nodes ?
A. $O(1)$
B. $O(\log n)$
C. $O(n)$
D. $O(n \log n)$

Q.21 Which of the following is an odd function?
A. $f(x) = x^2 - |x|$
B. $f(x) = \sin(x) + \cos(x)$
C. $f(x) = (x)(a^x + 1) / (a^x - 1)$
D. none of the above

Q.22 Choose the functions that are periodic.
A. $f(x) = x - [x]$; where $[x]$ stands for the greatest integer $\leq x$
B. $f(x) = |\cos(x)|$
C. Both (a) & (b)
D. $f(x) = \sin(1/x)$, if $x \neq 0$; 0 otherwise

Q.23 Method of communication in which transmission takes place in both directions, but only in one direction at a time, is called
A. simplex
B. four wire circuit
C. full duplex
D. half duplex

Q.24 Bit stuffing refers to
A. inserting a '0' in user stream to differentiate it with a lag
B. inserting a '0' in lag stream to avoid ambiguity
C. appending a nibble to the lag sequence
D. appending a nibble to the use data stream

Q.25 What uses a physical star topology ?
A. 10 base 5
B. 10 base 2
C. 10 base T
D. None of these

Q.26 The monitor station in what standard ensures that one and only one token is circulating ?
A. 802.3
B. 802.5
C. Both (a) and (b)
D. All of these

Q.27 What can happen at a Token Ring station
A. Examination of the destination address
B. Regeneration of the frame
C. Passing of the frame to the next station
D. All of these

Q.28 In Token Ring, when a frame reaches its destination station, then
A. message is copied
B. four bits in the packet are changed
C. message is taken of the ring and replaced by the token
D. both (a) and (b)

Q.29 Which of the following is not a transceiver function?
A. Transmission and receipt of data
B. Checking of line voltages
C. Addition and subtraction of headers
D. Collision detection

Q.30 The station-to-hub distance in which of the following is 2000 meters ?
A. 100 Base-TX
B. 100 Base-FX
C. 100 Base - T4
D. 100 Base - T1

Q.31 Ether LAN uses
A. polar encoding
B. diferential manchester encoding
C. manchester encoding
D. NRZ

Q.32 Which of the given below houses the switches in Token Ring ?
A. NIC
B. MAU
C. Nine-pin connector
D. Transceiver

Q.33 Which of the following uses an 8B/6T encoding scheme?
A. 100 Base-TX
B. 100 Base-FX
C. 100 Base-T4
D. 100 Base-T1

Q.34 Which topology requires a central controller or hub ?
A. Mesh **B.** Star **C.** Bus **D.** Ring

Q.35 Which topology requires a multi point connection?
A. Mesh **B.** Star **C.** Bus **D.** Ring

Q.36 Which of the following network access standard disassembler is used for connection station to a packet switched network ?
A. X.3 **B.** X.21 **C.** X.25 **D.** X.75

Q.37 How many characters per sec (7 bits+1 parity) can be transmitted over a 2400 bps line if the transfer is synchronous (1 start and 1 stop bit) ?
A. 300 **B.** 250 **C.** 240 **D.** 275

Q.38 A terminal multiplexer has six 1200 bps terminals and 'n' 300 bps terminals connected to it. If outgoing line is 9600 bps, then maximum value of n is
A. 4 **B.** 16 **C.** 8 **D.** 28

Q.39 Which memory is difficult to interface with processor ?
A. Static memory
B. Dynamic memory
C. ROM
D. None of these

Q.40 For a memory system, the cycle time is
A. Same as the access time
B. Longer than the access time
C. Shorter than the access time
D. multiple of the access time

Q.41 In comparison with static RAM memory, the dynamic RAM memory has
A. Lower bit density and higher power consumption
B. Higher bit density and low power consumption

C. Lower bit density and lower power consumption

D. None of these

Q.42 CPU has two modes privileged and non-privileged.In order to change the mode from privileged to non-privileged

A. A hardware interrupt is needed

B. A software interrupt is needed

C. Either (a) or (b)

D. A non-privileged instruction (which does not generate an interrupt) is needed

Q.43 The minimum number of comparisons required to determine if an integer appears more than n/2 times in a sorted array of n integers is

A. $\Theta(n)$　　**B.** $\Theta(\log n)$　　**C.** $\Theta(\log^* n)$　　**D.** $\Theta(1)$

Q.44 The running time of an algorithm T(n), where 'n' is the input size, of a recursive algorithm is given as follows.is given by

$T(n) = c + T(n - 1)$, if $n > 1$

d, if $n \leq 1$

The order of this algorithm is

A. n^2　　**B.** n　　**C.** n^3　　**D.** n^n

Q.45 Six files Fl, F2, F3, F4, F5 and F6 have 100,200,50,80, 120, 150 number of records respectively. In what order should they be stored so as to optimize access time? Assume each file is accessed with the same frequency.

A. F3, F4, Fl, F5, F6, F2

B. F2, F6, F5, Fl, F4, F3

C. Fl, F2, F3, F4, F5, F6

D. Ordering is immaterial as all files are accessed with the same frequency

Q.46 The time that depends on the input: an already sorted sequence that is easier to sort.

A. Process　　　　**B.** Evaluation

C. Running　　　　**D.** Input

Q.47 An algorithm is made up of 2 modules M1 and M2. If order of M1 is f(n) and M2 is g(n) then the order of the algorithm is

A. max (f(n) ,g(n))　　**B.** min (f(n) ,g(n))

C. f(n)+g(n)　　　　　**D.** f(n) x g(n)

Q.48 A text is made up of the characters a, b, c, d, e each occurring with the probability .12, .4, .15, .08 and .25 respectively. The optimal coding technique will have the average length of

A. 2.15　　**B.** 3.01　　**C.** 2.3　　**D.** 1.78

Q.49 The running time of an algorithm is given by

$T(n) = T(n - 1) + T(n - 2) - T(n - 3)$, if $n > 3$

n, otherwise.

A. n　　**B.** log n　　**C.** n^n　　**D.** n^2

Q.50 Consider an empty binary search tree. The elements 22, 25, 13, 4, 16, 30, 10, 14 are inserted in an empty binary search tree in the given sequence. Let h be the height obtained. The element at the 4th level(level-1 is top level) is

A. 25　　**B.** 16　　**C.** 4　　**D.** 10

Q.51 Which of the following algorithms solves the all-pair shortest path problem?

A. Dijkstra's algorithm

B. Floyd's algorithm

C. Prim's algorithm

D. Warshall's algorithm

Q.52 For merging two sorted lists of sizes m and n into a sorted list of size m + n, we require comparisons of

A. O(m)　　　　　　　**B.** O(n)

C. O(m+n)　　　　　　**D.** O(log(m) + log(n))

Q.53 Which one of the following statements is false?

A. Optimal binary search tree construction can be performed efficiently using dynamic programmmg.

B. Breadth-first search cannot be used to find connected components of a graph.

C. Given the prefix and postfix walks of a binary tree, the binary tree cannot be uniquely reconstructed.

D. Both (b) and (c)

Q.54 The number of edges in a regular graph of degree d and n vertices is

A. maximum of n,d　　**B.** n+d

C. nd　　　　　　　　**D.** nd/2

Q.55 A_______search begins the search with the element that is located in the middle of the array.

A. Serial　　　　　　**B.** Random

C. Parallel　　　　　**D.** Binary Search

Q.56 The time complexity of linear search algorithm over an array of n elements is

A. $O(\log_2 n)$　　　　**B.** $O(n)$

C. $O(n \log_2 n)$　　　　**D.** $0(n^2)$

Q.57 To sort many large object or structures, it would be most efficient to

A. Place reference to them in and array an sort the array

B. Place them in a linked list and sort the linked list

C. Place pointers to them in an array and sort the array

D. Place them in an array and sort the array

Q.58 Average successful search time for sequential search on 'n' items is

A. n/2　　　　　　　**B.** (n-1)/2

C. (n+1)/2　　　　　**D.** None of these

Q.59 The average search time of hashing, with linear probing will be less if the load factor

A. Is far less than one

B. equals one

C. is far greater than one

D. none of these

Q.60 Consider the given function F(A,B,C,D) = Σm(2,3,5,6,8,9,11,14) then what is the value connected at input I1 in the figure shown below if the select lines are connected to

B & D respectively?

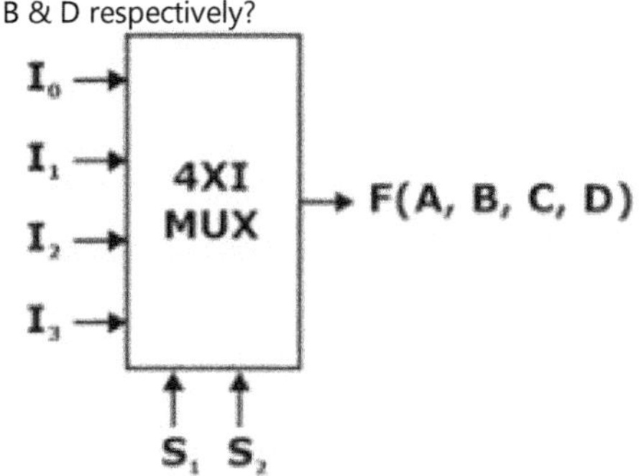

A. A+C
C. A'+C'
B. A EX-OR C
D. A'C+AC'

Q.61 Consider a program which stores the frequency of marks of student in a particular subject say Mathematics. The marks is in the range [0...100] and there are around 500 students. But there is one condition we only want to record frequency if the student has passed in the exam, the passing marks being 40. What is the best way to store the frequency of marks above 40?

A. An array of 500 numbers
B. An array of 100 numbers
C. An array of 40 numbers
D. An array of 60 numbers

Q.62 Let m, n be positive integers. Define Q (m, n) as

Q (m, n) = 0, if m > n

Then Q (m, 3) is (a div b, gives the quotient when a is divided by b)

A. a constant
B. p x (m mod 3)
C. p x (m div 3)
D. 3 x p

Q.63 The average number of comparisons performed by the merge sort algorithm, in merging two sorted liss of length 2 is

A. 8/3 **B.** 8/5 **C.** 11/7 **D.** 11/6

Q.64 Which of the following sorting methods will be the best if number of swappings done, is the only measure of efficiency?

A. Bubble sort
B. Selection sort
C. Insertion sort
D. Quick sort

Q.65 The maximum number of comparisons needed to sort 7 items using radix sort is (assume each item is 4 digit decimal number)

A. 280 **B.** 40 **C.** 47 **D.** 38

Q.66 The five items:A,B,C,D, and E are pushed in a stack, one after the other starting from A.The stack is popped four times and each element is inserted in a queue.Then two elements are deleted from the queue and pushed back on the stack.Now one item is popped from the stack.

The popped item is

A. E **B.** B **C.** C **D.** D

Q.67 If memory for the run-time stack is only 150 cells(words), how big can N be in Factorial(N) before encounterring stack overflow?

A. 24 **B.** 12 **C.** 26 **D.** 30

Q.68 In eveluating the arithmetic expression 2*3-(4+5),using stacks to evaluate its equivalent postfix form, which of the following stack configuration is not possible?

A. 4 6 **B.** 5 4 6 **C.** 9 6 **D.** 9 3 2

Q.69 Consider a language L which is described as a deterministic pushdown automaton with empty stack. Which of the following problem is undecidable by Language L?

A. Emptiness problem (Is L=∅ ?)
B. Finiteness problem (Is L is finite or Not?)
C. Complement of L is same type or not.
D. Intersection of two language of same type.

Q.70 L and $\overline{L}$ are 2 complementary languages, consider the following statements:

(RE : Recursively Enumerable)
(REC : Recursive)
S1 : Both are REC
$S2$: Both are RE
$S3$: One is REC, other is RE
S4 : Both are RE but not REC
$S5$: One is REC and other is not RE
S6 : One is REC, other is RE but not REC.
S7 : One is not RE, other is RE.
How many of the above statements are false__________

A. 1 **B.** 2
C. 3 **D.** None of the above

Q.71 Stack is useful for implemeting

A. breadth first search
B. depth first search
C. recursion
D. Both (b) & (c)

Q.72 A binary tree in which every non-leaf node has non-empty left and right subtrees is called a strictly binary tree. Such a tree with 10 leaves

A. Cannot have more than 19 nodes
B. Has exactly 19 nodes
C. Has exactly 17 nodes
D. Cannot have more than 19 nodes

Q.73 If the post order traversal gives a b - c d * + then the label of the nodes 1, 2, 3 ... will be

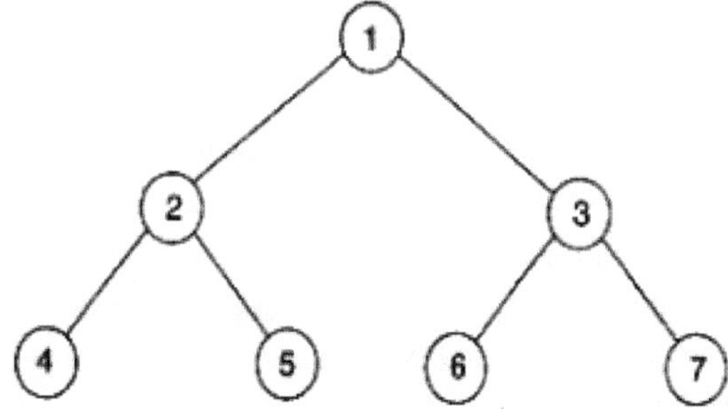

A. +, -, *, a, b, c, d
B. a, -, b, +, c, *, d
C. a, b, c, d, -, *, +
D. -, a, b, +, *, c, d

Q.74 Consider the following tree

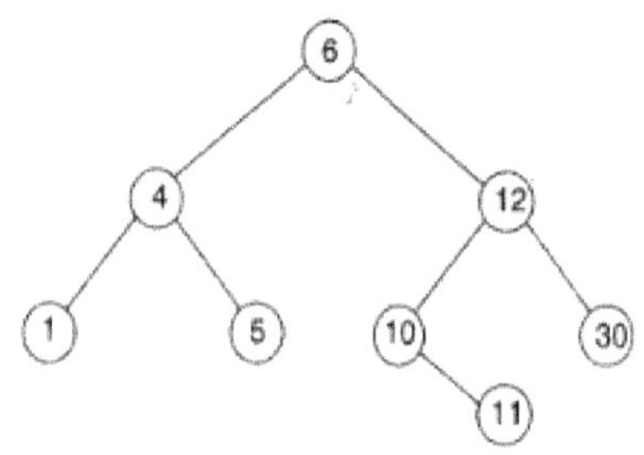

If this tree is used for sorting, then a new number 8 should be placed as the

A. left child of the node labeled 30
B. right child of the node labeled 5
C. right child of the node labeled 30
D. left child of the node labeled 10

Q.75 The number of possible ordered trees with 3 nodes A, B, C is

A. 16   **B.** 12   **C.** 6   **D.** 10

Q.76 Consider the following statements about L:

1) L is accepted by multi-tape Turing machine, M1

2) L is also accepted by a single tape Turing Machine, M2

Then which of the following is correct?

A. Acceptance by M2 is slower by $O(n^2)$
B. Acceptance by M2 is slower by $O(n)$
C. Acceptance by M1 is slower by $O(n)$
D. Acceptance by M1 is slower by $O(n2)$

Q.77 The depth of a complete binary tree with 'n nodes is (log is to be base two)

A. $\log (n+1)-1$ **B.** $\log(n)$
C. $\log (n-1) + 1$ **D.** $\log(n) + 1$

Q.78 Which one of the following fields of an IP header is NOT modified by a typical IP router?

A. Checksum   **B.** Source address
C. Time to Live(TTL)   **D.** Length

Q.79 Choose the correct security attack for integrity and availability.

A. Modification and sniffing
B. Modification and spoofing
C. Modification and DOS
D. Sniffing and DOS.

Q.80 For the IEEE 802.11 MAC protocol for wireless communication, which of the following statements is/are TRUE?

I. At least three non-overlapping channels are available for transmissions.

II. The RTS-CTS mechanism is used for collision detection.

III. Unicast frames are ACKed.

A. All I, II, and III   **B.** I and III only
C. II and III only   **D.** II only

Q.81 In an Ethernet local area network, which one of the following statements is TRUE?

A. A station stops to sense the channel once it starts transmitting a frame.

B. The purpose of the jamming signal is to pad the frames that are smaller than the minimum frame size.

C. A station continues to transmit the packet even after the collision is detected.

D. The exponential backoff mechanism reduces the probability of collision on retransmissions.

Q.82 Consider the following problems , which among them can be implemented on a Turing machine :

S1 : Calculating GCD of two numbers

S2 : Copying string

S3 : Predicting the result of tomorrow's cricket match

S4 : Calculating surface area of a given cone dimensions

A. S1 , S3 and S4
B. S1 , S2 and S4
C. S2 and S4
D. All of the statements

Q.83 Which of the following is true for proxy server ?

I] Proxy server is a program running on same machine working as a browser.

II] Proxy server is a program running on a separate machine.

III] Caching is a different concept and proxy server is not aware of it.

A. I- True, II-False, III- True.
B. I- False, II-True, III-True.
C. I-False, II-True, III-False
D. I-True, II-True, III- False.

Q.84 Which of the following are used to generate a message digest by the network security protocols?

(P) RSA

(Q) SHA-1

(R) DES

(S) MD5

A. P and R only   **B.** Q and R only
C. Q and S only   **D.** R and S only

Q.85 Internet Assigned Numbers Authority allocates _______for TCP/UDP to be used by SMTP.

A. Port 45   **B.** Port 80   **C.** Port 55   **D.** Port 25

Q.86 When RANDOMIZED-QUICKSORT runs, how many calls are made to the random number generator RANDOM in the worst case :

A. $\Theta(n)$ **B.** $\Theta(n^2)$
C. $\Theta(\log n)$ **D.** $\Theta(\log\log n)$

Q.87 Banks often record transactions on an account in order of the times of the transactions, but many people like to receive their bank statements with checks listed in order by check number. People usually write checks in order by check number, and merchants usually cash them with reasonable dispatch. The problem of converting time-of-transaction ordering to check-number ordering is therefore the problem of sorting almost-sorted input. Which sorting algorithm is best in this case ?

A. Quick Sort
B. Merge Sort
C. Insertion Sort
D. All are same

Q.88 If f(n) = O(n) and g(n) = Ω(n) , then what can be correct about f(n).g(n) ?

A. O(n)
B. O(n²)
C. Ω(n)
D. Both b and c

Q.89 The property of _____ is static in nature, compile time early binding and user friendly.

A. Stack
B. Array
C. Queue
D. Linked List

Q.90 Number of nodes of degree 2 given that the tree is a binary tree having N leaf nodes

A. Log_2N
B. N
C. N-1
D. N+1

Q.91 Which of the following statement is false?

A. In linked list implementation of queue, if new nodes are inserted at the beginning of linked list, then in pop operation, nodes must be removed from end.
B. In linked list implementation of queue, if new nodes are inserted at the end of linked list, then in pop operation, nodes must be removed from beginning.
C. In linked list implementation of stack, if new nodes are inserted at the beginning of linked list, then in pop operation, nodes must be removed from end.
D. In linked list implementation of stack, if new nodes are inserted at the end of linked list, then in pop operation, nodes must be removed from end.

Q.92 For two relations R (A, B, C) and S (D, E), relation S maintain a foreign key for D on attribute A of relation R. Consider the following statements:

A) Each record of R is related to 0 or more record of S.

B) Each record of S is related to 0 or more record of R.

C) Each record of S is related to 0 or 1 record of R.

D) Each record of R is related to 0 or 1 record of S.

Which of the following is true?

A. Only a
B. Only b
C. Both A and C
D. Both A and D

Q.93 Consider the following action:

Transaction.....

Commit;

Rollback;

What does Rollback do?

A. Undoes the transactions before commit
B. Clears all transactions
C. Redoes the transactions before commit
D. No action

Q.94 Which classes are used for connection-less socket programming?

A. Datagram socket
B. Datagram packet
C. Both A and B
D. None of the above

Q.95 Which of the following is true?

A. Token bus is adopted in ethernet to solve the disadvantages of token ring.
B. Acknowledgement is piggy backed in token ring.
C. There are no possibilities of collision in token ring.
D. Preamble and start frame delimiter are part of data link layer header.

Q.96 Which of the following are tasks of Data Link Layer?

A. Move packets from source to destination and provide inter-networking.
B. Job of maintaining proper communication by establishing, managing and terminating sessions between two computers.
C. Organizes bits into frames and ensures hop to hop delivery.
D. Decides how much information should be sent at a time.

Q.97 Arrange the following configuration for CPU in decreasing order of operating speeds

1) Hard wired control

2) vertical microprogramming

3) Horizontal microprogramming

A. 1>2>3
B. 1>3>2
C. 2>3>1
D. 3>2>1

Q.98 Suppose a DRAM memory has a 5K rows in its array of bit cells, it's refreshing period is 20ms and 4 clock cycles are needed to access each row. What fraction of memory time is spent performing refreshes, if clock rate is 133 MHz?

A. 9 %
B. 3%
C. 2%
D. 5%

Q.99 Which of the following statements are true:

S1: If a Privileged Instruction is executed in User Mode, then it will not be executed and will be treated as an illegal instruction

S2: To change the mode from Privileged to Non-Privileged, a Privileged Instruction is required that does not generate any interrupt.

S3: Generating any Trap Instruction is a Privileged Instruction.

A. Both S1 and S3
B. Only S1
C. Both S1 and S2
D. Only S3

Q.100 If we give a string of length 'n' as an input then which one of the following will give output of length 'n+1',

A. Mealy machine
B. Moore machine
C. In both (A) and (B)
D. Neither in (A) nor (B)

// Smart Answer Sheet //

Correct | Percentage of students who answered correctly. **Skipped** | Percentage of students who skipped.

Q.	Ans.	Correct / Skipped	Q.	Ans.	Correct / Skipped	Q.	Ans.	Correct / Skipped	Q.	Ans.	Correct / Skipped	Q.	Ans.	Correct / Skipped
1	A	17.02 % / 19.15 %	17	C	25.53 % / 65.96 %	33	C	10.64 % / 63.83 %	49	A	10.64 % / 65.96 %	65	A	19.15 % / 65.96 %
2	A	21.28 % / 63.83 %	18	C	19.15 % / 65.96 %	34	B	31.91 % / 65.96 %	50	D	12.77 % / 65.95 %	66	D	19.15 % / 65.96 %
3	A	2.13 % / 65.96 %	19	C	17.02 % / 44.68 %	35	C	10.64 % / 65.96 %	51	B	19.15 % / 65.96 %	67	C	17.02 % / 65.96 %
4	C	17.02 % / 65.96 %	20	C	17.02 % / 65.96 %	36	C	29.79 % / 65.95 %	52	C	27.66 % / 65.96 %	68	D	12.77 % / 65.95 %
5	C	14.89 % / 65.96 %	21	D	2.13 % / 63.83 %	37	A	21.28 % / 65.95 %	53	D	17.02 % / 65.96 %	69	D	4.26 % / 65.95 %
6	C	4.26 % / 65.95 %	22	C	19.15 % / 65.96 %	38	C	23.4 % / 65.96 %	54	D	17.02 % / 65.96 %	70	C	21.28 % / 65.95 %
7	D	12.77 % / 65.95 %	23	D	27.66 % / 61.7 %	39	B	8.51 % / 65.96 %	55	D	23.4 % / 65.96 %	71	D	17.02 % / 63.83 %
8	D	23.4 % / 65.96 %	24	A	14.89 % / 65.96 %	40	B	10.64 % / 65.96 %	56	B	21.28 % / 65.95 %	72	B	27.66 % / 65.96 %
9	C	17.02 % / 65.96 %	25	C	23.4 % / 65.96 %	41	B	21.28 % / 63.83 %	57	B	10.64 % / 65.96 %	73	A	17.02 % / 65.96 %
10	A	31.91 % / 63.83 %	26	B	6.38 % / 65.96 %	42	B	6.38 % / 65.96 %	58	C	19.15 % / 65.96 %	74	D	23.4 % / 63.83 %
11	C	17.02 % / 65.96 %	27	D	27.66 % / 63.83 %	43	B	19.15 % / 65.96 %	59	A	12.77 % / 65.95 %	75	B	14.89 % / 65.96 %
12	C	23.4 % / 65.96 %	28	D	17.02 % / 65.96 %	44	B	8.51 % / 65.96 %	60	A	10.64 % / 65.96 %	76	A	6.38 % / 65.96 %
13	C	23.4 % / 65.96 %	29	C	17.02 % / 63.83 %	45	A	27.66 % / 63.83 %	61	D	0 % / 100 %	77	A	8.51 % / 65.96 %
14	B	8.51 % / 65.96 %	30	B	14.89 % / 65.96 %	46	C	10.64 % / 65.96 %	62	C	19.15 % / 65.96 %	78	B	17.02 % / 65.96 %
15	C	19.15 % / 65.96 %	31	C	19.15 % / 65.96 %	47	A	17.02 % / 65.96 %	63	A	6.38 % / 65.96 %	79	C	17.02 % / 63.83 %
16	D	21.28 % / 65.95 %	32	B	4.26 % / 65.95 %	48	A	19.15 % / 65.96 %	64	B	12.77 % / 65.95 %	80	B	8.51 % / 65.96 %

Q.	Ans.	Correct		Q.	Ans.	Correct		Q.	Ans.	Correct		Q.	Ans.	Correct		Q.	Ans.	Correct
		Skipped				Skipped				Skipped				Skipped				Skipped
81	D	14.89 %		85	D	17.02 %		89	B	23.4 %		93	D	4.26 %		97	B	14.89 %
		63.83 %				65.96 %				65.96 %				65.95 %				65.96 %
82	B	6.38 %		86	A	8.51 %		90	C	17.02 %		94	C	21.28 %		98	C	17.02 %
		65.96 %				65.96 %				65.96 %				65.95 %				65.96 %
83	D	6.38 %		87	C	19.15 %		91	C	17.02 %		95	B	12.77 %		99	B	0 %
		65.96 %				65.96 %				65.96 %				65.95 %				100 %
84	C	23.4 %		88	C	12.77 %		92	C	12.77 %		96	C	19.15 %		100	B	17.02 %
		65.96 %				65.95 %				65.95 %				65.96 %				65.96 %

//Hints and Solutions//

1. x+i means increment in value of X not in address of X so it cant represent address of X.

& x[i] means address of the ith element.

So & xi-1] defines address of i-1 element .sizeof(int) defines size of an element

So &x[i-1] + size of(int) means the address of i-1 element plus size of an element that means the address of ith element.

It cant be option c as x+i is not representing any address.

 x+i means increment in the value of X not in the address of x so it cant represent the address of x.

So option (A) is correct.

2. scanf("%s", S) only scans first parameter of input stream .

So Option (A) is correct.

3. Consider the following declaration

double balance = {1000.0, 2.0, 3.4, 17.0, 50.0};

If you omit the size of the array, an array just big enough to hold the initialization is created.

So, the correct option is (A).

4. One element takes three memory words so memory location 1120 , 1121 , 1123 stores first element.

A[49] will be stored at location 1264 , (1120+(48×3)).

Hence, the correct option is (C).

5. Only element 70 violates the rule. Hence, it must be shifted to its proper position.

Step1: swap(10, 70)

Step2: swap(40, 70)

Hence, only 2 interchanges are required.

Hence, the correct option is (C).

6. 263 in binary form is 100000111. If one tries to print an integer as a character, only the last 8 bits will be considered - the rest chopped off. So, in this case the ASCII value of 00000111 will be printed, Look in the ASCII table. It is ringing a bell !

Hence, the correct option is (C).

7. Let ab be 0 x MN. N&f should yield 7 i.e. N & 1111 should produce 0111. So, N should be 0111, i.e., 7.

Similarly, M can be found to be 2.

So, ab is 0 x 27.

Hence, the correct option is (D).

8. The else clause has no brackets i.e., {and}. This means the else clause is made up only one statement.

So, printf ("a < = b"); will be executed anyway, i.e. if a>b a< = b.

Hence, the correct option is (D).

9. r+ - If is opened successfully fopen( ) loads it into memory and sets up a pointer which points to the first character in it. Returns NULL, if unable to open the file.Operations possible - reading existing contents, writing new contents, modifying existing contents of the file

r - Searches file. If the file is opened successfully fopen( ) loads it into memory and sets up a pointer which points to the first character in it. If the file cannot be opened fopen( ) returns NULL.

Operations possible – reading from the file.

Hence, the correct option is (C).

10. Which means a function will be manipulating a copy of the local variable, passed as argument.

So. any change will be local and hence will not he reflected in the calling routine.

Hence, the correct option is (A).

11. If y = 11, the expression 3 × (y - 8) / 9 becomes 3 × 3 / 9. which evaluates to 1. But the expression (y - 8)/ 9 × 3 becomes 3 / 9 * 3. which evaluates to 0 (since 3 / 9 is 0).

Hence, the correct option is (C).

12. y * = 2 means y = y * 2 i.e. y = 4, in this problem. So. the expression is equivalent to x = 4 + 4, which is 8. So, 8 will be printed. However, the order in which the operands are evaluated is implementation-dependent. If the right operand is evaluated first, the result will be 6.

Hence, the correct option is (C).

13. PCB Consists of:

1. Process Id: Process Id is a unique Id that identifies each process of the system uniquely.

A process Id is assigned to each process during its creation.

2. Program Counter: Program counter specifies the address of the instruction to be executed next.

3. Process State: Each process goes through different states during its lifetime.

Process state specifies the current state of the process.

4. Priority: Priority specifies how urgent is to execute the process.

Process with the highest priority is allocated the CPU first among all the processes.

5. General Purpose Registers: General purpose registers are used to hold the data of process generated during its execution.

6. List of Open Files: PCB maintains a list of files used by the process during its execution.

7. List of Open Devices: PCB maintains a list of open devices used by the process during its execution.

Hence, the correct option is (C).

14. WIFI (IEEE 802.11) operates at Data link layer.

Hence, the correct option is (B).

15. 5-2-3*5-2 will yield 18, id it is treated as (5-(2-3))*(5-2). i.e., if - has precedence over* and if it associates from the right.

Hence, the correct option is (C).

16. Coercion is the automatic conversion between compatible types and it is done by compiler. Coercion takes place if an operator has operands of different types. Operands are the objects that are manipulated and operators are the symbols that represent specific actions.

Hence, the correct option is (D).

17. Using a pointer variable, without initializing it, will be disastrous, as it will have a garbage value.

Hence, the correct option is (C).

18. Scaling factor that is use in header extension length field of routing extension header in IPv6 data packet is 8.

Hence, the correct option is (C).

19. Redundant instructions may be discarded during the final stage of compilation by using a simple optimizing technique called peephole optimization.It is a kind of optimization performed over a very small set of instructions in a segment of generated code. The set is called a "peephole" or a "window". It works by recognising sets of instructions that can be replaced by shorter or faster sets of instructions and it uses some common techniques : Constant folding.

Hence, the correct option is (C).

20. For skewed binary search tree on n nodes, the tightest upper bound to insert a node is O(n).

Hence, the correct option is (C).

21. $f(x) = x^2 - |x|$ and $f(x) = (x)(a^x + 1)/(a^x - 1)$ are even functions, because

$f(x) = f(-x)$. $f(x) = \sin(x) + \cos(x)$ is neither even nor odd as $f(x) \neq f(-x)$ and $-f(x) \neq f(-x)$.

Hence, the correct option is (D).

22. For $f(x) = x - [x]$; where $[x]$ stands for the greatest integer $\leq x$,

solving the equation $f(x+T) = f(x)$,

we get T=1 as the period.

$f(x) = |\cos(x)|$ is periodic with period π

$n.f(x) = (x)\cos(x)$ and

$f(x) = \sin(1/x)$

if $x \neq 0$; 0 otherwise are not periodic.

Hence, the correct option is (C).

23. A half-duplex (HDX) system provides communication in both directions, but only one direction at a time (not simultaneously). Typically, once a party begins receiving a signal, it must wait for the transmitter to stop transmitting, before replying (antennas are of trans-receiver type in these devices, so as to transmit and receive the signal as well).

A full-duplex (FDX), or sometimes double-duplex system, allows communication in both directions, and, unlike half-duplex, allows this to happen simultaneously. Land-line telephone networks are full-duplex, since they allow both callers to speak and be heard at the same time, the transition from four to two wires being achieved by a hybrid coil. A good analogy for a full-duplex system would be a two-lane road with one lane for each direction.

Hence, the correct option is (D).

24. Bit stuffing is required when there is a flag of bits to represent one of the incidents like start of frame, end of frame, etc, If same lag of bits appear in the data stream, a zero can be inserted. The receiver deletes this zero from the data stream.

Hence, the correct option is (A).

25. 10 base T cable is also called as Twisted-pair-Ethernet. A star topology LAN using unshared twisted pair instead of coaxial cable.

Hence, the correct option is (C).

26. Here 802.3 is Ethernet, it uses CSMA/CD. But 802.5 is Token ring. It will have only one token in circulation. These are IEEE standards but FDDI is ANSI standard.

Hence, the correct option is (B).

27. In a token ring each station with capture the token and checks the destination address if it is addressed to any other station then the frame will be regenerated and passed to the next station.

Hence, the correct option is (D).

28. In Token ring, when a frame reaches its destination station, the entire message is copied and four bits in the packet are changed.

Hence, the correct option is (D).

29. Transceiver is an acronym for transmission receiver, which receives data after checking the line voltage, hence it can't add headers.

Hence, the correct option is (C).

30. The distance between station-to-hub in 100. Base-TX is 100 meters. But in 100-Base-FX design. The distance between station-to-hub is 2000 meters.

Hence, the correct option is (B).

31. Base band Ethernet LAN uses Manchester encoding.

Hence, the correct option is (C).

32. MAU (Multistation Access Unit) : Individual automatic switches are combined into a hub called a multistation access unit (MAU) and MAU can support up to eight stations. Token ring uses the MAU.

Hence, the correct option is (B).

33. 100 base-T4 requires four pairs of unshielded twisted pair cable to reduce baud rate of transmission (number of signal changes) 8B/6T (eight binary / six ternary) is used in which each block of eight bits is transformed into six bauds of three voltages levels.

Hence, the correct option is (C).

34. Star topology and tree topology requires central controller or hub. Mesh, ring, bus topologies doesn't need hubs.

Hence, the correct option is (B).

35. Bus topology requires a multipoint connection. Because, in this there is a single communication channel, that is shared by all the systems in a net work. So bus topology require multipoint connection.

Hence, the correct option is (C).

36. For windows above 9 frames, the full 64 kbps is used.

Hence, the correct option is (C).

37. Start and stop bits are not needed in synchronous transfer of data.

Hence, it is 2400/8=300.

Hence, the correct option is (A).

38. Since there are six 1200 bps terminals, therefore

6 x 1200 + n x 300 = 9600

n = 8.

Hence, the correct option is (C).

39. Dynamic memory refreshes periodically so due to refreshment it is difficult to interface it.

Hence, the correct option is (B).

40. For Memory Access Cycle time=Latency time+Transfer Time Latency time is overhead of finding the right memory location and preparing to access it Transfer Time = Time required to transfer the data. Hence cycle time is longer than access time.

Hence, the correct option is (B).

41. Dynamic memory uses capacitor for storing information, so it doesnt need constant power but it has higher bit density due to its configuration.

Hence, the correct option is (B).

42. A software interrupt is initiated by some program module which need some CPU services, at that time the two modes can be interchanged.

Hence (B) is correct option.

43. Since it is a sorted array, we can use binary search to identify the position of the first occurence of the given integer in (logn) steps. If at all this integer repeats, its appearance has to be continuous because the array is sorted.

Hence, the correct option is (B).

44. By recursively applying the relation we finally arrive at

T(n-l) = c(n-l) + T (1) = c(n-l)+d

So, order is n.

Hence, the correct option is (B).

45. Since the access is sequential, greater the distance, greater will be the access time. Since all the files are referenced with equal frequency, overall access time can be reduced by arranging them as in option (a).

Hence, the correct option is (A).

46. The running time depends on the input: an already sorted sequence is easier to sort. The running time is given by the size of the input, since short sequences are easier to sort than the longer ones. Generally, we seek upper bounds on the running time, because it is reliable.

Hence, the correct option is (C).

47. By definition of order, there exists constants c1, ec2, n1, n2 such that

T(n)≤c1 x f(n), for all n≥n1.

T(n)≤c2 x f(n), for all n≥n2.

N=max (n1, n2) andC = max (c1, c2). So,

T(n)≤C x f(n) for all n≥N

T(n)≤C x g(n) for all n≥N

T(n)≤C/2 x (f(n)+g(n))

Without loss of generality, let max (f(n), g(n)) =f(n) .

So, T(n)≤C/2 (f(n)+f(n)) ≤ C x f(n) .

So, order is f(n) , which is max (f(n), g(n)) , by our assumption.

Hence, the correct option is (A).

48. Using Hoffman's algorithm, code for a is 1111; b is 0; c is 110; d is 1110; e is 10. Average code length is

4 x.12 + 1 x .4 + 3 x.15 + 4 x.08 + 2 x.25 = 2.15

Hence, the correct option is (A).

49. Let us find what is T(4), T(5), T(6) is.

T(4) = T(3) + T(2) - T(1) = 3 + 2 - 1 = 4

T(5) = T(4) + T(3) - T(2) = 4 + 3 - 2 = 5

T(6) = T(5) + T(4) - T(3) = 5 + 4 - 3 = 6

By induction it can be proved that T(n) = n.

Hence order is n.

Hence, the correct option is (A).

50. The element at the 4th level is 10.

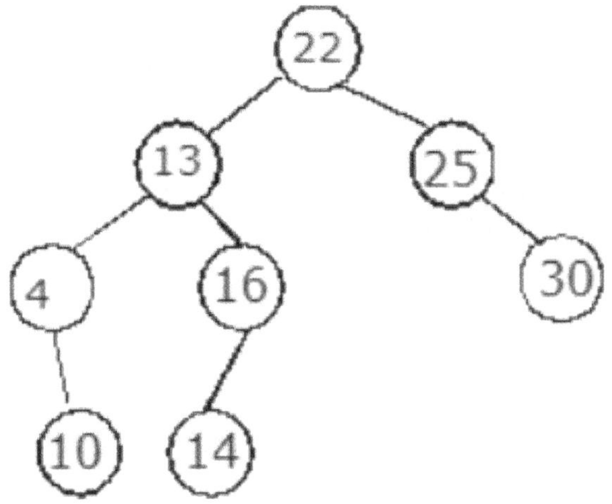

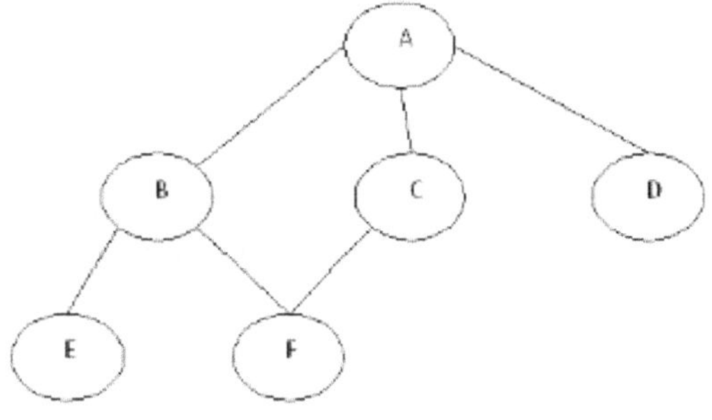

Hence, the correct option is (D).

51. Dijkstra's algorithm solves single source shortest path problem. Warshall's algorithm finds transitive closure of a given graph. Prim's algorithm constructs a minimum cost spanning tree for a given weighted graph.

Hence, the correct option is (B).

52. Each comparison will append one item to the existing merge list. In the worst case one needs m + n - 1 comparisons which is of order m+n.

Hence, the correct option is (C).

53. Here option (B) is also false because BFS and DFS both algorithm are used to find connected component. For example: In BFS, a search that begins at some particular vertex 'v' will find the entire connected component containing v (and no more) before returning. To find all the connected components of a graph, loop through its vertices, starting a new breadth first search whenever the loop reaches a vertex that has not already been included in a previously found connected component. For example:If we do the breadth first traversal of the above graph and print the visited node as the output, it will print the following output. "A B C D E F". The BFS visits the nodes level by level, so it will start with level 0 which is the root node, and then it moves to the next levels which are B, C and D, then the last levels which are E and F.

In BFS, a search that begins at some particular vertex v will find the entire connected component containing v (and no more) before returning. To find all the connected components of a graph, loop through its vertices, starting a new breadth first search whenever the loop reaches a vertex that has not already been included in a previously found connected component. so ans is both 'A' and 'C'

Hence, the correct option is (D).

54. In a regular graph, all the vertices will be of the same degree. Total degrees of all the vertices is nd. Each edge will be increasing the total degree by 2.

So, totally ndl/2 edges.

Hence, the correct option is (D).

55. Binary Search algorithm can do this because it firstly searchs the middle element. If required element is less than the middle one, then search the middle element in the less than part. If required element is greater than the middle one, then search in the greater part.

Hence, the correct option is (D).

56. inear search has linear-time complexity; binary search has log-time complexity.

Here is a table that provides some intuition about the running speeds of algorithms

Logarithmic: Linear:

array size	N
8	8
128	128
256	256
1000	1000
100,000	100,000 ....

Binary search and other divide-and-conquer algorithms have logN time complexity; we say O(logN)

Linear search have linear time complexity: O(N).

Hence, the correct option is (B).

57. • Dynamic structure (Memory Allocated at run-time).

• We can have more than one datatype.

• Re-arrange of linked list is easy (Insertion-Deletion).

• It doesn't waste memory.

Hence, the correct option is (B).

58. If search key matches the very first item, with one comparison we can terminate. If it is second, two comparisons, etc.

Average =[n (n + 1)] / 2.

Hence, the correct option is (C).

59. Load factor is the ratio of number of records that are currently present and the total number of records that can be present. If the load factor is less, free space will be more. This means probability of collision is less. So, search time will be less.

Hence, the correct option is (A).

60. The diagram is as shown below -

	B'D'	B'D	BD	BD'
A'C'	0	1	5	4
A'C	2	3	7	6
AC	10	11	15	14
AC'	8	9	13	12

Therefore, the expression for I1 is A'C+AC'+AC{Taking common from last 2 terms}

= A'C+A{Applying distributive property}

= A+C

Hence, the correct option is (A).

61. For this purpose, we can ignore the below forty numbers and have an array of 60 index to store the individual frequencies from 40 to 100.

Hence, the correct option is (D).

62. Let m>n yield a quotient x and remainder y. So, m= n*x+y and y<m div 3 is the quotient when m is divided by 3.

So, that many times p is added, before we terminate recursion by satisfying the end condition Q (m,n) = 0 if m<n.

Hence the result p x (m div 3).

So, the correct option is (C).

63. Merge-sort combines two given sorted lists into one sorted list. For this problem let the final sorted order be- 1, b, c, d. The two lists (of length two each) should fall into one of the following 3 categories.

(i) a, b and c,d

(ii) a, c and b, d

(iii) a, d and b, c

The number of comparisons needed in each case will be 2, 3, 3.

So, the average number of comparisons will be (2+3+3)/3= 8/3

Hence, the correct option is (A).

64. Because in selection sort algorithm we randomly access data rather than a list in which we can easily swap data which we want to swap and it takes less time.

Hence, the correct option is (B).

65. The maximum number of comparison is number of items ´ radix ´ number of digits i.e., 7×10×4 = 280.

Hence, the correct option is (A).

66. In queue elements are deleted from front (FIFO) and in stacks elements are popped from top (LIFO)

Hence, the correct option is (D).

67. Given that, the size of a run time stack is of 150 cells (words). The arguments to be evaluate the factorial are placed on the stack. A function call is made to calculate the factorial. Subroutine is executed for each time the function call is made. Each funcall creates a stack frames of co words (Cells), 2 words for n, 2 words for program counter (PC) and 2 words for some other information.

The value of n should be such that, the size of stack should not exceed 150 cells. If we consider the value of n to be 26, it executes 25 procedure calls each of it with 6-word stack frame.

In this case totalnumber of words of stack space would be 150 (6 words × 25 procedure calls = 150) cells.

Therefore, value of n will be 26 is n! before encountering a stack overflow for the stack of size 150 cells (words).

Hence, the correct option is (C).

68. The postfix equivallent is 2*3-(4+5).

For evaluating this using stack,starting from the left,we have to scan one by one, if it is an operand push.

If it is an operator, pop it twice,apply operator on the poppedout entries and push the result onto the stack.

If we follow this,we can find configuration in option(d)is not possible.

Hence, the correct option is (D).

69. A language L is deterministic context free language according to describes above.

And we know that DCFL is not closed under Intersection.

Hence, the correct option is (D).

70. Pre - Requisite Knowledge for this question :

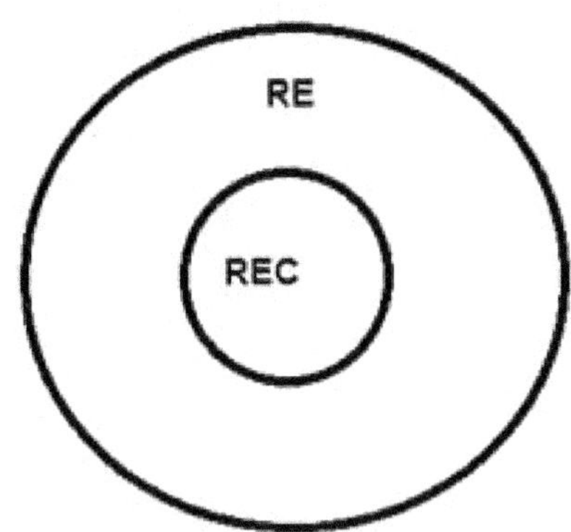

REC is a subset of RE.

If L is REC then $\overline{L}$ is also REC If L is RE then $\overline{L}$ may or may not be RE If L is not RE then $\overline{L}$ is also not RE
Using these three statements we can solve our problem.
S1: Both are REC, true
S2 : Both are RE, true in case when both are REC, because some RE are REC also.
S3 : One is REC, other is RE, true because every REC is RE.
S4 : Both are RE but not REC, False
$S5$: One is REC and other is not RE, False
S6 : One is REC, other is RE but not REC, False
S7 : One is not RE, other is RE , True, one is not RE if there is RE but not REC.
Hence total 3 statements are false.

71. Breadth first search needs Queue for implementaion.

Hence, the correct option is (D).

72. A strictly binary tree with 'n' leaves must have (2n - 1) nodes. Verify for some small 'n'. This can be proved by the principle of mathematical induction.

Hence, the correct option is (B).

73. Post-order traversal yields 4, 5, 2, 6, 7, 3, 1. Comparing with a, b, -, c, d, *, +, we get the labels of nodes 1, 2, 3, 4, 5, 6, 7 ans +, -, *, a, b, c, d respectively.

Hence, the correct option is (A).

74. If it is to be used for sorting label of left child should be less than the label of the current node. Coming down the tree we get left child of node labeled 10 as the correct slot for 8.

Hence, the correct option is (D).

75. It is 12. The tree may be of depth 2 or 1. if the depth is 2, we have 6 possible trees. This is because one of the three nodes A, B, C may be the root and the next level may be one of the remaining two nodes. If the depth is 1, the root may be one of the 3 nodes A, B, C. Corresponding to a root, say A, two trees as possible as this.

Hence, the correct option is (B).

76. Acceptance by M2 is slower by O(n²)

While simulating multi tape TM on a single tape TM, the head move at least 2K cells per move, where k is the number of tracks on single tape TM.

Hence, the correct option is (A).

77. If the depth is d, the number of nodes n will be 2 $^{(d+1)}$-1

So, n+1 = $2^{(d+1)}$ or d = log (n+1)-1.

Hence, the correct option is (A).

78. Length and checksum can be modified when IP fragmentation happens. Time To Live is reduced by every router on the route to destination. Only Source Address is what IP address can not change.

Hence, the correct option is (B).

79. Modification is the security attack against the integrity while Denial of service attack is the attack for availability.

Hence, the correct option is (C).

80. In collision avoidance, we use RTS-CTS mechanism but not in collision etection, only statement II is false.

So only 1st and 3rd statements are true.

81. The concept of binary exponential backoff algorithm The exponential backoff mechanism reduces the probability of collision on retransmissions.

Hence, the correct option is (D).

82. According to Church Turing Thesis , every problem which can be logically solved using some algorithm can be implemented on a Turing machine.

Hence ,now these statements can be analyzed :

S1 : For calculating GCD , we have algorithm , hence it can be implemented on a Turing machine

S2 : Copying string have algorithm , hence it can be implemented on a Turing machine

S3 : Predicting a tomorrow's match result is undecidable and it has no algorithm. Hence it cannot be implemented on a Turing machine

S4 : Calculating surface area of a cone has also logic behind it , a formula has to be used , hence it can be implemented on a Turing machine

So ,the correct option is (b).

83. Proxy server can be a program running on the same machine working as a browser or it can be a separate machine. Proxy server knows concept of caching, it collects and stores all the pages passing through it.

Hence, the correct option is (D).

84. SHA1 and MD5 algorithms are used to generate a message digest by the network security protocols.

So, (C) is the correct answer.

85. In computer network, SMTP serves as independent transmission subsystem which uses reliable ordered data stream channel. It is noted that Internet Assigned Numbers Authority allocates port 25 for both TCP and UDP for use by SMTP.

Hence, the correct option is (D).

86. RANDOM is called once for each time RANDOMIZED-PARTITION is called, so we can just consider the calls to RANDOMIZED-PARTITION by RANDOMIZEDQUICKSORT. The worst case behavior occurs when the partitioning produces one sub-problem of size (n-1) and one of size 0 each time it is called. Therefore, in the worst case, T(n) = Θ(n).

Hence, the correct option is (A).

87. As the array is almost sorted , hence quicksort will give worst case performance i.e. O(n2).

Insertion sort will be best for this case , => O(n).

Hence, the correct option is (C).

88. The least value of f(n).g(n) is $\Omega(n)$ as g(n) is $\Omega(n)$.

We cannot comment on the maximum value as upper bound of g(n) is not available.

Hence, the correct option is (C).

89. This is the basic definition of array.

Hence, the correct option is (B).

90. Given that number of leaf nodes are N. We know that number of nodes of degree two will be one less than number of leaf nodes.

Hence, the correct option is (C).

91. In linked list implementation of stack, if new nodes are inserted at the beginning of linked list, then in pop operation, nodes must be removed from end.

Correct statement is:

In linked list implementation of stack, if new nodes are inserted at the beginning of linked list, then in pop operation, nodes must be removed from beginning.

Hence, the correct option is (C).

92. Option A is correct because relation S is allowed to take only those value which are part of relation R. hence, R is related to 0 or more record of S.

Option C is correct, since relation S is going to have only those values which are part of R. hence, it is related to inly 1 value of R. but the field with NULL is related to 0 value of R. Hence, Option B and D are false.

Hence, the correct option is (C).

93. Rollback can undone the transation before it commits. But here rollback occur after commit.

Hence, the correct option is (D).

94. Both A and B, Both Datagram Socket and Datagram Packet are used for connection-less socket programming.

Hence, the correct option is (C).

95. Token ring is adopted to eliminate the disadvantages of token bus topology ethernet. There is one scenario where collision can happen in token ring, when every station is down and just monitor is active. Then there can be collision, if ring length is not enough for token (24 bits). Acknowledgement is piggy backed in token ring. Preamble and SFD are added as physical layer header.

Hence, the correct option is (B).

96. DLL is responsible for organizing bits into frames and ensuring hop to hop delivery. This is the layer on which the Switches operate on. Since routers operate at the network level, hence we can say that the MAC address resides at the data link layer. All the computers in a specific network get plugged into a switch so that they can communicate with each other.

Move packets from source to destination and provide inter-networking - Network Layer

Job of maintaining proper communication by establishing, managing and terminating sessions between two computers - Session Layer

Decides how much information should be sent at a time - Transport Layer.

Hence, the correct option is (C).

97. Micro programmed control unit uses microinstructions for generating control signals.

Hence, the correct option is (B).

98. No. of cycles needed to refresh all the rows = 5 x 1024 x 4 = 20480 cycles.

clock rate is 133 MHz, therefore

time needed to refresh all the rows = 20480 / (133 x 106) seconds

= 153.98 microseconds or 0.153 ms

Thus, refreshing overhead = 0.153/64 = 0.0024

Hence only 2% of the memory's time is spent on refreshing.

Hence, the correct option is (C).

99. S1: If any attempt is made to execute a Privileged Instruction in User Mode, then it will not be executed and treated as an illegal instruction. The Hardware traps it to the Operating System.

S2: In order to change the mode from Privileged to Non-Privileged, we require a Non-privileged Instruction that does not generate any interrupt.

S3: Various examples of Non-Privileged Instructions include:

Reading the status of Processor

Reading the System Time

Generating return from Trap Instruction

Sending the final printout of Printer.

Hence, the correct option is (B).

100. In case of Moore machine, if we provide a string of length 'n' as input then it will give output of 'n+1' symbols.

Hence, the correct option is (B).

Q.1 Which of the following is the original purpose of SQL?

A. To specify the syntax and semantics of SQL data definition language

B. To specify the syntax and semantics of SQL manipulation language

C. To define the data structures

D. All of the above.

Q.2 What are the notations used in Evaluation of Arithmetic Expressions using prefix and postfix forms?

A. Polish

B. Reverse Polish

C. Both A and B

D. None of the above

Q.3 It is necessary to sort a file before searching a particular item

A. True

B. False

C. May or may not be true

D. None of the above

Q.4 Which of the following is not a database object in MS Access?

A. Reports

B. Relationships

C. Tables

D. Queries

Q.5 A certain telecom company 'A' has a linear bandwidth of 8000 Hz. The signal to noise ratio is 35db. The capacity of the channel would be

A. 40860.42 bps

B. 28001.099 bps

C. 93017.64 bps

D. 80000 bps

Q.6 Consider a 32-bit register which stores floating point number in IEEE single precision format. The value of the number ___ in decimal if 32-bit sequence is given as

| 0 | 100000011 | 1100.............0 |

where first block represents sign bit, second block represent biased exponent value and third block represent value of mantissa.

A. 25   **B.** 26   **C.** 27   **D.** 28

Q.7 Which physical connection is the fastest?

A. Coaxial cable

B. Infrared

C. Microwave

D. Fiber-optic

Q.8 How long is an IPv4 address?

A. 128 bytes

B. 32 bits

C. 32 bytes

D. 128 bits

Q.9 Consider the following statements regarding user - level and kernel - level thread-

1) Context switching is faster with kernel supported threads

2) User-level threads can be scheduled independently

3) User level threads are not transparent to kernel

Which of the above statements are true?

A. Only 3   **B.** 1 and 2   **C.** 1 and 3   **D.** Only 2

Q.10 What is the out put of this program?

```c
main()
{
char *p; p = "Hello";
printf ("%cn", *&*p);
}
```

A. H

B. Hello

C. Compilation error

D. H E L L O

Q.11 #define clrscr() 100

```c
main()
{
clrscr();
printf( "%dn", clrscr() );
}
```

A. 100

B. 0

C. Compilation error

D. Exception occurs

Q.12 Public abstract interface Frobnicate { public void twiddle(String s); }

Which is a correct class?

A. public abstract class Frob implements Frobnicate { public abstract void twiddle(String s) { } }

B. public abstract class Frob implements Frobnicate { }

C. public class Frob extends Frobnicate { public void twiddle(Integer i) { } }

D. public class Frob implements Frobnicate { public void twiddle(Integer i) { } }

Q.13 #include

```c
int main()
{
    int max-val=100;
    int min-val=10;
    int avg-val;
    avg-val =( max-val + min-val ) / 2;
    printf( "%d", avg-val );
    return 0;
}
```

A. 55

B. 105

C. 60

D. Compilation error

Q.14 #include

```c
int main()
{
int a = 10;
void *p = &a;
int *ptr = p;
printf("%u",*ptr);
```

return 0;
}

A. 10   **B.** Address
C. 2   **D.** Compilation error

Q.15 What will be output when you will execute following c code?

```c
#include <stdio.h>
enum actor
{
    SeanPenn=5,
    AlPacino=-2,
    GaryOldman,
    EdNorton
};
void main()
{
    enum actor a=0;
    switch(a)
    {
        case SeanPenn:  printf("Kevin Spacey");
                break;
        case AlPacino:  printf("Paul Giamatti");
                break;
        case GaryOldman:printf("Donald Shuterland");
                break;
        case EdNorton:  printf("Johnny Depp");
    }
}
```

A. Kevin Spacey   **B.** Paul Giamatti
C. Donald Shuterland   **D.** Johnny Depp

Q.16 What is the behavior of following one i/p Flipflop 'X' ?

A. D - Flipflop
B. T - Flipflop
C. Inverted D - Flipflop
D. Inverted T - Flipflop

Q.17 What will be output when you will execute following c code?

```c
#include <stdio.h>
void main()
{
    switch(2)
    {
        case 1L:printf("No");
        case 2L:printf("%s","I");
```

            goto Love;
        case 3L:printf("Please");
        case 4L:Love:printf("Hi");
   }
}

A. I   **B.** IPleaseHi
C. IHi   **D.** Compilation error

Q.18 The number of min-terms after minimizing the following Boolean expression is________.

[D' + AB' + A'C + AC'D + A'C'D]'

A. 1   **B.** 46   **C.** 56   **D.** 76

Q.19
```c
main()
{
fork();
printf("Hello World!");
}
```
Output for the above unix program is

A. Hello World!
B. Hello World!Hello World!
C. Hello World
D. None

Q.20 Default read write and execute permissions given to a file for owner, group and others are

A. 6-4-4   **B.** 6-4-2   **C.** 6-4-6   **D.** 6-6-6

Q.21 Unreachable code would best be found using

A. code inspections
B. a static analysis tool
C. code reviews
D. a test management tool

Q.22 What is the effect on line utilization if we increase the number of frames for a constant message size?

A. Lower line efficiency
B. Higher line efficiency
C. No change in line efficiency
D. No relation between line efficiency and frame size

Q.23
```c
main()
{
float me = 1.1;
double you = 1.1;
if(me==you)
printf("yes");
else
printf("No");
}
```

A. Yes   **B.** No
C. Both   **D.** Compilation error

Q.24 Which of the following is not part of performance testing?

A. simulating many users
B. measuring response times
C. generating many transactions

D. recovery testing

Q.25 Which of the following is TRUE?

A. Every subset of a regular set is regular.

B. Every finite subset of a non–regular set is regular.

C. The union of two non–regular sets is not regular.

D. Infinite union of finite sets is regular.

Q.26 The transport layer protocols used for TFTP, SNMP, SMTP, RIP?

A. TCP, TCP, TCP, UDP

B. UDP, TCP, TCP, UDP

C. UDP, UDP, TCP, UDP

D. UDP, UDP, UDP, UDP

Q.27 Impact analysis helps to decide

A. How many more test cases need to written.

B. How much regression testing should be done.

C. Different Tools to perform Regression Testing

D. Exit Criteria

Q.28 The Boolean expression B'+A'C is equivalent to which of the following expression -

A. A'B'C' + AB' + A'B'C + A'BC

B. A'B'C' + AB + A'C

C. A'C + AB' + A'BC'

D. B'C + BC' + A'C

Q.29 Configuration management is not concerned with

A. maintaining versions of software

B. controlling documentation changes

C. controlling changes to the source code

D. choice of hardware configuration for an application

Q.30 A data dictionary is a special file that contains

A. The width of all fields in all files

B. The data type of all fields in all file

C. The name of all fields in all files

D. All of the above

Q.31 Which of the following describes a relational database?

A. It retrieves data related to its queries

B. It provides a relationship between floats

C. It provides a relationship between integers

D. It consists of separate tables or related data

Q.32 Test & Set Lock is not free from ?

A. Mutual Exclusion   **B.** Progress

C. Deadlock   **D.** Bounded Waiting

Q.33 If we have to send 7 bits of data then the number of redundant bits need to be added before send the data is ___.

A. 2   **B.** 3   **C.** 4   **D.** 5

Q.34 A packet whose destination is outside the local TCP/IP network segment is sent to?

A. File server   **B.** DNS server

C. Default gateway   **D.** DHCP server

Q.35 Which of the following services use TCP?

1) DHCP

2) SMTP

3) HTTP

4) TFTP

5) FTP

A. 1 and 2   **B.** 2, 3 and 5

C. 1, 2 and 4   **D.** 1, 3 and 4

Q.36 A subset of the database which contain virtual data that is derived from the database files but is not explicitly stored is called

A. Touple   **B.** View   **C.** Relation   **D.** Key

Q.37 Consider GBN protocol having sender window size of 8. The minimum number of bits require for sequence is

A. 2   **B.** 3

C. 4   **D.** None of the above

Q.38 Which of the following is not a static testing technique?

A. Inspections   **B.** Data flow analysis

C. Error guessing   **D.** Walkthrough

Q.39 What does the following code do to the parameter n?

```
int studytree(Tree* tree, int &n) //Tree is a structure
{
if(tree != NULL) {
n++;
studytree(tree->left, n);
studytree(tree->right, n);
}
}
```

A. Returns the height of the tree

B. Returns the number of leaves in the tree

C. Returns the number of nodes in the tree

D. Returns (total nodes -1)

Q.40 Statement coverage will not check for the following

A. Dead Code   **B.** Unused Statement

C. Missing Statements   **D.** Unused Branches

Q.41 Of the following tree structure, which is, efficient considering space and time complexities?

A. Incomplete Binary Tree

B. Complete Binary Tree

C. Full Binary Tree

D. None

Q.42 In a network that has maximum packet size of 129 byte, a maximum packet lifetime of 30 second and a 8-bit packet sequence number, What is maximum rate per connection?

A. 1700   **B.** 1579   **C.** 8806   **D.** 8809

Q.43 The capacity to change the conceptual schema without having to change external schemas or application programs is called

A. Physical Data Independence

B. Logical Data Independence

C. Both A and B

D. None

Q.44 Does the minimum spanning tree of a graph give the shortest distance between any 2 specified nodes?

A. Yes   **B.** No
C. May be Yes or No   **D.** None

Q.45 Transmission data rate is decided by

A. Transport layer   **B.** Network layer
C. Physical layer   **D.** Data link layer

Q.46 Consider a 16-bit register of following format to store a Floating Point number:

Mantissa, M is denoted as normalized signed magnitude fraction.

Exponent, E is expressed in excess-64 form.

Base of system is Let's say 2a is the difference(q-p) between first smallest positive number, say p and 2nd smallest positive number, say q. Then what is the value of a?

A. 2^{-72} **B.** 2^{-70} **C.** 2^{-68} **D.** 2^{-66}

Q.47 Application layer protocol defines

A. message format, syntax and semantics
B. rules for when and how processes send and respond to messages
C. types of messages exchanged
D. All of the above

Q.48 Where is a hub specified in the OSI model?

A. Data link layer   **B.** Session layer
C. Application Layer   **D.** Physical layer

Q.49 Which layer 4 protocol is used for a Telnet connection?

A. UDP   **B.** IP   **C.** TCP   **D.** TCP/IP

Q.50 By default, a Linux user falls under which group?

A. same as userid (UPG)
B. system
C. staff
D. others

Q.51 If every functional dependency in set E is also in closure of F then this is classified as :

A. FD is covered by E
B. E is covered by F
C. F is covered by E
D. F plus is covered by E

Q.52 Considering relational database, functional dependency between two attributs A and B is denoted by:

A. $A \rightarrow B$ **B.** $B \leftarrow A$ **C.** $AB \rightarrow R$ **D.** $R \leftarrow AB$

Q.53 Which of the following statements is true?

A. A weak entity set may exist without participation in any relationship.
B. A weak entity should participate in a relationship with another weak entity set.
C. A weak entity should participate in relationship with atleast one strong entity set.
D. None of these

Q.54 A network schema is used to :

A. Restrict to many-to-many relationship
B. Permit to store data in a database
C. Help in storing one-to-one relationships
D. Permit many-to-many relationships

Q.55 The decimal equivalents of 01440000 a 32- bit hexadecimal representation of IEEE single-precision floating point number is

A. $1.11 \times 2 - 125$ **B.** $1.53 \times 2 - 125$
C. $1.68 \times 2 - 124$ **D.** $1.88 \times 2 - 129$

Q.56 Which command undo all the updates performed by the SQL in the transaction?

A. Rollback   **B.** Commit   **C.** Truncate   **D.** Delete

Q.57 Which of the following is true?

A. Wait-die scheme of deadlock prevention strategy is non preemptive
B. Wound-wait scheme of deadlock prevention strategy is preemptive
C. Both a and b
D. Neither a nor b

Q.58 Which among the following information is correct forcomposite index?

A. It is built by default on unique key columns and has database for its internal use
B. It is a combination of index on two or more columns
C. It can never create by data row
D. It has a structure which is different from data rows

Q.59 B tree and B+ tree are used for:

A. Implementing indexed sequential file
B. Data sequencing
C. Data manipulation
D. Rearranging leaf nodes

Q.60 Which among the following process involved in arrangement of data in logical sequence?

A. Sorting   **B.** Classifying
C. Ordering   **D.** Summarizing

Q.61 Word processor is normally used for:

A. Account tracking
B. Media center
C. Inventory management
D. Typing a letter

Q.62 Which of the following statements are TRUE about an SQL query?

P : An SQL query can contain a HAVING clause even if it does not have a GROUP BY clause

Q : An SQL query can contain a HAVING clause only if it has a GROUP BY clause

R : All attributes used in the GROUP BY clause must appear in the SELECT clause

S : Not all attributes used in the GROUP BY clause need to appear in the SELECT clause

A. P and R   **B.** P and S   **C.** Q and R   **D.** Q and S

Q.63 Which of the following scheduling algorithms is non-preemptive?

A.   Round Robin

B.   First-In First-Out

C.   Multilevel Queue Scheduling

D.   Multilevel Queue Scheduling with Feedback

Q.64 Consider the methods used by processes P1 and P2 for accessing their critical sections whenever needed, as given below. The initial values of shared Boolean variables S1 and S2 are randomly assigned.

Method Used by P1

while $(S1 == S2)$;

Critica1 Section

$S1 = S2$

Method Used by P2

while $(S1 != S2)$

Critica1 Section

$S2 = \text{not} (S1)$

Which one of the following statements describes the properties achieved?

A.   Mutual exclusion but not progress

B.   Progress but not mutual exclusion

C.   Neither mutual exclusion nor progress

D.   Both mutual exclusion and progress

Ques (65-66): A processor uses 2-level page tables for virtual to physical address translation. Page tables for both levels are stored in the main memory. Virtual and physical addresses are both 32 bits wide. The memory is byte addressable. For virtual to physical address translation, the 10 most significant bits of the virtual address are used as index into the first level page table while the next 10 bits are used as index into the second level page table. The 12 least significant bits of the virtual address are used as offset within the page. Assume that the page table entries in both levels of page tables are 4 bytes wide. Further, the processor has a translation look-aside buffer (TLB), with a hit rate of 96%. The TLB caches recently used virtual page numbers and the corresponding physical page numbers. The processor also has a physically addressed cache with a hit rate of 90%. Main memory access time is 10 ns, cache access time is 1 ns, and TLB access time is also 1 ns.

Q.65 Assuming that no page faults occur, the average time taken to access a virtual address is approximately (to the nearest 0.5 ns)

A. 1.5 ns   **B.** 2 ns   **C.** 3 ns   **D.** 4 ns

Q.66 Suppose a process has only the following pages in its virtual address space: two contiguous code pages starting at virtual address 0×00000000, two contiguous data pages starting at virtual address 0×00400000, and a stack page starting at virtual address 0×FFFFF000. The amount of memory required for storing the page tables of this process is

A. 8 KB   **B.** 12 KB   **C.** 16 KB   **D.** 20 KB

Q.67 In the index allocation scheme of blocks to a file, the maximum possible size of the file depends on

A.   The size of the blocks, and the size of the address of the blocks

B.   The number of blocks used for the index, and the size of the blocks.

C.   The size of the blocks, the number of blocks used for the index, and the size of the address of the blocks.

D.   None of the above

Q.68 Which of the following implementation may waste CPU cycle.

A. Busy waiting   **B.** sleep and wake

C. both A and B.   **D.** neither A and B

Q.69 SCAN algorithm is applied to following request queue 98,183, 37,122, 14, 124, 65, and 67 with head at 53. Now if 10 is inserted in the queue before it started moving towards Zero or Left. Then at which position it will be serviced.

A. 3rd   **B.** 4th   **C.** Last   **D.** Never

Q.70 Which of the following is not the disc scheduling algorithm.

A. C-SCAN   **B.** FCFS

C. C-LOOK   **D.** SJF

Q.71 Which of the following statements is correct when user level threads are compared to Kernel level threads.

A.   User level threads require memory management where Kernel threads do not.

B.   User level thread scheduling is faster than Kernel thread scheduling.

C.   Both A. and B.

D.   Neither A. nor B.

Q.72 Which of the following is true regarding kernel level threads?

A.   It is easier to implement the kernel level thread as compare to user level thread.

B.   Context for kernel level thread is smaller as compared to user level thread

C.   Blocking of one kernel level thread block all the related thread of that program

D.   Scheduling of the kernel level thread requires hardware support.

Q.73 Match the following groups

Group-I

A) FCFS

B) Round Robin

C) SRTF

D) Priority scheduler

Group-II

1. Important processes get execute first.

2. Minimize the average waiting time

3. The processes run in the order they arrived.

4. Every process get a chance to execute.

A. A-1 B-2 C-3 D-4   **B.** A-4 B-3 C-2 D-1

C. A-3 B-4 C-2 D-1   **D.** A-2 B-1 C-3 D-4

Q.74 Assume time quantum of RR scheduler is greater than longest CPU burst time of all processes.

Which of the following is correct?

A. RR scheduler is better than FCFS

B. FCFS scheduler is better than RR

C. RR scheduler is same as FCFS

D. No comparison between RR and FCFS

Q.75 Match the following geoups

Group-I(Scheduler)

A) Long-term scheduler

B) Medium-term scheduler

C) Short-term scheduler

Group-II(Trnsition of process)

1. New to ready state

2. Ready to running state

3. Suspended to blocked

A. A-1 B-2 C-3

B. A-1 B-3 C-2

C. A-3 B-1 C-2

D. A-2 B-3 C-1

Q.76 Which of the following statements is true for time-sharing system?

A. Only one process can be active on the system.

B. Aims to minimize the user response time.

C. Other processes cannot be executed, when a process wait for I\O.

D. The execution of process has always be within a time constraints.

Q.77 There are six processes waiting ready queue with the brust time are 9, 7, 4, 2, 1 and x, In what order should they run to minimize the average waiting time when the value of x is either 5 or 6.

A. 1, 2, 4, x, 7, 9

B. 9, 7, x, 4, 2, 1

C. x, 7, 9, 4, 2, 1

D. Order can not decided

Q.78 A uni-processor computer system only has two processes, both of which alternate 10 ms CPU bursts with 90 ms I/O bursts. Both the processes were created at nearly the same time. The I/O of both processes can proceed in parallel. Which of the following scheduling strategies will result in the least CPU utilization (over a long period of time) for this system?

A. First come first served scheduling

B. Shortest remaining time first scheduling

C. Static priority scheduling with different priorities for the two processes

D. Round robin scheduling with a time quantum of 5 ms

Q.79 In classful IP addressing, NID & HID part contain number of bits

A. 16,16

B. 8,24

C. 4,28

D. None of the above

Q.80 Consider the following work load.

Process	P_1		P_2	P_3		P_4	P_5
Arrival time	0		3	1		2	2
Burst time	2		4	3		2	4
Priority	1(highest)		4	5 (lowest)		2	3

Processes are scheduled with priority scheduler. Assume that priority scheduler is non-preemptive.

What is the turnaround time with the priority scheduler?

A. 6.3 **B.** 6.5 **C.** 6.6 **D.** 6.8

Q.81 Let WT_i be the waiting time of process 'i', TAT_i be the turnaround time of process i, BT_i be the burst time of process i. Then find which of the following is correct.

A. $WT_i = TAT_i - BT_i$

B. $TAT =_i WT_i - BT_i$

C. $WT_i = BT_i - TAT_i$

D. None of these

Q.82 Consider the following Scheduling Strategies:

1) Longest Job First Scheduling

2) Longest Remaining Time First Scheduling

3) Shortest Job First Scheduling

4) Shortest Remaining Time First Scheduling

5) Priority Scheduling

6) Multilevel Queue Scheduling

7) First Come Fist Serve Scheduling

Which of the following do not suffers from starvation?

A. 2 Only **B.** 7 Only

C. 2 & 7 Only **D.** 2, 7 & 5 Only

Q.83 Consider a block set associative cache consists of 64 blocks, which are divided into 8 block sets. The main memory consists of 2048 blocks, each consists of 128 words of 16 bit length. Find the number of bits in main memory.

A. 2^{18} **B.** 2^{22} **C.** 2^{21} **D.** 2^{24}

Q.84 The simplified form of the Boolean expression $Y = \left(\overline{ABC} + D\right)\left(\overline{AD} + \overline{BC}\right)$ Can be written as.

A. $\vec{AD} + \vec{B}\vec{C}D$

B. $AD + BCD$

C. $\left(\vec{A} + D\right)\left(\overline{BC} + \overline{D}\right)$

D. $A\overline{D} + BC\overline{D}$

Q.85 In a two-level cache system, the access times of L_1 and L_2 caches are 1 and 8 clock cycles, respectively. The miss penalty from L_2 cache to main memory is 18 clock cycles. The miss rate of L_1 cache is twice that of L_2. The average memory access time (AMAT) of this cache system is 2 cycles. This miss rates of L_1 and L_2 respectively are:

A. 0.111 and 0.056 **B.** 0.056 and 0.111

C. 0.0892 and 0.1784 **D.** 0.1784 and 0.0892

Q.86 The stage delays in a 4-stage pipeline are 800, 500, 400 and 300 picoseconds. The first stage (with delay 800 picoseconds) is replaced with a functionally equivalent design involving two stages with respective delays 600 and 350 picoseconds. The throughput increase of the pipeline is ________ percent.

A. 3.33   **B.** 33.33   **C.** 42.33   **D.** 2.33

Q.87 What is the hexadecimal machine code for the instruction MOV AX, [BX]?

A. 8907   **B.** 8B07   **C.** 8938   **D.** 8B38

Q.88 Serial communications involves interfacing of data among:

A. Microprocessor and peripherals
B. Memory and peripherals
C. Data and interface
D. Microprocessor and microcontroller

Q.89 A processor needs software interrupt to

A. test the interrupt system of the processor
B. implement co-routines
C. obtain system services which need execution of privileged instructions
D. return from subroutine

Q.90 How many 32K x 1 RAM chips are needed to provide a memory capacity of 256 K-bytes?

A. 8   **B.** 32   **C.** 64   **D.** 128

Q.91 Consider a 4–way set associative cache consisting of 128 lines with a line size of 64 words. The CPU generates a 20–bit address of a word in main memory. The number of bits in the TAG, LINE and WORD fields are respectively:

A. 9,6,5   **B.** 7,7,6   **C.** 7,5,8   **D.** 9,5,6

Q.92 The figure shows the arrangement of addressing mode. Identify its type?

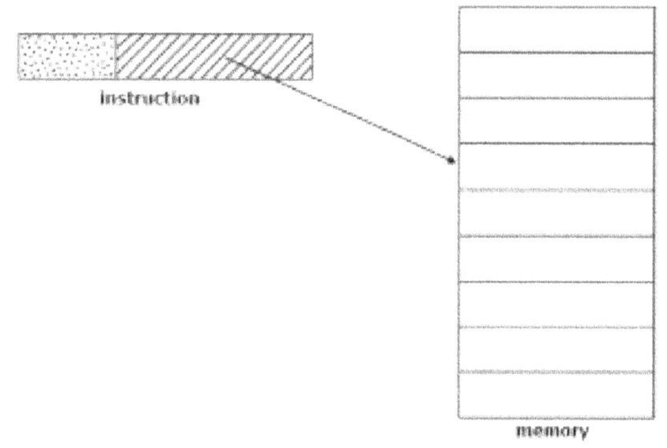

A. Direct addressing
B. Indirect addressing
C. Relative addressing
D. Immediate addressing

Q.93 IEEE 754 single precision format is used to store floating point numbers. Let X be the smallest number representable using implicit normalized form and Y is largest number representable using fractional form. Then the value of $(X-Y)2150$ is _____.

A. 0   **B.** 1   **C.** 2   **D.** 3

Q.94 Which of the following options is correct?

A. The main reason to have multi-level page is to speed up address translation.
B. Using a multi-level page table increases TLB hit time.
C. The main reason to have a hardware TLB is to speed up address translation.
D. There is a limit on the number of level that can be used to create multi-level page table.

Q.95 If the UDP header is given as

$(FFF0OO35FFEEFFEE)_{16}$

Which type of request is made by this UDP header?

A. Client to Server   **B.** Server to client
C. Client to Client   **D.** Invalid Request

Q.96 Consider the two statement regarding Data Link Layer:

Statement 1: Data Link Layer attaches header as well as trailer to the data

Statement 2: Only Error Correcting Codes are attached as trailer at the data link layer

Which of the following is true regarding the above statements?

A. Statement 1 is true and Statement 2 is the reason being S1 true
B. Statement 1 is false and Statement 2 is the reason being S1 false
C. Statement 1 is true but S2 is not the correct explanation for statement 1
D. None of these

Q.97 Suppose the maximum Sequence no which is possible with Go-Back N, Stop and Wait and Selective repeat protocol is k. What is the size of Senders window for each protocol respectively?

A. K, 1, K+1/2   **B.** K+1, 1, k+1/2
C. K, 1, K+1   **D.** K, 1, K/2

Q.98 Consider the following statements about the application layer protocols.

a. Telnet protocol is used to communicate with a remote device or system.

b. FTP and POP3 are stateless protocol while HTTP is a stateful protocol.

c. FTP is out of band protocol while HTTP is in-band protocol.

d. HTTP uses port number 80 while SMTP uses port number 20.

Which of the following is correct?

A. a and b only.   **B.** b and c only.
C. a, b and c only.   **D.** a and c only.

Q.99 During message transfer between two computer system, which is variable?

A. Address of LAN card
B. IP address
C. Port address
D. None

Q.100 You have a class B network with 12 bit subnet How many subnets and how many hosts per subnet are available ?

A. 14, 14   **B.** 14, 4096   **C.** 4096, 14   **D.** 4094, 14

// Smart Answer Sheet //

| Correct | Percentage of students who answered correctly. | Skipped | Percentage of students who skipped. |

Q.	Ans.	Correct / Skipped
1	D	78.0 % / 0.0 %
2	C	79.59 % / 0.0 %
3	C	83.15 % / 0.0 %
4	B	84.09 % / 0.0 %
5	C	81.82 % / 0.0 %
6	D	76.18 % / 0.0 %
7	D	88.41 % / 0.0 %
8	B	79.04 % / 0.0 %
9	A	88.82 % / 0.0 %
10	A	81.71 % / 0.0 %
11	A	83.44 % / 0.0 %
12	B	89.28 % / 0.0 %
13	D	77.32 % / 0.0 %
14	B	84.51 % / 0.0 %
15	D	89.8 % / 0.0 %
16	A	85.78 % / 0.0 %
17	C	85.73 % / 0.0 %
18	A	81.01 % / 0.0 %
19	B	80.5 % / 0.0 %
20	A	77.53 % / 0.0 %
21	C	82.6 % / 0.0 %
22	C	76.83 % / 0.0 %
23	B	79.76 % / 0.0 %
24	D	85.48 % / 0.0 %
25	B	80.29 % / 0.0 %
26	C	83.21 % / 0.0 %
27	B	82.79 % / 0.0 %
28	A	86.28 % / 0.0 %
29	D	79.83 % / 0.0 %
30	D	76.86 % / 0.0 %
31	D	81.01 % / 0.0 %
32	D	84.46 % / 0.0 %
33	C	84.78 % / 0.0 %
34	C	82.96 % / 0.0 %
35	B	82.53 % / 0.0 %
36	B	80.35 % / 0.0 %
37	C	76.04 % / 0.0 %
38	C	79.9 % / 0.0 %
39	C	87.82 % / 0.0 %
40	C	85.94 % / 0.0 %
41	B	79.6 % / 0.0 %
42	C	79.03 % / 0.0 %
43	B	82.47 % / 0.0 %
44	B	88.56 % / 0.0 %
45	C	89.97 % / 0.0 %
46	A	85.85 % / 0.0 %
47	D	77.57 % / 0.0 %
48	D	79.31 % / 0.0 %
49	C	84.57 % / 0.0 %
50	A	83.32 % / 0.0 %
51	B	84.49 % / 0.0 %
52	A	87.27 % / 0.0 %
53	C	88.25 % / 0.0 %
54	D	89.25 % / 0.0 %
55	B	77.29 % / 0.0 %
56	A	81.46 % / 0.0 %
57	C	89.48 % / 0.0 %
58	B	82.17 % / 0.0 %
59	A	84.01 % / 0.0 %
60	A	85.49 % / 0.0 %
61	D	79.15 % / 0.0 %
62	B	76.42 % / 0.0 %
63	B	81.02 % / 0.0 %
64	A	85.22 % / 0.0 %
65	D	85.12 % / 0.0 %
66	C	84.02 % / 0.0 %
67	C	86.57 % / 0.0 %
68	A	79.07 % / 0.0 %
69	A	88.19 % / 0.0 %
70	D	80.87 % / 0.0 %
71	B	78.26 % / 0.0 %
72	D	85.13 % / 0.0 %
73	C	79.81 % / 0.0 %
74	C	85.41 % / 0.0 %
75	B	85.31 % / 0.0 %
76	D	89.69 % / 0.0 %
77	A	84.37 % / 0.0 %
78	D	88.42 % / 0.0 %
79	D	82.35 % / 0.0 %
80	C	89.51 % / 0.0 %

Q.	Ans.	Correct		Q.	Ans.	Correct		Q.	Ans.	Correct		Q.	Ans.	Correct		Q.	Ans.	Correct
		Skipped				Skipped				Skipped				Skipped				Skipped
81	A	88.01 %		85	A	82.82 %		89	C	82.8 %		93	C	86.42 %		97	A	78.71 %
		0.0 %				0.0 %				0.0 %				0.0 %				0.0 %
82	C	78.0 %		86	B	86.2 %		90	C	82.5 %		94	C	82.3 %		98	D	89.21 %
		0.0 %				0.0 %				0.0 %				0.0 %				0.0 %
83	B	88.04 %		87	B	87.48 %		91	D	89.03 %		95	A	76.45 %		99	A	85.2 %
		0.0 %				0.0 %				0.0 %				0.0 %				0.0 %
84	A	76.05 %		88	A	89.28 %		92	A	79.19 %		96	C	88.44 %		100	C	85.53 %
		0.0 %				0.0 %				0.0 %				0.0 %				0.0 %

//Hints and Solutions//

1. SQL is a domain-specific language used in programming and designed for managing data held in a relational database management system, or for stream processing in a relational data stream management system.

Purpose of SQL are :-

To define the data structures

To specify the syntax and semantics of SQL manipulation language

To specify the syntax and semantics of SQL data definition language

2. Polish and Reverse Polish are the notations used in Evaluation of Arithmetic Expressions using prefix and postfix forms.

3. If less work is involved in searching a element than to sort and then extract, then we don't go for sort

If frequent use of the file is required for the purpose of retrieving specific element, it is more efficient to sort the file.

Thus it depends on situation.

4. Queries, reports and tables are all related to database and relationships are not the database object and it is related to functions in mathyematics.

5. SNR = 35 dB = $10\log_{10}$(S/N)

$\log_{10}$(S/N)= 3.5

S/N = 3162.28

Channel capacity

C = B $\log_2$(1+S/N)

= 800 log2(1+3162.28)

= 93017.64 bps

6. In IEEE single precision format, decimal value can be find using the formula

$$(-1)^S(1.M) \times 2^{E-127}$$

Where s is sign bit value, M is mantissa part and E is biased exponent part.

So value of above bit sequence $= (-1)^0(1.11) \times 2^{131-127} = 1.11 \times 2^4 = 28$

7. Fiber-optic physical or wired connection is the fastest communication onnection.

8. Internet Protocol version 4 (IPv4) which defined an IP address as a 32-bit value

IPv4 is in contrast to IPv6, which defined an IP address as a 128 bits value.

9. Kernel - level threads can be scheduled independently not the user level threads.

User-Level threads are invisible to the OS they are not well integrated with the OS.The kernel knows nothing about user-level threads and manages them as if they were single-threaded processes.

10. * is a dereference operator & is a reference operator. They can be applied any number of times provided it is meaningful. Here p points to the first character in the string "Hello". *p dereferences it and so its value is H. Again & references it to an address and * dereferences it to the value H

11. Preprocessor executes as a seperate pass before the execution of the compiler. So textual replacement of clrscr() to 100 occurs.The input program to compiler looks like this :

main ()

{

100;

printf("%d\n",100);

}

Note: 100; is an executable statement but with no action.

So it doesn't give any problem.

12. B is correct, an abstract class need not implement any or all of an interface's methods

13. We cannot use special character – in the variable name.

Variable name can have only underscore.

14. Void pointer can hold address of any data type without type casting. Any pointer can hold void pointer without type casting.

15. Default value of enum constant

GaryOldman = -2 +1 = -1

And default value of enum constant

EdNorton = -1 + 1 = 0

Note: Case expression can be enum constant.

16.

X	Qn	Qn+1	T - FF (X ⊕ Qn)
0	0	0	0
0	1	0	1
1	0	1	1
1	1	1	0

→ Qn+1 = X

Therefore it is D-Flipflop.

17. It is possible to write label of goto statement in the case of switch case statement.

18. Given Boolean expression is:

[D′ + AB′ + A′C + AC′D + A′C′D]′

Step 1: [D′ + AB′ + A′C + C′D (A + A′)]′

(taking C'D as common)

Step 2: [D' + AB' + A'C + C'D]'

(as, A + A' = 1)

: [D' + DC' + AB' + A'C]' (Rearrange)

Step 3: [D' + C' + AB' + A'C]' (distributive law - D'+DC = (D'+D)(D'+C))-> (D'+D)=1

(Rule of Duality, A + A'B = A + B)

: [D' + C' + CA' + AB']' (Rearrange)

Step 4: [D' + C' + A' + AB']'

(Rule of Duality)

: [D' + C' + A' + AB']' (Rearrange)

Step 5: [D' + C' + A' + B']'

(Rule of Duality)

:[(D' + C')'.(A' + B')']

(Demorgan's law, (A + B)'=(A'. B'))

:[(D''.C'').(A''.B'')] (Demorgan's law)

:[(D.C).(A.B)] (Idempotent law, A'' = A)

: ABCD

Hence only 1 minterm after minimization.

19. The fork creates a child that is a duplicate of the parent process. The child begins from the fork(). All the statements after the call to fork() will be executed twice(once by the parent process and other by child).

The statement before fork() is executed only by the parent process.

20. Default permissions given to a file are:

Owner - read write and execute - 6

group - write - 4

others - write - 4

21. Code review is a software quality assurance activity in which one or several humans check a program mainly by viewing and reading parts of its source code, and they do so after implementation or as an interruption of implementation.

22. In both the following cases, line utilization remains the same-

• Whether the entire message is sent as a single entity

• Or the entire message is divided into frames and then frames are sent.

This is because line contains the same amount of data in both cases.

So,

• If the number of frames are increased by dividing the message, there is no change in line efficiency.

• The line efficiency remains the same.

Thus, Option (C) is correct.

23. For floating point numbers (float, double, long double) the values cannot be predicted exactly. Depending on the number of bytes, the precession with of the value represented varies. Float takes 4 bytes and long double takes 10 bytes. So float stores 0.9 with less precision than long double.

24. In software engineering, performance testing is in general, a testing practice performed to determine how a system performs in terms of responsiveness and stability under a particular workload.

25. Every finite subset of a non–regular set is regular. Choice A cannot be correct as any formal language is a subset of E* which is a regular set. Choice C cannot be correct as the union of two non regular can be cfl, a cfl and its complement is necessarily regular e.g. take all the palindromes over some alphabet. A formal language can be looked upon as the infinite union of singleton sets consisting of one string in the language,

So D cannot be correct.

26. • Trivial File Transfer Protocol (TFTP) process includes flow and error control. It can easily use UDP.

• UDP is used for management processes such as SNMP.

• SMTP uses TCP.

• UDP is used for some route updating protocols such as Routing Information Protocol (RIP).

27. Impact Analysis is used in software testing to define all the risks associated with any kind of changes in a product being tested.

Impact Analysis is nothing but analyzing the impact of changes in the deployed product or application. It gives the information about the areas of the system that may be affected due to the change in the particular section or features of the application.

Why Impact Analysis is done :

1. It is done to understand the possible outcome of implementing the change. Inducing too much functionality into a product can reduce the overall performance of the product.

2. To identify all the files, documents and models that might have to be modified if team decides to implement the change in product

3. To estimate the effort needed behind implementing the change

4. To identify the task required to implement the change

5. It will list the dependencies on a specific element

The impact is analyzed on Requirements, Design & Architecture, impact on Test and impact on schedule.

28. Trying with the first option -

=A'B'C' + AB' + A'B'C + A'BC

=A'B'C' + A'B'C + AB' + A'BC {Rearranging the expression}

=A'B'[C'+C] + AB' + A'BC {Taking common from first two terms}

=A'B' + AB' + A'BC {C'+C =1 By the Boolean properties}

=A'B' + A'BC + AB' {Rearranging the expression}

=A'[B'+BC] + AB' {Taking common from first two terms}

=A'[B'+C] + AB' {By distributive law}

=A'B' + AB' + A'C {Rearranging the expression}

=B'[A'+A] + A'C {Taking common from first two terms}

=B' + A'C

Therefore, option A is correct.

29. Configuration management is not concerned with the choice of the hardware configuration for an application.

Configuration management is concerned with the development of procedures and standards for cost-effective managing and controlling charges in an evolving s/w system.

It includes:-

1)software versions maintenance

2)controlling changes in documentation

3)controlling changes to the source code

4) management activities

30. A data dictionary is a special file that contains a set of information describing the contents, format, and structure of a database and the relationship between its elements, used to control access to and manipulation of the database.

31. A relational database is a digital database based on the relational model of data, a database structured to recognize relations between stored items of information. A software system used to maintain relational databases is a relational database management system.

Computer database in which all data is stored in Relations which (to the user) are tables with rows and columns. Each table is composed of records (called Tuples) and each record is identified by a field (attribute) containing a unique value. Every table shares at least one field with another table in 'one to one,' 'one to many,' or 'many to many' relationships. These relationships allow the database user to access the data in almost an unlimited number of ways, and to combine the tables as building blocks to create complex and very large databases.

32. There is no limit on the number of times a process can enter into critical section after it has made request to enter critical section and before that request is granted. Therefore bounded waiting is not followed in Test & Set Lock.

33. we need to satisfy the condition

$2^r >= m+r+1$ where r is number of redundant bits and m is number of data bits that needs to be send.

The smallest value for r=4 is satisfying the condition.

Hence the answer is 4.

34. A default gateway server act as access point to IP router that network computer uses to send information to a computer in another network or internet.

35. SMTP, HTTP and FTP use TCP.

36. A view may be a subset of the database or it may contain virtual data that is derived from the database files but is not explicitly stored .

37. in GBN, receiver window size $(w_R)= 1$

As we know, number of sequence numbers require = sender window size(w_S) + receiver window size (w_R)

$=8+1 =9$

So minimum number of bits require = ceil of $\log_2 9 =4$.

38. Explanation:

Static Testing, a software testing technique in which the software is tested without executing the code. This Techniques provide a powerful way to improve the quality and productivity of software development by assisting engineers to recognize and fix their own defects early in the software development process.

It has two parts as listed below:

Review - Typically used to find and eliminate errors or ambiguities in documents such as requirements, design, test cases, etc.

Static analysis - The code written by developers are analysed (usually by tools) for structural defects that may lead to defects.

In this software is tested without executing the code by doing Review, Walk Through, Inspection or Analysis etc.

Hence, **Error guessing** is not a static software testing technique.

39. Total number of nodes that are present in the tree are calculated using the above code.

40. Statement coverage is a white box test design technique which involves execution of all the executable statements in the source code at least once. It is used to calculate and measure the number of statements in the source code which can be executed given the requirements.

41. Full binary tree loses its nature when operations of insertions and deletions are done. For incomplete binary trees, extra storage is required and overhead of NULL node checking takes place. So complete binary tree is the better one since the property of complete binary tree is maintained even after operations like additions and deletions are done on it.

42. Maximum number of packets that can be transmitted in 30 sec = 2^8 = 256

Data size = 256 × 129 bytes

= (256 × 129 × 8) bits

In 30 sec, (256 × 129 × 8) bits are transmitted

In one second number of bits transmitted

= (256 × 129 × 8)/ 30

= 8806.4 bps

43. LDI is the capacity to change the conceptual schema without having to change external schemas or application programs.

44. No.Minimal spanning tree assures that the total weight of the tree is kept at its minimum. But it doesn't mean that the distance between any two nodes involved in the minimum-spanning tree is minimum.

45. The speed of the transmission data is generally determined by the cables or connectors we use for data transmission. In networking, layer-1 the physical is which deals with the network cables like pins, usb, connectors, etc. We use for data transmission.

46. Here S, sign bit $= 1$
$E = 7$ as bias is given as 64
$M = 8$
$p = $ first smallest + ve number: $(-1)^0 \times 1.00000000 \times 2^{0-64} = 2^{-64}$

$q = $ second smallest +ve number: $(-1)^0 \times 1.00000001 \times 2^{0-64} = 1.00000001 \times 2^{-64}$
Now , $q - p = (1.00000001 - 1.0) \times 2^{-64}$
$= 0.00000001 \times 2^{-64}$
$= 2^{-8} \times 2^{-64} = 2^{-72}$

47. Application layer protocol defines types of messages exchanged, message format, syntax and semantics and rules for when and how processes send and respond to messages.

48. Hubs are specified or operate at Layer1 i.e, the physical layer in the OSI model. Hubs regenerate electrical signals. A hub sends data packets (frames) to all devices on a network, regardless of any MAC addresses contained in the data packet.

49. Telnet uses TCP at layer 4. It uses IP at layer 3. We know that Telnet uses TCP/IP protocol, but in the question, it is asked specifically at layer 4 what is used in Telnet. So it is TCP at layer4 and IP at layer 3.

50. Linux is a family of open source Unix-like operating systems based on the Linux kernel, an operating system kernel. By default, a Linux user falls under same as userid (UPG) group.

51. In case if a functional dependency in set E comes under the closure of F then it is classified as E is covered by F.

52. Functional dependency between two attributs A and B is showed as A Ã B.

53. Weak entity depends on the strong entity for its existence.Weak entity always have total participation. it must relate to the strong set via a one-to-many relationship set.

54. A network schema or a network data model can be best described by the data structure GRAPH. A graph's node (I.e. any tuple) can be linked to as many other nodes as possible. So, the network schema basically helps in representing many-to-many relationship.

55. 01440000
OIOOO OOO1 OI1OO O1OO OOOO OOOO OOOO OOOO
1st bit sign = +ve

next 8 bits $-x$ -cess 127 bias so exponent $= 2 - 127 = -125$
mantissa
$10001 = (1.10001) = (1 + 1/2 + 1/32) = 49/32 = 1.53$
$1.53125 \times 2 - 125$

56. Rollback is used to erase all data modofications made from the start of transaction or to save a point. It also free resources held by the transaction.

57. Wait-die-scheme is non-pre-emptive as older transactions may wait for younger one to release data item, but younger ones never wait for older ones, they are rolled back instead.

Wound-wait-scheme is preemptive as older transactions forces rollback(wounds) of younger transactions instead of waiting for it.Younger transactions may wait for older one.

58. A composite index is an index on two or more columns of a table. In case of a non-clustered index the structure is separated from the data row and has key values containing a pointer to data row.

59. It is seen that both these trees are used to implement indexed sequential file. In case of B+ tree, we see that such tree is balanced and sort all the nodes that are at similar distance where only leaf node contains real value which is convenient for searching any record in no time. In this tree, the insertion and deletion of index files doesn't take much time which forms an efficient method of storing the records.

60. It is seen that sorting is the process of rearranging of letters and numbers. It involves the arrangement of data items in required order. It is noted that many times the data gets arranged in alphabetical sequence which further transforms into information.

61. It is noted that word processor is similar to operations of MS word, where the words or numbers are conveniently typed. It does not involved in any sort of operations nor in calculations.

Since it is part of Microsoft used for typing.

So among the four options, option (D) is correct.

62. When group by is not present, having is applied to the whole table A grouped table is a set of groups derived during the evaluation of a <group by clause> or a <having clause>. A group is a multiset of rows in which all values of the grouping column or columns are equal if a <group by clause> is specified, or the group is the entire table if no <group by clause> is specified. A grouped table may be considered as a collection of tables. Set functions may operate on the individual tables within the grouped table." it shows that P is indeed correct.

63. A) Round Robin - Preemption takes place when the time quantum expires.

B) First In First Out - No Preemption, the process once started completes before the other process takes over.

C) Multi Level Queue Scheduling - Preemption takes place when a process of higher priority arrives.

D) Multi Level Queue Scheduling with Feedback - Preemption takes a place when process of higher priority arrives or when the quantum of high priority queue expires and we need to move the process to low priority queue

So, B is the correct choice.

64. Mutual Exclusion:

Conditions for **deadlock** to occur. **Mutual Exclusion** : At least one unsharable resource - processes claim exclusive control of resources they need. Hold and Wait : Process holds one resource while waiting for another.

Progress Requirement:

If no process is executing in its critical section and there exist some processes that wish to enter their critical section, then the selection of the processes that will enter the critical section next cannot be postponed indefinitely.

P1 can enter critical section only if S1 is not equal to S2, and P2 can enter critical section only if S1 is equal to S2. But here Progress Requirement is not satisfied. Suppose when S1=1 and S2=0 and process p1 is not interested to enter into critical section but p2 want to enter the critical section. P2 is not able to enter critical section in this as only when p1 finishes execution, then only P2 can enter (then only S1 = S2 condition be satisfied).

65. Average access time = Average address translation time + Average memory access time= 1ns (TLB is accessed for all accesses)+ 2*10*0.04(2 page tables accessed from main memory in case of TLB miss)+

Average memory access time = 1.8ns + Cache access time + Average main memory access time = 1.8ns + 1 × 0.9 (90% cache hit) + 0.1 × (10+1) (main memory is accessed for cache misses only) = 1.8ns + 0.9 + 1.1 = 3.8 ns.

So it will be option D i.e 4.

66. First level page table is addressed using 10 bits and hence contains 210 entries. Each entry is 4 bytes and hence this table requires 4 KB. Now, the process uses only 3 unique entries from this 1024 possible entries (two code pages starting from 0x00000000 and two data pages starting from 0x00400000 have same first 10 bits). Hence, there are only 3 second level page tables. Each of these second level page tables are also addressed using 10 bits and hence of size 4 KB. So,

total page table size of the process

= 4 KB + 3 * 4 KB

= 16 KB

67. In the index allocation scheme of blocks to a file, the maximum possible size of the file depends on the size of the blocks, the number of blocks used for the index, and the size of the address of the blocks.

In Index allocation size of maximum file can be derived like following :-

No of addressable blocks using one Index block (A)= Size of block / Size of block address

No of block addresses available for addressing one file (B) = No of Maximum blocks we can use for the Index * No of addressable blocks using one Index block (A).

Size of File = B × Size of Block.

68. Busy waiting approach is easy to implement and less overhead if the wait time is short (no context switch), but here is a possibly waste of CPU cycles due to the active until the chance to enter the critical section.

Sleep and wake approach is more over head due to the context switches, but no waste of CPU cycle due to sleep.

69. If the disk arm is moving toward 0, the head will service 37 then 14 and then 10 thus 10 will server at 3rd Place.

70. In operating systems, seek time is very important. Since all device requests are linked in queues, the seek time is increased causing the system to slow down. Disk Scheduling Algorithms are used to reduce the total seek time of any request.

TYPES OF DISK SCHEDULING ALGORITHMS

Although there are other algorithms that reduce the seek time of all requests, I will only concentrate on the following disk scheduling algorithms:

First Come-First Serve (FCFS)

Shortest Seek Time First (SSTF)

Elevator (SCAN)

Circular SCAN (C-SCAN)

LOOK

C-LOOK.

71. User level thread scheduling is faster than kernel thread scheduling. Both user level threads and kernel level threads require memory management. User level threads are scheduled by thread library (user-level) and kernel level threads are scheduled by OS (kernel-level).

72. a- it is false, since implementation of kernel level thread require hardware support and it is difficult as compared to user level thread.

b- It is false since kernel level threads are independent from each other. Hence, context will be larger.

c- Since each and every kernel level thread is independent of each other so there is no need of blocking of all the other threads.

d- It is true regarding kernel level threads.

73. FCFS: The process run in the order they arrived.

RR: Every process get a chance to execute

SRTF: Minimize the average waiting time.

Priority: Important processes get execute first.

74. If time quantum is greater than the longest CPU burst time of all processes then no job will be preempted and hence RR works same as FCFS.

75. Long-term scheduler can create a new process and make a transition from new to ready or new suspended ready.

Medium-term scheduler makes a transition from either suspended ready or suspended block to blocked. Short-term scheduler makes a transition from ready/blocked to running.

76. Each task is given some time to execute, so that all the tasks work smoothly. Each user gets time of CPU as they use single system. These systems are also known as Multitasking Systems.

77. Ascending order of process gives minimized average waiting time.

X is either 5 or 6.

Scheduling order: 1,2,4,x,7,9.

78. Consider process P and Q.

Say P utilizes 5ms of CPU and then Q utilizes 5ms of CPU.

Hence after 15ms P starts with I/O And after 20ms Q also starts with I/O.

Since I/O can be done in parallel, P finishes I\O at 105th ms (15 + 90) and Q finishes its I\O at 110th ms (20 + 90).

Therefore we can see that CPU remains idle from 20th to 105th ms.

That is when Round Robin scheduling is used,

Idle time of CPU = 85 ms

CPU Utilization = 20/105 = 19.05%

When First Come First Served scheduling or Shortest Remaining Time First is used

Say P utilizes 10 ms of CPU and then starts its I/O.

At 11th ms Q starts processing. Q utilizes 10 ms of CPU.

P completes its I/O at 100 ms (10 + 90)

Q completes its I/O at 110 ms (20 + 90)

At 101th ms P again utilizes CPU.

Hence, Idle time of CPU = 80 ms

CPU Utilization = 20/100 = 20%

Since only two processes are involved and I\O time is much more than CPU time, "Static priority scheduling with different priorities" for the two processes reduces to FCFS or Shortest remaining time first.

Therefore, Round robin will result in least CPU utilization.

79. In classful addressing, class D and E is not partitioned into NID and HID.

80.

Process	P_1	P_2	P_3	P_4	P_5
Arrival time	0	3	1	2	2
Burst time	2	4	3	2	4
Priority	1(highest)	4	5 (lowest)	2	3

$$TAT_1 = 2 - 0 = 2$$

$$TAT_2 = 12 - 3 = 9$$

$$TAT_3 = 15 - 1 = 14$$

$$TAT_4 = 4 - 2 = 2$$

$$TAT_3 = 8 - 2 = 6$$

Average TAT $= \dfrac{2+9+14+2+6}{5} = \dfrac{33}{5} = 6.6$

81. Waiting time of a process can be computed by removing burst time from the turnaround time of a process.

$$\therefore \; WT_i = TAT_i - BT_i$$

82. Longest remaining time first do not suffer from starvation as if longer process keep on coming, then memory will be full.

First Come First Serve do not suffers from starvation because fixed time bound exist for execution of each process.

83. Number of bits in main memory = number of blocks × number of words per block × number of bits per word

= 2048 × 128 × 16

$= 2^{11} \times 2^7 \times 2^4$

$= 2^{22}$

84.
$$Y = (\bar{A} + D)(\bar{A}D + \bar{B}\bar{C})$$
$$\quad BC$$
$$= \bar{A}BCD + \bar{A}D + \bar{B}\bar{C}D$$
$$\{[A'D(BC + 1)] - > A'D\}$$
$$= (\bar{A}D + \bar{B}\bar{C}D)(A + 1 = 1)$$

85. Access time of L_1 = 1

Access Time of L_2 = 8

miss penalty L_1 cache (2×L_2) = 18×2 = 2×a

miss penalty L_2 cache say a = 18

AMAT (average memory access time) = 2

AMAT = Access time of L1 + (MissRate L_1 × miss penalty L_1) where miss penalty L_1 = Access time of L_2 + (MissRate L_2 × miss penalty L_2)

2 = 1+ 2×a × (8 + a × 18)

Solving the equation,

a=0.111

86. Old design= $t_0 = 800$

New design= $t_0 = 600$

Throughput= $\dfrac{800-600}{600} \times 100\% = 33.33\%$

87. The problem is solved using registerindirect addressing. BX has displacement rather than data.

The first 6 bits is opcode for MOV which is 100010. The next is D value. Since direction is "To Register", D = 1. Next bit is W value.Since data is word, W = 1. Next 2 bits are MOD value.

MOD value for BX register without any displacement is 00. Next twobits are register value. Registervalue for AX = 000. Next three bits are R/M value. R/M value for [BX] is 111

The 16 bit binary code is therefore, 1000 1011 0000 0111. The hexadecimal equivalent of it is 8B07

88. It exhibits serial exchange between microprocessor and peripherals such as printers, external drives, scanners or mice. The interface has parallel-to-serial converter which serves as data transmitter and serial-to-parallel converter which serves as data receiver.

89. Software interrupts are required by CPU to obtain System services which need execution of privileged instructions. A software interrupt is caused either by an exceptional condition in the processor itself, or a special instruction in the instruction set which causes an interrupt when it is executed. The former is often called a trap or exception and is used for errors or events occurring during program execution that are exceptional enough that they cannot be handled within the program itself.. An interrupt alerts the processor to a high-priority condition requiring the interruption of the current code the processor is executing. The processor responds by suspending its current activities, saving its state, and executing a function called an interrupt handler (or an interrupt service routine, ISR) to deal with the event. This interruption is temporary, and, after the interrupt handler finishes, the processor resumes normal activities.

So C. is correct option

90. Number of hips required = $\dfrac{256\times1024\times8}{32\times1024\times1}$ =64 chips

91. 4 way set associative cache

The cache address is divided in to tag, set, word fields.

The word field consists of 6 bits as 26 = 64

The set field consists of 5 bits

Number of sets = $\dfrac{128}{4} = 32 = 2^5$

So the number of bits in the tag field = 20 – (number of bits for set field + number of bits for word field) 20 – 11 = 9 bits

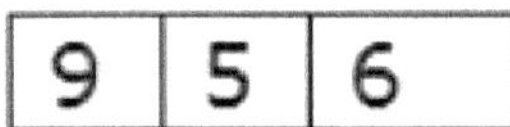

Hence (D) is correct option.

92. It is a direct addressing mode as the value gets stored in memory obtained directly by retrieving it from another memory location. It is used for destination addresses in control instructions and for scalar operands in simple expressions.

93. $X = (1.M) \times 2^{E-127} = (1.0) \times 2^{1-127} = 2^{-126}$

$Y = (0.M) \times 2^{-126} = (1 - 2 - 23) \times 2^{-126}$
$X - Y = 2^{-126} - (1 - 2^{-23}) \times 2^{-126} = 2^{-149}$

So,

$$\alpha - \gamma \times 2^{150} = 2$$

94. Considering each statement:

• Multi-level page tables are there to save space in memory.

• TLB-hit time is not affected by page table structure.

• TLB is used to cache address translation and hence it will speed up the entire process.

• No, there is no limit on the number of levels that can be used to create multi-level page table.

95. The UDP header is specified as

Source Port NO (16 Bit)	Destination Port No (16 Bit)
Total Length (16 Bit)	Checksum (16 Bit)

For given format, Source Port No= (FFF0)$_{16}$= 65520, which is a dynamic port address.

Destination Port No= (0035)$_{16}$ = 53, which is a fixed port

Hence the request is made by a client to the server.

96. Statement 1: data Link layer attaches header for adding the information about preamble and trailer to store the data about error correction and detection codes.

Statement 2: is false as data link layer attaches the detection code also, as the trailer.

97. Sender window size for stop and wait protocol is always 1.

And, for go back it is on less than no of sequences which are possible. if N be the total no of sequences possible, than, K = N-1, i.e., Size of sender's window= K

For Selective repeat protocol, No of sequences which are possible= (Sender window size+ Receiver window Size)/2

Also, Sender Window Size= Receiver Window Size

Hence, Sender Window Size= (K+ 1)/2

98. (a) First statement is true, Telnet protocol is used to communicate with a remote device.

(b) Statement second is false, FTP and POP3 are stateful protocol While HTTP is stateless protocol. A stateless protocol is a communications protocol in which no information is retained by either sender or receiver.

(c) Statement 3 is true, In FTP we have two different dedicated paths to send the data and command separately. That is why it is out of Band protocol.

(d) Statement 4 is false. Because SMTP uses port number 25. While port no. 20 is used by FTP.

99. Mac address is the address of LAN card present in router. message transfers between two computer system through a no. of router, one router to another router.

So source & destination router changes, MAC address attached to message as source & destination router changes.

100. Even through your parent subnet is of class B, your network nodes extends beyond the Class B/ Class C border (24-bit) because you are using 12 bit subnets. Basically you are taking this big network and splitting it into many little subnetworks.

Number of subnets = 2^{12} = 4096 subnets

Number of hosts per subnet = 2^4-2 = 14 hosts

// Notes //

// Notes //